The
GUINNESS
Legend

The GUINNESS Legend

Michele Guinness

HODDER AND STOUGHTON
LONDON SYDNEY AUCKLAND TORONTO

British Library Cataloguing in Publication Data

Guinness, Michele
  The Guinness legend.
  1. Guinness, (Family), history
  I. Title
  929'.2

ISBN 0-340-53669-1

Published by Hodder and Stoughton, a division of Hodder and Stoughton Ltd, Mill Road, Dunton Green, Sevenoaks, Kent TN13 2YA. Editorial Office: 47 Bedford Square, London WC1B 3DP.

Typeset by Hewer Text Composition Services, Edinburgh.
Printed in Great Britain by Richard Clay Ltd., Bungay, Suffolk

For Peter Grattan

who made me part of his illustrious clan

Contents

Illustrations

Family Trees

Plates

Between pages 154 and 155

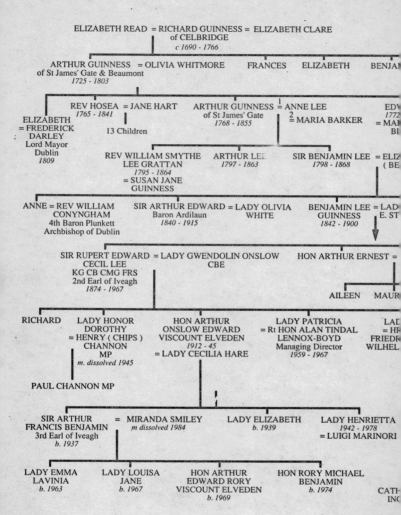

ELIZABETH READ = RICHARD GUINNESS = ELIZABETH CLARE
of CELBRIDGE
c 1690 - 1766

ARTHUR GUINNESS = OLIVIA WHITMORE   FRANCES   ELIZABETH   BENJAM
of St James' Gate & Beaumont
1725 - 1803

REV HOSEA = JANE HART   ARTHUR GUINNESS = ¹ ANNE LEE   EDV
1765 - 1841   of St James' Gate   ²   1772
                          1768 - 1855   = MARIA BARKER   = MAI
ELIZABETH   BI
= FREDERICK   13 Children
DARLEY
Lord Mayor
Dublin
1809

        REV WILLIAM SMYTHE   ARTHUR LEE   SIR BENJAMIN LEE = ELIZ
        LEE GRATTAN   1797 - 1863   1798 - 1868   (BE
        1795 - 1864
        = SUSAN JANE
        GUINNESS

ANNE = REV WILLIAM   SIR ARTHUR EDWARD = LADY OLIVIA   BENJAMIN LEE = LAD
CONYNGHAM   Baron Ardilaun   WHITE   GUINNESS   E. ST
4th Baron Plunkett   1840 - 1915   1842 - 1900
Archbishop of Dublin

SIR RUPERT EDWARD = LADY GWENDOLIN ONSLOW   HON ARTHUR ERNEST =
CECIL LEE   CBE
KG CB CMG FRS
2nd Earl of Iveagh
1874 - 1967
                                                            AILEEN   MAUR

RICHARD   LADY HONOR   HON ARTHUR   LADY PATRICIA   LAD
           DOROTHY   ONSLOW EDWARD = Rt HON ALAN TINDAL = HF
           = HENRY (CHIPS) VISCOUNT ELVEDEN LENNOX-BOYD FRIEDR
           CHANNON   1912 - 45   Managing Director WILHEL
           MP   = LADY CECILIA HARE 1959 - 1967
           m. dissolved 1945

PAUL CHANNON MP

SIR ARTHUR   = MIRANDA SMILEY   LADY ELIZABETH   LADY HENRIETTA
FRANCIS BENJAMIN m dissolved 1984   b. 1939   1942 - 1978
3rd Earl of Iveagh   = LUIGI MARINORI
b. 1937

LADY EMMA   LADY LOUISA   HON ARTHUR   HON RORY MICHAEL
LAVINIA   JANE   EDWARD RORY   BENJAMIN
b. 1963   b. 1967   VISCOUNT ELVEDEN b. 1974
                           b. 1969   CATI
                                                          INC

THE BREWING LINE

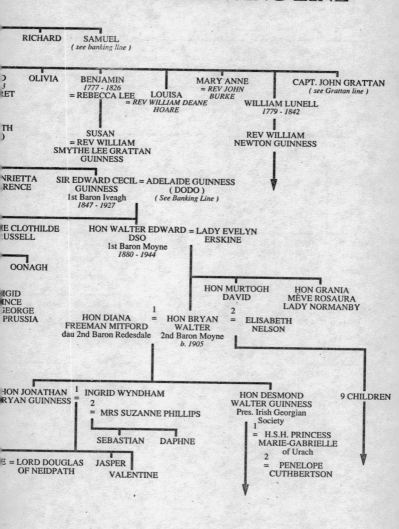

RICHARD   SAMUEL
(see banking line)

OLIVIA   BENJAMIN
1777 - 1826
= REBECCA LEE

LOUISA
= *REV WILLIAM DEANE HOARE*

MARY ANNE
= *REV JOHN BURKE*

CAPT. JOHN GRATTAN
(see Grattan line)

WILLIAM LUNELL
1779 - 1842

SUSAN
= REV WILLIAM SMYTHE LEE GRATTAN GUINNESS

REV WILLIAM NEWTON GUINNESS

SIR EDWARD CECIL = ADELAIDE GUINNESS
GUINNESS   (DODO)
1st Baron Iveagh   *(See Banking Line)*
1847 - 1927

HON WALTER EDWARD = LADY EVELYN
DSO   ERSKINE
1st Baron Moyne
1880 - 1944

OONAGH

HON MURTOGH DAVID

HON GRANIA MÈVE ROSAURA LADY NORMANBY

HON DIANA
FREEMAN MITFORD
dau 2nd Baron Redesdale

1

HON BRYAN WALTER
2nd Baron Moyne
b. 1905

2

ELISABETH NELSON

HON JONATHAN BRYAN GUINNESS

1

INGRID WYNDHAM

2

= MRS SUZANNE PHILLIPS

SEBASTIAN   DAPHNE

HON DESMOND WALTER GUINNESS
Pres. Irish Georgian Society

1

= H.S.H. PRINCESS MARIE-GABRIELLE
of Urach

2

= PENELOPE CUTHBERTSON

9 CHILDREN

= LORD DOUGLAS OF NEIDPATH

JASPER
VALENTINE

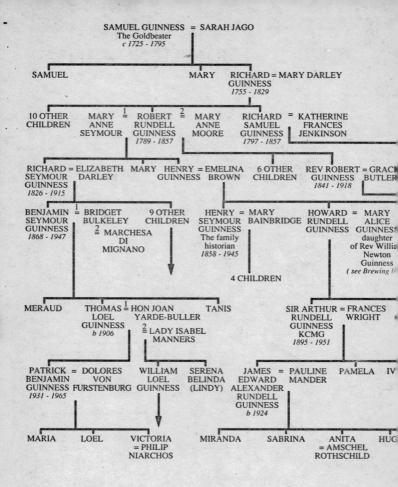

THE RUNDELL BANKING LINE

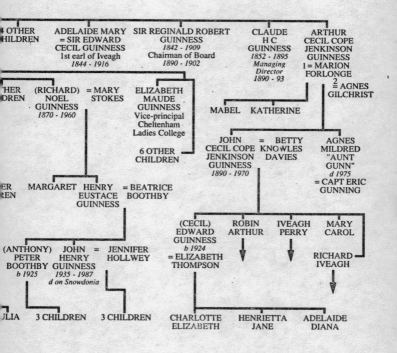

OTHER CHILDREN

ADELAIDE MARY = SIR EDWARD CECIL GUINNESS 1st earl of Iveagh 1844 - 1916

SIR REGINALD ROBERT GUINNESS 1842 - 1909 Chairman of Board 1890 - 1902

CLAUDE H C GUINNESS 1852 - 1895 Managing Director 1890 - 93

ARTHUR CECIL COPE JENKINSON GUINNESS 1 = MARION FORLONGE

2 = AGNES GILCHRIST

OTHER CHILDREN

(RICHARD) NOEL GUINNESS 1870 - 1960 = MARY STOKES

ELIZABETH MAUDE GUINNESS Vice-principal Cheltenham Ladies College

6 OTHER CHILDREN

MABEL   KATHERINE

JOHN CECIL COPE JENKINSON GUINNESS 1890 - 1970 = BETTY KNOWLES DAVIES

AGNES MILDRED "AUNT GUNN" d 1975 = CAPT ERIC GUNNING

OTHER CHILDREN

MARGARET   HENRY EUSTACE GUINNESS = BEATRICE BOOTHBY

(CECIL) EDWARD GUINNESS b 1924 = ELIZABETH THOMPSON

ROBIN ARTHUR

IVEAGH PERRY

MARY CAROL

(ANTHONY) PETER BOOTHBY b 1925

JOHN HENRY GUINNESS 1935 - 1987 d on Snowdonia = JENNIFER HOLLWEY

RICHARD IVEAGH

JULIA   3 CHILDREN   3 CHILDREN

CHARLOTTE ELIZABETH

HENRIETTA JANE

ADELAIDE DIANA

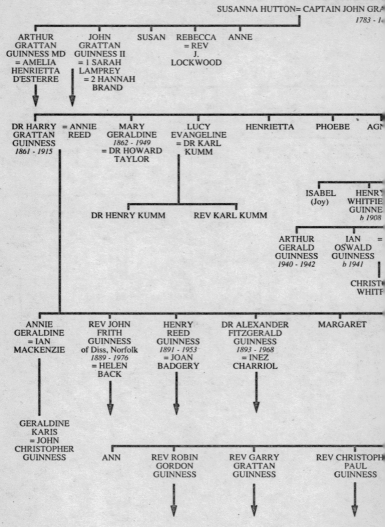

THE GRA

SUSANNA HUTTON = CAPTAIN JOHN GRA
1783 - 1

ARTHUR GRATTAN GUINNESS MD = AMELIA HENRIETTA D'ESTERRE

JOHN GRATTAN GUINNESS II = 1 SARAH LAMPREY = 2 HANNAH BRAND

SUSAN

REBECCA = REV J. LOCKWOOD

ANNE

DR HARRY GRATTAN GUINNESS 1861 - 1915 = ANNIE REED

MARY GERALDINE 1862 - 1949 = DR HOWARD TAYLOR

LUCY EVANGELINE = DR KARL KUMM

HENRIETTA

PHOEBE

AGN

DR HENRY KUMM

REV KARL KUMM

ISABEL (Joy)

HENRY WHITFIE GUINNE b 1908

ARTHUR GERALD GUINNESS 1940 - 1942

IAN OSWALD GUINNESS b 1941 =

CHRISTO WHITF

ANNIE GERALDINE = IAN MACKENZIE

REV JOHN FRITH GUINNESS of Diss, Norfolk 1889 - 1976 = HELEN BACK

HENRY REED GUINNESS 1891 - 1953 = JOAN BADGERY

DR ALEXANDER FITZGERALD GUINNESS 1893 - 1968 = INEZ CHARRIOL

MARGARET

GERALDINE KARIS = JOHN CHRISTOPHER GUINNESS

ANN

REV ROBIN GORDON GUINNESS

REV GARRY GRATTAN GUINNESS

REV CHRISTOPH PAUL GUINNESS

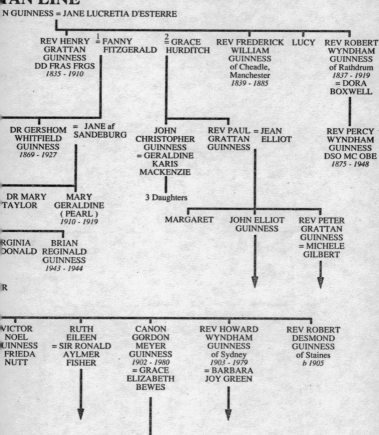

TAN LINE

N GUINNESS = JANE LUCRETIA D'ESTERRE

REV HENRY GRATTAN GUINNESS DD FRAS FRGS *1835 - 1910* = 1 FANNY FITZGERALD

2 = GRACE HURDITCH

REV FREDERICK WILLIAM GUINNESS of Cheadle, Manchester *1839 - 1885*

LUCY

REV ROBERT WYNDHAM GUINNESS of Rathdrum *1837 - 1919* = DORA BOXWELL

DR GERSHOM WHITFIELD GUINNESS *1869 - 1927* = JANE af SANDEBURG

JOHN CHRISTOPHER GUINNESS = GERALDINE KARIS MACKENZIE

REV PAUL GRATTAN GUINNESS = JEAN ELLIOT

REV PERCY WYNDHAM GUINNESS DSO MC OBE *1875 - 1948*

DR MARY TAYLOR

MARY GERALDINE (PEARL) *1910 - 1919*

3 Daughters

MARGARET

JOHN ELLIOT GUINNESS

REV PETER GRATTAN GUINNESS = MICHELE GILBERT

RGINIA DONALD

BRIAN REGINALD GUINNESS *1943 - 1944*

R

VICTOR NOEL GUINNESS FRIEDA NUTT

RUTH EILEEN = SIR RONALD AYLMER FISHER

CANON GORDON MEYER GUINNESS *1902 - 1980* = GRACE ELIZABETH BEWES

REV HOWARD WYNDHAM GUINNESS of Sydney *1903 - 1979* = BARBARA JOY GREEN

REV ROBERT DESMOND GUINNESS of Staines *b 1905*

DAWN

HOSEA'S LINE
(New Zealand Branch)

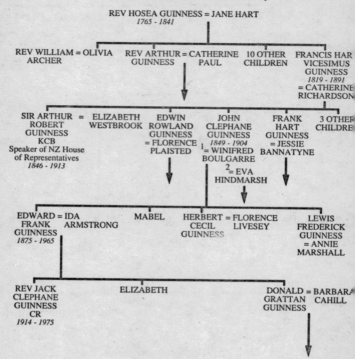

REV HOSEA GUINNESS = JANE HART
1765 - 1841

REV WILLIAM = OLIVIA ARCHER
GUINNESS

REV ARTHUR = CATHERINE PAUL
GUINNESS

10 OTHER CHILDREN

FRANCIS HART VICESIMUS GUINNESS
1819 - 1891
= CATHERINE RICHARDSON

SIR ARTHUR ROBERT GUINNESS KCB
Speaker of NZ House of Representatives
1846 - 1913
= ELIZABETH WESTBROOK

EDWIN ROWLAND GUINNESS = FLORENCE PLAISTED

JOHN CLEPHANE GUINNESS
1849 - 1904
1 = WINIFRED BOULGARRE
2 = EVA HINDMARSH

FRANK HART GUINNESS = JESSIE BANNATYNE

3 OTHER CHILDREN

EDWARD FRANK GUINNESS
1875 - 1965
= IDA ARMSTRONG

MABEL

HERBERT CECIL GUINNESS = FLORENCE LIVESEY

LEWIS FREDERICK GUINNESS = ANNIE MARSHALL

REV JACK CLEPHANE GUINNESS CR
1914 - 1975

ELIZABETH

DONALD GRATTAN GUINNESS = BARBARA CAHILL

Preface

I was walking down O' Connell Street in Dublin, enjoying an hour of sightseeing before speaking at a Women's Luncheon Club, when the strap on my sandal snapped. It was the only pair of shoes I had with me and my resources could not possibly rise to a new pair. My hostess, an American missionary, shared my state of financial embarrassment and we rushed into the first shoe repair shop we could find.

"Could you do them now, this minute," I pleaded.

The assistant shook her head slowly, unmoved by my predicament. "There's a long waiting list. Sure, you'll have to wait your turn, and it'll take two days."

"But it only needs a stitch."

There was no response and I would have left the shop there and then, were it not for the fact that it is impossible to go anywhere wearing only one shoe.

"Name?" the shop assistant asked.

"Guinness," I responded.

There was a moment's silence. Then without looking up the assistant said, "Your shoes will be ready in five minutes, Mrs Guinness."

"Oh gee!" said the American as we left the shop a few minutes later, my strap sewn in place.

I echoed her sentiment. My name had never had that effect before and I was slightly punch-drunk with the experience. True, when my husband and I became engaged and he handed me a copy of his pedigree, I was impressed. It was heady stuff for one descended from immigrant Jewish peasant stock. But though the present Viscount Elveden at his birth in 1969 was reputed to be worth £7 million, heir to an empire worth about £90 million, my husband was then earning his living as a schoolteacher. Great-grandson of the founder of the brewery's youngest son he may have been, but his existence was remote from the brewing and banking branches of the family. "All the members of the world-famous Guinness family are reputed to be worth a fortune in the region of £200 million", said the *Daily Express*,[1] with more than the usual journalistic overstatement. If that was so I never saw any of it! Small wonder the prestige of the name meant very little to me.

During the first years of our marriage, within the circle in which we moved, I met a number of people who regarded the name with awe, not because of its business connections but because of the associations of the youngest, or Grattan, branch of the family with the Church and missionary enterprise. In fact at one conference I was asked so many times whether we were related to Canon Gordon, or Howard, or Henry, or Desmond, or Os, that I threatened to pin a copy of the family tree to my back.

But a sense of belonging to the wider clan was reserved for that moment in the shoe shop in Dublin. Suddenly the sight of the name emblazoned high above the city over the St James' Gate Brewery made me feel I had come home. For the first time I understood something of the pride with which my husband regarded his heritage.

Since then, in what has become a time-honoured tradition not only of the Grattan branch of the Guinnesses, he has become a clergyman, the nineteenth member of the family to be ordained. It was with a deep sense of shock that he and his cousins received the news of the 1987 scandal. Their pride rested in a family business renowned for its uprightness and honesty, and lauded for its philanthropy and benevolence in Ireland and England.

The arrest of the former Chairman of the brewery was in fact one of a series of tragedies to rock the family since the 1940s, leading some to speculate about a Guinness "curse". Such were the number of family deaths in the 1970s that my parents began to wonder whether their schoolteacher son-in-law had been watching the film *Kind Hearts and Coronets* on the television and was making a bid for the baronetcy by removing the obstacles one by one. Ironically it was Alec Guinness, who took his name from a member of the family, who played each one of the victims.

Sadness haunted the family almost from the start. The first Arthur Guinness did not live to see three of his grandchildren become alcoholics or two in mental institutions or several more reduced to begging and insolvency. It was left to his son, the second Arthur, to deal with the constant demands of his profligate nephews and nieces. And though harassed and disappointed, he closed ranks around them, giving his relatives the benefit of his support and protection. That same sense of patriarchal duty has protected and steered the family through tragedy and failure ever since.

It has been said that the Guinnesses are:

almost Oriental about losing face among themselves. They would do anything rather than admit to another member of the family that they had made a wrong decision. And while they will be relieved when someone else takes the responsibility from them, if they find the most minute indiscretion – such as a mistake in the milk bill – they hit the roof.[2]

The charges brought against the former Chairman in March 1987 amounted to more than a mistake in the milk bill. It was alleged that certain irregularities had appeared in transactions leading up to the acquisition of Distillers'. In 225 years of business it was the first doubt to be cast on an otherwise unimpeachable reputation. The first Arthur must have been turning in his grave. His son, the second Arthur, kept a Bible open on his desk at the brewery. For both men and for their successors wealth brought inescapable, divinely-appointed responsibility expressed in a life of ruthless integrity and open-handed philanthropy.

"Guinnessty" would make a more exciting, if less credible, television soap opera than any created so far. Life often leaves fiction behind. But the Guinnesses, though they may appear to be the stuff of which soap operas are made, are more like an Old Testament tribe, with the first Arthur an Abrahamic figure setting out towards Dublin, not knowing, when he bought a derelict brewery in St James' Gate, how it would turn out. And if ever there was a Guinness "curse", there was also a covenant, such as the Almighty once made with the children of Israel: "I call heaven and earth to witness against you this day that I have set before you life and death, blessing and curse; therefore choose life, that you and your descendants may live."

Never has the struggle between God and mammon been so obviously fought out as in the Guinness tribe. While many of them became wealthy businessmen and many clergymen, there were not always clear lines of demarcation as to who served which. Some of the businessmen were very devout, and some of the clergymen very worldly.

One member of the family stands out with a special lustre. He was Henry Grattan Guinness, grandson of the first Arthur. He gave away his inheritance, became a minister and preached to thousands outside the brewery. He founded the Grattan line of Guinnesses who as clergymen, missionaries and doctors travelled the world and in a series of hair-raising adventures proved that the earnestness and determination which earned the brewers their millions could be as well used in God's employment. Because of the wealth of hitherto unpublished material collected by the author, this is primarily their story.

Difficult choices have had to be made. The tribe has multiplied and spread out through the earth to such a degree that it is impossible to follow all its branches. But with the Guinnesses one branch can never be fully cut off from the rest of the family tree. Whatever their final destiny all drank from the same source, all blossomed from the same root.

1 *Daily Express*, Monday, August 11th, 1969.
2 Sally Brompton in the *Daily Mail*, May 6th, 1978.

Acknowledgments

Detective work is never much fun when done single-handed. I am indebted to several people who gave me their time, advice and help as I scoured the country for clues to the mystery of the Guinness legend.

Lord Moyne took time from his exceedingly busy schedule – delivering speeches in the House of Lords, writing book reviews, working tirelessly for the Guinness Trust – to write me several detailed letters full of anecdotes and reminiscences. He checked my description of his father's tragic assassination and I am grateful for his help.

The writer and historian Piers Brendon allowed a complete stranger access to his home, to his book on Rupert Guinness, born of much hard work and never circulated publicly, and to his copious notes on the family, made at Farmleigh. When, to my dismay, I discovered that the archives at Park Royal were empty, the files on the family missing, he came to my rescue. Without his help this book would have been much the poorer.

Many others have made their own special contribution. I am grateful to the Rev. Alan Munden for sharing with me some of his own research on Cheltenham in the past century; to the Rev. Desmond Guinness of Staines, who wrote me a long and detailed account of his childhood memories; to Dr Henry Kumm of Pennsylvania for his mother's letters; and to Karl Kumm the third, who dared to entrust his grandmother's precious diaries to the GPO and an unknown cousin on the other side of the Atlantic. The staff of the headquarters of the Regions Beyond Missionary Union looked after me royally as I pored over the old minute books of the Harley Institute. Jim Broomhall took time from a demanding writing schedule to send me letters from the China Inland Mission archives, which he calls affectionately "Hudson Taylor's bones".

It was my late father-in-law Paul Grattan Guinness, the last surviving great-grandson of Arthur, founder of the brewery, who first attempted to record a brief history of the family. He felt that as new generations were born, particularly in the Grattan line, there was a danger they might lose sight of their roots altogether. He collected and began to edit a vast amount of Grattan memorabilia. But even he had no idea of the treasure concealed in a vast trunk in the rooftop study of his Ibiza home: letters written by his mother in her younger days, graphically describing her love for Henry Grattan Guinness, a man over forty years her senior. Their discovery made me decide it was time to write. He was so proud of his ancestry. I am sad that he has not lived to see the book.

Finally and above all I am indebted to C. Edward Guinness, for fifteen years Chairman of Harp Lager, one of Guinness' subsidiaries. Despite other demands on his time he has worked tirelessly on my behalf. Every request was treated with graciousness and courtesy. He provided the photographs of the family portraits, many anecdotes and the insights into the running of a brewery, as well as contributing to the postscript. I have been inspired by his wholehearted, though not uncritical, admiration for the family. With his warmth and humour he typifies all that is best in Guinness and, knowing him, I doubt there is any compliment he would prefer.

M.G.

1

1759–1803

Arthur the First, Founder of a Dynasty

1

It is January 1803. A gentleman of considerable means is being carried home to his roots in the soft rich soil of the Irish countryside, several miles west of the thriving, bustling little city of Dublin. In the funeral procession leaving Beaumont, his serene and stately home on the north side of Dublin Bay, roll the carriages of the mighty, the strength of wealthy mercantile Dublin. On a clear summer's day the Welsh hills can be seen across the bay, rising majestically from the horizon, but in winter the Irish Sea is a churning, angry grey, merging with the sky. It exhales an all-pervading damp which hangs over the city as a dense mist, clinging to the body and penetrating the bones. The employees lining the route stand with heads bowed in silent respect, shawls pulled in tight to keep out the winter cold.

The procession continues on its way inland until the spire of the old parish church of Oughterard comes into view. The carriages slow down and eventually stop and a coffin, draped in crimson and bearing the right hand and golden lion of the Magennis coat of arms, is hoisted on to the shoulders of four middle-aged men. With all the pomp and circumstance attending the departure of a man of standing, Arthur Guinness esquire, brewer, philanthropist and public citizen, is carried by his sons to his last resting place.

He has come home to County Kildare where the legend was born nearly fifty years before, long before his name conjured up power and prestige, before there was a brewery at St James' Gate or sons to carry his coffin and read the funeral service, before the respectable burghers of Dublin, the Darleys, the Smythes or the LaTouches would have deigned to share his company, let alone attend his funeral. But if he was not quite gentleman enough to socialise with the Anglo-Irish gentry who danced to the tune of the English Viceroy, safely garrisoned in Dublin Castle, yet he was the official purveyor of their beer, a man of influence and substance. That much his wife's relatives were forced to concede. When Olivia Whitmore married the young brewer, bringing him a thousand pounds and the prestige of her family connections, it was said that the unknown merchant had done quite well for himself. Olivia had not done badly out of the match either.

The Whitmores, Darleys and LaTouches were builders and bankers, Protestant merchants of long-standing well-to-do Dublin families. Their cousin Henry Grattan was Ireland's greatest orator and foremost politician. Arthur Guinness' origins on the other hand were a mystery. But brewing was becoming a respectable trade and his wife's relatives chose to ignore uncertainties surrounding his pedigree. He quietly adopted the coat of arms and crest of the Magennises of County Down, one of Ireland's oldest and most powerful Catholic clans, the hereditary earls of Iveagh, and his in-laws encouraged him to do so. At his wedding they presented him with a silver cup, engraved with the Magennis arms superimposed upon those of Whitmore. But whether he was entitled to them, how the name became Guinness and he a Protestant, no one knew for certain, not even his own children for he never spoke of his parents or grandparents.

But as rumours filtered down to the city from County Kildare, Dublin workers told their own tale. The Reads, his mother's people, they whispered, had always maintained that against their wishes their daughter Elizabeth had eloped with the family groom, one Richard Guinness. After their marriage he became agent and receiver to Rev. Dr Price, Vicar of Celbridge and later Archbishop of Cashel. Richard Guinness may have been a Magennis, but the locals in Celbridge, where Dr Price built his residence, Oakley Park, preferred their story, that he was the illegitimate son of a soldier left behind after the Battle of the Boyne, and a country girl. The girl, so they said, left her offspring to be raised at the foundling hospital at Leixlip.[1] The gossip was never substantiated and rent collectors are notoriously unpopular.

So are the successful, especially when regarded as upstarts. A hundred and fifty years later a LaTouche, blind drunk in a Dublin bar, holes in the elbows of his jacket and the soles of his shoes stretched out on the chair in front of him, held up his pint of Guinness and said, "My ancestor's butler was responsible for this."[2] But Arthur Guinness was never a butler.

What is sure is that when the old Archbishop of Cashel died in 1752 he left a hundred pounds to his faithful servant Richard Guinness, whose delicious home-made black brew had made the old ecclesiastic a favourite host among the local gentry. Richard Guinness became proprietor of the Bear and Ragged Staff, a popular coach stop in Celbridge.

It so happened that the Archbishop also left a hundred pounds "to my servant Arthur Guinness, his son". From such beginnings sprouted a dynasty of peers, brewers and missionary-adventurers, whose influence would spread throughout the world. For with that hundred-pound bequest the son of Richard Guinness opened a small brewery in Leixlip. Many before him had experimented in brewing, but only Arthur Guinness succeeded in making a porter the like of which no man had tasted, and no one knew his secret. Some said it started as an accident, that his father burnt the malting barley and the caramelised result was stronger and better than had ever been brewed before. Some whispered that Arthur had stolen the recipe from some monks whose home-made beer could make hairs grow on a man's chest. Others suspected there was magic in the water of the St James' Gate well and it was the Liffey which gave Guinness porter its distinctive taste. All anyone knew for sure was that one day Arthur left the Leixlip Brewery in the hands of his younger brother Richard, packed up his few belongings and set off to seek his fortune in the big town. On that day the story really began.

2

When the thirty-four-year-old Arthur Guinness arrived in Dublin in 1759 there were not as yet the wide boulevards, elegant squares and dignified buildings which were to grace the town in later years. The dilapidated state of the disused brewery he leased in St James' Gate was not unusual. The preacher John Wesley, who had already visited Dublin several times, was struck by the abundance of ruined and unfinished buildings and put it down to "the amazing fickleness of this people".[3] Rather than evidence of an inherent character defect it probably suggested a certain lack of national pride.

Apart from a brief interlude Ireland had been dominated by the English for over a hundred years, from the time when Oliver Cromwell rode in and devastated the entire country. He took possession of the great estates and gave them to his anti-papist British followers, creating an aristocratic ruling class as blind and ignorant to the needs of the poor as they were in England. Ireland remained deeply divided into those who had everything and those who had nothing. The latter were by far the greater number.

At the top of the pile sat the great Anglo-Irish landowners, the descendants of Cromwell's beneficiaries. They lived a sheltered existence in Dublin, fawning upon the English at the fashionable Viceroy's court in Dublin Castle. At the bottom, squeezed down by a rigid system of tenant farming, were the peasants, utterly dependent on the humble potato to eat and pay the rent. Techniques in caring for the land were primitive. The landowners, many of them absentees, were largely uninterested. The peasant had neither the means nor the education to improve his lot. He was caught in the vicious spiral of his lack of motivation, high rents, arrears and ultimate eviction. Unlike his landlord, he was Catholic. The amount of land a Catholic was allowed to own was strictly limited.

For men like Arthur Guinness, somewhere in the middle of the pile, the latter half of the eighteenth century was a time of qualified, yet definite potential. At Dublin Castle the aristocracy was bored and looked for amusement. Their wealth began to stimulate a host of service industries: building, banking and brewing, and a rising professional and trading class gradually emerged. For a brewer the opportunity was limited because England controlled Ireland and it was English, not Irish prosperity, which interested the English parliament. Irish beer was heavily taxed.

But for a man of such enterprising stock as Arthur Guinness, high export duties were a minor hurdle. His father Richard invested his legacy well, brother Benjamin would one day become a successful merchant and brother Samuel a goldbeater of some repute, but Arthur outshone them all. After all had he not heard John Wesley preach of the rewards awaiting those who embraced thrift and diligence? "We must exhort all Christians to gain all they can, and to save all they can, that is, in effect to grow rich," said the preacher. Arthur Guinness had every intention of fulfilling his Christian duty.

In the three years since he started brewing in Leixlip his business had expanded, but Dublin was the place to make a man. When Arthur fell upon the property in St James' Gate, he knew it was a calculated risk. If the brewery itself was poky, suffering from the neglect of some nine years and consisting only of a copper kieve, a mill, two malthouses and a loft to hold 200 loads of hay, the house and land amply made up for it. He leased the entire property for 9000 years at an annual rent of £45, and found himself master of a substantial dwelling with spacious gardens, a fish pond, a summer-house and stables. It was the first step towards becoming a gentleman. The next was to find a wife, preferably one with an income which would enable him to extend and improve the brewery. If she had influential connections, so much the better. It was as a man of property that he was introduced to Olivia Whitmore just two years later. She was a ward of William Lunell of Dublin and had inherited over a thousand pounds from her father. In other words she was a lady of some fortune.

That his suit was so readily accepted suggests that his potential was obvious from the first. Arthur Guinness was not a handsome man, but personable and striking none the less. His high forehead and aquiline nose conveyed an adequate suggestion of aristocratic refinement. His face was open and kindly, so that only the most discerning would detect an occasional glint of steel in the eyes or notice the way his lips would draw together in a fine line, revealing a man who made his mind up and kept to it. When he married Olivia he did not guess how important a connection he had acquired in her cousin, the politician Henry Grattan.

The match served him well in every respect. Within two years he was deemed suitable to be elected Warden of the Dublin Corporation of Brewers and as a singular honour, represented his corporation in the annual civic ceremony of "Riding the Franchise" in 1764. The same year he bought Beaumont, his country house, a symbol of his new status. After only six years in business he was well enough known in Dublin for *Freeman's Journal* to report that the "eminent brewer" who had died recently in James' Street was a Mr Ennis and not Arthur Guinness as some of the papers had previously stated.[4] It must have been an embarrassing journalistic error. Arthur Guinness may well have succeeded in fulfilling what for many a man was a lifetime's ambition, to be regarded as a gentleman, but he had only reached the first level, and by no means the pinnacle of his life's achievement.

His business success was based on more than luck or instinct. He was shrewd in the extreme. The main attraction of the brewery at St James' Gate, which he noticed the moment he saw it, was its position in regard to the city watercourse. From the Dublin mountains, ten miles from the city, water flowed down plentifully into the Liffey and was carried by pipes right up to the western side of his property. Those who maintained that Liffey water was the magic in the Guinness recipe were not altogether wrong. Soft water made the best beer.

When Arthur Guinness signed the lease he made absolutely certain that he had also acquired the water rights. A free supply of plentiful water was a brewer's dream, and he took his full share – more than his fair share, said the City Corporation when they discovered he had enlarged the pipes and made new breaches in the watercourse walls. In a fit of pique the corporation decided that the lease had been misunderstood. Mr Guinness had no rights whatsoever to the watercourse and it must be recovered for the city immediately. This meant filling up the channel from which Guinness drew the brewery's water supply. He would be ruined overnight.

The might of the corporation duly descended on St James' Gate to remind the brewer of his duty as a citizen to render unto Caesar what was Caesar's. The officers, anxious to be respectful and courteous, would graciously overlook his past faults if he heeded their warning. Of course they realised he needed time, for it could hardly be easy for a brewer to be without water!

Guinness was not intimidated. He was incensed. Before God and man, his conscience was clear: the water was his. He would defend it by force if necessary. They said they had their duty to perform and would do it. Let them try, Guinness retorted, they would see how far they got.

Nothing daunted, back came a body of men behind the City Sheriff, with shovels and other tools and instructions to fill in the breach. Guinness was not there, but his loyal employees caused a lengthy obstruction, and only gave way when the Sheriff threatened to take them all to Newgate Prison. Suddenly, in a volley of language which took everyone by surprise, Arthur Guinness himself appeared, snatched a pickaxe from one of his amazed workmen and promised them that if anyone dared to fill up the breach he would open it up again. The City Sheriff stood his ground for a while and shouted back, then, watching the formidable brewer wielding the pickaxe high above his head, finally decided that diplomacy might succeed where force had failed and beat a hasty retreat.

There followed a protracted lawsuit, which gave Guinness several years of grace. Next time the officers arrived to inspect the state of his pipes, they met with a brick wall, this time a literal one. To the corporation's immense relief the brewer finally settled for all the water he needed for an annual sum of ten pounds. By then he was Master of the Dublin Guild of the Corporation of Brewers, official brewer to Dublin Castle, and not a man to cross.

3

However impressed Arthur Guinness may have been with Wesleyan teaching, its influence never seemed to tempt him towards teetotalism. The temperance campaigns of the time were mainly levelled against spirits. Whiskey was the real demon, robbing the working man of his senses and making him lazy and unproductive. It never seems to have entered Arthur Guinness' head that any man could drink himself into a Guinness-induced stupor. Perhaps the idea was too upsetting to contemplate. Perhaps, as a man who deplored excess of every kind, he assumed that no one would be able to drink beer in such quantities. To be fair to the brewer, it was certainly not a habit at the time. Beer was regarded more as a fortified lemonade than a tame spirit. A nourishing form of beer might even turn a man away from spirits and thus perform a public service. At least, that was Arthur Guinness' argument.

Unlike the nineteenth century, the eighteenth was not outst
in religious piety. In England church attendance was little mor
a social convention for the landed gentry. The clergy did as ...ie
as possible unless it was hunting, shooting, swearing, drinking and
gambling. When they did preach, their sermons were so bad that
there was generally nobody in the pews to hear them. In that
context John Wesley was dynamite. He invested the working man
with integrity and value.

Wesley visited Ireland several times and loved the country. When
it came to the evils of indolence and the joys of hard work, no one
could accuse him of not practising what he preached. Sometimes
he was up and preaching by five in the morning, with a discipline
which amazed the Irish. Arthur Guinness must have been still a
young man when he heard him for the first time. Unlike the
landed gentry Arthur was not offended to hear that the heart of
a gentleman was as black and sinful as that of any labourer. It
appealed to his innate sense of equality and fair play. Throughout
his life he gravitated between the dissenting chapel and the Church of
Ireland: nonconformism satisfied his integrity, the Church of Ireland
his ambitions. Men with aspirations needed influence among their
Protestant peers and nonconformism was still too novel. It was the
working man's religion. A little convention went a long way.

The Church of Ireland was as bedevilled by social convention as
its English counterpart, except that the working classes missing from
its pews were Roman Catholics. It was in this respect that Arthur
Guinness was unusual for his time and his Protestant background.
He was not so governed by expediency that he could not bend for
the sake of his conscience. He treated his employees with dignity,
and unlike many other Protestant merchants, publicly supported
the Catholics in their struggle for equality and justice, as long as
they went about it in the proper way, his way. It was the way of
non-violence, said that mighty wielder of the pickaxe. When local
gossip said he had opposed a man's election to the freedom of the
city on religious grounds he issued a public denial, claiming he had
gone out of his way to solicit votes on the man's behalf.[5]

There are few anecdotes about the first Arthur Guinness other
than the saga of preserving his water rights, but one thing is clear:
he was not a hypocrite. He ruthlessly refused all bribes, which were
commonly offered at the time. His honesty bordered on austerity.
And though he did not suffer fools or sinners gladly, rigour was
tempered with genuine humanity and charity. In his religion he
followed the dictates of his own conscience, unaware of the struggle
between the claims of humility and aggrandisement that waged war
for his soul. When his eldest son Hosea announced his intention
to become a Church of Ireland minister, his initial disappointment

7

that he was lost to the brewery was later matched by his pleasure on Hosea's appointment to St Werbergh's, one of the most socially prestigious churches in Dublin.

As the brewery expanded, so did his reputation and standing in Dublin society. If he now lived as a merchant gentleman in his stately home, surrounded by fine portraits, elegant furnishings and well-mannered children, did it not signify the gracious hand of the Almighty? But he was too vigorous, too motivated a man to settle for a life of smug satisfaction, enjoyed from the comforts of his favourite armchair. Wealth brought responsibility and moral obligation. It was not to be squandered selfishly, nor was it an excuse for excess. How else did a man amass and maintain a private fortune, then pass it on to his children? Indeed he once confessed that had it not been for the necessity of "providing for ten children now living out of one and twenty born to us, and yet more to come," he might never have been so enterprising in the first place.[6]

Spes Mea in Deo, "My hope is in God", was Arthur's chosen motto. It might equally have been "Moderation in all things". This was not reflected in the spirit of the Dublin of the 1780s. In 1782 England had granted Ireland her own parliament. Henry Grattan stood beneath the magnificent chandeliers of the parliament building at College Green and held everyone spellbound with his oratory. "Ireland is now a nation," he proclaimed, and the spirit of national pride to which he gave voice burst out in a time of unequalled building, draining, trading and frolicking. Dubliners had never known anything quite like it. The professional and merchant classes which gave birth to men like Arthur Guinness were tired of being treated like uncultured provincials. They coveted the elegance and status of the upper classes and built a city worthy of their aspirations and fine taste, with elegant houses, dignified churches, wide boulevards for their coaches, and spacious squares and parks. Well may the English treat them as some tiresome, backward colony: now they had a capital fit for an independent nation.

But much of the sophistication was skin deep. When it came to food and drink, elegance had a habit of giving way to Bacchanalian ribaldry. This was something of an Irish tradition. Dean Swift and John Wesley were both appalled by the gluttony and drunkenness they found in Ireland. Self-indulgence, they said, was Ireland's besetting sin. Brewer though he was, Arthur Guinness was inclined to agree. As a vigorous, often outspoken member of the Dublin Council, he felt that men in public office should set an example and was appalled by the behaviour of his fellow councillors. By long tradition a newly-elected Alderman treated the City Corporation to a lavish banquet. Guinness thought it an indulgence of the worst order, carousing at the expense of the poor: let fifty guineas be given instead to the Blue Coat Hospital. The city fathers were put out. Why should a killjoy like Arthur Guinness inflict his rigorous standards on them and spoil all the fun? They rejected his proposal and saved face by declaring that "good eating and above all, good drinking, were strong bonds of good fellowship and unity". Hospitality and good living were the very essence of their charter and they "must stand or fall together".[7]

Guinness' anti-gluttony campaign was not the only one of his attempted reforms to fall on stony ground. As secretary of the Friendly Brothers of St Patrick he was a dedicated opponent of duelling. Many people, particularly Wesleyans, were now opposed to an upper-class practice which was rapidly becoming a plague in Dublin, spreading to the middle classes. Motivation for the duels was often petty, a ridiculous insistence on personal honour which ended in a waste of life. But many years would pass before a halting of the trend, and as irony would have it one of Ireland's most famous duels would one day have lasting repercussions for Arthur's youngest son.

Some of the causes which aroused his indignation were successfully resolved in his lifetime. He was outspoken in his demand for penal reform. In 1765 a man was burnt alive at St Stephen's Green for keeping a brothel. A year later a priest was hanged, drawn and quartered for expressing sympathy with the peasants. Excess was always deplorable, even in punishment. Guinness could not tolerate barbarism, whoever the perpetrator. He lent his voice to the increasing volume of public protest, and slowly the law was modified.

It was as an old man, a respected elder of the city, that Arthur Guinness was invited by Henry Grattan to appear before the Irish parliament to plead for the repeal of the excise duties on beer. Grattan was concerned to introduce any measure which would improve Ireland's chances in the trade war with England. The brewers had had a long and hard campaign. Never, Guinness told the parliament, had the brewing industry been at such a low ebb. With the consumption of spirits and the high price of malt it was hardly surprising. None of the members, it seems, was moved unduly. Instead they called in an English brewer, who had just moved to Dublin because he found conditions in Ireland advantageous. During his evidence, notice was given to the House that the roof was on fire and the dome about to collapse. Within two hours the beautiful parliament building was burnt to the ground. Whether because they thought the fire an act of God or, more likely, because the English brewer let it be known that enormous profits could be made in brewing, the Commons decided not to repeal the taxes when they met in the Coffee House the following month.

Four years passed before Arthur Guinness appeared before the parliament again. This time he knew how to pitch his argument. Drunkenness was rising in Ireland at an alarming rate, he claimed. This was a matter of the utmost seriousness and there was no doubt that whiskey was the real culprit. It was an instigator of turbulence, violence, faction fighting, and worse! There was only one sensible, wholesome alternative, and that was beer.

With most of Ireland's problems – health, moral, political and religious – firmly attributed to whiskey, parliament had no alternative but to adopt what now appeared a vital piece of social reform and abolish the excise duty on beer. So began a particular piece of the legend, popular in the missionary branch of the family, that Guinness beer was first brewed in the spirit of true Christian altruism, to combat the whiskey-drinking of Ireland.

However dubious the argument may seem today, it appeared to convince Guinness himself and Henry Grattan too. "It is at your source", said the politician to the brewers, "the Parliament will find in its own country the means of health with all her flourishing consequences and the cure of intoxication with all her misery."[8] Beer, he said, was "the natural nurse of the people", a philosophy echoed by many a beer-drinker down the ages. The Irish brewing industry never looked back, and for all his increased prosperity Arthur Guinness was grateful to God, Henry Grattan and the distinctive extra strong porter he now began to brew, using a higher proportion of brown malt.

Wesley's warnings of the evils of drink may well have been diluted to suit Arthur Guinness' convenience, yet ironically four of his grandsons had to be dismissed from the brewery for drunkenness and drink-related misdemeanours. From the first a strange dualism followed the clan. For some of the Guinnesses alcohol was the elixir of life, for others it soon became their poison. But Arthur Guinness the patriarch never lived to see it. It would have broken his heart.

4

Over the years as sales increased steadily, success had never taken Arthur Guinness by surprise or gone to his head. Had he not always fulfilled his God-given responsibilities to the best of his ability? Work, public duty, charitable institutions and his family, these had preoccupied his mind and in that order. Righteousness had reaped its own rewards. He had become one of the principal employers in Dublin, and the business thrived at St James' Gate as did the flour mills he had built at Kilmainham in 1790. He had sorted out the finances of the Meath Hospital and placed that charitable institution firmly on its feet. His own money had been put to good use enabling the Dean of St Patrick's Cathedral to repair the Chapel Schools. The Sunday school he founded, the first in Dublin, was flourishing. In fact he had made a veritable career of philanthropy, sowing the seeds of a long family tradition.

And his family was all he could have wished. Should Arthur Guinness have witnessed the ceremonials attending his own departure there is no doubt that he would have been satisfied. The Rev. Hosea Guinness, presiding at the funeral, was a solid, dignified and liberal-minded man, if a little lacking in fire and imagination. Never had Arthur anticipated that the Church would deprive him of his natural heir. Perhaps it was his eldest son's first name which made him a scholar from birth and robbed him of a head for business. To Hosea he bequeathed Beaumont, the family home – his son, as he remarked drily in his will, "not being in any line of life whereby he is likely by Industry to enlarge his Property".[9] One clergyman in the family might well be a blessing, as long as it was only one.

He need not have feared. Arthur, his second son, was as like him in nature as he was in name. Facially the resemblance was remarkable, the same long pale face, exaggerated by the receding hairline and aquiline nose. The eyes, more hooded than his father's, glinted beneath the heavy lids, daring any adversary to cross him. The set of the jawline spoke of dignity and determination. Only the mouth, curving almost involuntarily at one corner, betrayed a store of carefully controlled generosity. Such was Arthur's trust in this son that he bequeathed him the precious silver salver which had been presented to him as a mark of particular respect by the Corporation of Brewers. Arthur the second, wearing his father's mantle, stepped into his elder brother's role, assumed the running of the brewery, and with it the headship of the family. It was the first time, but not the last, that God had come between a Guinness and his natural inheritance.

If Arthur manifested the same business flair and genius of his father, there was little sign of it in Edward, the third son. Edward already appeared weak and indecisive, easily enticed by gracious living, without enough self-discipline to earn it. They had tried him out in the business without success. With one son already in the Church, law appeared to be the answer, but at thirty-one Edward had not yet distinguished himself in any way. Life was the problem. It failed him, or so he complained. Every family has a black sheep and Edward was the first of a long line. Unlike his brother Arthur and two younger brothers, William Lunell and Benjamin, who had proved their reliability in business, Edward's penalty in his father's will was the exclusion from any rights in the brewery.

It was however the youngest son, John Grattan, who worried Arthur the most. At twenty he had decided that the pedestrian life of a brewer or a miller was not for him. This most dashing and handsome of his sons was adventurous to the point of recklessness. Nearly killed at fifteen, he had still not developed a sense of self-preservation and his craving for adventure seemed inexhaustible. The last of ten children, only a child when his brothers Hosea and Arthur were married, it sometimes seemed as if John Grattan felt he was under their shadow and had something to prove.

In 1798, fired by the influence of the French Revolution, the Catholic working classes revolted against English domination and tried to set up an Irish Republic. There were uprisings all over the country, the most serious in County Wexford. Dublin raised a yeomanry to defend the city from the revolutionaries. Despite his sympathy with the Catholic cause, old Arthur Guinness felt things had gone too far. Violence could never be condoned. He came out of semi-retirement to keep a fatherly eye on the brewery while two of his sons, William Lunell and Edward, volunteered at once. Arthur the younger and Benjamin continued their work at the brewery to the latter's intense pique:

> I think myself unfortunate that I am so situated at this time that I cannot join the yeomanry but really attendance required now in Dublin is such that if both Arthur and I went into the yeomanry the Business here must be entirely stop'd . . . £80 which we sent by the Canal for Athy the day before the Disturbances broke out has fallen into the hands of Rebels and is all gone.[10]

John Grattan could not resist the scent of danger. In vain they told him he was too young to join his brothers, that at fifteen he should be studying, not manning the defences of Dublin. His enthusiasm got the better of him and he was severely wounded carrying dispatches. The very next year he volunteered for the English army's East India Company. Better, old Arthur decided, simply to leave him £1500 in his will and see what he would make of himself.

There was no doubt that life had smiled very kindly on the old brewer. He had enjoyed all his faculties to the last, shrewd and alert in business matters, vigorous in all his dealings, active in mind as he was in body. He enjoyed appearing at the brewery for an hour or two every morning, just to see that Arthur, Benjamin and William Lunell were coping, and then for exercise he would ride out to the Hibernian mills at Kilmainham. As he rode towards the western edge of the city he would stop and look down. Below him the Liffey wound its way, slow and sluggish, thick like the vital ingredient of a rich green pea soup, not of a dark, full-bodied drink of stout. In miniature Dublin looked more like a child's plaything than a sophisticated cultural centre, none the less old Arthur savoured the ever-increasing influence of his family into the political, religious and social life of that bustling city. His eldest son was curate of the prestigious St Werbergh's. His eldest daughter Elizabeth was married to one of the wealthy, influential Darleys. Edward Smythe, his wife's cousin, was minister of Bethesda Chapel, the leading Nonconformist Church, and though as a result of the uprisings England had ended the Irish parliament by the Act of Union, Henry Grattan's influence in Dublin was still substantial.

When Arthur Guinness died in 1803 his estate was valued for probate at £23,000, a small fortune for the time. That shrewd business sense, married to a morality and sense of duty unusual for a man of the eighteenth century, had enabled him to turn a poky, neglected brewery into the biggest business enterprise in Ireland. "A successful manufacturer had to navigate the shoals of religious faction, of civil disturbance and political corruption",[11] and he had successfully managed to do all three.

With three sons to follow him in the brewery and the mills, one in the Church, one in law and one in the army, and his daughters married into well-established Dublin families, he could afford to be well satisfied with his achievement. Everything was as it should be. He could now sink peacefully to his rest in the family vault. "The worthy and the good will regret him", said the *Dublin Evening Post*, "because his life has been useful and benevolent and virtuous."[12]

2

1803–1842

Captain John the Gentleman Soldier

1

India at the beginning of the nineteenth century was as turbulent and war-torn as Ireland. In fact it was home from home for many an Irishman with military aspirations.

When John Grattan Guinness arrived there as a raw recruit of the East India Company, the 250-year-old Mogul Empire had fallen into decay and the country was divided into many warring princely states. The European empires, ever ready to take advantage of a potentially lucrative situation, had pushed their way through the continent and ruthlessly exerted their hold.

The East India Company was created in 1600 when Elizabeth I granted a charter to a group of London merchants, giving them permission to trade in the East Indies. But times had changed. By 1765 the so-called "Trading Company" had managed to become the official administrator of the vast province of Bengal, reducing the great princes to mere ruling dependants. By the turn of the century everyone in the company, its directors, civil servants, army, merchants, the native Indian rulers, Muslim sultans and Hindu rajas, every thug and bandit plaguing the villages like locusts, all regarded India as their El Dorado. Small wonder that the army of the East India Company had such a large Irish contingency. Life could be no worse than in Ireland. In fact it might be a lot better if there was a fortune to be made.

The most famous of all Irish soldiers, Arthur Wellesley, later Duke of Wellington, was sent to India in 1798 to bring the rebellious Raja of Mysore, Tippu Sultan, to heel. For Wellesley the appointment came as a welcome relief after the excruciating boredom of life at Dublin Castle. He was tired of handing the ladies of the Anglo-Irish ascendancy in and out of their carriages and had long awaited an opportunity to demonstrate his military prowess. India held out unlimited possibilities.

The situation was becoming increasingly tense. England and France were at war in Europe. Long-time rivals in India, they naturally played out their struggle there too. Indian princes like Tippu Sultan quickly realised that they could exploit the situation to their own advantage and it was with the French that Tippu made a treaty.

Wellesley at once laid siege to Tippu's capital, Seringapatam, and that was where the seventeen-year-old John Grattan Guinness was posted when he joined the 12th Regiment Native Infantry of the Madras army. The tall, rather handsome young man, hungry for excitement, found plenty to satisfy his appetite. The siege of Seringapatam was a baptism of fire. Soldiers who had the misfortune to be captured had nails driven into their skulls or their necks wrung by the Hindu strongmen, known as Jetties. John Grattan's nerve was strained to its limit, but he survived to see his commander triumph.

Wellesley installed himself as the official governor of Seringapatam and appointed a new raja. Peace reigned, but not for long. A brigand from the Mahratta region with the unlikely name of Dhoondiah Waugh had managed to escape from Tippu Sultan's dungeons during the British assault. Gathering a bunch of Tippu's wild men around him he fled from the Mysore province into Mahratta territory and made a series of lightning raids across the border. Eventually the British had had enough and sent Wellesley to find him and hang him from the highest tree.

In years to come John Grattan regaled his family with the romantic story of how he followed the great Wellington in his long chase across Mahratta territory. In truth there was little romance about it. Day after day they marched, mile after mile in the intense heat of the Indian sun. The nights were bitterly cold. Wellesley expected a stamina and courage from his men to match his own. When they finally caught up with Dhoondiah, Wellesley himself headed four regiments in a swift and fierce charge which routed the enemy. Dhoondiah was killed and Wellesley marched his men back to Seringapatam where for the first time he received the widespread recognition of his military abilities he knew he deserved.

John Grattan was garrisoned at Seringapatam for two more years, watching his commander restore law and order to the province of Mysore. The natives were easily controlled compared to the troops, who engaged in looting, quarrelling and debauchery the moment Wellesley's back was turned. His own officers often mistreated the locals, bullying and threatening them, or set them a bad example in their futile drunken brawls and squabbles. It was not the sort of behaviour the son of Arthur Guinness was used to. Having inherited his father's self-restraint and high moral principles, he soon realised that the Honourable East India Company, with its tendency to overlook and even encourage greed, theft and rapacity, was not quite as honourable as he had anticipated. Small wonder that the man who would become England's most famous soldier earned his undying respect.

In 1803 the British finally decided to deal once and for all with the fractious, violent princes of the Mahratta states, now trained, armed, and their ranks swelled by the French. Once again John Grattan found himself following Wellesley across Mahratta territory in the same gruelling conditions. But if the British had assumed that this war would be as easily won as the last they were mistaken. The French had effectively transformed marauding hordes into an intelligent and disciplined army, with modern equipment and skills. The British had to navigate the treacherous system of river tributaries and the enemy took full advantage of their ignorance. At Assaye there was carnage and the British sustained severe losses. Still, it was better to die in battle than to be taken alive and tortured barbarically.

By the end of the year the princes were finally subdued and metamorphosed into puppet rulers. And John Grattan, an ardent soldier and skilful horseman, had won his commission. Wellesley was always on the lookout for "forward young men with dash" and Guinness fulfilled the ideal. He was competent and fearless. Furthermore Wellesley insisted his officers be gentlemen and soldiers, in that order, a principle John Grattan never forgot. According to his commander only discipline and vigilance could save his men from their besetting sin, intoxication, and the brewer's youngest son could not have agreed more. But Captain John Grattan's moment of recognition was tinged with disappointment. His father did not live to see it.

In 1805 Wellesley was called back to England. Despite the removal of his inspiration no thought of returning home occurred to the young captain. One day a letter arrived from his brother Edward, enthusing about the potential of two large ironworks at Palmerston and Lucan. Despite his father's lack of confidence in his business ability, Edward knew he was not destined for a life at the bar and was sure he could turn the ironworks to his advantage. It was a failsafe venture. But there was a problem. His own inheritance of £1500 was insufficient for such a project. Brothers Arthur, William and Benjamin were too involved in the brewery to help, but John Grattan had received the same sum from their father. What did he want with such an inheritance while he was out in India? He ought to consider investing it, and where better than with his own brother? By the time John Grattan was ready to settle down he,

Edward, would see to it that his brother's inheritance was worth twice as much. John Grattan, naïve in all but military matters, was easily convinced. Flushed with the success of his chosen career, easy-going about money, he willingly handed over his legacy to his brother. Whatever shrewd business sense the first Arthur Guinness possessed was appropriated by the rest of the family before it reached the youngest of his sons.

He never thought again about his legacy, until he came home on leave in 1810 and met Susanna Hutton, daughter of a Dublin alderman. Only then did the comforts of a quiet life begin to appeal to his adventurous nature. He married Susanna, but any thoughts of settling down were soon shattered. The iron works collapsed and brother Edward, hounded by creditors and the threat of debtors' prison, fled to Dundalk with his wife, Margaret, and their many children. There, filled with self-pity and terror at the possibility of imprisonment for bankruptcy, he besieged his brewing brothers with requests for help.

They complied. They could hardly stand back and watch their brother's family starve, though brother Arthur did have some stringent questions about their high standard of living. But Edward explained away his expensive house and two servants. His children needed a garden to play in. He could not expect his wife to do without a carriage. Money matters were making her ill. It fast became apparent that Edward's needs were becoming a bottomless pit.

Worn down and not a little irritated by his constant barrage of requests, Arthur finally acknowledged defeat and instructed the brewery to buy his brother out of bankruptcy for the exorbitant sum of £5900. It cost the brewery dear at a time when they could least afford it. In fact it placed its very future in jeopardy. It was 1815, the year Wellington finally defeated Napoleon at Waterloo. For Ireland the end of the Napoleonic wars heralded a major economic upheaval.

As for Captain John Grattan, no one seems to have been too concerned with his financial problems, as long as he stayed with the army in India. Now he had little choice: there were few ways for a gentleman to make an honourable living and the army was one of them. India would rob him of his health and another fourteen years of his life.

2

In 1815, as Wellington marched on Napoleon and Captain John Grattan was sweating out his days beneath a scorching Indian sun, an event occurred in Dublin which was to have lasting consequences for the young captain of the Madras army. It caused such a furore in the Irish capital that, a hundred years later, when people gathered round a warm fire they told the story of O'Connell's duel with D'Esterre with relish, far more than the tales of O'Connell's victories fighting for the emancipation of his people.[1]

In the icy winter of 1814–15 frustration ran high among the Catholic population of Dublin. The political equality they craved seemed as distant as ever, despite the pressure they had exerted upon Westminster. The Protestant-controlled Dublin Corporation, without the moderating presence of old Arthur Guinness, terrified that the government might be tempted to grant concessions to the Catholic majority, presented an anti-emancipation petition to the English parliament.

The Catholic population had long since needed a popular hero and they found it in Daniel O'Connell. He was a large, genial Irishman whose gift for blarney disguised a brilliant legal mind. The bigotry of the corporation infuriated him. It was at best "a beggarly Corporation", he said, which, given the extent of the injury and the man's reputation for deadly invective, was hardly the worst abuse he could have employed.

A certain member of the corporation, one John Frederick D'Esterre, a pork butcher by trade, took exception to the remark. O'Connell was becoming intolerable and the time had come to silence him once and for all. It was not that D'Esterre was such a narrow-minded Protestant. In fact he had opposed the passing of a previous anti-Catholic resolution. Nor was he as "gallant, but unfortunate"[2] as his wife's family were to say of him in later years. He was motivated by self-interest rather than any genuine sense of injustice. Lacking the clear head and application necessary for a successful merchant he found himself bankrupt and worried sick about providing for his wife and young family. As a last resort he was standing for the post of City Sheriff, which, if he were elected, would confer instant relief from his financial anxieties. It was therefore imperative to demonstrate his suitability for the job with a display of anti-Catholic muscle. He rather fancied himself as the champion of the Protestant cause.

D'Esterre sent O'Connell a letter of protest containing a veiled threat and a demand for immediate satisfaction. O'Connell replied, refusing to eat his words. "No terms attributed to me," he wrote, "however reproachful, can exceed the contemptuous feelings I entertain for that body in its corporate capacity, although doubtless it contains many valuable persons."[3] He failed to challenge D'Esterre to a duel, so the butcher wrote to him again and this time received his note back unopened.

By then the entire city, in an agony of suspense, was buzzing with rumour and gossip. D'Esterre spread most of it himself. The weedy little man strutted up and down the centre of Dublin with whip and pistols in hand, telling everyone that the mouth of the great O'Connell was to be silenced for ever. He threatened to horsewhip O'Connell in Grafton Street, or at the Four Courts where he practised law. O'Connell was almost twice his size and Dublin citizens might have been amused, were it not that D'Esterre was known to be a deadly shot. Before settling down to his prosaic and impecunious existence in Dublin he had been an infantry captain in the Indian army, like John Grattan, and before that a naval officer when mutiny broke out on his ship. He had refused to join the mutineers. They gave him one last chance and with the rope around his neck he shouted, "Hang away, and be damned!" His Irish bluster changed their minds.

Still no challenge came from O'Connell. "The man is a poltroon and will not fight," claimed D'Esterre. O'Connell had tried to stay calm, to ignore the whole ridiculous affair, but there is a limit to the endurance of any man. He marched out of the courts to meet the alderman, who by this time was waiting for him outside the draper's shop in College Green, O'Connell's normal route home.

Tension in Dublin was high. Terror for O'Connell's safety had risen to near panic and the people provided him with a formidable bodyguard, which would not permit any confrontation between the two men. A judge followed O'Connell and he was bound over to keep the peace. Undaunted he proceeded to the home of Major MacNamara, a wealthy Protestant landlord with Catholic sympathies, and asked him to be his second. MacNamara was something of a dandy, but more important, he was a practised duellist.

Early the following morning Sir Edward Stanley, D'Esterre's second, called on MacNamara and yet again demanded an apology. MacNamara refused point blank. Then with a speed which left Stanley dumbfounded he accepted the challenge and insisted on a duel to be fought without further delay at three o'clock the same afternoon. Stanley tried to negotiate a postponement but MacNamara's only concession was that since it was not a private quarrel a single shot should be sufficient.

"No Sir!" stormed Stanley, who finding his voice lost his temper, "If they fire twenty shots each, Mr D'Esterre will never leave the ground until Mr O'Connell makes an apology."

MacNamara replied: "Well then, if blood be your object, blood you shall have, by God!" and stormed out of the room.[4]

It was a bitterly cold February day and snow lay thick upon the ground as O'Connell's carriage rolled slowly into the field in

Bishop's Court, County Kildare, a spot some twelve miles west of Dublin, where the duel was to be fought. Duelling, though not illegal for another thirty years, was socially unacceptable, thanks to the efforts of men like Arthur Guinness who regarded the victors as little better than common murderers. But it still exerted ghoulish fascination. The news had spread through the surrounding area and crowds of peasants turned out to watch, the women huddled in threadbare shawls, their breath freezing and fingers aching in the glacial winter air.

It was almost dark when D'Esterre's carriage arrived nearly an hour late, accompanied by a procession of carriages and gigs belonging to virtually the entire Dublin Corporation. He had barely climbed down and proceeded to choose his pistol when false rumours reached a delighted Dublin Castle that O'Connell the Liberator, the thorn in their flesh, was no more. The army was called out into the streets of Dublin to quell any riot or insurgence. A squadron of cavalry was despatched to County Kildare to protect D'Esterre from the fury of the people and escort him safely home.

Meanwhile at Bishop's Court the seconds were still wrangling over details. More than half an hour was spent in preliminaries. D'Esterre appeared completely calm and walked about nonchalantly twirling his cane while Stanley measured the ground. O'Connell tried to appear relaxed and catching a glimpse of his tailor in the crowd shouted, "Ah, Jerry, I never missed you from an aggregate meeting," but his easy chatter belied his anxiety. MacNamara, his second, instructed the inexperienced O'Connell to remove his white neckerchief as it made an easy target, and his fob because if it were hit it would inflict a ghastly wound. O'Connell was shaken by such grisly preparations.

D'Esterre won the toss and the two men moved into position, ten paces from each other. As the handkerchief fell D'Esterre stepped to one side and fired. His shot was extraordinarily bad and ricocheted off the ground at O'Connell's feet. A second later O'Connell fired and D'Esterre fell writhing to the ground. He had been shot through the groin.

O'Connell was appalled. He stood motionless, muttering, "I aimed low, I aimed low," over and over again. He wanted to go over and see if D'Esterre was all right but MacNamara led him quickly away.

It was the people's turn to rejoice. The town erupted into a frenzy of joy and relief. Bonfires burned in the streets, but O'Connell refused to appear or enter into the celebration. He was morose and silent. When he did speak he simply repeated "I aimed low", shaking his head in disbelief and demanding to know whether his friends thought he had killed the man.

The next morning the *Dublin Journal* carried the following announcement:

> Yesterday, at four o'clock in the evening, a meeting took place at Bishop's Court, between Mr D'Esterre, one of the Representatives of the Guild of Merchants in the Common Council of Dublin, and Counsellor O'Connell, when we lament to say, the former was wounded in the hip. The cause of quarrel was some insolent words used by Counsellor O'Connell at one of the Popish Meetings, as against the Corporation of Dublin. These words Mr D'Esterre resented, and desiring an explanation, was answered by further insolence, which induced him to press the meeting.
>
> Mr D'Esterre's wound is considered dangerous: the ball has not been extracted.[5]

The following day D'Esterre died, managing to utter some last words of forgiveness, like a true gentleman. But O'Connell never forgave himself. Remorse pursued him for the rest of his life. It was said that whenever he approached the sacrament he wore a black glove on the hand which had fired the fatal shot. Passing D'Esterre's house in Bachelor's Walk on his way to the Four Courts, he would stop to pray for mercy for the dead and forgiveness for the living. He went to see the young widow to offer her a share in his income and was greatly struck by her beauty. She refused his help, and her dignity only pained him more. Eventually he persuaded her to accept a small annuity for her daughter, which he paid until his death thirty years later.

3

The first Jane Lucretia D'Esterre knew about the duel was the moment her dying husband was carried into the house. She was eighteen years old, the mother of two small children, penniless, and completely alone. Her husband was her only close relative. Both her parents were dead. There was a half-brother who lived in London, Johann Baptist Cramer, a world-famous pianist, composer and music publisher, but they had not been raised together and he was something of a stranger.

The Cramers had been musicians for generations. Jane Lucretia's paternal grandfather, Jacob Cramer, was a flautist, a native of Sachau in Silesia in the south of Germany. His son Wilhelm showed exceptional brilliance on the violin and was accepted as a pupil by Johann Stamitz and Christian Cannabich, the foremost violin teachers of the day. Playing in the Mannheim orchestra did not provide adequate expression for his creative genius and when his son, Johann Baptist, was only a year old the family sailed for England. George III quickly recognised Wilhelm's outstanding qualities as a musician and made him leader of the Court Band, the Opera and the Pantheon. But it was his role as leader of the Handel festivals at Westminster Abbey which brought him real recognition. For a while he was without rival in England as a solo player. In time Wilhelm's son, Johann Baptist, established an international reputation as a pianist. According to Beethoven's correspondence he appears to be the only pianist of whom the great composer had any opinion at all. "All the rest went for nothing."

It was rumoured that the Cramers were Jews, but if this was so they chose to ignore it once they had left Germany behind. Their Jewishness may well have been the reason for Wilhelm's lack of success there and he did not care to suffer the same disadvantage in England. When his first wife died and he married for the second time, he chose a Miss Madden, daughter of a well-established Protestant Dublin family, who was many years his junior. Jane Lucretia was born to them in 1797 and two years later Wilhelm died. Her mother took the little girl back to Dublin and brought her up there as a member of the comfortable Protestant ascendancy.

When she was fourteen Jane Lucretia took bourgeois Dublin society by storm. Her beauty was legendary. She possessed the classic Celtic skin colouring, long locks of dark hair falling in waves over her shoulders. Her eyebrows arched gently over a pair of penetrating dark eyes and her rather large mouth and full, expressive lips which curled up at the corners betrayed an impish sense of humour. So did the dimple in her chin. Not only was she vivacious and beautiful, she had also inherited the creative and musical gifts of her father's family. She could play the piano like one inspired and the effect at any soirée was magnetic. In a society where the Protestant middle classes constantly sought to ape and better the Anglo-Irish aristocracy by making a display of their fine culture and taste, Jane Lucretia was a rare prize. Young men flocked to her. Though Irish through and through, with all the warmth and geniality of the Celtic temperament, she inherited the more intense, reflective disposition of her German ancestors. In short, she was Irish enough for people to feel at home with her and just foreign enough to exercise a certain fascination.

Flattery is heady stuff at any age, but at fifteen a woman is too young to be discerning. Coquettish and wilful, she was easily swept off her feet by the dashing, worldly D'Esterre, who was richer in swagger than common sense. What he lacked in stature he made up for in bravado. He pretended to be a wealthy merchant with prospects, easily convincing Jane Lucretia and her mother. Jane would have him at any cost. But there were money problems from the first. Every one of the three years they were married was blighted by fear and anxiety. Poverty and shame robbed her of some of her looks and her sparkle. The small amount her mother left her when she died was soon swallowed up by her husband's debts. His death left her virtually destitute with two small children to support.

Before D'Esterre's body was cold the bailiffs were knocking on the door. They burst into the house and appropriated all his goods, then left, threatening to come back the next day for his body too. They wanted their money and if there was nothing else to sell a body could always raise something in the anatomy department at the hospital. Besides it would save her the cost of a burial, which she could not afford anyway.

There was no time to grieve. Jane Lucretia had to act quickly. She managed to rally one or two friends and late that night they stole out of the house with shovels and the body. Down the cobbled Dublin back streets they crept by lantern light, in terror of being caught, until at last they were out of the town and into the hills. There they could give the unfortunate man a burial of sorts. John Frederick D'Esterre, whose only claim to fame was that he was killed by the legendary O'Connell, was laid to rest in an unknown grave.

For his widow despair came close. To escape Dublin, the bailiffs and the wagging tongues, she took a house in Ecclefechan in Scotland. One day, feeling more listless than ever, she set off on her own, intending to sit and read by the riverside. She sat staring into the water for some time, too unhappy to settle to her novel. What was the point of going on? Nothing deadened the pain for long. Before her lay the only permanent escape. The still, deep waters seemed to lure her with their offer of peace and an end to the bitter weariness.

She looked up and her gaze fixed on a young ploughman, about her own age, who had appeared in the field on the other side of the river, totally absorbed in his work. She watched him, fascinated despite herself, marvelling at his zest and determination. He seemed to find real enjoyment in an ordinary, mundane task. She felt rebuked for her apathetic self-pity. Here she was with two small children relying on her completely and she was so wrapped up in her own misery that she could even contemplate evading her responsibilities. Work would be her salvation. She got up, dusted herself down and with fresh determination to face the future, however hard it might be, set off for Dublin.

Some weeks later she sat in the gallery of St George's Church, as she did every Sunday, listening half-heartedly to the preacher. His text was "God so loved the world that he gave his only begotten son". They were familiar words, but suddenly they impressed her as if she were hearing them for the first time. The realisation dawned on her that she was not as completely alone as she had assumed. God in His divine providence would be father to her fatherless children. Perhaps life would not be such a comfortless, intolerable burden after all.

With a new confidence and fierce pride she refused all offers of help, including Daniel O'Connell's. Like the Ecclefechan farmer's son she would "find her task and stand to it". Her duty was to support her family, which she would do by giving music lessons. She turned down the many proposals of marriage which came her way – her widow's garb with its stand-up, frilled white collar and long black lace veils only enhanced her attractions. Years later, studying a portrait of her in her widow's weeds, one of her sons commented that she looked "as if formed to win admiration and affection".[6] Somehow she managed to ward off all suitors for a further fourteen years. When she did eventually marry she followed her heart once again, and not the dictates of financial good sense.

4

In 1829 Jane Lucretia D'Esterre met Captain John Grattan Guinness at the York Street Chapel in Dublin. The attraction was mutual and instant. They had a great deal in common. Life had been traumatic and difficult for both of them in recent years. Each was resigned to the fact that the joy and tranquillity which eluded them was meant only for others. Falling in love as they did was an unexpected surprise.

John Grattan had been invalided home, sick and exhausted, five years earlier. For twenty years, under the command of Lord Moira, the infantry captain had led his mercenary Indian troops against the remaining Mahratta princes, until all of them, including the Peshaw, Raja of Poona, were placed under British control. Conditions were appalling, the food inadequate and the constant massacres he witnessed began to oppress his spirit. The conquest of northern Burma in 1824 was the last straw. He could no longer cope with the climate, the conditions or the behaviour of his fellow human beings.

This disillusionment predisposed his positive response to the Wesleyan teaching he heard in the officers' mess. Wesley himself had been dead for some time, but his message was as alive and influential as ever, proclaimed by a host of new preachers and their large dissenting congregations. In England the Wesleyan movement was largely working class and therefore treated with fear and suspicion by the political and religious establishment.

The ruling aristocracy was terrified that religious liberty might give a taste for social freedom and provoke a French Revolution in England. Established Church leaders watched their dwindling congregations and lost revenue with dismay. Wesleyanism was socially outlawed. In 1810 and 1811 some of its leaders were beaten and imprisoned. Meetings were broken up, but under pressure the new movement spread like wildfire. It sparked a growing evangelical influence within the Church of England, particularly among the gentry, producing men of large heart and social conscience like the future Earl of Shaftesbury. It gave birth to an entirely new breed in the Indian army, a generation of officers of high moral calibre and integrity. They were the sort of men John Grattan Guinness respected most. Their piety appealed to him too. He had after all been raised as an Irish Protestant, even if his religion had been a formality in recent years. Unlike his father and his elder brother Arthur, who kept their feet in both the established and dissenting church camps, John Grattan became a Nonconformist.

As far as his brewing brothers were concerned, John Grattan gave no cause for concern until he left the army. They were occupied enough with brother Edward and his incessant demands. Under such pressure the well of sympathy was fast running dry. Besides, the brewery was just emerging from the most traumatic economic crisis of its history. The Napoleonic wars had played havoc with Ireland's economy. As far as his youngest brother was concerned out of sight was very much out of mind, until he arrived home, unwell, with a wife and four children to support and an army pension of £1000 a year, already modest by Guinness standards. Furthermore while it was not unusual for members of the family to be Wesleyan by persuasion, none of them had ever appeared to snub brother Hosea by leaving the established Church altogether.

Despite his youngest brother's break with family convention, despite his own financial anxieties, Arthur Guinness immediately found John Grattan work. His conscience would not allow him to do less. He sent him to Liverpool to take over a Guinness agency there at 29 Manesty Lane. He was to have two partners, Bewley and Nevill, and the business was to be totally self-supporting and separate from the brewery. Arthur Guinness did not believe in charity. This was to be John Grattan's great opportunity.

The retired soldier did his best, but he was made of too gentle stuff. The agency only dealt with beer as a sideline. Its main business was importing Irish whiskey, anathema to the Nonconformist. He wanted to sell beer primarily and replace the whiskey with another commodity, possibly some sort of food. His grand ideas did not work out. In business noble principles do not always make the best financial sense. His partners knew that from the start, but how could they argue with the brother of Arthur Guinness? Bewley and Nevill stayed in business but John Grattan withdrew after only a year. He was sorry to let his brother down but felt it better to let the agency manage without him than destroy it altogether.

A few months later his wife Susanna died. It was a terrible blow. Arthur, unable to stand back and watch his brother's near despair, did what he could. He took John Grattan's younger son John into the brewery as an apprentice.

His failure as a soldier and at business finally decided John Grattan that he was obviously destined for the leisurely, unpressurised life of a retired officer and Christian gentleman. Fast approaching middle age, he was still a handsome man with an erect, military bearing and a strong, dignified face, set off by the high white collars and silk cravats he loved to wear. His hair was as dark as ever. There was no hint of grey, not even in his long sideburns and the only suggestion of the past years of trauma was in the extraordinary pallor of his complexion. Despite his vigour and courage as a soldier, socially he was a shy man who often hid behind his spectacles, preferring the simple, solitary pleasures of reading and walking to the high life of Dublin society. In this quiet, gentle man Jane Lucretia D'Esterre found the qualities she most admired. She had waited a long time. He had been in India at the time of the duel, had missed the publicity and was ignorant of the gossip which still surrounded her wherever she went. He saw beyond the mystique still conferred upon her by her past, beyond the beauty and charm for which she was so admired, to the depths of her character, born of hard experience and moulded by her Christian faith. Both were Nonconformist. Their children were almost grown up. It was an ideal partnership. He needed her vivacity to stir him from his lethargic tendencies, and she needed his quiet strength. That, it would seem, was the only security he had to offer, for Jane Lucretia was destined to marry men without the capacity to earn a regular income.

After their marriage in 1829 they led a nomadic existence, wandering between Dublin, Clifton and Cheltenham. They always hoped their children by their first marriages would be fond of each other and to their great delight in 1835 John Grattan's eldest son Arthur married Amelia D'Esterre, Jane Lucretia's daughter. It seemed a providential blessing on their union. In the same year, when John Grattan was fifty-two and Jane Lucretia thirty-eight, while they were still living in Monkstown, Dublin, a child of their own was born. They called him Henry Grattan after John Grattan's cousin, Ireland's most celebrated politician. He was dedicated to God at the York Street Chapel. It was a year when Halley's Comet visited earth's solar system, a propitious omen for their firstborn.

Three more children followed, Robert Wyndham in 1837, Frederick William in 1839 and Lucy in 1841.

John Grattan had no particular occupation, except occasional housebuilding, which was a vital necessity since they moved so often. Their favourite resort was Cheltenham, where they settled for some time as the children were growing up. With its sheltered position and mild climate, Cheltenham had become a veritable oasis for retired officers of the East India Company; it was said that "you couldn't fire a shot-gun in any direction without hitting a colonel".[7]

It was a gracious, beautiful town with tree-lined avenues, exclusive clubs, and villas with open verandahs and porches, a replica of life in India. The spa waters were reputed to do wonders for liver and digestive systems disordered by the highly spiced diet of years overseas. That in itself was enough to attract John Grattan, who was far from strong in health. But the Madras army officers had also imported their piety into the town, making it the gentleman's evangelical mecca of England. The charms of Cheltenham were irresistible indeed.

The most powerful figure in the town was the Rev. Francis Close, vicar of St Mary's parish. He was known locally as "the Pope", such was his ability to mould public thinking. Being low church and evangelical by persuasion he must have regarded it as nothing less than a snub when John Grattan passed his church by in favour of the Nonconformist Congregational chapel. The minister there, Dr Archibald Brown, though equally outstanding a preacher, was less establishment and more liberal in his politics, a quality which would appeal to the son of old Arthur Guinness.

The couple were blissfully happy in their series of elegant town houses, John Grattan at his pottering, Jane Lucretia chivvying him along, reminding him of his responsibilities both to his first and second family, taking upon her own shoulders all the practical details of running the home. Fortunately she was used to it. It would appear that Guinness men were either intensely shrewd and practical or spiritual and other-worldly, and when they were the latter they were hopelessly impractical. Arthur Lee, brother Arthur's eldest son, had just bowed out of the brewery, and to his father's dismay had retired to a country estate to live like a Greek god and write romantic verse. John Grattan, said his son Henry Grattan, in later years was a man of "a decidedly religious turn". In fact there were similarities between father and son. Both lived half in this world and half in the next, and left the lesser, mundane necessities of life, such as food and finance, to the practical good sense of their spouses.

On more than one occasion Jane Lucretia had to rebuke her husband for his lack of commonsense. He seemed to imagine that she could just pack up and follow him wherever he chose to go But although John Grattan treated houses like toys, Jane Luc: felt a home and four children were a responsibility which could not be delegated. The one letter between them still extant was written by Jane Lucretia when they were living in Clifton and John Grattan was away on one of his many trips to Ireland to see his first family. It reveals a woman who knew how to handle her husband's rather impractical, petulant demands with charm and tact.

Clifton, August 9th, 1842. 5 Carlton Place
My own dear John
Your very welcome letter I have just received and am delighted to find you appear in such perfect health and spirits. I also much rejoice in the great kindness and affections of all friends and that you have had such an opportunity of seeing so many whom you love, especially your dear children, Arthur and Rebecca and Nan. In all this pleasure I sympathise with my dear partner and although I so much wish to see you again, yet I would not on such a selfish account have you shorten your absence from home even one day when so many and such urgent claims are heaping upon you. I shall be much more satisfied when I think you are in the path of duty and of pleasure and shall patiently wait until you find it suitable to come to your little wife again.

As to your affectionate invitation, would you really like to see the house, 5, Carlton Place, which I believe is yours, completely turned outside the windows and the children after it! "On horror's head, horrors accumulate!" I would as soon put a little lap dog over my house and family as the lady you mention . . . "Tell it not in Gath" that a lady of my sapient time of life should elope without ever the temptation of a lover's attendance. I have the Demon of Ruin to wave his wand over my domicile!

Jane Lucretia was witty, and coquettish rather than scolding. She knew how to tease and it worked. Both were quite satisfied with this arrangement. By day, when he was not away on one of his many visits, he indulged in his little projects, while she performed acts of charity all over the neighbourhood, visiting the sick, gathering poor children together into a ragged school and, Bible in hand, stopping to talk to people in the street, especially Jews, about their eternal destiny. She worked intensively to found an institution for the reclamation of fallen women. In the evening while he sat and read, she wrote letters, painted in oils or took out her harp and played for him. For Jane Lucretia, with her brilliant temperament and great musical and intellectual gifts, life in both Clifton and Cheltenham after Dublin must have been something of a cultural wilderness.

She never complained of frustration but was determined none the less to inspire in her children a deep appreciation of music, poetry and painting. Years later Henry was to say, "Whatever love I have had for nature, for history, and for literature, has been derived from her, and also whatever gift I may possess as a public speaker."

Such was her personal magnetism and zest that life could never be any other than interesting when Jane Lucretia was around. She trained her children in the art of lively conversation. To watch her was the only instruction they needed. Although her greatest source of news and excitement were the goings-on at their local chapel, in Jane Lucretia's case even these were not allowed to be commonplace. The gentle teasing which could woo and win a husband was put to a greater challenge when a visiting minister became her target. "Well, what next?" she writes to her husband, "Your friends are about you like bees, not stinging but infusing their honied kindness into your heart and still you contrive to send a thought across the waters to poor me! But I have no news to tell except what I will reserve for you on your return and which would not be worth entering upon now." But then she tells him the story of her little contretemps and it appears that there was no question who gained the upper hand:

Mr and Mrs Robertson of book-selling memory are here at present. I persuaded them to go with me to Hope (Chapel) on Sunday and there they were really delighted with Gregory. He preached a most lovely sermon from these words "will ye also go away?" I thought much of it was pointed at me for we have had a desperate quarrel, paper war, and I have expected my forgiveness since then, all the while I mean to make him smart a little. I sent him a most funny letter in answer to his angry one turning the whole thing into ridicule and saying that notwithstanding all his explosions there is nothing in all the artillery he lacks against me but powder and that the noise has frightened me into good behaviour. It was last Thursday he wrote the angry letter towards evening. I was vexed of course and was determined not to speak to him. At the singing class accordingly I was making my way out of the room by a circuitous route in order to avoid him but no, he intercepts my way, serries my hand, smiles in my face and says, "I hope you all very good." I must suddenly close or shall be late. The children all well. Love to Mr and Mrs Burke. Gregory desired his love to you. Mine to dear Arthur, Amelia and husband.

Your affectionate wife Jane Guinness.

The only real threat to their serenity was the behaviour of John Grattan junior, Captain John's youngest son by his first marriage.

One day he arrived on their doorstep in disgrace. Uncle Arthur had dismissed him from his apprenticeship at the brewery for drunkenness and mixing in degraded company. It was the first they knew that any of their children had gone astray and it came as a severe shock.

3

1815–1855

The Life and Times of Arthur the Second

1

John Grattan the younger was only one of many relatives to be a source of bitter disappointment to the second Arthur Guinness. Since the bankruptcy of his brother Edward there was always a steady stream of brothers, sisters, nephews and nieces tugging at his purse, if not his heart strings. As the tribe spread throughout the land and multiplied Arthur Guinness found that the patriarchal mantle often hung heavily on his shoulders. He felt, he said to one nephew, "pressed upon by claims on the part of the multiplied branches of our large (and from various circumstances) needy family to an extent of which even you, though not altogether ignorant, can hardly form adequate conception".[1] To his niece Olivia, Hosea's daughter, he wrote: "May I recommend, my dear Olivia, that you keep a systematic account of all your expenditure for in that way you may more easily judge." It was a recurrent theme in his letters to the younger members of the family.

If ever Moses was emotionally spent at the hands of the wayward children of Israel, Arthur Guinness must have thought he suffered more at the hands of his ever-increasing family. He was adviser, provider, counsellor and benefactor, and above all banker. Like his father he was far too shrewd, too conscious of the value of hard work, to give in to pressure without receiving any evidence of real appreciation. For years Edward was given the minimum to see whether or not he could make something of himself. But instead of working he went on begging on behalf of his poor children and in the end, under pressure from his brothers, Arthur paid Edward's many debts.

Arthur Guinness' natural sense of duty would not allow him to see any of his family destitute. Besides he was not unfeeling. He loved his family. He was one of ten children and he and his brothers and sisters had always been close. When Captain John wrote to him saying that his son was now a reformed character, begging him to give the boy another chance, what could Arthur do? He set him up on his own in a small brewing business in Bristol. If he was reformed, then let him prove it! When his eldest sister Elizabeth came to him, telling him that her husband Frederick Darley, a former lord mayor of Dublin, was in desperate financial straits, he helped her at once and took on their son as an apprentice. The Darleys were too distinguished a Dublin family to suffer disgrace.

A veritable army of nephew-apprentices were now working at the brewery with a view to developing their managerial potential and keeping the business in the family. They were carefully supervised and woe betide them if their behaviour did not enhance the reputation of the brewery. Arthur Guinness' charity would not tolerate any impugning of the firm's good name. His nephews were sent packing first, as the young John Grattan discovered to his cost.

Like his father, the second Arthur Guinness was a man who did what he felt was right, however much he might suffer for it. It was that integrity at any price which provoked the most precarious moment in the brewery's existence.

The first years of the nineteenth century had been boom years. Arthur, with his inherited flair for enterprise, took advantage of the war with France to extend his sales across the Bristol Channel. What better way to put strength into the young men resisting Napoleon's steady advance across Europe? In 1815 Napoleon was defeated, the war was won and 300,000 men were suddenly released from the army. Contracts for weapons were cancelled. Unemployment rose and the United Kingdom experienced severe economic depression. Ireland, as ever, was the worst affected. The brewing trade slumped. To compound problems in 1817 and 1819 the potato crop failed.

The Guinness brothers were appalled by the poverty and human misery they saw. They were already serving on a host of charitable committees. With foresight unusual for the time, Arthur had been a founder member of the Society for Improving the Conditions of Children Employed as Chimney Sweepers, and William Lunell served on a committee trying to put a stop to begging. But charitable committees could do nothing to alleviate the distress. A radical economic policy was needed. Arthur, who had risen through the ranks of the Bank of Ireland to be its Governor, felt as banker rather than brewer that deflation and revaluation of the Irish currency was the only solution. Financial stability must be achieved whatever the consequences for the brewery. And suffer the brewery did. The vast amount paid out to settle brother Edward's debts compounded the problem. Surviving against the economic odds was a close-run affair, but principles were more important than material success. Writing to his teenage son Benjamin Lee, Arthur noted with pleasure the improvement in his handwriting and the care he was taking with his schoolwork, but added this proviso: "but my dear Ben . . . recollect that although diligence in our worldly calling is our indispensable duty as Christians, yet we have higher than these to engage our attention for we have a Heavenly calling in Christ Jesus and to this our supreme diligence is required."[2]

In 1821 George IV went to see the bank as part of his state visit to Ireland. As Governor it was Arthur Guinness who received him and showed him round. For the first time the path of the Guinness family crossed British royalty. For his own part Arthur was not unduly impressed by royal patronage. Years later he would decline the privilege of "Purveyor of Porter" to Queen Victoria on the grounds that "it would be a useless feather, and, I think, not even a respectable feather."[3] Later generations happily enjoyed more than a token feather.

At first Arthur Guinness' colleagues at the bank were pleased with the skilful way he handled the country's finances, but their pleasure diminished rapidly when he vetoed a rise in salary for the Governor and directors. He was afraid the public might get the wrong impression and presume that the currency reforms were intended to line the Governor's own nest. "Abstain from all appearance of evil", said the Bible and the Wesleyan teaching which were second nature to him even more than to his father. To forgo a rise in salary was a small price to pay. Virtue brought its own rewards, whatever his colleagues thought. Like his father before him, who found the excesses of the Dublin Corporation distasteful, the second Arthur Guinness was austere in his standards for men in public office. The difference was that he was now in a powerful enough position to enforce them.

The problems of being the nation's chief banker were slight compared with those of being the "Guinness Family Banker", as Arthur began to call himself. Benjamin died in 1826 and left his brother Edward £1865, but despite his inheritance and an annuity from the firm Edward still kept coming to Arthur for money. What hurt the most was the way he played the brothers off against each other, so that Hosea had the gall to suggest that Edward was entitled to more than Arthur had given him. Arthur remonstrated firmly:

My dear Hosea
I feel myself placed in a painful and delicate situation when called upon to address my Elder Brother, and a Brother who I so sincerely love and respect upon the subject of his pecuniary concerns but my situation by which I am unavoidably obliged to

act as the Family Banker forces me to speak plainly . . . What claim had Edward upon the Trade? Had he rendered any service to the Trade to entitle him to an annuity, and was it for a given period of years? Certainly not; upon what could he have founded "expectation of future advantage from continuance in the House". Surely upon nothing.[4]

Hosea himself was not above asking for a supplement to his stipend. He could not afford to run the country house at Beaumont and he gave it to Arthur. It was more in keeping with his brother's lifestyle. But that still did not ease his financial situation. When his daughter Olivia, who had married a clergyman, became mentally ill it was to brother Arthur he turned for financial support.

Arthur had three sons and six daughters of his own by his first wife, Anne Lee. Shortly before her death in 1819 their eldest son William Smythe Lee Grattan announced his intention of going into the Church rather than the brewery. For the second time a Guinness heir gave up his inheritance for the Church. And once again there were more sons at home. Arthur Lee and Benjamin Lee both joined their father at the brewery.

When Anne Lee died Arthur Guinness married her close friend Maria Barker. Maria was not a young woman and there were no children of their union, which was perhaps as well, because Arthur's hands were full enough with the problems of his brothers' and sisters' offspring. The potential he expected from his apprentice nephews was sadly lacking. Like young John Grattan, Richard Lyons Darley, his sister Elizabeth's son, turned out to be a waster and left Dublin in disgrace. So did Arthur Burke, son of his youngest sister Mary Anne and her clergyman husband. Neither of their sons amounted to much. Arthur Burke's brother John was a drunk, as for that matter was John Guinness, one of Hosea's sons. If that was not enough, one of brother Edward's sons, Richard, had to be committed to a mental institution like his cousin Olivia. Small wonder that Arthur wrote to his sister-in-law Jane Lucretia, who was starting again with a young family, "Early control can alone secure, under God's blessing, obedience and steady conduct."[5]

When outsiders demanded financial help too, he became completely exasperated:

It appears from your letter to be your opinion that I am extremely wealthy and my children so independent that on making my will I shall have much property to spare for others. Now you have formed a very mistaken estimate on both points. I have from various casualties, which have in the act of the Lord's Providence fallen out, chiefly affecting the property of my many dear Relations, had several individuals and families depending on me solely or partially for support . . . so that although the Lord has been pleased to prosper mine and my sons' industry, I have not been accumulating as you suppose, and indeed, I think I could not have done so acting as a Christian man . . .[6]

The family may well have given birth to a number of drunks and wasters, but it was producing or acquiring just as many clergymen. Arthur's eldest son, Hosea's eldest son and William Lunell's only son all became Church of Ireland ministers. Three of Arthur's daughters married clergymen. The Guinness clergy often seemed as feckless as the black sheep. Their demands were endless. They were accustomed to a very reasonable standard of living and for that they depended on their stipends. Stipends came from tithes. The Act of Union between England and Ireland, which had disbanded the Irish parliament, had united the established Church. The Catholic community were forced to pay tithes to a Church they despised. As relations between Protestant and Catholic deteriorated those tithes were often withheld as a means of protest, leaving the clerical Guinnesses in dire financial straits.

With so many clergy and black sheep in the family it became increasingly difficult to ensure a succession of reasonable managers for the brewery. As if this were not problem enough, both sorts of Guinness pursued the chief brewer as if his purse were bottomless. Any tussle for his soul between God and mammon was doomed from the start by a clan who knew how to manipulate his Christian conscience.

2

The Guinness brothers were ambivalent in their attitude towards the Act of Union. Members of the Protestant middle classes though they were, they possessed a strong sense of justice and national pride. They identified more easily with the Irish people than the Anglo-Irish gentility. Besides, the Irish parliament under Henry Grattan's influence had served them well. But like their father they had no sympathy with violence and no desire to see a repeat of the upheaval caused by the Peasants' Revolt. After all their youngest brother was almost killed. And most Irish Protestants were only too aware how near they came to a repeat of the carnage of the French Revolution. If Ireland's parliament was the price to be paid for peace, then so be it.

Arthur Guinness also genuinely believed that the British government would grant Catholic emancipation. But as the years rolled by and the promises remained unfulfilled he became increasingly frustrated. No broadminded, liberal thinker who believed in the inherent equality of all men before God could stand impassive before such gross injustice. Wherever he had any influence Arthur Guinness tried to instil a more reasonable attitude. He fought hard for the right of Catholics to be admitted to the Court of the Bank of Ireland. It hardly made him popular with his fellow Protestants. Nor did it allay Catholic suspicion either. In the tense atmosphere of nineteenth-century Dublin the Guinness family simply could not win.

From time to time various extreme anti-papist groups, terrified that concessions might be granted to the Catholics, sent petitions to the British government. In 1812 one such petition contained among other forgeries the signature of Guinness. Rumour spread quickly round the town that this was the master brewer himself.

Incensed, the brothers offered a reward of five hundred pounds for the prosecution of the instigators. Who would dare to suggest that they would sign a petition against "the claims of our Catholic brethren"? In a public statement published in the *Dublin Evening Post* they said that the petition was in total opposition to their principles. They, like their father before them, would go on fighting for full emancipation.

The Catholic Board was embarrassed by the whole affair and passed a resolution, stating not only that the signature was a forgery but that the Guinness family was entitled to the "confidence, gratitude and thanks of the Catholics of Ireland".

That was not the end of the saga. There were some who could neither forget nor forgive remarks made by Arthur Guinness during the Peasants· Revolt. An editorial appeared in *Cox's Irish Magazine* in June 1813 accusing the Catholic Board of fawning to their "superiors":

We hope that Mr O'Gorman does not mean to interweave brewing into the catholic bill, nor make it one of the terms of our emancipation that we do give security to drink Guinness' porter . . . If Councillor Guinness will get us porter for nothing, as he gave us character for nothing, when he called us a felonious rabble, we may deal with his porter, but until some domestic arrangement is agreed on, we will drink what we like, and whenever we can.

This was followed in October 1813 by a nasty piece of doggerel in a satirical journal called the *Milesian Magazine*:

To be sure did you hear
Of the heresy beer

That was made for to poison the Pope?
To hide the man a sin is
His name is Arthur Guinness
For salvation he never can hope.

A certain Dr Brennan claimed that in order to make their magic brew the Guinnesses had impregnated it with heretical poison by pouring in 136 thousand tons of Bibles and 501 thousand cartloads of hymn books and Protestant catechisms. His analysis showed beyond doubt that anti-popery porter was subverting the Catholic faith for it produced "a disposition to bowels particularly lax, an inclination to pravity, and to singing praises of the Lord through the nose".[7] The latter was a dig at evangelicalism and its hymn-singing with an English accent. However, Dr Brennan concluded, there was no need to worry unduly about the effects of too much Guinness. Pim's ale was the perfect antidote.

The Guinness brothers were not amused. Irresponsible journalism inflamed the prejudices of the ignorant and susceptible, who knew no better. Little trade was lost, but the family became aware that negotiating their way through the religious factions and political turmoil of Dublin was like walking barefoot through a field of broken glass.

It was Hosea who, gauging the way the wind blew, perceived that the blast was becoming increasingly glacial in all directions and decided to do something about it. Until the end of the eighteenth century there had been positive advantages in an Anglo-Irish pedigree. It was one way of getting on. But an all-pervading hatred of everything English was steadily gaining momentum. Besides, Hosea was embarrassed, as any true liberal clergyman would be, that his income was extracted forcibly from a resentful Catholic majority. The time had come to take certain steps his brother had overlooked, but which he from his vantage point in the established Church knew were not only necessary but vital.

In 1814 he wrote to Sir William Bethan, the deputy Ulster King of Arms and Herald of all Ireland, and asked him to confirm to all the descendants of his grandfather Richard Guinness, the right to use the Magennis crest and coat of arms. Sir William Bethan replied tartly that the first Arthur Guinness had been using them anyway. There were no records to suggest he was entitled to them, which was just as Hosea suspected. Fortunately for the Guinnesses they were granted a new coat of arms, which, but for a minor change, happened to be the Magennis crest. As long as the contents of Sir William Bethan's letter were not made public the Guinness family could now confidently claim to be descended from the hereditary earls of Iveagh. For the present Hosea was satisfied. He had simply wanted some sign for the Irish people of the family's genuine Irish descent. The alternative was that Richard Guinness was the direct descendant of a Cromwellian soldier, and who in their right mind in nineteenth-century Dublin would care to admit to that?

But Hosea's efforts could not spare the Guinnesses a certain amount of unpopularity. It was almost inevitable for any Protestant family in the public eye. The Catholic cause had found a charismatic, intelligent leader in Daniel O'Connell. Although he had duelled with Alderman Frederick D'Esterre in 1815 his relationship with Alderman Guinness was always cordial. When O'Connell won a by-election in County Clare it was with Arthur Guinness' support. Terrified of mass unrest, the British government passed the Roman Catholic Relief Act in 1829, granting Catholics the right to sit in parliament, and Arthur Guinness went to a meeting to celebrate, where he said publicly:

> I am much joyed at the final adjustment of the "Catholic Question", as it is wont to be called – but more properly the Irish Question – for hitherto although always a sincere advocate for Catholic freedom, I never could look my Catholic neighbour confidently in the face. I felt that I was placed in an unjust, unnatural elevation above him; and I considered how I would have felt if placed in a different position myself. Sorrow always excited my mind by such a contemplation.[8]

His joy was premature. Qualification for voting was quickly raised from a two pound to a ten pound freehold and most of O'Connell's supporters were disenfranchised.

Undaunted, Arthur Guinness still worked towards parliamentary reform and in the struggle was given to yet more grandiose oratory. It was folly to deprive Catholics of their legitimate rights, he said, but a great change was taking place all over the world. Men were awakening. Reason and intelligence were upon their majestic way and everywhere the grand principle was beginning to be asserted that governments were instituted only for the benefit of the people. Even in empires where despotic sway had long been exercised, the principle of liberty had begun to be extended, the struggle of popular power had loosened the iron hold of tyranny and prostrated the oppression that would seek to build itself on the oppression of the human race.[9]

The Reform Act was eventually passed by a Whig government in 1832. But whatever satisfaction the brewer felt at the time was slowly eroded over the next few years. Instead of being satisfied with their achievement, O'Connell's Catholic Association, to his mind, became more and more extreme, calling for an end to the Union altogether. As far as Arthur Guinness was concerned equality was one thing, republicanism quite another. In the General Election of 1835, a mere five years after he had obliquely accused the British government of tyranny and oppression, Guinness not only opposed O'Connell, he even considered a request to stand against him. "I think", he is reported to have said, "the time has come when it is the bounden duty of every man to speak his sentiments and to declare whether he is for the destruction or preservation of the constitution."[10] In the end he decided not to stand but signed a petition to unseat O'Connell.

O'Connell and his supporters were devastated by this sudden inexplicable change of heart. Arthur Guinness was one of their key Protestant supporters. The *Pilot*, O'Connell's newspaper, described how for years he had publicly resisted intolerance, registering his disapproval of the Orange system. He was a man "who never committed but this one public error", and why he had done so, no one knew.

Arthur Guinness denied any change of political allegiance. He was not an Orangeman, though it could hardly have escaped notice that his youngest brother had not long since married the widow of that notorious Protestant loud-mouth, Frederick D'Esterre. The marriage had not appeared to affect O'Connell's relationship with the Guinnesses. His only explanation for his friend's betrayal were that it was thanks to the influence of those clerical relatives of his who had "got about him".[11] It was a stab in the dark, but it may well have been nearer the truth than even he could have guessed.

In all probability what disturbed Guinness more than O'Connell's "extremism", for the seeds had been there for years if he had cared to see them, was that the Whig government, not satisfied with parliamentary reform, had touched the untouchable and was about to reform one area the Guinness family considered sacrosanct, the Church of Ireland.

In 1830 Catholics refused to pay their tithes. Tithe cattle were branded and maimed. For the Church of Ireland clergy the situation was desperate. How could they live? Since eight members of the Guinness family were clergymen, Arthur can hardly have been pleased. The Church robbed the brewery of management potential, then relied on it to keep its clergy. And in divorcing the Irish Church from its English counterpart it appeared that the Whig government intended to make this a permanent state of affairs.

O'Connell may well have been right. Here was a logical explanation for Arthur Guinness' sudden change of political bias. In the end the projected reforms forced a General Election and brought the Tories back to power and Arthur Guinness heaved a sigh of relief. O'Connell bitterly regretted the end of their association but limited his attack to the verbal variety. Some of his supporters allowed their fervour to run away with them and in an attempt to boycott Guinness trade, made several attacks on the brewery itself. The *Pilot* condemned the attacks. Revenge was counter-productive and O'Connell urged his supporters to remember that unlawful behaviour would not affect Guinness as his property was insured, but they would feel the pinch when a grand jury found them guilty of malicious damage. And after all Guinness' behaviour was merely the senile aberration of an old man, who had been on their side "when in the full strength of his intellect, and in the youthful vigour of his mind".

It was as well that Arthur Guinness was not a man who courted popular approval. His precarious balancing-act on a ridge between two valleys might satisfy his own sense of tolerance with moderation, but it rarely satisfied anyone else. O'Connell now referred to him as "that miserable old apostate",[12] while eminent Protestants smugly proclaimed that he had seen the light at last. One thing was clear, the narrow middle path did not allow for the slightest shift in position to one side or another without running the risk of a fall, and great was the drop on either side. Small wonder that some years later when his son Benjamin Lee was invited to stand for a Dublin seat Arthur urged him to decline:

> You will recollect that on two occasions a similar suggestion was conveyed to me, backed on both occasions by offers on the part of gentlemen who were candidates themselves and who offered to resign in my favour. I then felt, and now feel, that the office of sitting in Parliament for a great city and especially such a city as Dublin where party and sectarian strife so signally abound and more especially if filled by one engaged in our line of business, is fraught with difficulty and danger.[13]

However his actions may have been interpreted, Arthur Guinness believed that he had never left the narrow path. It was everyone else who moved. O'Connell shifted left, which put him on the right; it was just far enough right to impair the balance for posterity. Never again would the Guinness family climb their way back into the Liberal fold and one potentially moderating voice in the Catholic cause was stilled for ever.

3

Any expectation Arthur Guinness may have had that his last years would be spent in a calm and tranquil serenity were doomed to disappointment. His vigour and strength of character had enabled him to weather many storms, but none were so deeply personal or pained him as much as the major family crisis of his old age.

In 1838 he celebrated his seventieth birthday. He was as alert and sprightly as his father had been at the same age, managing his affairs both public and private in a way that would put a much younger man to shame. There was no sag to his chin, the jawline was as set and determined as ever. His receding hairline made his forehead seem higher and nobler, but the shock of white hair which framed his face gave a hint of softness to an otherwise rather severe appearance. He wore his sideburns long according to the fashion and tended to wear black, having had the misfortune to lose a second wife. Although a distinguished gentleman, respected for his philanthropy and for the wisdom and moral integrity he displayed in fulfilling his civic responsibilities, he never took advantage of his position or his wealth to gain entry into the upper echelons of Dublin society. His lifestyle, like his dress, was simple, almost austere. There were too many crises, too many demands on his pocket to permit a life of unbridled luxury – not that the latter was ever a real temptation. He was rather too abstemious for that, and besides it was contrary to his understanding of the Christian faith. His family provided him with all the satisfaction he required, and more than enough anxiety too.

He lived quietly at Beaumont with his five unmarried daughters, entertaining rarely, and then usually family. Occasionally he paid an extended visit to Rathdrum, where his eldest son William Smythe Lee Grattan had his first incumbency. William had married his cousin Susan and they had three sons. They were Arthur's only grandchildren at that time and provided him with a great deal of pleasure. While he was away his other two sons, Arthur Lee and Benjamin Lee, managed the brewery. Lee, his first wife's maiden name, had become an adopted family name within the brewing line.

Arthur Lee was forty-two, a bachelor who lived alone at St James' Gate. Benjamin Lee, though the youngest son, was most like his father in ability and personality. He had recently married Elizabeth, daughter of his demanding, bankrupt and recently deceased Uncle Edward. Bessie, as she was known, was his father's favourite niece. Despite her impecunious state Arthur Guinness was pleased with the marriage. Intermarriage within the family was always welcome. In fact it was fast becoming a Guinness tradition.

At the brewery business was booming. The Irish Nationalists had ceased to attack brewery property, thanks to O'Connell's calming influence, and there was no noticeable alteration in sales. "The Guinness Persecution" as it was called in the Protestant press, fizzled out. The papists manifestly preferred their porter to their principles. Having survived a series of physical attacks the brewery

41

then had to contend with a sustained verbal attack, which it managed to turn into a very acceptable advantage.

Temperance campaigns were fast becoming a feature of Irish life. Alcohol was a major social problem. Since there seemed little sense in wishing for the moon, the campaigners had tended to denounce spirits rather than beer. That always meant a sudden rise in the sales of beer, so the brewers smiled happily on the Temperance cause. Campaigner Father Matthew was different. He condemned alcohol of every kind and inveighed against it with such passion and fury that his preaching began to show frightening results for brewers and distillers alike. Arthur Guinness and his sons saw their precious commodity join the black list and heard it called an affront to Christianity right outside the brewery. They had the wisdom to keep quiet and issue no defence, which ultimately proved the most sensible course of action. Total abstention was an unreasonable demand and in the end the campaign served to establish beer as the favourite drink of the working classes. The brewery had reached another major landmark. Sales were never in doubt again.

The tranquil retirement Arthur Guinness anticipated was on the horizon. Nothing prepared him for the blow to come. Within a few months of sending his young nephew John Grattan back to his parents, his own son Arthur Lee came to him and begged to be released from his partnership at once. He felt unable to manage the brewery. Worse, he could not even manage his own affairs and was hopelessly in debt. He was mortified by his failure and begged his father's forgiveness. Arthur, to whom the very idea of overspending and mismanagement was anathema, forgave his son and dealt with his debts as generously as he had dealt with those of the rest of the family. Arthur Lee was pained almost more by his father's forgiveness and compassion than he would have been by his anger. On June 13th, 1839 he sent him a note:

My dear Father
I well know it is impossible to justify to you my conduct if you will forgive me, it is much to ask, but I already feel you have and I will ever be sincerely grateful . . . I know not what I should say, but do my dear Father believe me I feel deeply . . . the extreme and undeserved kindness you have ever, and now, more than ever shown me.

Believe me above all that "for worlds" I would not hurt your mind, if I could avoid it – of all the living. Your feelings are most sacred to me, this situation, in which I have placed myself, has long caused me the acutest pain and your wishes on the subject must be religiously obeyed by me . . .[14]

The practicalities were not so simple. If Arthur Lee withdrew his shares from the partnership, they constituted such a large amount of capital that Ben, his brother, might not be able to continue. In the end he took only enough to enable him to buy Stillorgan Park just outside Dublin and rebuild the house there. He heaved a sigh of relief and abandoned materialistic pursuits for the aesthetic pleasures of the soul. He retired to Stillorgan to collect paintings, compose pantheistic verses and write letters, sealed with the designs of a young Greek god. Dark, slim and good-looking, his attempt to play the part made him look more like a fop than a classical deity. Nor was he quite ethereal enough to avoid embarrassing his father and brother with his recurrent financial problems and strongly pro-Catholic political sympathies.

A man of fervent faith, whose Bible was often left open on his desk and who liked to close every interview with prayer, Arthur was deeply disturbed when his son rejected Christianity. He longed to see "some token of his being awakened to a sense of the value of the Gospel of the Lord Jesus and to an embracing of those invaluable truths".[15] He urged him to discipline his tendency towards self-gratification and his "inordinate passion" for beautiful things. Material possessions were all very well but he ought to "lay something by against the evil day".

But even if he did turn his back on Christianity Arthur Lee was kindly and well meaning. The problem was that he had inherited his father's generosity of spirit without the prudence and discretion which made it feasible.

The brewery survived this latest crisis and Arthur Guinness breathed a sigh of relief and prayer of thankfulness to Almighty God that for every business skill his second son lacked, his youngest son seemed amply to compensate. The whole affair had been the making of Benjamin Lee, who now took over the running of the brewery, showing an exceptional flair for the job. The famous black stout even found its way to the Holy Land. Arthur Guinness was a key member of the Hibernian branch of the Church Missionary Society, which in 1842 sent out Alexander as first Protestant Bishop to Jerusalem. From his new diocese he wrote to his "faithful friend": "We are daily enjoying your excellent porter, which I think has done much to keep up our strength. I regret to say we have lost some on the voyage. I have no doubt that you will be pleased that your excellent beverage has found its way to Jerusalem."[16]

At last Arthur could retire into the role of adviser. Once again, in this last major crisis of his life, he had revealed that he was a man who could hold lightly to his purse and his business when other priorities became apparent. Shrewd he may have been but hard-hearted, never. When within a few years Ireland was ravaged by famine, the likes of which had never been seen in Great Britain, the old man immediately recognised yet another major call on his resources.

4

In the autumn of 1845 the potato crop failed. Famine spread slowly from the south-eastern counties through half of the country. The following year, to the despair of the poor cottiers, the leaves of the fresh crop showed the unmistakable black markings of blight. They were utterly helpless. Few in authority seemed to appreciate the magnitude of the disaster. The British government refused to acknowledge a problem or believe the reports of starvation and disease which were beginning to reach them. While millions died the government played political games, naïvely shifting all responsibility on to the landlords. It was their duty to feed their tenants. Many landlords, particularly the Anglo-Irish, rejected such an idea. They stayed in Dublin, as oblivious to the problem as the proverbial ostrich, ejecting their tenants when they did not pay the rent. Whole families were left starving and destitute, some to die in the middle of the road without a roof over their head. The stench of disease and rotting bodies filled the countryside. But only those who saw the famine-ridden areas for themselves fully understood the extent of the misery.

Meanwhile Dublin's well-to-do continued to eat and drink and dance. Daniel O'Connell pressed the corporation to ban the export of foodstuffs and limit all brewing and distilling, which used up invaluable resources. The corporation refused. Benjamin Lee was largely ignorant of what was happening. It was Arthur who saw the newspaper reports while on holiday in England and was horrified by what he read. On March 12th, 1847, his seventy-ninth birthday, he wrote to his son from Torquay:

My dear Ben
Your kind letter of the 8th is before me and the continued good account of our Business calls for much thankfulness to Almighty God while we humbly ask for the infinitely higher blessings of His Grace in the Lord Jesus Christ. I have entered this day upon my 80th year. Surely it becomes me to speak of the Lord's patience and longsuffering towards one so utterly evil and sinful and to pray that I might be enabled through Grace to live every hour under the teaching of the Holy Spirit patiently abiding his time for calling me to that place of Everlasting Rest, the purchase of the precious blood of the Lamb of God for sinners. Amen.

It was Arthur's customary habit to open his letters on a spiritual note; now he went on: "How awful do the accounts from Ireland continue and how evident is it that the exertions of the Government need to be aided by those of private individuals." Arthur Guinness was never a man to expect of others what he was not prepared to do himself. There was no doubt that he regarded himself as one of those "private individuals" whose help was so necessary and his letter was a veiled hint to Ben that he should be offering his support too. But he could hardly tell a man of nearly fifty what to do with his money, even if he was his son.

The problem was that while the Guinnesses presumed that the government was actually exerting itself, they lived like most other well-to-do Dubliners under a fond illusion. The potato blight of 1848 completed the semi-devastation. Millions of Irish tried to emigrate. Many died on the crowded boats, carrying disease and plague with them. While again on holiday in Torquay Arthur Guinness noticed a letter in the *London Record* which shook him. He wrote to Ben with a fresh urgency:

In the *London Record* of last evening there is a letter from a correspondent who had been visiting Connemara and was just returned to another part of Galway, presenting a picture of the state of destitution in Connemara exceeding in horror and misery anything we have before observed. May the Lord in his infinite mercy direct our Government and all individuals also possessing means to do so to the use of measures to relieve if possible the sufferings of our wretched poor people. I wish to know of any mode in which we might be able to aid in the work. You know my dear Ben that my purse is open to the call.[17]

On May 9th he wrote again, burdened by the problem which faces any individual wanting to contribute towards famine relief, how practically to do it. He bitterly lamented the fact that "a fair honest movement independent of party spirit is not working towards relief of the prevailing destitution . . . if there were, I know our Firm would stand forward".

But in Dublin the usual well-heeled, well-fed social routine continued and no concerted effort was made to deal with the crisis. Few like Arthur Guinness were willing to be jolted out of their complacency by newspaper accounts. Deliberate ignorance was truly blissful. With the best will in the world Benjamin Lee could do little to alleviate a situation which seemed so remote.

It was Arthur Lee, who never had his feet on the ground, who most resembled his father in generosity of spirit. He, more than most landed gentry, did all he could for the peasants who worked on his estate. And they loved him for his efforts. In memory of his exertions and as a token of their appreciation they erected a small obelisk made of Connemara marble:

1847

TO ARTHUR LEE GUINNESS ESQ
STILLORGAN PARK

To mark the veneration of his faithful labourers who in a period of dire distress were protected by his generous liberality from the prevailing destitution.

This humble testimonial is respectfully dedicated consisting of home material.

Its colour serves to remind that the memory of benefits will ever remain green in Irish hearts.

As the years passed Arthur Guinness continued as alert and active as ever. "My bodily health and my mental vigour are both preserved to a degree very unusual at the age of nearly 84", he wrote with apparent surprise.[18] "Every step of my protracted journey has been marked on the part of my God with Mercy." He still served on the numerous philanthropic and civic committees he had supported throughout his life, the Farming Society of Ireland, the Dublin Ballast Board, which managed the docks, the Ouzel Galley Society, an exclusive business club, the Dublin Society, the Meath Hospital, and the Dublin Chamber of Commerce of which he had been president for many years. In 1855 *Freeman's Journal* called him "our most distinguished citizen". The brewery under Benjamin's leadership was more prosperous than ever and his father could write to him with some satisfaction, "We have much cause for continued thanksgiving to our God 'who giveth us all things richly to possess'."[19]

Shortly before his father's death Arthur Lee received a rather embarrassing visitor as far as the family was concerned. That was why it seemed most sensible that Arthur Lee should entertain him at Stillorgan, a little out of the way, though other senior members of the family, including old Arthur, were invited to dinner to meet him. Their guest was a certain Captain Edmund Henn-Gennys of Whitleigh House, Plymouth, a representative of the ancient family of Gennys of Cornwall. He was claiming to be a relative, which would have confirmed the Guinnesses' descent from a Cromwellian soldier. Fortunately Hosea had died some years earlier, so was spared an ordeal which would have brought on an attack of apoplexy. Arthur Guinness, physically frail at eighty-six but mentally as alert as ever, listened carefully to the captain's explanation of his extraordinary claim, and decided quite happily that there was no satisfactory evidence to suggest any connection.

When he died peacefully some months later the Magennis crest was in evidence as usual at his funeral. In some ways that seemed in keeping for a man who always instinctively felt himself more Irish than English. Sadly the minister of Bethesda Chapel failed to grasp this significant fact. He preached a rather back-handed eulogy in a patronising tone which Arthur Guinness would have deplored. "He was what is untruly called 'a Liberal'," said the minister. He then went on to explain that Arthur Guinness had developed these views, "partly, it might have been from his associations, partly from his circumstances, and with a judgement not yet fully enlightened in divine truth, and, therefore, without the perception of their error and evil tendencies". In other words his tolerance had been a temporary aberration of youth, abandoned with the wisdom of later years. But with what character, with what "fearless and undaunted resolution" did he then, "once convinced of his error", take "his stand on the opposite side – on that side which shall ultimately be pronounced true liberality by the voice of God".

This disappointing epitaph was no true reflection of Arthur Guinness' character. It was as well that the deceased could not be present. He at least was never a bigot. Nor was he that dogmatic about whose side God was on. "I am a friend to liberty," he had once said in his own defence, when under attack from O'Connell, "not the wild liberty . . . but the liberty connected with order, the liberty which gives not power to one party to trample on another."[20]

In following the dictates of his own conscience, he certainly hoped he was pleasing God, even if he could not hope to please anyone else. As to whether he succeeded, Irishmen would always differ in their opinion depending which side they were on.

The people of Dublin honoured him with a more generous elegy:

> Now Dublin City's into mourning thrown,
> Its leading member to the grave is cast!
> Is gone – for ever fled –
> This honor'd man is dead –
> of rich and poor throughout the land fam'd Guinness
>   was the pride.
> Dead – no – he lives on some more glorious shore,
> He lives – but ah! he lives to us no more.

The preacher at Arthur Guinness' funeral, not satisfied with religious bigotry, maintained that "God brought wealth also to his hand – and herein lay his greatest danger." Wealth never constituted any real danger to a man of Arthur Guinness' simple convictions. But it was a prophetic message for the later generations, who would either reject or succumb to the snare. At Arthur's death his family had arrived at the crossroads.

4

1855–1860

Henry Grattan and Benjamin Lee
Stars in their Ascendancy

1

Henry Grattan Guinness was twenty years old when his Uncle
Arthur died. Some young men would have been impressed by the
generous legacy of £400 his uncle left in trust for his twenty-first
birthday, but not Henry Grattan. Throughout his life money would
never be any more to him than a tiresome necessity, best left in
anyone's hands but his!

He did not know his Uncle Arthur well. As a child he had
visited Beaumont with his father on several occasions. Captain John
Grattan never stayed away from Ireland and his brothers and sisters
for long. He was especially fond of Mary Anne Burke, his youngest
sister, who lived with her clergyman husband in Galway. It was she
who kept a motherly eye on the children of his first marriage while
he was in Cheltenham.

Of all his uncles, Arthur Guinness made the deepest impression on
his young nephew. There was something about the old gentleman's
regal bearing which defied contradiction. He was kindly, but distant.
His nephew was not altogether comfortable in his presence. The
behaviour of his elder half-brother had caused a certain chill to
develop between the head of the family and his youngest brother's
line. Family loyalty triumphed, as it always did. Captain John begged
his brother to give his son John another chance. He was a good boy
at heart, if his uncle would let him prove it. And Arthur, always
ready to go the last mile where his family was concerned, bought his
nephew a brewery in Bristol, which the latter promptly bankrupted.
Captain John was ashamed of his son, but having no means to settle
the debts himself was forced to throw himself on his brother's mercy.

Whenever they went to Beaumont, as if to warn his nephew

against the follies of his half-brother, Arthur Guinness always made some comment about Henry Grattan's name, to the effect that if he had but a fraction of the honour, the dignity, the gift of oratory of his illustrious namesake and cousin, Ireland's greatest politician, then he would do more than well.

The child listened carefully to the many conversations he overheard about Irish politics. He was particularly interested in any mention of Daniel O'Connell, noticing how voices were lowered to a whisper whenever his parents were in the room. The escapades of the arch-villain who had killed his mother's poor, but "gallant", first husband were more exciting than any story-book. Cheltenham, though miles from the turbulence of Ireland, was something of an Irish colony and Henry Grattan Guinness grew up with a strong sense of his Irish identity and a deep love for the country of his roots.

Although Jane Lucretia kept in regular correspondence with her brother-in-law, there had been little contact between the Dublin and Cheltenham Guinnesses since Captain John died five years before, and Henry Grattan had rather rudely declined his uncle's well-meant invitation to an apprenticeship at the brewery. Arthur Guinness had assessed rightly that his youngest brother had not left his widow and four children well provided-for. Ever optimistic of discovering family flair, even in this branch which had hitherto proved so singularly fruitless, he was prepared to hold out one last chance. But Henry Grattan was fifteen, a boy raised in a society of retired military gentlemen who whiled away the hours weaving fantasies of faraway, exotic places. Brewing by comparison seemed mundane and commonplace. He had other, far more adventurous plans.

His father's death was a bitter blow. Henry Grattan had suddenly become aware of how little he knew this reserved and godly man and now the chance was gone for ever. Their similar temperaments had kept them apart. They were both solitary by nature, both dreamers. Henry Grattan was a romantic from childhood. He had an instinctive love of nature which his mother encouraged. He could spend hours collecting fossil ammonites and belemnites, or staring at the shadows made by the sun on the walls of an old castle. He would wander alone for hours, or become completely absorbed in a book. But though their pleasures were similar, father and son rarely shared them together. Only one occasion really stood out in Henry's memory, and he held on to it as if it were the last lingering note of a symphony.

One Sunday night he read to his father from the book of Revelation, and he remembered:

the light of the street lamp shining into the quiet room, where we sat together, and the solemn and beautiful imagery of the chapter relating to the New Jerusalem seeming to shed over the scene a purer and loftier light. Though but a child at the time, I think I entered more or less into my father's profound admiration for the passage; and felt with him the vibration of the soul attuned to eternal realities.

When Captain John died Henry Grattan became a familiar figure in the seediest of the town's taverns. But they only provided a temporary relief from his abiding sense of futility. He needed some stronger excitement.

Jane Lucretia had worked hard at providing her second family with a secure, loving home and strong Christian values. She was deeply disturbed by her son's behaviour and her anxiety was compounded when he decided to follow his brother Robert Wyndham to sea. Having lost her husband she was now faced with the possibility of losing two of her sons.

It was as a midshipman that the sixteen-year-old Henry Grattan sailed to Mexico. Some of the crew deserted on the way home, leaving the ship short-handed. This meant he had to stand at the wheel for hours at a stretch, wrestling to keep the vessel on course in gale-force winds. It would have exhausted and shaken most men, but Henry Grattan found the excitement he craved. It was a challenge to manage the steering in such conditions and an exhilarating sensation to watch the wind fluttering the edge of the sails when the ship was close hauled. Years later in his dreams he would still feel the jerk of the wheel as the vessel bounded over the billows, leaning to leeward before a stiff breeze. He would relive the almost intoxicating sense of danger of clambering up the mast to the topsail and battling single-handed to furl it before a rising storm.

But even at his height of exultation he would be suddenly overcome by the sickening sense that this was escapism, not real life. Like his father he craved adventure, finding it at sea, not in India. But in the end the army had broken his father, and Henry Grattan had no desire to remain at sea until sickness or disillusionment overcame him. No particular career took his fancy. Emigration to the new colonies was much in vogue. Since the idea of brewing left him colder than ever, it seemed the only option though he was never filled with any sense of certainty that he had found his destiny – not until one night in 1854.

It was two o'clock in the morning and the house in Cheltenham was in total darkness. Jane Lucretia had visitors to stay and everyone had been in bed some hours. They were rudely awakened by a sudden hammering at the front door. Wyndham was standing on the doorstep in a state of high excitement. He had arrived home unexpectedly after sixteen months on the *Francis Ridley*. Unfortunately Wyndham's own bed was occupied by one of the visitors. Henry, desperate to hear his brother's adventures at sea, offered him half of his bed and Wyndham gratefully accepted.

But to Henry's surprise Wyndham had little to say about the countries he had visited or the sights he had seen. Instead he held forth at length about the extraordinary chief mate, a man called Peek. From the first day he had made no attempt to hide his Christian convictions, and even tried to convert the rest of the crew. They laughed him to scorn, as hardened old sailors would, never missing a chance to abuse him verbally if they could. Then one day a gale-force wind arose with a fury such as Wyndham had never known before. Disaster seemed certain and the crew was terrified, all except Peek. He fell to his knees and prayed for the storm to subside. The crew was too petrified to laugh at him this time. When his prayer was answered, mockery turned into a grudging respect.

At first Wyndham had laughed at Peek like the others. But in a moment of real extremity, where was the man that did not remember his mother's prayers? How he had failed her expectations. Peek had backbone. That was what he lacked, until he became the first convert of the voyage.

Wyndham's voice gradually tailed off and he fell into a deep sleep. But Henry Grattan lay awake for hours. He began to look back over his own life and suddenly felt confronted by his own utter aimlessness, as if it were a yawning empty pit, defying all his efforts to fill it. Long-forgotten memories, successfully buried until now, suddenly floated back into consciousness. He remembered having the measles, he must have been about ten at the time, lying in his tiny, darkened room with the blinds drawn, and his half-sister Rebecca talking to him of the beauty of heaven. In the strange half-light her face seemed illuminated with an other-worldly serenity and he sensed that the presence of Christ was real for her in a way he had never experienced. He wanted that for himself, that "mental vision of moral loveliness such as I had never seen before". But the vision and any desire to hold on to it evaporated with restored health, until tonight as he lay in the darkness listening to Wyndham's even snoring from the other side of the bed.

When he came down for breakfast the following morning his sister Lucy could not take her eyes off him. He was "a changed man", she told her mother. When Wyndham asked him if he had slept well, he simply said, "little", and left it at that. But the whole family noticed that he began to read *Hawker's Morning and Evening Portion*, scribbling copious notes about the Bible passage for the day in pencil in the margins.

If Jane Lucretia anticipated that her two sons would now settle down to a life of relative calm she was sadly disappointed. News came that Chief Mate Peek had been promoted to captain and was looking for a crew to sail with him on a voyage half-way round the world. The brothers volunteered at once. Peek was glad of their company, Henry Grattan noted in his journal, that his "crew on this occasion was a most ungodly one, the mouths of the men in the forecastle being filled with cursing and bitterness". The ship had only got as far as Lowestoft, when Henry had had enough. It anchored in an evening calm and as he stood watching Yarmouth spire rising from the trees, silhouetted against a glowing sunset sky, he longed to escape from the blasphemy around him into some secluded, tranquil spot.

His wishes were granted sooner than he expected. He became so ill that when the vessel anchored at Hartlepool he had to be put ashore and sent home to Cheltenham. Once home his health improved, and he began to think positively about a career. His longing for solitude and open spaces made farming an interesting prospect; where better to learn than in his beloved Ireland?

It was in County Tipperary, in a little village several miles from Cashel, that he found a farmer willing to take him in. The farm was some way from the town, which Henry welcomed since it would prevent his being tempted by the pleasures of the flesh. But no one had warned him of the snares of the outdoor life. Farming was tedious. There was much more fun to be had wandering the countryside in one's own company, gun in hand. A minor accident brought him up with a start and altered the whole course of his life.

One morning he set off as usual for a day's shooting. It was a lovely spring day and oblivious of time he wandered for miles, until he came to a large ditch. For some reason he never understood, he misjudged it completely and instead of slinging his gun over his shoulder, kept it in his hand. He leapt, lost his balance and unable to break the fall with his hand, landed heavily on one of his ankles. It was badly sprained and he lay in the ditch for some time before he could summon up enough strength to crawl home in great pain. Instinct told him it was a sign, a judgment, and when he reached the farmhouse he hung the gun on its hook and vowed he would never take it down again.

The hours he spent on his back over the next days gave him a chance to think and he began to feel that up to that point his existence had been utterly selfish. He had wasted twenty precious years and longed for something better. When he began to get about again he sought out solitary places in the woods. And gradually the peace for which he yearned came:

The future was lighted with hope. The gates of glory and immortality opened to my mental vision and there shone before me an interminable vista of pure and perfect existence in the life to come. It was the marriage of the soul; the union of the creature in appropriating and self-yielding love with Him who is uncreated, eternal love.

This "marriage of the soul" became Henry's driving force. He suddenly became aware that all around him were the "miserable and abject slaves of Romish superstition", and he resolved to loosen their chains. It was the dawning of his preaching career, which began not in a church, but in the environment where it would always have the greatest impact, out in the open, in the marketplaces, fields and crossings, wherever men and women would stop and listen.

News of Henry's preaching soon reached the ears of the local priest, a certain Father H, who determined to silence the young Protestant upstart once and for all. He set out on horseback to find him, whip in hand, and nearly had a fit when he saw his own flock listening with rapt attention to the handsome young preacher. From a rather gawky boy, Henry Grattan had turned into a striking-looking young man with a mane of shoulder-length dark brown hair and large dark eyes.

"How dare you disturb the peace of the country!" the priest raged at him, nearly purple with anger.

Henry said quietly that he had come not to disturb the peace, but to offer the people real peace.

"Your religion is false," the priest retorted, "a cursed lie. I challenge you to prove the truth of the Bible on which you say it is founded."

Henry was about to do so, when the priest turned his horse, called back over his shoulder that he would denounce the madman from the altar that very Sunday and galloped off in a fury.

Father H was true to his word. The following Sunday the people were instructed to kick the young preacher out of doors if he tried to gain entrance to their cottages, to splash him with sink water if there was some to hand, or to throw him into the nearest convenient puddle. The farmer with whom Henry was staying was warned that if he did not silence his guest his hayricks would be burnt.

But there was no silencing Henry. He had found his life's work. He was stirred by the ignorance of the villagers. They told him that Protestantism had been invented by Henry VIII who had imprisoned Mary Queen of Scots and married his own daughter, so that he could have as many wives as he pleased. The priests seemed to delight in keeping the people in ignorance, filling their minds with fears and superstitions which subjected them and enslaved them in a grinding, miserable poverty. "These people are unconvertible," warned the Protestant governess of the family with which Henry was staying. A while later he noted in his diary, "Thank God, she was, through my poor testimony, converted herself shortly afterwards."

As the priests stirred the people up, threats soon turned to violence. Henry needed a permanent bodyguard and was not allowed to go out after dark. It was at this time that the news of his Uncle Arthur's death reached him. In all probability he went to Dublin for the funeral, but there is no record of it. One thing is certain, his presence at the farmhouse was becoming increasingly unwelcome. He was not a great source of help on the farm and was constantly borrowing money from the farmer; now his very presence constituted a risk.

The future was once again a blank page. A legacy due in just over a year opened up all kinds of possibilities, but none of them filled him with enthusiasm. The idea which appealed the most had been germinating in his mind for some time. He had read the story of Captain Gardiner who had died in his attempt to take the gospel to the Patagonians, and was greatly impressed. Life on the wild shores of South America held great romance. He knew how to shoot, fish, row and ride, could sail a boat in a stormy sea, was a passable carpenter and not afraid to rough it. He even went to the local cobbler's for lessons in shoe-making. The ideal missionary must be omni-competent.

He wrote to his mother to ask her what she thought of his plans, but South America was definitely not what Jane Lucretia had in mind for her eldest son.

2

Jane Lucretia's response to her son's letter arrived in Tipperary on August 11th, 1855, his twentieth birthday.

1 Buckingham Villas, Cheltenham. August 11th, 1855
My very dear Henry
I write this on your birthday! Many many happy returns of this day to you. May you, my ever dear Son, find this coming year the best you have ever experienced. Your twentieth year has just closed – in other words you are now twenty years of age – and if spared till this day twelvemonth will be of age. I would therefore dearest Henry strongly and affectionately advise you to seek in constant prayer, guidance as regards your future course. Various plans have no doubt presented themselves to you from time to time as to your future path in life and it appears

that you now have a prospect when of age, which is new and encouraging. The sum of money which by your late kind uncle's will is in reserve for you will enable you if you are desirous to make a favourable commencement in the line of life for which you are now preparing. But if your mind has undergone any change relatively to engagement in the Farming line, I do not see to what purpose you would continue your residence, beyond the present year, where you now are. I know, dear, that you will go to the House of grace with your plans and desires, and I do much wish, as far as I am concerned, not to influence you to anything which might be detrimental in the least to your happiness.

Having said that she was quite prepared to leave any future decisions in Henry's hands, she went on to wonder why the Patagonians should need to hear his message more than his fellow countrymen. Could he not be a missionary at home? "In this happy and favoured land – England – the towns and villages especially, are so many moral deserts. The towns corrupt, the villages in a state of brutish ignorance." And if he was determined to spend his life preaching, ought he not to spend some time studying for the ministry? Her argument was not devoid of maternal self-interest, but it made sense.

With the birthday money she sent, Henry paid off his debts, as she begged him to do. How could a son of hers incur debts? Then he packed his bags, said goodbye to Ireland, for the time at least, and went home to Cheltenham, to a diet of "farinaceous food", his mother's latest nutritional fad. Word soon came from Wyndham that he and Captain Peek were shortly due home. If Henry wanted a surprise he should meet the ship when it docked.

Henry rushed to London and was staggered to hear "the very men who had been bold blasphemers sing the songs of Zion with such stentorian strength that it seemed to me they might have meant to blow the roof off the deck-cabin in which they held their prayer meeting". If hardened sailors could be such changed men, anything was possible.

There was no time to be lost. He was a man possessed by a driving force. Even the months spent waiting for a place to study theology at New College, St John's Wood, were taken up with preaching in the chapels and on the street corners of Cheltenham. Since the days of Whitefield and Wesley, street preaching had become a common social phenomenon.

The night before Henry left for college he walked the streets in a state of utter dejection, convinced that theological study would be his ruin. Theological institutions had a way of turning zeal into torpor and the very thought horrified him. Before he went to bed he made up his mind to walk in the footsteps of Whitefield and Wesley. Nothing would be allowed to extinguish the sacred fire which burned in his soul.

Prolonged bouts of academic study did not come easily to Henry. He balked at what appeared to be a waste of precious time. At weekends and in the evenings, when his fellow students settled down to their essays, he went out into the street to hold open-air services. Gathering a congregation was never a problem. The tall, handsome young student with the penetrating eyes and intense expression had magnetic appeal. His deep voice had a musical quality and rose and fell as if he were speaking in verse. The more he preached, the more he became aware of a growing ability to hold a congregation in the palm of his hand.

Ordinary people may have been enthralled by his preaching, but his tutors were not. He preached his first official sermon for them in the Congregational Church, Kentish Town. "His voice was too loud," they said. "People would not be frightened into heaven."

"I am sure I should not attempt to do any such thing," Henry replied, "but if I could be enabled to point out their danger, scare any away from the pit, I should indeed rejoice."

Neither the College, nor the Congregational Church was impressed with his argument and no more formal opportunities to preach in church came his way.

Nonplussed at first, Henry soon got over his disappointment and continued to preach in the open air. To the other students he was a familiar sight hobbling back into college after miles of tramping around the district. His feet were especially blistered and painful on Sunday nights, because he refused to ride at all on the Sabbath. By the time the summer came and he had completed his first year he was preaching more and more and attending his classes less and less. There was a sigh of relief all round when he finally decided to go home and not return.

Back in Cheltenham he immediately started preaching in the streets. "He'll be a very useful man when he cools down," his minister said to Wyndham.

"Did he say that?" Henry asked indignantly. It made him more determined than ever that there would be no cooling down. The proof of it was in his preaching.

Whenever he preached he invited anyone who wanted to talk to him privately to come to his house. Day after day "enquirers" queued up to see him, as many as seventy at a time. Jane Lucretia could barely move in her own home. Enough was enough. Henry respected her feelings and managed to hire a room in the Cheltenham Town Hall. No more preaching in the rain on the Promenade. Soon the crowds began to fill the Town Hall. He was euphoric. On his twenty-first birthday he noted in his diary that his only ambition was "to live preaching and to die preaching; to live and die in the pulpit; to preach to perishing sinners till I drop down dead".

The legacy of £400 left to him by Arthur Guinness was now his to do with as he pleased, and he gave it to his mother. He hated seeing her scrimp on an army widow's pension. When she said that "farinaceous food" was better for the constitution than meat, he was not taken in. She could not afford meat, that was the truth of the matter. But now he could leave her to live in a little more style.

His reputation was spreading and the preaching invitations denied him at college had begun to pour in. His own personal assets amounted to half a crown and with that in his pocket he set off for Birmingham. From the Midlands he travelled on to many English towns, and wherever he went his preaching had the same dramatic effect. Never since Wesley and Whitefield had anyone elicited so many temperance pledges. These were the months leading up to a sudden revival of religious interest, when theatres, music-halls, concert-halls, any buildings capable of seating an audience, were filled with people, some of them waiting from early morning to get places at an evening service. Good preachers were in great demand. But acclaim did not bring Henry Grattan security. It was a hand to mouth existence, for he never knew where he would find the next meal or bed for the night.

In April 1857 he was invited to preach at the famous Moorfields Tabernacle in London, base of the great Whitefield. The young man who had been a failure at theological college now stood in the pulpit of the most prestigious Nonconformist church in England, feeling overawed at the thought of his illustrious predecessor. There in the vestry was the life-size portrait of the great preacher, arms uplifted and countenance glowing with divine emotion; there was the pulpit from which he preached, the pews and galleries which held his hearers; the windows which met his gaze, the walls which echoed his wonderful voice, the roof which sheltered his vast congregation from sun and rain. His presence seemed to pervade the place and impart to it a unique and sacred character.

Wyndham sat at the back of the gallery, waiting anxiously to pick up the reaction to his brother's first sermon. In front of him sat two elderly ladies, one of whom turned to the other and said, "My dear, there ought to be a committee appointed to choose a suitable wife for this young preacher!"

There was no doubt that Henry Grattan now constituted a serious risk to unattached young ladies. He was more handsome than ever. When he preached his whole expression became animated and his voice had a resonance which would quicken any female heart. Mothers of marriageable daughters rushed to seize an opportunity to entertain the young man.

In fact he took the Moorfields Tabernacle by storm. The elders, the official leaders of this Nonconformist church, were so impressed that they invited him to be their minister. The offer was tempting. It held out a security and prestige Henry had never known. After a lengthy inner struggle he declined, saying that he could not continue his wider ministry if he were tied to one church. The eldership conceded and on July 29th they ordained him an itinerant, interdenominational evangelist. The following day he left London, went to Cheltenham to say goodbye to his mother and set off on preaching tours of France, Switzerland, Wales and Scotland.

In Wales he preached in eighty different locations, 140 times, to a total of about 100 thousand people. In Aberdare his audience was so enthusiastic that they tried to mob him. The platform on which he was standing collapsed and he narrowly escaped with a minor leg injury. But it was while in Scotland that he received the most enticing invitation of all, to Dublin.

3

In the Dublin of 1857 Benjamin Lee Guinness was not only head of the thriving Guinness Brewery, he was also the recognised leader of the city's merchant class. His was a rapid, meteoric rise in status. Born in 1798 at his father's house at the brewery, he was only sixteen years old when he became an apprentice there. Six years later he was made a partner, and such was his obvious business flair that his father entrusted him with the running of the brewery whenever he was absent. It was Benjamin Lee who presided over its sudden dynamic expansion after 1840. Until then stout was chiefly bought for home consumption, but Benjamin Lee pushed forward a massive increase of the firm's export trade and it made him the richest man in Ireland.

In 1851, four years before his father died, he had been elected Lord Mayor and was inaugurated with enormous pomp and ceremony. He manifestly did not share his grandfather's scruples about the self-indulgence of men in public office, for he marked the occasion with a magnificent civic banquet, inviting the Lord Lieutenant and all the important dignitaries and gentry of the city. The great famine was barely over, but it was the rural areas which suffered its appalling effects, not comfortable Dublin.

If Arthur Guinness was concerned by his son's lavish hospitality he had the wisdom to keep quiet, recognising that unlike the two preceding generations Benjamin Lee had a duty to behave in a manner befitting his new elevated station. When Arthur did choose to give Benjamin the benefit of his advice his son usually took it. That was why he allowed him to make the ultimate decisions. In 1851 when asked to persuade his son to contest a Conservative Dublin seat, Arthur refused on the grounds that Benjamin Lee was "the devoted husband of a wife suffering extreme delicacy of health", and that he had enough on his hands with the heavy demands "from the pressures of peculiar family and other relative claims".[1] Benjamin Lee agreed with his father. His cousin-wife Bessie, whom he had married in 1837 and adored, was never strong. She had however managed to provide him with four children, Anne in 1839, Arthur Edward in 1840, Benjamin Lee in 1842 and Edward Cecil, the future Earl of Iveagh, in 1847. But it was not only consideration for Bessie which decided him not to stand. Shrewd as he was, Benjamin Lee was prepared to bide his time. The moment had not yet come for a Guinness Member of Parliament. Outspoken political allegiance could damage trade. Arthur, who knew only too well the pitfalls of political involvement and was never a Conservative, sighed with relief and blessed God for "the measure of his Grace which has led you to this happy decision".

Once Arthur had died, Benjamin Lee adjusted his lifestyle. He already owned a country estate, St Anne's in Clontarf, but for a man with his social commitments a decent town house was an absolute necessity. His home at 1 Thomas Street was totally inadequate, so in 1856 he bought 80 St Stephen's Green, a property in one of Dublin's most fashionable squares. It was an elegant, three-storey residence with a projecting, four-columned portico, the first in Dublin. He later bought the adjoining house, number 81, dismantled the dividing wall and made one large and lavish mansion, later known as Iveagh House. It was here that he began to entertain regally and the legendary Guinness hospitality was born.

Moving into St Stephen's Green, to a house with about thirty bedrooms and accommodation for twenty servants, marked the barely subtle, inevitable rise from tradesman to gentry. Benjamin Lee could afford to look a little pleased with himself, as his portrait suggests. He had the same determined chin, "the prototypic Guinness jaw"[2] and aquiline nose of his father and grandfather, the same tight-lipped smile, but there was something about the regal manner in which he held his head which suggested a man confident enough to look the Anglo-Irish aristocracy firmly in the eye.

But Benjamin Lee was never as frivolous as the aristocracy. Temperamentally he manifested the uneasy ambivalence which would haunt successive generations of Guinness brewers. Success necessitated a certain gregariousness, but innate shyness sought refuge in privacy and solitude. That was why he loved to escape to St Anne's, his quiet house overlooking Dublin Bay. Entertaining was at best his duty, at worst a necessary evil, especially when he wanted to be alone with his family. Besides he was far too dignified a Christian gentleman for frivolity. The low church influence of his childhood left him with an abstemious streak. To squander money was a sin, to spend it wisely the sign of fundamental virtue. Two generations of Guinness brewers had regarded their wealth as a sacred trust. So did he. He was exceedingly generous in caring for impoverished relatives like his errant brother Arthur Lee, and he funded a host of worthy causes. Aware of the value of the grand gesture he also financed the complete renovation of St Patrick's Cathedral, which would have crumbled into ruins without his help.

If the entrepreneurial and philanthropic spirit was as alive as ever in the third Guinness to inherit the precious silver salver, then so was the tradition of piety. Benjamin Lee's religious observance was more formal than his father's and owed less to nonconformism, but with Prime Minister Gladstone threatening the Church of Ireland with disestablishment, it needed a staunch defender. Besides evangelicalism did not blend with increased sophistication. Within his own home the daily prayers for family and servants, which had been Arthur's delight, were slowly becoming a ritual, to his wife's deep concern.

Bessie was a devout woman whose faith had sustained her through long years of illness. While her husband was drawn towards a high church expression of his faith, she went on attending Bethesda Chapel, taking her four children with her. The less earnest Benjamin Lee appeared in matters religious, the more she feared for his eternal soul. She was painfully aware of the moral snares which lay in wait for such a man. Prosperity made the greedy and ambitious gravitate towards him like moths to a light, especially feckless women seeking position and prestige. The fast and fashionable society in which they now moved did not deceive her, but she was never so sure of her husband and sons. Benjamin Lee might be left an eligible widower at any moment, without her protection and guidance, and what then? She expressed her concerns to her son Arthur Edward:

Do my darling avoid bad company, I mean worldlings, for there will be plenty anxious to come here, and do guard darling papa from designing worldly women, for he will be much set on and might easily be taken in. I do not mean that he should not marry, but that he should get one who would help him on to that future world and not lead him to think of or live for the present . . .[3]

Although *Spes Mea in Deo* was the family motto, Benjamin Lee's trust in a gospel of self-help often appeared greater than his trust in God. Work was what counted, discipline and duty, a concerted, collective effort to get Ireland back on its feet after the famine. He was the first to achieve "the serene equipoise between God and Mammon which has ever since been the hall-mark of the family".[4] Like his father and grandfather before him and the great Quaker proprietors of Victorian England, Benjamin Lee was renowned for his benevolence as an employer. Astute and able at business, he was also a gentle, thoughtful man. As the brewery expanded, propelling him from the safe base of a wealthy man to the dizzy heights of a millionaire, he never abused his workforce, but provided job security, pensions and better housing. Wages were higher than anywhere else, bearing in mind that brewing required a smaller workforce than most other industries. Throughout Dublin a job at Guinness was regarded as gold.

Small wonder that the town began to buzz with the news that a certain member of the Guinness family was exciting great curiosity throughout the rest of the British Isles with the extraordinary power of his preaching. "Is it a meteor or a real star?" the people asked. Dr Urwick, minister of York Street Chapel, the city's leading nonconformist church, who had baptised the young man nearly twenty three years before, decided it was time to find out.

4

On January 15th, 1858, the *Daily Express* announced Henry Grattan Guinness' imminent arrival: "We understand that our fellow citizens will shortly have an opportunity of hearing this now celebrated preacher, as he is about to visit Dublin."

Even the pro-Catholic *Dublin Evening Post* showed a great deal of interest. Protestant preachers were weighed against each other like professional boxers. On January 28th it referred to Henry Grattan as a rival to the celebrated Mr Spurgeon. The *Liverpool Mercury* had apparently carried a glowing account of one of his sermons. The Liverpool Concert Hall had been packed to capacity, albeit with a congregation "of very mixed character", for many remained with their heads uncovered. The preacher's personal appearance was described in detail:

A modest unassuming young man of twenty one, of middle stature, wearing a frock coat that reaches to the knees and is buttoned almost up to the neckerchief. Long black hair, parted in the middle, and when the eyes are heaven-directed, reaching to the shoulders, forms the natural background and enclosure of the face, to which it lends a classic or poetic grandeur, intensifying as it does every expression. His language is of the most childlike simplicity.

Henry Grattan Guinness arrived in Ireland in February 1858 to enormous acclaim. Only 22 per cent of the population of Dublin was Protestant, but she was proud of her sons, particularly a Guinness son and full cousin of Benjamin Lee. The newspapers revived the story of the duel, surrounding the son of D'Esterre's widow in an aura of romance and adventure. Dr Urwick noted in his journal: "Unwonted excitement possessed all classes of what is called the religious public, and spread fast to numbers beyond it. To prevent serious disorder, admission was regulated by tickets; yet under that restriction the chapel was thronged to its utmost capacity of even standing room, long before the hour for commencing the worship."

Miraculously, after such a build-up, Henry Grattan Guinness was not a disappointment. In him all the drive and forcefulness of the entrepreneurial Guinness spirit mingled with the creative, magnetic qualities of the Cramers. It was an irresistible combination and Henry was learning how to employ those qualities to the fullest effect. He had but to walk into a room to command attention. He was a deeply intense young man, unable to laugh easily, which boded ill for his nervous health, but to all he met, intensity added drama to his personal charm.

On February 8th the *Daily Express* carried a full report of his first public appearance.

> He appears to be not more than one and twenty years of age, his figure rather slight, and his features regular and complexion somewhat pale, which, combined with dark hair, worn long and thrown back from the forehead, tend to give him a striking and interesting appearance. In the pulpit his manner is quiet and unaffected, and characterised by an earnest simplicity which forcibly impresses itself on the listener. His gesture is remarkably graceful and appropriate, without the smallest approach to elocutionary display, and in addition to these, his voice is musical and well-modulated.

The journalist then went on to say that his discourse was "earnest, solemn and impressive, fully realising the expectations which had been formed of his powers from the notice of his efforts in England". In fact he so fulfilled all expectations and more that the cream of Dublin society, from the ruling Protestant ascendancy to the leading professionals in the town, deigned to grace a nonconformist chapel with their presence, in order to catch a glimpse of this latest phenomenon. By Monday, February 15th he was commanding the front page of the Irish *Daily Express*:

He has now delivered nine discourses in this city since his arrival; and the interest which he has excited, so far from abating, has daily increased, and will probably continue to do so during the present week . . . Few preachers have ever addressed congregations more select. They consisted of the élite of all denominations, including a considerable number of the Established Clergy. The wealth, the respectability, the cultivated intellect, as well as the evangelical piety of the city, have been represented in a measure unprecedented, we believe, on such an occasion in this country. Judges, members of Parliament, distinguished orators, Fellows of College, the lights of the various professions, and, to a considerable extent, the rank and fashion of this gay metropolis, have been drawn out to a dissenting chapel which was thronged, even on weekdays, by this new attraction. On Wednesday morning the Lord Lieutenant was present, with the gentlemen of his Excellency's household; and yesterday morning we observed among the audience the Lord Chancellor, the Lord Justice of Appeal, and Baron Pennefather. . . .

Although the Lord Lieutenant had graced the young preacher with his presence, no mention was made of Benjamin Lee and whether he came to hear his cousin preaching temperance, the folly of riches and the need for a new birth. But John Grattan junior, living in penury since his failure in the Bristol brewery and hearing of his half-brother's enormous success, decided his moment had come. He sued the brewery for wrongful dismissal twenty years earlier.

Henry Grattan had by then left Dublin for a preaching tour of the whole of Ireland. His reputation went before him. Wherever he went the story was the same. His striking appearance, beautiful voice and ability to "preach in pictures" ensured him vast audiences. Dr Urwick noted:

Without an exception the welcome he met with in the provinces resembled that in Dublin. Altogether nothing to compare with it had been known in Ireland within living memory. An announcement that he was to preach was enough to put the population on the move. The largest buildings available for his use failed to accommodate the numbers who thronged to hear him. A tidal-wave of popularity bore him along day after day. The local press everywhere chronicled and commented on his appearances as leading topics of interest.

There was no doubt that in an era before television and the cinema Henry Grattan Guinness was wonderful entertainment, happily filling the role of the later screen heroes. On the basis of those few months, one historian would later refer to him with Spurgeon and D. L. Moody, as one of the three great preachers of the nineteenth century. But he did not whip up the emotions of his audience. The *Daily Express* said that there was no "cunning exhibition of oratorical fireworks, a dazzling stage effect, or theatrical contrivances to work up a 'galvanic' revival". The preaching was simplicity itself. That was what was so extraordinary. Yet people of all ranks and classes responded, generally the non-religious, so that years later Henry Grattan himself could say "it was scarcely a matter of preaching". There was no need for "hanging back", no "introducing the subject in a delicate way for fear of giving offence". He had never experienced anything like it, nor would he again. "Everyone wanted to hear."[5] His popularity, so the *Daily Express* reported, was only "because all his powers, intellectual and moral, are pervaded by a consecrating influence from on high". In other words he was the right man at the right time.

The world of 1858 was in political turmoil. The philosophies of the day were largely materialistic and had nothing to offer the pervading sense of gloom and despondency. Here and there an individual raised a voice of protest against the evils of sweated labour, ignorance, dirt and the slums, but most people were indifferent. The established Church was silent. Some explosion was necessary to break through the prosperity of the middle classes and their complacent accumulation of wealth. Some hope was needed for the working classes who lived a life of drudgery in order to provide it. The country was ripe for religious revival and it came, sweeping through England, Scotland and Wales, affecting every rank and class, giving birth to some of the greatest pioneering movements for social reform. It would flicker on for many years. From factories to society drawing-rooms everything would stop for prayer:

> Clergy and ministers were unable to cope with the demands of their people, and services lasting from three to four hours were sometimes followed by harrowing scenes – men and women agonizing on the floor under conviction of sin, groans mingled with shouts of praise as this one or that proclaimed himself delivered from the bondage of Satan and the wrath to come.[6]

For sectarian reasons Ireland was notoriously resistant. Henry Grattan's preaching heralded a new dawn. Revival of religious fervour broke out in a blaze. It was a predominantly Protestant movement, inevitably affecting Ulster the most, but the Catholic population was by no means immune. When in April Henry Grattan publicly maintained that Protestants were in as much need of conversion as their Catholic compatriots and had no business to denounce Romanism when they were in darkness themselves, he was overwhelmed with Catholic acclaim. The *Dublin Evening Post* quoted him in full in an article entitled, "Reverend Grattan Guinness on religion in Ireland":

In the North I saw a great deal of rancour and Orangeism, but very little true Christianity. One clergyman told me that a man applied to him for Church membership and to be allowed to take the sacrament, stating that he believed himself to be a Christian. The minister said to him, "What makes you think you are a Christian?" "Ah well Sir" said he, "I think I could eat a Roman Catholic" (laughter).

The journalist wondered what Lord Eglinton, the Viceroy, would make of Henry Grattan Guinness' remarks. After all he had just appointed two loyal Orangemen as his chaplains: "The Rev. Guinness will however have accomplished a great good for society and religion, if his disinterested advice be followed . . . 'Before Protestants seek to convert Roman Catholics, let them seek to convert themselves'."

Ireland was a notoriously fickle admirer and it was as well that Henry, in the full flush of adulation, could not foresee what lay ahead. Looking back at those days, remembering the deep hush, the spellbound audiences, the tears they shed, he would one day say wistfully: "I can almost listen to him, that evangelist of other days, and wonder, WAS IT I?"

He left Ireland for a few months in the summer of 1858, at about the time that his half-brother's claim for compensation received a public hearing. Benjamin Lee gave evidence and the suit was dismissed. Whatever embarrassment Henry felt, it did not prevent his triumphant return to the country in the following year. This time he preached predominantly in the open air, dispensing with the chapels and their ticket system which limited his audiences to the well-to-do. In Ulster he had to be hoisted on to the roof of a cab so that the twenty thousand who had turned up could see him. Certain English newspapers, including *The Times* and the *Lancet*, were indignant. To fill the streets of Belfast with prostitutes and drunken revellers was nothing more than "a moral epidemic and contagious hysteria".

A similar "epidemic" broke out in the United States and Henry Grattan was invited to Philadelphia. He arrived in November to a punishing schedule, preaching as often as thirteen times a week. The County Prison disturbed him dreadfully. All 246 prisoners were kept in solitary confinement, locked behind two doors. Only the outer doors were opened slightly and Henry had to shout down a 400 foot iron framework corridor, so that the prisoners could hear him. It was a gloomy December day and the utter hopelessness of the place weighed him down. In the twilight of one of the cells he sat for some time with a man who had murdered his wife. He "seemed filled with the gloom of mental wretchedness and despair, and only stared at the floor, shook his head and said, 'I believe all that'". It was the first time Henry allowed himself to feel defeated by his circumstances and a sign of how tired he was.

Despite his growing fatigue he went on to New York and several other American and Canadian towns, preaching a minimum of nine sermons a week for six or seven months. When he returned to Ireland in June 1860 expecting to continue where he had left off almost a year earlier, exhaustion had driven him to the edge of breakdown and he was good for nothing. A holiday was imperative. Norway was what he had in mind but his plans fell through and he had to settle for Ilfracombe. It was the most fortunate disappointment of his life.

5

On an Ilfracombe down one drowsy summer afternoon three young women in wide-brimmed sun hats sat reading and sketching on a grassy clifftop. Below the cliff fell away in a sheer rocky drop to the sea, which shimmered and sparkled in the August sun. Mabel, the eldest of the sisters, was engrossed in her book. Laura, the youngest, looking pretty in the new muslin dress she had bought for her holiday and unable to settle to anything for very long, was trying to distract her. Fanny, the plainest of the three, stopped her sketching for a moment and stared out to sea, marvelling at the way its deep azure seemed to melt into the sky on the distant horizon.

She was a slight, sallow-faced, almost fragile-looking woman, well past the first bloom of youth. But her apparent frailty belied the wiry inner strength which circumstances had forced upon her. Her dress, in stark comparison with her sisters', was dark and unfashionable, buttoned to the neck in the plain, simple style of the Quakers. A high forehead, emphasised by dark brown hair parted in the middle and pulled severely into ringlets bunched on either side of her face, was wrinkled into an almost permanent expression of anxiety.

For a moment as she gazed out to sea the frown dissolved into a smile of satisfaction. The murmur of the waves, the taste of the salt on her lips and the feel of the warm sun on her back had driven away the bitter disappointment of this particular holiday, a poor second-best arranged at the last moment when plans to go to Paris fell through. She drew in a deep breath, bent her head to her sketch pad and worked industriously. Whatever she did, she did earnestly and well.

For some time she had been vaguely aware that Laura was talking to Mabel about young Mr Guinness – again! She had talked of little else since she heard him preach the first Sunday they were in Ilfracombe. Fanny smiled, and seeing it Laura said in a hurt tone, "You missed something, Fanny! Why on earth didn't you come?"

Fanny felt like saying that there was hardly any point since Laura had insisted on giving her such a detailed account, but Laura had relapsed into reverie.

"Such speaking, such a voice, such a manner!" she sighed ecstatically. "You never heard anything like it, I am certain, in your life. And you didn't care even enough to go!"

Fanny laughed and shook her head. "Oh, I shall hear him, child, some day, no doubt. And, after all," she said loudly, teasing her youngest sister, "it doesn't much matter whether I hear him or not."

Fanny returned to her sketching, unaware that the colour had suddenly drained from her sister's face. Directly below on the silvery water a boat had swiftly appeared around the corner of the cliff. It was a light craft manned by a strong, solitary oarsman, close enough for her to be able to identify the rower.

"It's him!" Laura whispered to Mabel in a panic. "Do you think he heard her?"

The two girls were irrepressible. Their panic quickly dissolved into excited giggles as they stared at the rower, observing his skill and vigour with admiration.

"Look, Fanny! Do look quickly, there he is!"

"Who?" Fanny asked, obtuse to the end.

"Mr Guinness!"

With a sigh of resignation Fanny looked down at the sea and caught a glimpse of a tall, dark-haired young man as he disappeared again around the cliff. "That youth!" she said dismissively, and went on with her sketching.

And that was how, years later, Fanny Guinness described her first sight of her future husband to their children.

Fanny's had been an unhappy, chequered history. Her father, Major Edward Marlborough Fitzgerald, was a member of one of Ireland's most illustrious aristocratic families. Theirs was a long line of adventurers and fighters dating back to the time of Henry II, when they had crossed over from England and played a leading part in the conquest of Ireland. In recent years however they had not been entirely unsympathetic to the Catholic cause. A Fitzgerald had played a leading role in the Peasants' Revolt of 1798, during which the fifteen-year-old John Grattan Guinness had been badly wounded. But intermarriage with the Catholic population was another matter. The family disowned Edward Marlborough when he made a match considered beneath his station, to a Roman Catholic girl from the lower middle classes. The marriage was a disaster and ended in divorce. Even though Edward Marlborough went on to lead a distinguished military career, taking for his second wife Mabel, the daughter of Admiral Stopford, family pride prevented any reconciliation.

The second marriage was a happy one, until Mabel died of tuberculosis, leaving her grief-stricken husband with five children to care for. Gerald, the eldest, was only ten and then there were four little girls, of which Fanny was the second. She had a dim recollection of being held in her mother's arms, an impression of long, waving brown hair and beautiful eyes. She remembered too a summer garden by the Thames, her wonderful Papa coming home, so handsome with his twirling military moustaches, and of running to meet him in a shining white dress to show him her new ribbons. She would have been about three at the time.

The happy memories ended there. Fitzgerald never got over the loss of his wife and found it difficult to socialise. Although he became a distinguished journalist, the editor of one newspaper and leader-writer of another, it did not pay well. He worked hard to look after his young family, but there were always financial difficulties. Fanny remembered the evenings at the house they had moved to in Glasgow, the huge square table bedecked in tiny, twinkling candles, and Papa writing, always writing.

A smallpox epidemic broke out. Fanny succumbed to it and was desperately ill for weeks. Through the haze of a high fever she heard the bells pealing louder and louder and was aware of something stiff and unfamiliar being carried out of the room. She was too ill to ask what it was, but a while later, feeling better, she asked for her brother. Her father took her into his arms and told her that Gerald had died the day the bells rang out for the wedding of Queen Victoria.

Some months later in a London city office Arthur West, actuary, was sitting at his desk reading the morning paper. A rather old-fashioned gentleman, he had that air of quiet gravity which often distinguished the Quakers. One particular story had caught his attention that morning. A certain military man, broken by his circumstances, had taken a one-way ticket on a Channel steamer, and half-way across had thrown himself overboard, leaving four motherless little girls totally alone and unprovided for. As he sat thinking how sad it was, the door opened and his partner came in, a letter in his hand.

"I cannot understand this, West," he said, waving the letter in the air. "What do you think it means?"

West took the letter and read it. It was addressed from a Channel steamer and contained a few words of farewell, begging whoever read it to see to the needs of his children. "Before this reaches you," the letter ended, "I shall be out of reach of any answer."

West handed his partner the morning paper, took the letter and put it in his pocket.

That evening he told the story to his wife Mary, and showed her the letter. The Wests had no children and that had always been a source of great regret for Mary. Their pleasant home and garden in Stamford Hill seemed empty. With true Quaker prudence she listened in silence, but the following morning before her husband left for work she put her hand in his and said, "My dear, I have been thinking that thee and I perhaps might help to care for those fatherless little ones."

"I had thought the same myself from the first moment," he replied. "God bless thee for thy loving heart."

Mary West put on her bonnet and paid a series of calls on well-known members of the Tottenham Friends Meeting House. Before the day was over she had found good homes for three of the girls. Eight-year-old Fanny was to live with them.

The Wests were a kindly, though reserved couple and Fanny "with the high spirit and passionate blood of old Anglo-Irish Barons running in her veins", did not always find it easy to submit to their rather narrow, quiet, Quaker ways. Fortunately the Friends were also cultured and well-read, and Fanny, who, with her square brow and penetrating blue-grey eyes bore a striking resemblance to her father, and had inherited his literary and mental abilities, found an outlet in the open debate and discussion which the Quakers enjoyed.

In the 1840s the Society of Friends was strongly influenced by an exciting new movement known as "the Brethren". Once the Methodists had set a precedent in breaking away from the established Church, other reactionary sects felt free to follow, leading to several new denominations. Brethrenism began in Plymouth with a group of dissatisfied evangelical Anglicans who wanted to dispense with the hierarchical system of priest and people and return to a simple communion service in which everyone could participate on an equal basis. This emphasis on brotherhood and the equality of all believers was a radical challenge to the social, as well as the religious establishment, and had a profound influence on the embryonic Trade Union movement. Brethrenism brought a new warmth and freedom to the Church, challenging rigid formality and stereotyped attitudes. Fanny Fitzgerald's keen, enquiring mind was stirred by the questioning it provoked. This was before the 1860s, when the Brethren movement itself, with no central authority, became hidebound by restrictive rules and regulations and divided into two factions, "Exclusive" and "Open".

During Fanny's teenage years the Wests moved to Exmouth and later, ironically, to Dublin. Though this was a return to her ancestral roots, Fanny never contacted her father's family. She could well have done with their help. Arthur West, exhausted by years of over-exertion in the Quaker struggle against slavery, had a stroke and was left severely incapacitated and unable to earn a living. For years both his wife and adopted daughter nursed him devotedly. In order to make ends meet Fanny took a job as a teacher, pursuing her own studies in whatever spare time she could snatch. Eventually Mary West's health broke down too. The family moved to Bath, where Fanny continued her teaching and looked after both of them. It was a terrible blow when, like her natural father, Arthur West took his own life.

By the time she was twenty-nine hard work and slender means had taken their toll. Whatever brilliant mental powers Fanny possessed were hidden behind her wan, sober appearance. Necessity, which had robbed her of her youth, had made her capable and competent, but never cold or hard. There was too much of the Irish in her for training to curb her fire and zest completely. When she opened her mouth to speak there was a sudden warmth and vivacity about her which commanded attention. The little tea parties of the Quaker and Brethren circles in which she moved tended to be dull, but one of the old ladies was overheard to say, "My dear, I do assure thee when Fanny Fitzgerald comes into the room she breaks the ice in a moment. Thou knows the way she has with her! Sets everyone talking, and puts the stiffest people at ease."

Henry Grattan Guinness felt at ease in her presence from the moment they met. They were introduced by a mutual Brethren acquaintance one evening in Ilfracombe. Fanny blushed remembering her comments on the clifftop a few days before, but if he had heard them he chose to ignore the fact. He asked if he could call on the sisters one evening before he left. Romance was the last thing in Fanny's mind. She had long abandoned any hope of matrimony and was sure that the young preacher was falling in love with Laura, who stood beside her in great excitement. Laura was twenty-five, his age, beautifully dressed and lovely to look at. Her adoptive parents were wealthy and had provided her with every accomplishment a young lady should have.

But when the young preacher did pay them a visit it was Fanny who received his attention. Something about her attracted him at once, so that after one evening together he could say quite simply, "I felt that I had found, for the first time in my life, a woman with a mind and soul that answered to my own. When with her I no longer felt alone."

Nevertheless when, within a day of returning home, she received his proposal it came as a complete surprise. He made no secret of the fact that marriage to a man in his position, who had no financial security, would not be easy. She replied almost at once, "It is a life worth living, worth suffering for, a life worth resigning all else for . . . Were it to cost a hundredfold more than in all probability it will, I would not resign the prospect or exchange it for the brightest lot earth could offer."

Two months later, on October 2nd, 1860, they were married at the Princes Street Meeting House in Bath. The chapel was packed. On the plain unpolished benches the women sat in their shawls and poke bonnets, their tight ringlets nestling neatly beneath the wide brims. There were no flowers, no decorations, no organ or harmonium, no pulpit or platform, no minister or functionary, nothing except a table in the centre of the room and two vacant chairs for the bride and groom.

At her home in Widcombe Crescent Fanny had risen early and supervised the preparation of the wedding breakfast. Mary West was too infirm to cope and too upset at the thought of losing the daughter on whom she relied. The appearance of the wrong table-cloth on the principal table distressed her terribly. Fanny reassured her that all the guests would be far too interested in the bridegroom to notice. But Mary West was still worrying about it when the maid announced the arrival of the old man who was to give her daughter away.

Fanny heaved a sigh of relief and looking radiant in her plain white dress ran downstairs to greet him. For the first time in years the sense of heavy restraint lifted from her shoulders and she felt relaxed.

A hush descended on the congregation as the bride and groom walked in together and took their seats in silence. There were no bridesmaids, and no bridal bouquet. It was to be the simplest of Quaker services. Someone suggested a hymn and after it was sung, unaccompanied, the bridegroom rose to his feet and began the meeting with a prayer. Other hymns and readings were selected spontaneously by members of the congregation and then there was a long, meaningful pause. The bride and groom took their cue, nodded at each other and rose to their feet. Henry took Fanny's hand, placed a plain gold ring on her finger and announced in his resonant voice that this was to signify that she was hereafter his wife. Fanny, in her turn, made her promises and then the pair knelt while the meeting united them with a prayer.

Years later when her children and grandchildren gathered round her feet, begging her again to tell the story of her wedding, they would always ask the same question, "Did no one marry you? Nobody at all?" And Fanny would reply with a radiant smile, "Father married us, darlings. Father did everything – except the registrar's work. We didn't need anybody else."

5

1860–1872

Trials and Testings

1

With no home and no income, Henry and Fanny both knew that their honeymoon could be little more than a carefree interlude, but they lived as if it would last for ever. For several blissfully happy weeks in Clevedon, on the pretty north Somerset coast, they revelled in the simple life, Fanny playing at keeping house in their quaint lodgings. They bought bread and other basic provisions and carried them home, enjoying the warmth and cosiness of a meal alone together as the early autumn twilight closed in around them. By day they wandered hand in hand along the sandy beach at the entrance to the Bristol Channel, and watching the vast expanse of churning sea stretching out until it met the distant grey horizon, wondered where it would carry them. Few couples begin their married life with such an uncharted future.

It was perhaps as well that they were unaware of what lay ahead, so that nothing could mar the untroubled, almost childlike enjoyment of those days. Once over, they would never be recaptured. Anxiety would be a constant companion. Immense popularity of the kind Henry Grattan had enjoyed could not last for ever. Though neither of them knew it, the tide was slowly turning.

Henry Grattan was undergoing a change of direction himself. In the weeks after their honeymoon, before they were due to sail for the United States, Fanny brought him into contact with her Brethren friends. The simplicity of their worship had impressed him for some time. But it was their fascination for prophecy which influenced him the most.

Interpreting world history in the light of the apocalyptic books of the Bible was not original. Throughout the Middle Ages and particularly at the time of the Reformation, Christians breaking away from the established Catholic Church had interpreted Daniel's "Great Beast", who oppressed the saints, as the Church of Rome. The preface of the King James version of the Bible, published in 1611, stated clearly that "the Man of Sin" of the book of Revelation, was none other than the Pope. And indeed history had witnessed a succession of popes as cruel and corrupt, if not more so, than any other temporal dynasty of the time. It was the prophecies of the "Beast's" ultimate downfall which enabled its victims to endure persecution and even martyrdom.

By the beginning of the nineteenth century, when Protestants were no longer a persecuted minority, that interpretation was not quite so popular, not until a triumphant Napoleon conquered Italy and destroyed the Holy Roman Empire, making the Pope a virtual prisoner in the Vatican. Protestants well-read in biblical prophecy began to feel it was being fulfilled before their very eyes. The temporal power of the Pope had been all but decimated overnight. The "Beast" was losing its iron grip. It was a heady turn of events. The impossible had happened just as the books of Daniel and Revelation predicted. That being so what other great political events had the Bible foreseen?

From the sixteenth century it had been the driving force and justification for the early Zionists. In the nineteenth century, from his study of the Old and New Testaments Lord Ashley, the future Earl of Shaftesbury, an outstanding pioneer of social reform, became convinced that the return of the Jews to Palestine was part of the divine plan. In 1839 he managed to persuade Lord Palmerston, the Foreign Secretary, that Palestine should become a Jewish national homeland, with Jerusalem as its capital, under Turkish rule but with British protection. It was an extraordinarily premature vision. The scheme came to nothing, but Zionism was at least considered a viable political proposition, and one which Henry Grattan Guinness would take up years later.

The series of revolutions all over Europe in 1848 compounded the growing interest in prophecy. These were unsettling days. Governments appeared and disappeared, Europe was in turmoil. The world appeared to be changing faster than ever before. People wanted to understand the nature of the times in which they lived and believed that the Bible held the key.

As an Irish Protestant who had experienced first-hand both the superstition and the fury of the Roman Catholic Church, Henry Grattan was predisposed to an interest in the subject. He now lamented his lack of formal education and those wasted years at theological college. He undertook to teach himself history, theology and ancient Hebrew, and was immersed in his studies. Early in 1861 his first pamphlet on prophecy and world history was published, but by then he and Fanny were en route for America, the scene only months before of some of his greatest triumphs.

It was a very different America they found when they landed, no longer a "United States". England, under Wilberforce's rallying call, had banned Negro slavery in 1833. Twenty-eight years later the American government was about to do the same, but for fierce opposition from eleven cotton-picking southern states, who asserted their right to secede from the union. In just a few months revival fever gave way to war fever.

Henry and Fanny were stunned by the sudden change, but no more than Henry's American friends were surprised by the change in him. He seemed more subdued, more contemplative. Whenever he preached, it was about prophecy, and to the Americans it seemed as if the old fire had dwindled to a few desperate sparks. Doors which had been flung open to him a few months earlier were now slammed in his face. Of the thirty churches in Philadelphia which once welcomed him, only three were prepared to let him preach.

The problem was that his marriage to Fanny and subsequent association with the Plymouth Brethren had earned him a reputation for sectarianism. In England and the United States the exclusivity of the Brethren was now provoking hostility and suspicion. They practised a form of "Christian democracy" in which every member of the congregation, rather than one priest, had the right to decide on policy. This was a threat to ministers of the more established denominations. Besides there were grave dangers inherent in such a system. In her book *Silas Marner*, George Eliot described how things can go tragically wrong when a community imagines that a consensus of opinion necessarily implies a correct moral judgment. American ministers were terrified that Henry Grattan Guinness would turn their church members against them. When he began to baptise his own converts it confirmed their worst fears.

Henry Grattan could not understand their sudden coldness. He admired certain aspects of Brethrenism, but saw its shortcomings too. Never throughout his life was he entirely committed to one denomination. When it came to truth, none of them held a monopoly. But the Brethren had influenced him more than he knew. Shortly before he left England they had told him that his great gift of oratory was not divinely inspired. It stemmed from his own desire for popularity and attention. Henry Grattan, young and naïve, believed them implicitly. He was devastated. More than anything else he coveted real holiness of character. He decided to trim away every suggestion of histrionics in the pulpit, assuming that the results of his preaching would be unchanged. But he was deceived. His style was cramped. Like Samson when his hair was shorn, his power vanished. And no matter how hard he tried he never fully regained it. When, many months later, he realised he had been misled, it was too late. It was a loss he was to lament for the rest of his life.

Sensitivity to the prevailing climate would never be one of Henry Grattan's strong points. Unaware of the reasons for his waning popularity or the strength of feeling behind them, he launched into a full-scale attack on the senseless emotional manipulation which was driving the United States towards civil war. It was not that he did not advocate the abolition of slavery. Wilberforce and those who spear-headed the English abolitionist campaign had been evangelicals, strongly supported by the Quakers. The suppression of slavery had long been regarded as a Christian cause. It could even be argued that Henry Grattan's own preaching in America several months earlier had added fuel to the abolitionist fire there. But he did believe that whatever the provocation, Christians should never fight.

The Peace Society published a letter he wrote entitled, "The Duty of Christians in the Present Crisis", to howls of derision from the American press. The pamphlet suggested that Christians were within their rights to disobey any government which urged them to draw the sword. It rubbed some raw nerves. Coming from a foreigner and an Irishman, that was rich indeed. Was he so naïve that the lesson of Napoleon had not taught him that "heaven was on the side of the strongest artillery"? Most parsons in the north and south believed that "while the New Testament may enforce a conviction, still the rifle is not to be entirely neglected". Mr Guinness was evidently suffering from pique that the American public had more interesting demands on their attention than his preaching. He was nothing more than a "cowardly poltroon", who "when human sentiment is properly developed, should be tried by a Court Martial, presided over by the Rev. chaplain of the Brooklyn Phalanx".[1]

Not content with public defamation, the newspapers called for his removal from the northern states. The *World* demanded that he make a public retraction or go and take up residence in the Southern Confederacy.

Such vitriol was devastating for Henry Grattan. No one had ever before questioned his integrity. Nor had he experienced such a bitter personal attack. He realised too late that he had overestimated his popularity. The papers were right. His suggestions would have about as much success in altering public opinion as turning "the current of the Niagara with a pitchfork". It was time to leave America to its self-inflicted destiny. Fanny was pregnant and must not be further upset. They needed a safe haven where the baby could be born in peace. America no longer welcomed them, but as that door closed another opened in the form of a request from Canada.

As they travelled the news reached them that war had been declared. They had left the country just in time. For four years America tore itself apart in a futile conflagration, so that the words of the newspaper, written before the war as a condemnation of Henry Grattan's stance, take on a strange irony and in retrospect sound almost like a eulogy.

Reiterating our advice that Mr G. had better depart for a more profitable vineyard, we place him on the record as among the first clergymen who advocated peace, and the only Irishman who ever so far forgot his nationality as to interfere to prevent a quarrel that promises in a military sense, to be in all respects so interesting as that we have now at hand.

2

On his parents' first wedding anniversary, October 2nd, 1861, young Henry Grattan Guinness was born in Toronto. He was always known as Harry to distinguish him from his father and to Fanny's relief he was a healthy baby, not adding to the burdens she already had to bear.

Canada had not received her husband with any greater warmth than America. They found his preaching disappointing and Henry was slowly sinking into self-doubt and near despair. The fact that Fanny was in great demand as a speaker compounded her anxiety for her husband. Preaching was not something she had ever anticipated or desired. In fact it was a radical thing for a woman to do. When she was first invited to address some meetings in the eastern states of America the prospect filled her with alarm. After much persuasion she gave in and was such a success that Henry encouraged her to preach at his side wherever he went, even with the increasingly evident signs of her pregnancy.

Neither had experienced a freezing Canadian winter before. It wore Henry down even further. By January Fanny realised that to preserve her husband's mental health she had to get him back to England as soon as possible. That was a problem. They were now in Quebec. The nearest embarkation point for England was Portland in America which would mean crossing the frozen St Lawrence River and braving the dangers of a country at war, all with a three-month-old baby. In the end she had little choice. Travelling would only become more hazardous in the next few months as the weather deteriorated. She wrapped up her tiny baby and they set off.

"The crossing of the St Lawrence is a frightful and exciting exploit," she wrote in her diary. "I was terrified in going over to Quebec, expecting each moment to be swallowed in the surging ice." On the return journey she hugged her baby close, expecting the worst, but miraculously it only took half an hour instead of the usual two hours, and was much less cold. The rest of the journey passed smoothly and by April they were in England.

Any hopes that Henry's spirits would be restored once he was on familiar territory were soon dashed. The stigma of sectarianism had followed him home. Preaching invitations were scarce. In his journal he expressed an aching longing for those earlier days when preaching had been so easy and had such impact. The people had turned against him and he could not understand why.

Just as Fanny was becoming acutely anxious about how they were going to live without any income, a generous friend provided for her to take Henry on a prolonged holiday abroad. Harry was left in an English nursery and they spent four months touring the Middle East. The pure wonder at seeing so many sacred sights, the awesome sense of walking on hallowed ground was to have a profound effect on Henry's later ministry, but when they first returned to England his mental health seemed little better. His confidence was so shaken that the thought of addressing a large meeting brought him out in a cold sweat. Yet he had a family to support and Fanny was pregnant again. When the congregation of Byrom Hall, a small chapel in the Waterloo area of Liverpool, asked him to be their minister, he accepted with relief.

It was there on Christmas Day 1862 that Mary Geraldine was born. He called her Minnie and from the day of her birth felt that she had been endowed with an unusual, inner strength, foretelling some special destiny. In later years she was to feel that those months her parents spent visiting the holy places of Palestine had left their mark upon her while she was still in the womb, imbuing her with a heightened spiritual awareness and a profound natural reverence for eternal mystery and beauty.

Little beauty was to be found in Liverpool. The poverty of the people was evident, but in the seven months Henry Grattan spent there they responded to him with warmth and rebuilt his confidence. Soon he was travelling again, preaching all over England, Ireland and Scotland, his family following him, taking cheap lodgings wherever he went. In Bury, Lancashire, in April 1863 Fanny noted in the cover of her husband's large black Bible:

We think it undesirable to determine beforehand on the length of our stay in any place; this should be regulated by results. A definite period in view, especially if it be a short one tends to hinder earnest, whole-hearted labours and preclude large expectations.

It may also tend to longer tarriance in a place than is wise (as at Boston). One step at a time!

Not seeing the results they had once seen, they never stayed long in one place. It was not like the old days. Any preacher of worth was invited by the Earl of Shaftesbury to preach on a Sunday evening to the thousands who crammed into the Exeter Hall in London. But the man once heralded as Spurgeon's rival received no invitation.

Dublin alone had not forgotten him. Such was his reputation for abstinence that "Mr Guinness is not for Guinness" became a popular saying around the town in the 1860s. By a cruel irony, a distinguished Irish minister was soon to make a bitter attack upon him in the newspapers: he was accused of bribing his converts with money from the Guinness brewery. His preaching tour came to a standstill in Edinburgh in the bleak November of 1863. Henry was to look back at those months as the worst in his life. All preaching engagements were cancelled on the spot. The shock made him ill again. He had no home, no money and no means of earning an income. Though pregnant once more Fanny did her best to support and comfort him. She went into labour prematurely and their baby, a little girl, was stillborn. Before their savings ran out altogether they left Edinburgh and went to Dundee where the lodgings were cheaper. There they stayed cold and alone for some weeks, "strangers amongst strangers and with only seventeen shillings in hand". They were almost at the end of their tether when, just in time for Christmas, they were offered the use of Mount Catherine, a beautiful country house in glorious surroundings three miles from Limerick.

Fanny fell in love with Mount Catherine at once and revelled in a degree of normal family life at last. They had a happy family Christmas and the children were deluged with presents from kind friends. Fanny wrote:

Harry went to a Christmas Tree and saw a little boy teasing a little girl. He marched up and collared him, saying, "I'll tell you what, sir, if you tease that lady fair, I'll put you in prison or shoot you dead!" Where he had heard such an expression I have no idea, but it sounded absurdly gallant from a little three-year old.

In Harry's case the child was father to the man. He was a knight errant by instinct. Each of Henry and Fanny's children reflected something of the circumstances of their birth and early childhood. Harry was the son of their Canadian adventure and would grow up the most extrovert of their children, and an inveterate globe-trotter.

Settled in Mount Catherine, Fanny's trials were by no means over. Henry, against her better judgment, was risking life and limb preaching to large crowds of Catholics in Limerick. It was a

matter of time before the tolerance of the authorities was pushed
to its limit. One day she was called out of the women's meeting she
was leading to find Henry had returned home badly cut and bruised.
Apparently a large crowd had gathered to hear him and were listening peaceably when one or two trouble-makers began to hustle and
stone him. He tried to make his escape but the crowd followed the
ringleaders, hurling stones and abuse. He would have got away, but
two burly men, one a butcher, set upon him and beat him over the
head. The blows knocked him over and mercifully he fell into a cart,
otherwise he could have been trampled to death. At that moment an
army officer happened to ride by, his uniform bedecked with medals
for bravery won during the Crimean War. He leapt down, collared
the butcher and harangued the crowd for their cowardice in setting
upon one defenceless man. It gave Henry time to make his escape.
The Times reported the incident on May 6th, 1864, revealing that
the officer who had saved Mr Guinness from the vengeance of the
populace was a Captain Jones of the depot battalion.

Henry and Fanny were both extremely shaken. Irish Protestants
they may have been, but they were not blinded by bigotry. They
had no quarrel with individual Catholics, but rather with the Roman
institution and its priests, which kept the people in poverty and
ignorance. The experience confirmed what Henry had been thinking
for some time, that as far as his life's work was concerned he was
travelling down the wrong track. Soon he would be thirty. For
several years now every door had slammed shut in his face. All
over the country the great religious revival appeared to be past its
height, its ardour dampened by the work of Charles Darwin. *On the
Origin of Species*, published in 1859, began to shake the moral and
religious foundations of society. Henry Grattan became increasingly
concerned for the many people whose faith was so vulnerable it could
never resist such an onslaught. What was needed was an army of
young men sufficiently versed in the evidence for Christianity to be
able to hold off the enemy invasion. Perhaps instead of preaching it
was time to train others. Fanny's heart sank for she knew what that
meant. There would be no point in starting some kind of training
class for would-be preachers and missionaries at Mount Catherine,
tucked away in the Irish countryside miles from civilisation. Once
Henry made up his mind there would be only one thing to do, give
up Mount Catherine and head for the city of his birth, Dublin.

3

The Dublin to which Henry returned in 1865 had changed very
little in the seven years since he caused such a stir there. It was

still a divided city: the wealthy, largely Protestant, living in their elegant mansions; the poor, largely Catholic, living in squalor. Tom Barnardo, a young man of Italian extraction, who became Henry Grattan's first pupil, said that:

> whiskey drinking, added to the vicious tendencies of the people who dwell in these wretched hovels, have demoralised them to the lowest degree. The Corporation of Dublin have reason to be utterly ashamed that such fever dens and loathesome sources of moral contagion are allowed to remain in a city which boasts of so many noble streets and imposing public buildings.[2]

The first Arthur Guinness' dream of a moral victory for stout over whiskey had evidently not yet been fulfilled. None the less in seven years the Guinness brewery had continued to expand. John Purser junior, son of the wily old John Purser and the second Arthur's junior partner, died in 1858 and was succeeded by his son, John Tertius Purser, a particularly gifted chief brewer who left Benjamin Lee free to develop his own style of leadership in business and public life, while maintaining a tight, informed and caring control at St James' Gate. Benjamin's every initiative proved fortuitous. With a stroke of genius he transformed Guinness from one of Ireland's ordinary industries into the natural heritage of the Irish people. And all it took was one simple, inspired gesture. In 1014 at the Battle of Clontarf, the site of Benjamin's St Anne's Estate, Brian Boru the legendary Irish king and national hero had conquered the pillaging Norsemen. Benjamin decided to adopt Boru's harp as the Guinness emblem. It was a timely move. Nationalistic pride was growing. So was the demand for Home Rule. Fenianism was on the horizon.

As business blossomed, so did Benjamin Lee's social standing. He bought a magnificent country estate, Ashford in County Galway. In 1863 his eldest child Anne Lee brought the first title into the family by marrying the treasurer of St Patrick's Cathedral, William Conyngham, fourth Baron Plunkett. Like many of her female Guinness descendants she chose a clergyman, and this one would become the Archbishop of Dublin.

In 1865 Benjamin Lee's wife Bessie died. On her deathbed she was as concerned as ever about her three boys, now young men, and the negative effects that a worldly, wealthy existence might have on their souls. She wrote to her eldest son Arthur Edward, "All tho' the Lord has given me peace and joy in believing . . . if I were well assured that my darling children were safe in Jesus. Oh! How happy I should be – well, I think they are the Lord's, but I want to SEE it."[3] Evidently there was some doubt. As far as their mother was concerned their behaviour did not match up to her nonconformist conceptions of the godly life, as another letter to Arthur Edward suggests: "I hope you do not smoke and that if Lee must smoke sometimes, which I wish he would not, it is not vile tobacco or cigars."[4] Poor Bessie never had the joy of seeing her sons safely married to women of faultless pedigree, nor of witnessing their exemplary, charitable destinies. Future generations might have been a source of despair to her, but her own sons did not fail their mother's expectations.

The widower Benjamin Lee did not marry again. He embraced the political life instead and was elected Conservative-Unionist MP for Dublin. The political restraint advocated by his father was now irrelevant. Fourteen years earlier it may have been counter-productive from a business point of view to show allegiance to one particular party. The brewery was now so well established that he no longer feared antagonising his political enemies. His father had been Liberal in his politics, whereas he, as the most prominent and successful figure in Irish business life, was quite naturally Conservative and Unionist; Conservative because the Tories were the official "liquor party", and Unionist because the Protestant establishment was genuinely afraid of the Fenians and their demand for a republic. It would have been strange for him to have been anything else.

When Henry Grattan arrived in Dublin, this time with no fanfare or publicity, the repairs to a dilapidated St Patrick's Cathedral which Benjamin Lee had financed to the tune of £150,000 had just been completed. One of Ireland's great national monuments, once the home of Dean Swift, had been saved from disintegration and restored to the nation. The city was full of gratitude. Lord Wodehouse, the Lord Lieutenant of Ireland, said that "work which was too great for the Knights of St Patrick, or for the Ecclesiastical Commissioners, or the Bench of Bishops, which the Irish Parliament refused to undertake and which the British Parliament never entertained the thought of executing has been accomplished within four years by a single merchant"[5] It was this particular act of public service which earned Benjamin Lee a baronetcy two years later. He had preserved the national heritage and at the same time demonstrated his allegiance to a national Church which Whig Prime Minister Gladstone was still trying to disestablish. One window of the cathedral bore witness to the benefactor and was inscribed with a text which would amuse successive generations of tourists: "I was thirsty and ye gave me drink."

Henry and Fanny took 31 Upper Baggot Street, a large Georgian house in a run-down part of the town, scraping every penny to pay the rent. Within weeks of moving to Dublin Lucy Evangeline was born. "We called her Lucy – from lux, lumiere, light," Henry wrote, but several times the light was almost extinguished for she was a frail, delicate baby. She never seemed to bloom with health and it caused Fanny a great deal of anxiety. Harry was a strong, sturdy little boy, full of life and mischief. Minnie was rather prim and ladylike. At three she had her first portrait taken, wearing a voluminous pink dress with five deep tucks in the waistline and tiny puff sleeves trimmed with broad blue ribbons. Her hair, parted demurely in the middle, was curled around her head, making the two solemn eyes, which stared into the camera with wonder, seem enormous. Compared to the other two children Henry saw his Lucy "not as a hardy, vigorous plant, but frail like a clinging woodbine that hangs its blossom on a supporting bough". She drew from him his most tender, protective instincts. "When a child there was no place she loved better than her father's arms," he wrote, "and to him the delicacy of her frame and sensitiveness of her mind were no mystery, for trials which had preceded her birth seemed their explanation". His unspoken fear that at any moment he might lose her would be borne out years later.

While Benjamin Lee was now high church, an accepted member of the Protestant establishment, Henry accepted the position of elder at Merrion Hall, the newly built, socially unfashionable Brethren chapel. There was some contact between the two cousins but their paths had so diverged that they could live an almost unrelated existence within the same town. It was hard to believe that their fathers were brothers and close. They did share a love of their homeland and a hatred for Fenianism. A group of republicans, exiled to the United States, were constantly stirring up sedition and rebellion in Ireland. It was a movement "despicable in its objects, its resources and its courage",[6] said Benjamin Lee. Henry Grattan agreed. There was also a moderate nationalistic movement committed to working within the confines of law and order, but neither of the cousins appeared to take it seriously. The rumbles of revolution sounded ominously close. A sort of paranoia overtook the Protestant establishment. Nationalism of any kind threatened peace and stability.

But life continued and Henry Grattan pursued the purpose which had brought him to Dublin. It was at the Merrion Hall that he met Tom Barnardo, a Sunday school teacher, and was instantly drawn to the small, bespectacled, almost monkey-like character, who would later become famous for his work among homeless children. His unprepossessing appearance hid an irrepressible sense of fun. Barnardo for his part felt an instant admiration for this tall, striking man with his great charm and strong personal magnetism. The house on Upper Baggot Street became his second home.

Before long a group of eight or nine students gathered there four evenings a week after work to study Paley's *Evidences of Christianity*, a book designed to enable its readers to hold their own against Darwin and his supporters. There were Charles and Edward Fishe, the dashing sons of a retired colonel of the East India Company's Horse Artillery, and John McCarthy, a mature, thoughtful man, married with three children. Lively little Barnardo was the children's favourite. True to his Italian ancestry he was a great talker, waving his arms around as he held forth on whatever subject was filling him with righteous indignation at that particular moment, usually something to do with the injustices suffered by the poor. He had a special relationship with three-year-old Minnie, who was fascinated by him. Even Henry and Fanny, who had already become deeply concerned about the poverty and deprivation all around them, could not help but be moved by the passion with which he gave vent to his emotions.

On Monday, February 19th, 1866 the group met in a fever of anticipation. Henry Grattan had gone down to the Kingston ferry to meet a missionary-explorer whose fame had spread throughout the British Isles. It was during a visit to Liverpool that Henry Grattan was introduced to Hudson Taylor in the home of a mutual friend. The two men were drawn to each other at once.

Taylor had sailed to China in 1853, spent over ten years there and since coming home was writing and touring the country speaking of all he had seen. In the 1860s, due to voyages of exploration, geographical horizons were rapidly expanding. The far corners of the world, hitherto unknown, were gradually becoming accessible. The world map altered almost daily. It was a source of great fascination to the general public. All travel was regarded as an adventure, but there was no doubt that China had its own special mystique. There was a fairy-tale quality about its ancient dynasties, with their strange traditions and exotic culture. At the same time the religious revival had stirred up interest in missionary work. Both as an explorer and as a missionary Hudson Taylor attracted attention and established a reputation. He was also radical in his opposition to the patronising, colonialist tendencies of the British in the Far East. He demanded of his missionaries a willingness to sacrifice all comforts and identify completely with the people, in customs, lifestyle and dress. Pure Christianity implied a rejection of the twin scourges of imperialism and denominationalism with their inherent self-interest.

Henry Grattan invited him to Dublin to speak to the group of young men who met at his house, then to go on to address gatherings in Limerick, Cork and Belfast. He said he would accompany him to Cork and Limerick and take part in the meetings, "being better known in Ireland at present than you are".[7] This was not intended to be a put-down. It was a simple statement of fact. Taylor agreed and Henry promised to meet him at the ferry "at half-past six Irish time, seven o'clock, English, and to bring you on to our house".

In Baggot Street the tension rose. Minnie could hardly wait to see Dr Taylor. If Tom Barnardo said he was special, then he must be. Inside the large drawing-room Barnardo, McCarthy, the Fishe brothers and the others waited in silence; sitting stiffly in tight-fitting, sombre frock-coats, their collars barely visible above their coats, apart from the one or two rather old-fashioned members of the group who still preferred the high-winged, turned-down variety. The door opened, they looked up and Grattan Guinness' magnificent figure filled the doorway, totally shielding Hudson Taylor from view.

"Where is the great man?" Barnardo whispered to McCarthy, with a twinge of disappointment.

"I suppose he hasn't come," McCarthy whispered back.

Henry Grattan stood to one side and there appeared a slight, slim man, fair haired, in a dress coat and with an abundant white tie knotted at the neck. They ogled him for some time, more than a little bemused. They had never seen such dress before, possibly because Dublin was several years behind the London fashions, possibly because Taylor was years out of date. Either way the young men sat in an uncomfortable silence for what seemed an interminable few seconds, until Barnardo broke the ice. As Hudson Taylor came into the room he took full stock of his height, or the lack of it, and said loudly, "Well there's hope for me!"

By the end of the evening Barnardo was offering himself as a missionary for China. Hudson Taylor was unsure. Deeply perceptive, he liked Barnardo enormously and respected his drive and ebullience, but he wondered whether he was not too impetuous. He suggested that Barnardo should go to one of the London hospitals for a while to improve his medical knowledge. A party was to sail to China later in the year. If by then Barnardo still felt he wanted to go, then Taylor would seriously consider him as a possibility.

McCarthy volunteered as well, his one stipulation that as his wife was expecting her fourth baby the confinement should be over before they sailed. Hudson Taylor had no doubts about him, or about Charles Fishe who, still very young, promised to go as soon as he had his father's permission. Taylor's greatest surprise was yet to come.

While he travelled to Cork with Henry Grattan, the latter told him that he and Fanny were seriously considering sailing with him on the *Lammermuir*. Taylor was astonished, but gave the idea serious consideration when he went on alone to Belfast. By the time he returned to Baggot Street he had reached a decision and tried to tell them as gently as possible that in fact, since they were past thirty, they were too old. At their age they would find language study too difficult.

While Henry and Fanny struggled to accept this, Taylor looked round and noticed the little girl who stood at his side gazing up at him, her large almond-shaped eyes fastened on his and a most serious expression on her face. He bent down, picked Minnie up and sat her on his knee. He asked her how old she was and when she said, "three", told her he had a little boy her age called Howard. In fact he had a Herbert who was Harry's age, a baby Lucy's age and a big girl called Gracie too. Minnie forgot her shyness and bombarded him with questions.

Aware of Henry and Fanny's acute disappointment, Taylor begged them to stay in England and "train me the men and women". It was wise, if vague advice, but none of them could guess how fruitful it would eventually prove. A bond was sealed between them that day and the little girl who sat on Taylor's knee would one day be its visible sign. Forty years would turn the child into Hudson Taylor's biographer and greatest comfort.

4

"Lord and Lady Radstock request the pleasure of Mr and Mrs Henry Grattan Guinness at a reception on Thursday, March 8th at 30, Bryanston Square, London." When the invitation arrived, it filled Fanny with dread. Unlike her brewing cousins she was not used to great social occasions. What should she wear? She had not been able to afford a new dress for years. Yet she could not decline. Lord Radstock was renowned for his generosity to missionary societies. He arranged these glittering events whenever a good cause caught his imagination, inviting the élite of upper-class London society so that he could relieve them of their excess income. This particular reception was to be held in Mr Hudson Taylor's honour and her husband had been invited to share the limelight.

The Guinnesses made the long journey from Dublin to London. They were announced at Lord Radstock's and Fanny appeared in a new dress she could ill afford, bought for the occasion. Henry Grattan was in good form. His magnetic presence, brilliant conversation and what Hudson referred to as his "marvellous power", made him an enormous success. As Fanny looked round the room she was shocked by the *décolletages* of the ladies, but even more horrified that her own covered neck and shoulders made her appear old-fashioned and provincial. The evening was a strain and she returned to Dublin with a sigh of relief. To Hudson Taylor she wrote that she would do what she could for China, raising money from her own home. Taylor was horrified and wrote back to say so. To have the Guinnesses on one's side was a great advantage, but they could be a little overpowering. There was a danger that the horse would run away with the rider. It was his policy never to make demands for money. If God willed the project, the money for it would come in. Fanny took the point graciously and was to remember the lesson he taught her many times over the next years.

All their talk of China made Henry restless. A year in Dublin was enough. It was time to be on their travels. This time Fanny put her foot down. She wanted to buy her own home. Her mother was frail, so Bath seemed the obvious place. It was near enough to Cheltenham for Henry to take care of his mother too. In May they moved into their own home for the first time in seven years of marriage.

The whole family would remember that glorious summer of 1866. The Taylors were offered a lovely country house called Saint Hill, belonging to the benevolent Berger family, and they invited the Guinnesses to share it with them. The grounds were spacious and beautiful. The sun shone almost all the time. Romping together in the garden day after day the seven children got to know each other well. One morning, ignoring the nanny's instructions, Minnie rushed out on to the porch and down the stone steps, tripping and cutting her arm quite badly on the way. As it was bandaged up she was mortified to see the two fair-haired little boys, Herbert and Howard, so handsome in their long pinafores, watching her in shocked silence. She knew she had been naughty. Their look said it all.

Within weeks of the end of the summer holiday, the *Lammermuir* sailed for China with Hudson and Maria Taylor, their children, and sixteen others. The McCarthys decided to wait until October when their new baby would be a little older. Tom Barnardo also felt he needed more preparation time in London. Henry and Fanny felt desolate. To fill the emptiness Henry set off on a preaching tour of Yorkshire.

He was walking one evening through the streets of Keighley when he noticed a poster on the wall of a house. Hands behind his back and his high-crowned hat pushed to the back of his head, he examined it with rising indignation. It announced a series of lectures to be given by Mrs Harriet Law, a well-known exponent of Darwinism, who would prove beyond any shadow of doubt that the Bible and its claims were entirely false. Up to that moment Henry Grattan had presumed that the new scepticism was limited to the intelligentsia. If they chose their own spiritual disintegration so be it, but they had no business to dally with the faith of those whose limited education left them with few powers of reasoning.

When Mrs Law delivered her first lecture Grattan Guinness was there to defend the defenceless. Keighley had never known such entertainment. For several days the dreary little town throbbed with excitement as the Titans fought their oratorical battle. The challenge restored Henry's verbal genius. The people loved him and Mrs Law acknowledged defeat, albeit temporarily. Within a few miles, alone in his draughty parsonage since the death of his three famous daughters, lived the elderly, almost blind Rector of Haworth, Patrick Brontë. Henry Grattan's victory must have brought some cheer to his twilight existence.

In his journal Henry noted that in 1866 he preached a total of 230 times, and was ill only twice. It was a relief to have a permanent base. Fanny was preaching regularly too, to both sexes, still with misgivings, arguing out the pros and cons in her diary. The children were her greatest supporters. Returning from one meeting of which he was most appreciative, Harry said to the maid, "Ah, Susan, if you were to go with Mamma like me, then you'd know what PREACHING means." He then informed Fanny that he would rather like to have a go himself, only he would not let Papa hear, nor the PUBLIC, just Mamma and Minnie.

In September their fourth child, Henrietta, was born, but despite their new-found security and the special care Henry and Fanny gave their precious baby, she died five months later. Harry, Minnie and Lucy's clothes were edged with black crêpe, which was unlike Fanny, for her attitudes to raising children were usually quite advanced. The truth was she did not cope well with this bereavement. The morbid side of her Brethren upbringing rose to the surface. She was consumed with guilt, blaming herself for Henrietta's death. Though she never said it explicitly she felt God was punishing her for her materialism. The children deprived of a cosseted infancy, having their ailments in cheap boarding-houses and other people's homes, were well and strong while the only one born in their own home had died. This could only mean one thing. It was time to give up their home and move again. What did it matter if China was denied them? There was always the Continent, almost as spiritually blind as the great Eastern empire itself.

Shortly before they left for Europe Henry's mother, Jane Lucretia, died. A few weeks later on May 19th, 1868 Sir Benjamin Lee Guinness died too. He was seventy and had enjoyed complete control of the brewery only for the last ten years of his life. But those ten years were sufficient to build Guinness into the leading porter brewery in the industry, establishing its owner as the most prominent figure in Irish business life. His estate was valued at £1,100,000, making his will the largest proved in Ireland up to that date. It made provision for Anne, his married daughter, and for his second son, Lee, who had opted for a career in the Royal Horse Guards. The bulk of the estate went to twenty-seven-year-old Arthur Edward, his eldest son, and twenty-year-old Edward Cecil, the youngest. As far as the future of the brewery was concerned Benjamin Lee had thought of everything. It was left equally to his two sons, with the proviso that if one of the partners opted out he would receive not the value of his share, but a mere £30,000. This was the equivalent of striking him off without an inheritance. Recognising that great wealth might be a problem for future generations, Benjamin Lee had managed to do what many a rich man has longed to do and failed. He had found a way of controlling his fortune beyond the grave, preserving it from dispersion and dissipation, ensuring it remained in the business. The capital must be left intact so that there would never be a question of liquidation; the surviving partner would have the capital he needed to continue expanding.

In an uncanny way it was almost as if he had foreseen the future. There was no doubt he had a shrewd idea which of his sons most reflected his own aspirations. Arthur, an old Etonian, inherited the baronetcy, his father's parliamentary seat, St Anne's and the gracious Ashford Estate. Edward, who had been apprenticed to the business at fifteen, and educated himself at Trinity in his spare time, inherited 80 St Stephen's Green, the real status symbol of his father's prosperity and authority. It was Edward who seemed to demonstrate that flair, that intuitive business sense, which made him the obvious recipient of that most sacred of trusts, the silver salver.

Sir Benjamin Lee was buried in the family vault at Mount Jerome Cemetery. His funeral was described in *The Times* as "One of the most impressive demonstrations of public feeling ever seen in this city."[8] The family had intended a private funeral, but in the event, such was the public grief that this proved impossible. Five hundred Guinness workers, dressed in black, marched in front of the cortège. The hearse and coaches of the bereaved were followed by 239 private carriages including those of the Lord Lieutenant, the mayor, representatives of the gentry and every aspect of the professional and civic life of Dublin. Along the route shops were closed and the streets lined with silent mourners. It was a fitting tribute to a man renowned for his courtesy and kindness.

Neither wealth nor power ever fossilised Benjamin Lee's emotions. Like his father he remained unassuming and approachable, sensitive to the heavy demands made on his sympathy and his purse by the ever-increasing band of aunts, uncles, cousins and other relatives who felt they had some claim on his generosity. His father had begged him to take care of them and, encouraged by Bessie, he took his responsibility seriously. He was devoted to his wife. If her constant catalogue of ailments tried his patience he never said so. He loved his children. Though proud and dignified he was never aloof, and they returned his affection. He cared for his workforce and they in turn so respected him that when the Fenian uprising eventually came they disclaimed all association with it, and sent a deputation to their employer to assure him of their devotion and loyalty. They would defend the brewery if necessary.

The only discordant voice at his departure belonged to a certain Temperance Society. It produced a pamphlet entitled, *What it is to Die a Brewer: the burial of Sir Benjamin Lee Guinness*, which was circulated all round the city. The writer, J. A. Mowatt, expressed his disbelief that the Bishop of Cork, a known teetotaller, should feel able to deliver such a grand funeral oration. "Has the wealth of the brewery of St James' Gate blinded his eyes?" In a barbed attack Mr Mowatt concluded that the brewer deserved no eulogy. "Prior to the restoration of St Patrick's he was little known, except through his XX labels, which are the only famous literary works which he has left behind him; and they are read the world over with thick tongues, bloated countenances, bloodshot eyes and staggering gait."[9]

No record exists whether Sir Benjamin's temperance-preaching cousin Henry Grattan attended his funeral. He wrote to Sir Arthur Edward and polite contact was maintained at a distance: whatever Henry's financial constraints he did not want it to appear that he felt he had any claim on their resources. All drink was devilish as far as he was concerned and that included stout. He wanted nothing to do with it. When he gave away his legacy he intended the break with the brewery to be final. In many ways his departure to Europe was the end of an era. With the death of Sir Benjamin came the severance of his last real connections with Dublin, though not with the brewing family. As for the brewing side, new horizons were opening before them too, drawing them away from their Irish roots to the English metropolis and a dazzling world of peers, politics and royalty itself.

5

Henry and Fanny chose to settle in Paris, where Napoleon III and his beautiful Empress Eugenie held court in the glittering splendour of the Palace of Versailles. It was not the glamour of the city which attracted them. Like Ireland, France was a stronghold of Romanism. The home of Voltaire, it was also a centre for scepticism, and since his escapade in Keighley Henry felt equal to a challenge. There had been no religious revival in France. Even the Protestantism there was turgid and dreary with no Whitefield or Wesley to revitalise it. This was pioneer work. He could barely speak any French, but that was no deterrent to Henry Grattan Guinness. In a few months he addressed more than seven hundred meetings. Small wonder he was soon exhausted. His eyes became inflamed and Fanny ordered him to Switzerland for a rest. He travelled home through Spain and it was there that he had a bizarre experience which profoundly affected the future course of his life.

Some workmen in Madrid were constructing a new road near the city. As they cut through the top of a hill they noticed that between the usual layers of red gravel was a large stratum of soft black dust. When they examined the layer more closely they found bits of bone and hair and realised that they had discovered human remains. This was the site of the Quemadero, the burning place of the Spanish Inquisition. Thousands of Protestant "heretics" had been tortured and killed on this spot.

News of the finding spread quickly round the town and Henry, who happened to be in Madrid, went to have a look. The workmen went on digging, exposing yet more gruesome evidence of the most barbaric cruelty, rusty chains and nails, instruments of torture, the remains of two hands clasped in prayer and transfixed by a huge iron nail, the ribs of a victim with a spear protruding from them. Any attempt to separate the relics from the surrounding substances failed. They simply crumbled to dust.

As Henry stood in the ashes of so many martyrs, the tears welled up in his eyes. None of his study of church history had caused him the sense of grief and revulsion which he felt now as he touched and examined the ghastly evidence of religious cruelty. He collected a heap of ashes, folded them tenderly in a Spanish newspaper and took them home to his hotel.

There he poured his anger and outrage into a poem. He had written poems before, but none like this, lambasting the Church of Rome for her heartless cruelty:

TELL ME, THOU MURDERESS BLACK, WHAT MEAN THESE BONES?
    These bones before me, upon that hill,
    Who, what were these thus slaughtered by thy will?
    What did these helpless women? these poor men?
    Why didst thou shut them up in thy dark den?
    Why didst thou rack their limbs and starve their frames,
    And cast them bound into devouring flames?

At home he read the poem to Fanny and the children. Though she could not understand it, listening to her father's sonorous voice Minnie caught something of the emotion he felt and never forgot it. Nor did she forget the pile of human ashes lying on his desk. In the years to come they were to be a source of inspiration to her father, a symbol of his life's work and calling.

It was spring when Henry got back from Spain. Paris was breathtaking, the tree-lined avenues heavy with almond blossom, and the spring of 1869 was a particularly happy one, with little presage of the crisis to come. He found the children speaking French like the natives and Fanny, pregnant again, addressing various meetings in French with a fair degree of fluency.

Gershom Whitfield was born on April 25th. He was called Gershom like the son of Moses, "a stranger in a strange land", and Whitfield after the great preacher. But Paris hardly seemed a strange land any more. The Château de Foicy where the family were living had become home. Years later, thinking back to those days, Minnie wrote, "Love reigned in our home. Life seemed free and generous. All the changes didn't matter, there was home and happiness everywhere as long as we were together."

That sense of security was largely due to Fanny's influence. She was an extraordinary woman. Neither beautiful nor particularly artistic, she none the less had some indefinable charm which made people sit up and take notice of her. She was immensely capable, but not in an overbearing way. People relaxed in her presence. She radiated calm, which was essential for the wife of a man with so tempestuous a nature as Henry Grattan. One day a young woman called on her and went to wait in the nursery because its west-facing window commanded a glorious view of the Parisian sunset. Gershom began to scream and neither the nanny nor the young woman could do anything to placate him. They were almost beside themselves when Fanny swept graciously into the room, picked up the screaming baby, carried him to the window and said, "Look!"

There was instant silence [the woman wrote]. The child's mind was taken off himself entirely. It was not a vacant stare but a look of beautiful intelligence which lit up his eyes as he gazed at the glowing sky . . . as she stood there for quite three minutes she watched it intently, both of them bathed in the sunset glory. Then, without a word, she handed the quieted child back to the nurse and turned to me to speak of other things, not at all aware that she had given me one of the finest object-lessons of my life.[10]

Fanny could not forget the lesson she felt she had learned from Henrietta's death in Bath. Never again would any home be completely hers. It was to be shared with whoever needed her motherly care. When his wife died in China Hudson Taylor sent his children with Miss Blatchley, their nanny, to Paris to stay with the Guinnesses for a prolonged holiday on their way back to England. Only Fanny could provide the children with the love and security he knew they needed. Three extra children were no problem to her. She had them all fitted with French suits.

By the time Phoebe was born, only a year after her brother Gershom, the storm clouds were brewing over France. The halcyon interlude in Paris was almost over. Every day the streets were filled with ugly demonstrations, angry workmen in their caps and overalls screaming, "à Berlin, à Berlin!" They demanded war with Prussia, a war which the Empress Eugenie was to call "ma guerre", but it was to be her downfall. Some days because of the crowds the narrow cobbled streets were almost impassable and it became increasingly difficult to go anywhere. Harry, Minnie and Lucy were returning from their daily walk with their nurse when their way home was blocked by a noisy procession. The children were terrified by the din. The nurse, who held fifteen-month-old baby Gershom in her arms, tried to squeeze through the throng, when both she and the baby were thrown to the ground in the path of an oncoming carriage. None of the children was very sure of what happened next, but somehow both were dragged to safety just in time.

The children ran home to Fanny, who decided there and then that the situation was deteriorating so rapidly that it was time to return to England. With a heavy heart Henry handed over responsibility for the chapel he had founded in the rue Royale, between the Madeleine and the Place de la Concorde, to a pastor called Armand Delille. Throughout the war and the terrible months of the siege of Paris and of the Commune which followed, the chapel doors would stay open, making it a refuge for thousands of suffering civilians and soldiers.

By then the Guinnesses were back in the safety of Bath and following the devastating progress of the war from the daily accounts in the newspapers. They could hardly believe the photographs they saw: carefree, beautiful Paris, which they had come to love so much, suddenly surrounded by advancing Prussian armies, ensnared within a gigantic ring of artillery fire from which there was no escape, and Napoleon III fleeing for his life. The whole series of events began to appear apocalyptic, compounded by the fact that the very day before France had declared war on Prussia the Pope had issued the decree of his infallibility. As far as Henry Grattan was concerned this was not just heresy, it was tantamount to blasphemy. The pile of ashes on his desk begged for vindication. But justice was swift. The French troops in Rome, sorely needed at home, were evacuated, leaving the Vatican at the very moment of its highest self-exaltation, at the mercy of King Victor Emmanuel, whose aim was to rule a united Italy.

By the end of 1870, within a few short months, the temporal power of the Pope had been destroyed for ever, Rome was incorporated into a united Italian kingdom. France was lying in ruins and the world had seen the rise of Bismarck's powerful united Germany. A new era was dawning.

Henry Grattan was overwhelmed by the swiftness of events. His fascination for history and biblical prophecy returned with fresh vigour. So much of what had happened seemed part of an overall plan, but what was his role in it all?

The answer came when Fanny broke her leg. The doctor set it wrongly and it would not heal. Pregnant again, she was confined to a couch, unable to care for her five children. As far as Henry was concerned travelling was out of the question, but being at home proved unexpectedly opportune: it provided him with the time he had never had to think and write.

It was also a long-denied chance to get to know his children. Every night Harry, Minnie and Lucy climbed into his arms as he sat in the huge armchair in his study and in the firelight glow he read them whatever he had written, excerpts from the book which was to become *The Approaching End of the Age*. He explained to Harry and Minnie that they must not be afraid or surprised about what was happening in Europe. It all pointed to one thing, that Jesus Christ would soon return, "perhaps not in my lifetime, but he may come in yours," he said to Minnie. The idea kindled her vivid imagination, and remained a driving force in her life.

Subtly the dawn of a new age in Europe had heralded a new beginning in the life of Henry Grattan Guinness. The preacher was becoming a teacher, and as such he would influence the nation in a way he had not done before.

6

1872–1880

To the Great Metropolis

1

It was during a trip to Armagh in 1872 that the future course of Henry's life became clear. As he walked around in circles beneath the beautiful old trees in the city centre, turning the last years over and over in his mind, oblivious of the passers-by who stopped to stare at him, the vision came almost as a revelation. After years of uncertainty, of groping in the darkness and banging at doors which refused to open, the pathway suddenly materialised out of the mist. "The cloud moves," he wrote in his diary, with undisguised relief and exultation, "may I have grace to follow!"

Fanny was not as enthusiastic, for Henry had in mind a training institute for ministers and missionaries. To attend a theological college was a privilege normally reserved for the wealthy who could afford the fees. Hudson Taylor's appeal for workers had made it clear that the revival of the early sixties had produced many young men and women eager to do further theological training, but without the means to do so. Henry's vision was for a college which would require no fees. It would run by faith. God would provide the house, the staff, the students and the food to feed them.

Fanny knew only too well after twelve years of marriage that her husband was a visionary. He could inspire and teach, he could move men, but he had no idea of what it would take to make his vision possible. As far as she was concerned he was simply "brooding on great schemes" again, as hopelessly impractical as ever. Well may Hudson Taylor have urged them to train him the men. He was in China! It was abundantly apparent that the practical details of such a venture would be left to her and they were too enormous to contemplate. She had six children to care for, Agnes having been born in 1871. Besides Henry was an itinerant evangelist. He was called to preach, not teach.

Such were his powers of persuasion that, despite her misgivings, one cold December afternoon Fanny found herself with him, alighting from a horse-drawn tram in the raucous din of the Mile End Road in the East End of London. She was both fascinated and repelled by the sights which confronted her. The road itself was a broad thoroughfare, thronged with people heading home from work, pushing and shoving their way in and out of the cabs and around the horse dung, grimy and weary with their toil, or cocky like the factory girls in their jaunty feathered hats, dallying already outside the gin palaces. Every tenth building was a public house, alluring with its garish lights and promise of warmth. Underneath the flickering, hissing blue naphtha flares barrow-boys and pedlars sold their wares, yelling in competition for the attention of the passing crowds. The noise was deafening. Mingled with the clatter of the cabs on the cobbled street, the bell of the tram, the neighing of the horses, the shouting and raucous laughter of the costermongers, was the faint sound of a barrel organ.

The squalor and deprivation described for posterity by Charles Dickens was everywhere. Standing in their doorways women drew their threadbare shawls tightly around their shoulders. Filthy children in tatters, looking half-starved, played in the gutters, stopping their games to beg as Fanny walked by, a tiny frail-looking woman hanging on to the arm of her tall, imposing husband. Occasionally the mouthwatering smells of cooking wafted past her, but were soon drowned by the all-pervading odour of burning hops emanating from the vast grey edifice of Charrington's Brewery, casting its shadow the entire length of the road.

They turned at last into a narrow, ugly little street with brick houses on either side, protected by high spiked iron palings. This was Hayfield Passage, the approach to quaint old Stepney Green, popularised by the pen of Walter Besant. But those were in the days before the East End sprawl swallowed up the fields and meadows. With disappointment Fanny realised that Stepney Green was not nearly as attractive as Besant had described it. There were no trees or shrubs, simply a square of dilapidated three-storey mansions of which number 29 was the shabbiest. One quick examination by twilight convinced Henry that this was exactly what he was looking for.

The feelings Fanny expressed in her diary when she got home were rather different. With a sinking heart she knew that Henry was right, but the idea frightened her. It was a test of her faith and courage such as she had never before experienced. "I feel just like a would-be swimmer longing to strike out and feel the water up-bearing him, yet fearing to trust himself to do it," she wrote. Then she added, "But I shall swim yet," determination enabling her to take the plunge at last.

The family moved to London at the end of 1872. It took Fanny time to acclimatise to her new situation, not helped by the fact that many of her friends and acquaintances criticised her for taking her children to such an unsavoury area. What about their education, they demanded. There was no such thing as a local school. Fanny weighed it up carefully and knew what she was doing. "We have been amused at times," she wrote later, "at the hesitation with which some of our friends have treated an invitation to Bow. 'Is it not a – a VERY disagreeable neighbourhood?' 'Do you find it TOLERABLY healthy?' 'How do your dear children stand the close atmosphere?' etc, etc." Fanny's answer to such questions was:

True, its noise is trying, its dirt and dust disagreeable, and its atmosphere anything but invigorating. We sometimes gasp for a fresh breeze, and sigh for other sights than a never-ending succession of omnibuses and market-carts, and for other sounds than the shriek of the railway-whistle and the tinkle of the tram-bell. But when we recall the lot of our missionary friends in the narrow lanes and streets of undrained Chinese cities, unable to secure in their comfortless dwellings even privacy from rude and curious crowds, or freedom from fever-breeding odours . . . we feel that we have good reason to be content with such things as we have.

One reason for choosing the East End of London was that Henry felt no young man or woman could honestly say they could cope with missionary work in China or anywhere else, if they could not cope with life among London's poor. Another reason was that his old friend and student Tom Barnardo was there and had written to tell him of several exciting new projects in which Henry Grattan might be able to help him.

Barnardo had by now given up any idea of going to China. Hudson Taylor's suggestion that he trained at the London Hospital was farsighted. Barnardo was appalled by the London slums. They were worse than anything he had seen at Dublin Bay. It was the plight of the children which haunted him day and night. Many were treated like animals, kicked, starved and brutalised. The cholera epidemic of 1866 killed so many of them that their bodies were disposed of in out of the way, desolate places, lest seeing the cemeteries full to overflowing people in high places started to ask awkward questions. The source of embarrassment and focal point of protest were Christian gentlemen like Lord Shaftesbury, who had been fighting for years to improve the lot of the factory and mine children, the chimney sweeps and the poor in general.

Many factory and landowners regarded Shaftesbury and his Christian conscience as a threat. When Barnardo opened two small houses in Hope Place in 1868 as a ragged school, he also was scorned. The gentry of Victorian Christian England had seen the liberating effect of Methodism on the working man and feared it. Shaftesbury had managed to rally a small but influential group of evangelicals within the Church of England to work with him for humanitarian causes. They recognised that concern for a man's spirit was useless without doing something for his body. They were also prepared to support anyone with vision enough to improve the lot of the poor, and that included dissenters like Barnardo.

Desperately concerned for the children who were sleeping rough all over London, Barnardo opened his first residential children's home in 1870. But this was not enough. A man after Henry Grattan Guinness' heart, he dreamed up grandiose schemes by the moment. Two years later, without a penny of his own, he attended the auction of one of the largest gin palaces in London, and with the support of his patrons bought it outright. The pub was built like a castle, with turrets and a flag-pole. The interior was loud and garish, with nude statues in every corner, countless mirrors, coloured glass and brass. It was also the most famous music-hall in the area, renowned for its bawdy jokes. In went Barnardo and out went the statues, and the music-hall comics. The blazing lights, the glass and brass remained, so did the bar, and the gin palace was converted into the world's first coffee-palace.

Like Henry Grattan, Barnardo was unashamedly teetotal. He had seen too much evil perpetrated by drink. Some employers even paid their workers in the pubs, letting them take their wages in kind. But it was no good preaching teetotalism if you could not offer an attractive alternative. A Christian coffee-house had to be as gaudy and bright as any pub or club. The concert hall provided a ready-made auditorium and before long the Edinburgh Castle public house was converted into the Edinburgh Castle People's Mission Church, a world of colourful make-believe for the Guinness children. It was a strange mixture of Wesleyanism, Quakerism and Brethrenism, with aspects of the Baptist Church thrown in. But the local people loved it. It was their church. In its first year attendance was around three thousand and Barnardo could say with some satisfaction, "I unhesitatingly assert that those who tell us that the working-classes are inimical to Christianity are wholly misinformed."[1]

Barnardo was as enthusiastic about Henry Grattan's project as Henry was about his. It so happened he was looking for somewhere to live. The obvious solution was that he should become a co-director of the newly named Stepney Institute and live there as supervisor. It was situated near the Edinburgh Castle and it also meant that the Guinness family need not live over the job. They took a house in nearby Clapton.

29 Stepney Green turned out to be much more attractive than Fanny had first thought:

> Old and ugly though it be, 29 is not an uncomfortable house, as houses go in London nowadays; and it suits our purpose very well. In the first place, it is roomy; and as we want to pack a good many people into it, that is one great point. Why, it has a hall twenty three-feet long by ten feet broad! There are not many houses in London at £63 a year of which as much can be said. Then the dining-room, though not lofty will dine a party of twenty without difficulty. And there are three good studies – no little matter in a house intended for students. A broad and easy old staircase leads to a spacious landing, off which are ten bedrooms. True, nine of them are but ship's cabins in point of size, but each contains a bed and a chair, and a gaslight, if not a candle, so they answer their purpose as prophet's chambers. The beds only measure two feet six in width; but as the Duke of Wellington said to the young officer, who, on seeing his Grace's camp-bed, exclaimed, "Why, dear me! your Grace, there's no room to turn round in it!" "Turn, Sir? turn? when a man wants to turn, its time he turned out." So we think. We provide beds, not to soothe the restlessness of the slothful, but only to give rest to the weary, and two feet six is enough for that!

Another advantage of number 29 was that it had its own garden with trees at the front, "a square of sufficient dimensions to admit a fair amount of exercise". At the back was a large timber-yard. "But let anyone who has sighed over the dreary monotony of slated roofs and blank walls, or over the worse intrusion of smokey chimneys and windowed walls close to his house, judge whether an extensive timber-yard at the back of your dwelling is not something to be thankful for!"

The funds which made the purchase possible were not limitless. Fanny was always conscious of the sacrifice some had made to provide them and she could not abide extravagance. Strong chairs, well-stocked bookcases, warm coconut matting and curtains "to keep out the draughts which old-fashioned windows will let in", were all that were required. The house was comfortable, if a little spartan.

The first student volunteered at the beginning of 1873. He was an Asian from India by the name of Joshua Chowriappah. He spoke so little English that the Guinnesses decided he should live with them at Clapton. The children warmed at once to his sparkling dark eyes and mischievous grin and he quickly became part of the family.

While Papa went off on a recruitment tour all over the country the three elder children went to school at the indomitable Mrs Pennefather's. The Rev. William Pennefather, her husband, was Vicar of St Jude's, Mildmay, and founder of what was to become a vast complex known as the Mildmay Centre, consisting of a church, conference centre and hospital.[2] Years later when Minnie was asked whether Mrs Pennefather was not something to do with Mildmay, she retorted, "She was Mildmay!"

As Henry toured the country potential students began to arrive at Stepney Green, French, Spanish, Russian, German, Armenian and Kaffir, a hundred in the first year. Each had to serve a month's probation and were only accepted after careful testing. Of the hundred volunteers, thirty-two were passed, which meant that 29 Stepney Green was already full to capacity.

Donations amounting to £1500 were received. It was enough, but the budget, which fell into Fanny's capable hands, still had to be managed very carefully. "Deeming it wise that intending mission-aries be trained to independent and active habits," she wrote, "we keep no servants." This was revolutionary for a Victorian household. Men were never expected to do the housework. But she and Henry deplored the tendency among British expatriates, in government and the army, to turn the natives into their servants. The missionary himself should be the servant of those to whom he was called. If he could not respect their integrity, then it was better he did not go at all.

The schedule at the Institute reflected the Guinnesses' innovative attitude to theological training. The rising bell went at six, there was housework from six thirty for an hour, then worship until breakfast at eight. Classes began at nine and ended at one thirty with lunch at the Edinburgh Castle, to save cooking meals at the house. During the afternoon the students learned a trade or craft, mechanics, building, carpentry, basic medicine, cookery, botany and reading the compass and sundial. At seven in the evening they were out in the streets learning how to cope with both physical and verbal brick-bats as they preached in the open air, all this "to counter the deadening influence of study on their souls". Henry never forgot his own experience. He also recognised that letting students loose on the Mile End Waste would either make or break them. It could be rough. Local breweries, concerned that teetotalism would mean a loss of trade, often paid disrupters to stop the meetings. The students' long day ended with prayers at nine thirty.

The academic institutions of the time criticised Henry Grattan for offering an amateur, "short-cut" theological education. They were probably suffering from pique. Though life at the Stepney Institute often resembled an endurance test, the students seemed to thrive on it and applications came pouring in from all over the world. It became very clear to Henry and Fanny that the house in Stepney Green was far too small. Barnardo left in June to get married, and Fanny felt increasingly that the students were an extension of her own family, and she ought to be mother to the house. New accommodation was essential and by the end of 1873, only a year after the opening of the Institute, the Guinnesses and their students moved into Harley House in Bow.

One day, just before they left Clapton, the doorbell rang. Ten-year-old Minnie, still in a frilly pinafore, ran to open it and found Howard Taylor standing there with a letter for her father. It was from Hudson Taylor, who had returned to England to care for his children and was living with his family nearby. At eleven Howard felt very grown up to be entrusted with such an important errand. He found his way from Mildmay to Clapton, but was totally non-plussed when Minnie's face with its large blue eyes, framed by two long blonde pigtails, slowly appeared around the open door. They stared at each other for some time until Howard managed to find his tongue, and explained why he had come. Minnie invited him in and as far as she was concerned that was the end of the episode. Howard, however, was to say for the rest of his life that that was the moment when he fell in love with her.

2

The children were thrilled with their new home. Although Harley House faced the Bow Road with its constant din, the back garden was a secluded, magic world. From a window they could watch the fountain splashing gently in the middle of a spacious lawn. At the bottom of the garden stood an old pear tree with spreading branches, whose gnarled appearance soon made it a family friend. Beyond the pear tree was an unimpeded view of shrubs and fruit trees, giving a sense of open space and tranquillity, for the garden backed on to a paddock of about an acre of land, connected to Harley House by a bridge over a grassy ditch. One local visitor, stopping to admire the fountain, said to Fanny, "Shouldn't think, Miss, as 'ow you'd ever want to go to 'eaven – with that there waterspout!"

Harley House was ideally situated as far as Henry and Fanny were concerned, not only for the children, but also in terms of practical work for the students. It was surrounded by factories such as Bryant and May; within easy reach of the huge London Hospital, where many died alone and abandoned; near the Tower with its garrisons of soldiers, and the docks where bewildered immigrants were arriving daily. Right opposite stood the most imposing building in the area, the dreaded Union Workhouse. Opportunity for caring was limitless where so many thousands lived in real Dickensian hopelessness and despair.

The house itself was large and old-fashioned, dating from a time when Bow had been a pleasant London suburb. To find any house with such a garden in the East End of London was a source of delighted amazement to Fanny. There were some disadvantages, mainly the clatter of cabs and constant roar of the horse-drawn trams in their tracks at the front, so that even "at midnight, sounds that never disturb the echoes of the West End Squares are paining our ears". But, she said, ever ready to look on the bright side, "The noise is endurable when the windows are shut, and its inmates can hear each other speak even when they are open!" Fanny's ability to make the best of any situation, more than any other strength of character, enabled her to cope with the many demands inflicted upon her by her husband.

On the ground floor were the dining-room, classrooms and Fanny's study. Upstairs were the Guinness' living quarters, now that 29 Stepney Green served as a dormitory. Fanny needed a study because, as she had foreseen, her life suddenly became absorbed with accounts and general administration. Examination of the budget revealed that there were not enough funds to furnish Harley House. Furniture would have to be begged and borrowed wherever they could find it. But this did not worry her unduly. She could still say, "We would sooner live in the broad, cheerful, airy Bow Road than in many a dull, confined and built-up West End square, or in many an elevated cage-like apartment on the palace-lined Boulevards of Paris."

The brewery Guinnesses however were setting their sights on Fanny's "dull, confined" West End. In 1873, the year Henry and Fanny took Harley House, Edward Cecil Guinness, youngest son of Sir Benjamin Lee, married his cousin Adelaide. She was a daughter of the late Richard Samuel Guinness, MP, a descendant of Samuel Guinness, one of the first Arthur Guinness' younger brothers and ancestor of the banking side of the family.

Samuel Guinness had followed his brother Arthur to Dublin late in the eighteenth century. He chose goldbeating, rather than brewing, as his trade, for he had married Sarah Jago, the niece of a goldsmith. They produced two sons, both of whom became barristers. It was through Richard, the younger son, that the banking line was established. In the 1820s Richard's two sons, Robert Rundell and Richard Samuel, set up a small land agency and banking firm at 5 Kildare Street, Dublin. Private banking was a risky business in Ireland. There were no laws protecting investments and banks tended to rise and fall almost overnight. R. Guinness and Co. appeared to do well, until 1836. It was then that Robert Rundell, who had raised the initial capital, decided that his younger brother was living extravagantly, far beyond his means, and withdrew from the partnership. Events proved it a shrewd and timely decision.

There happened to be an apprentice at R. Guinness and Co. who showed exceptional flair in the business and coming from a very good Irish family had valuable connections with the landed gentry, vital for any successful land agent. His name was John Ross Mahon. Robert Rundell had spotted his potential at once and in 1836 invited him to be his partner in a new banking firm and land agency to be known as Guinness and Mahon.

The firm began at 26 South Frederick Street, an elegant four-storey Regency house not far from College Green, central and convenient for business. Robert Rundell had just lost his first wife, Mary Anne Seymour. He sent his children to boarding-school and lived a lonely existence in his large, candle-lit house. Both of his sons were apprenticed to the firm at the age of fifteen, Richard Seymour in 1841 and Henry Seymour in 1846. All through the Great Famine the firm progressed satisfactorily, if not startlingly, doing what it could to alleviate distress.

In 1854 premises were taken in College Green. The move was primarily of psychological importance. Guinness Mahon and Co.'s position in the shadow of the Bank of Ireland reflected its status as an established part of the city. When Robert Rundell died in 1857 he left a comfortable business to his two sons. It would not be long before there was talk of developing a London branch.

The wisest move Robert Rundell had made was to pull out of R. Guinness and Co. nearly twenty years before. He had perceived clearly that his brother Richard's wife, Katherine Jenkinson, second daughter of the tenth Baron of Hawkesbury, intended to live as she had been accustomed, which was way beyond what her husband's small land agency could provide. In July 1849 R. Guinness and Co. collapsed and left Richard Samuel a bankrupt. This was almost more than his wife could bear. That she, a cousin of the Duc de Montebello, should be forced to endure poverty and disgrace! Richard Samuel, who was known as "Old Pel", because the high collars he wore forced up his chin, giving him the air of a pelican, turned instead to politics. From 1847-8 he served as MP for Kinsale, and from 1854 until his death in 1857 was the member for Barnstaple in Devon.

When Adelaide, their fourth daughter, met and fell in love with her distant cousin Edward Cecil, Katherine was not pleased. She felt that "Dodo", as she was known, deserved better than yet another of these Guinness tradesmen. That Edward Cecil was rich and they were desperately poor, counted for little. Nor did the fact that thanks to his financing of the great Irish Exhibition he was now Deputy Lieutenant of the City of Dublin. Dodo had spent months in France at the court of the Duc de Montebello being groomed and trained to marry into the aristocracy, not into a brewery. Katherine finally gave way and gave her consent. By the time she died in 1881 she was forced to acknowledge that her aspirations for her daughter were much closer to fulfilment than she had foreseen.

In choosing Adelaide, despite her impecunious background, Edward Cecil made a wise and brilliant match. She was petite, but an extremely striking woman, forthright and interesting, her husband's equal in drive and determination. Charming and cultured, well-read, with a faultless command of French, she was, as her husband had guessed, the perfect hostess. The marriage heralded their dramatic entry into society. In 1874 Edward Cecil bought Farmleigh, a large estate adjoining the Phoenix Park at Castleknock and they spent their time gravitating between their estate, the house in St Stephen's Green, and 5 Berkeley Square in London. Wherever they were they entertained on a grand scale. The tasteful luxury of their homes, the sumptuousness of their hospitality and the brilliance of their circle soon became legendary in London society. It was a matter of time before they began to play host to royalty.

Unlike his elder brother, Edward Cecil never felt any tension between his aristocratic aspirations and the means which made them possible. Arthur Edward, on the other hand, as his father had foreseen, tried to stir up some interest in brewing for a while, but eventually lost heart. In 1871 he married the formidable Lady Olivia Charlotte White, daughter of the third Earl of Bantry, who would one day become famous in Dublin for her philanthropy and opposition to Irish Home Rule. Lady Olive had a profound distaste for "trade", which she passed on to her husband. Increasingly Arthur Edward seemed to regard the brewery as a source of income, enabling him to follow other pursuits.

In 1869 his political agents were accused of bribing the electorate. No evidence was found against him, but this first hint of corruption ever to affect the Guinness family cost him his Dublin seat. For five years he was kept out of parliament. In his frustration he helped Edward finance the Irish Exhibition, converted St Anne's, Clontarf into an Italian-style palazzo and transformed Ashford by planting a huge larch forest and making it the best woodcock shoot in the country, particularly attractive to the Prince of Wales. In 1874 he won his Dublin seat back. That was the final death-knell as far as his interest in the brewery was concerned. Rumour has it that one evening in 1876 he and Lady Olive were taking a walk through Dublin when a labourer, disgusted to find his bottle of Guinness had gone off, slung it over a wall and landed it at their feet. That, maintained Lady Olive, was the last straw. The following morning Arthur Edward resigned.

The truth is that for some time he had felt pushed out by Edward Cecil. The younger brother was quick and clever, intuitively making the right decisions. He was also intense and excitable and found it hard to have what he considered the obvious questioned. Collaboration with someone who was only interested in the financial benefits was a tiresome constraint and in the end he was happy to dissolve the partnership, making a generous settlement on his elder brother of £680,000, far more than his father's will had allowed. He could well afford to do so. Arthur Edward now devoted his life to the genteel pursuit of spending money, not making it, and this he did on countless philanthropic causes. The member for Dublin also needed a London base. Like their brother and sister-in-law the future Lord and Lady Ardilaun established a reputation for magnificent dinner parties and glittering soirées at their London home, 11 Carlton House Terrace.

Meanwhile their father's first cousin had chosen to live in the lively squalor of the other end of town, "unnoticed by the world of fashion, business or pleasure," Lucy was to write years later, "unknown in the world of literature, the prophetic and scientific works to follow in after-years being all as yet unwritten, poor with no organisation to rely on, no denomination or society at their back, and with absolutely nothing in hand to supply the needs of the missionary students". Henry never took a salary from the Institute funds:

Looking back over the ministry of those days I recall the fact that it was boldly undertaken in faith, and largely unrecompensed in character. It was wholly unsalaried. Never, as far as I remember, in the course of a long ministry, have I made any bargain for fee or reward. Four hundred pounds had been left me as a legacy by my uncle Arthur Guinness of Beaumont, and when my mother needed pecuniary help I gave her this sum, and went down to Birmingham to preach the gospel, knowing no one, and with half-a-crown in my pocket. When speaking there in the open air in what was called the Bull Run, a brother in the Lord came forward and asked me to his house, and from that day I have never lacked a home to shelter in, or provision for daily needs.

This was in stark contrast to his two elder step-brothers. In 1871 John Grattan, who had been dismissed from the brewery for "mixing in degraded company" and had then sued Benjamin Lee for wrongful dismissal, was found dead, lying in "the greatest misery and dirt imaginable". His elder brother, Dr Arthur Grattan, who had married Amelia D'Esterre, saw his opportunity to exert a little gentle blackmail. He wrote to Edward Cecil at the brewery, explaining how he had bribed the newspaper reporters with ten shillings not to publish the fact that the deceased was related to "the rich Guinness of Dublin . . . feeling sure that you . . . knowing my present circumstances would help me to pay it – it would indeed have been a terrible annoyance to have the particulars stated".[3] How Edward Cecil responded is unknown, but with such step-brothers small wonder that Henry Grattan was wary of social contact with his wealthy relatives. However difficult things might be financially, he would die rather than appear to be begging.

When it came to money Fanny could not always rise to her husband's heroic heights of faith. She kept the account books. There were over fifty students now and the more there were the harder it became to feed them. She abhorred being in debt. Henry set off happily on his preaching tours, leaving her with an empty cash-box. Sometimes she wrote to him in utter desperation, "in these days of high prices, money melts away rapidly," and back would come the maddeningly confident reply: "We are now in debt. Let us go without meat in the Institute for another week, and give ourselves to prayer and searching of heart . . ." And Fanny would have to stand before all the students, account book in hand, and tell them that even more stringent sacrifices would have to be made. Being of a more practical turn of mind she felt that prayer and effort were not antagonistic. "We cannot expect God to do by a miracle that which we can do for ourselves." For her that meant writing endless bulletins and reports to the Institute's supporters, making the work of the Institute known so that funds would come in. But time and again she had to admit that Henry was usually right. For no apparent reason the tide would turn and money would appear almost from nowhere. For the students it was a stretching experience. The quantity of food on their plates would vary from week to week. This Guinness household was definitely not 5 Berkeley Square or 11 Carlton House Terrace.

Though Harley House was not renowned for its lavish entertaining, it none the less had its share of exceptional visitors. The East End of London was becoming a centre for radical, nonconformist Christian workers committed to alleviating the lot of the poor. The Edinburgh

Castle was just across the road and Barnardo would often bring his preachers over for a meal. They were not the intellectual élite, but they were just as intriguing.

There was Harry Moorhouse, once Ireland's most notorious professional pickpocket until he was converted in the Irish revival. As the children sat round the mealtable, their father told them how he and Harry were one day riding with several others in an Irish jaunting car, which was a kind of a carriage. The others, being well-heeled and more than a little naïve, refused to believe the stories they had heard about Harry. "Look to your purses, gentlemen," he said. By the end of the journey, without any of them knowing when or how, he had divested them of the entire contents of their pockets. The children thought it was a marvellous story and plagued Harry with pleas to pick their pockets when they were not looking every time he came.

Other visitors included Richard Weaver and his wife, rough diamonds but both celebrated preachers; George Holland, a wealthy gentleman who had given up his comfortable existence to form a Ragged School and charitable work in Whitechapel known as the George Yard Mission; and Amy McPherson, who founded the first receiving home for destitute children. Later there were Spurgeon, the celebrated pastor of the Metropolitan Tabernacle; D. L. Moody, the famous American evangelist; William Booth, founder of the Salvation Army; and the gracious, elderly Earl of Shaftesbury himself.

The children would rush to the mealtable in anticipation, eager to see who was there. The mercurial Barnardo was a favourite. He spun some wonderful yarns, and Minnie watched him open-mouthed, the food untouched on her plate. It might even have been in the Guinness home that the legend was born, the story Barnardo loved to tell of the night he was invited to dinner by Lord Shaftesbury. The Earl, moved by Barnardo's tales of the countless numbers of destitute children sleeping rough in freezing temperatures, called for a carriage and asked Barnardo to take him so that he could see for himself. And when he had seen their pitiable state, he turned to Barnardo and said, "All England shall hear of this."

In all probability the incident never happened. By the time Barnardo arrived in London Shaftesbury was already only too aware of the plight of poor children. For years he had been fighting in parliament to introduce legislation which would improve conditions in the factories and mines, where small children were treated as slaves. In 1872 he had arranged what he called "a regular tea-fight" for sixty heads of missions in the lower parts of London, "to come and give me information respecting the progress of Christianity under those forms".[4] Henry Grattan was there. So was George

Holland. Catherine Booth represented her husband. Barnardo spoke publicly of his horror at the number of children without a roof over their heads at night and that may well have been the occasion on which Shaftesbury uttered his apocryphal remark. Barnardo loved to let his imagination wander.

Henry and Fanny themselves were gifted conversationalists, which ensured lively, animated debate at mealtimes. It was a stimulating environment for the children, for then there were the students too, bringing countless different cultures into their home. "Robinson Crusoe, Robin Hood and Cinderella are all very well in their way," Lucy said, "but – you should see the war dance of our two Kaffir brethren!"

Social history, economics and politics were topics of conversation the children overheard almost every day. Geography had a personal face because of the students. "Foreign missions were as real as Guy Fawkes, and quite as interesting," Lucy wrote of her childhood memories. "Curled up in a big armchair, one can feel oneself fascinated still by the spell of Stanley's journey through the dark continent. He was only Hans Andersen with bigger print, and a little more ponderous to hold." "Truth is stranger than fiction, little one!" Henry Grattan had once said to her, and Fanny had looked round from her desk and smiled.

Fanny was increasingly at her desk. In the evening before bed the children crowded round her for a last story, but then she returned to her work:

And this daily routine went on [Lucy said] until my childish conception of mothers was inseparably linked with the thought of correspondence and pressing literary work. It appeared to me natural and proper that people should go to bed at night-time – all people, children, nurses, governess, servants, men and women – but that MOTHERS should stay up, and start at about half past ten their hardest writing. I believed with a perfect faith that all mothers did this; that they worked on till one or two a.m., and came down to breakfast at eight o'clock next morning as regularly as the sun went round the earth.

With Fanny so much occupied with Institute matters, it was Minnie who took care of her two baby sisters, Phoebe and Agnes. She bathed them and played with them for hours, feeling more herself in the nursery with them. Fanny was unaware that Minnie was becoming increasingly withdrawn. She had always been a quiet child, but now at twelve years old her shyness began to be a problem. She often felt sluggish, dull and stupid. Her parents were so clever and gifted. Harry, her hero, was dashing and fearless. Lucy, with her large brown eyes set in a pale, oval face, was sensitive and interesting, and had inherited all the musical brilliance of the Cramers. But Minnie felt she had no inherited gifts or talents at all and there seemed only one obvious explanation for it.

Finally, when she could bear the uncertainty no longer, she waited hesitantly behind Fanny's desk, until Fanny laid down her pen and drew her into her arms. Then, fighting to find the words, she asked whether she was adopted. Fanny was stunned, but merely dismissing the idea was not enough. It had become so embedded in Minnie's mind that it took some time to convince her that she was her parents' actual flesh and blood.

As she sat looking at her daughter's serious expression, Fanny must have seen something of herself in this gauche, shy child. She too had lamented her lack of looks and accomplishments and even now often felt in the shadow of her brilliant, dynamic husband. Stroking Minnie's long pigtails, Fanny told her that she had qualities which the others lacked. She, more than any of the other children, seemed to understand why, as a family, they lived as they did, without luxuries or privacy, and just how much that cost her parents. Fanny also decided that the time had come to make some changes. Minnie needed an understanding governess, someone who would bring her out. And as for Harry, it was time his energy was harnessed. He was ready for school.

Shortly before Harry left for Tettenhall College near Wolverhampton, a school with a strong Methodist foundation, he, Geraldine and Lucy were baptised at the Edinburgh Castle. Ruben Saillens, a French student at Harley College said he had "never seen an audience more deeply stirred by religious emotion. Mr Guinness himself baptised his three eldest children. He did it in so touching a way, speaking to them with such tenderness and depth of meaning, in tones so vibrant, yet so calm, that there were few present who were not moved to tears." For Minnie it was the most important day of her life. She had found the courage to demonstrate her convictions in public.

3

Harry Guinness was thirteen when he arrived at Tettenhall College in 1874. "A most loveable boy, and a great favourite with masters and pupils,"[5] one of his tutors wrote. He distinguished himself more on the sports field than in the classroom, and that was sufficient to ensure his popularity. Although the sciences fascinated him, maths was a severe trial, but an overriding goal helped him scrape through. He was determined to become a doctor, in order to serve one of the countries he had heard about from the overseas students at Harley.

Herbert and Howard Taylor joined Harry at Tettenhall. Their father had remarried and with his new wife had once again set sail for China. Howard, known then as Fred, for his first name was Frederick, was a slight child with fair hair and blue eyes. His classmates promised themselves some sport with the soft-looking little new boy. On the first day of term, as soon as lessons were over a crowd gathered round him.

"What does your father do, new boy?"

"He's a missionary."

That promised well.

"What's your name?"

"Lazarus."

"Have you any sisters, Lazarus?"

"Yes, two, Mary and Martha."

To the gang's delight Howard answered all their questions in a plaintive little voice and they soon began to hustle and jeer him. Just then Harry's class was dismissed and he came dashing out on to the playground.

"Hi Fred," he shouted.

The gang turned to stare at him.

"Fred? This isn't Fred. It's Lazarus."

Harry caught Howard's eye and the pair burst out laughing. Throwing their arms around each other they marched off, leaving a very embarrassed group of boys who would never again try ragging Howard Taylor.

Raised in China, immersed in its culture, Chinese honour was a way of life to the Taylor brothers. Despite their age difference they were in the same class. Though Howard could have beaten him easily, Bertie was always top, for Howard kept his marks low and deliberately stayed in second place. Reverence for an elder brother required it. Howard was also an exceptionally unselfish child.

In London Minnie and Lucy had lessons for a while with Florence and Maud Charlesworth, daughters of the vicar of nearby Limehouse. Maud would later become Mrs Ballington-Booth, daughter-in-law of the founder of the Salvation Army. The Charlesworth girls were clever and vivacious. They made Minnie feel gauche and stupid. They preferred Lucy, but the extrovert Harry was their favourite and they eagerly looked forward to the school holidays.

The Guinnesses had no sitting-room at Harley House. There were not enough rooms, and the dining-room had to serve a dual purpose. A grand piano commanded pride of place and barely a meal went by without Harry leaping up from the table to play a musical accompaniment. If Florence was there they would play a duet and after the meal she would organise songs or charades and other games, insisting that everyone join in. It was agony for

Minnie. She thought the Charlesworth girls silly and giddy and they teased her for her earnestness.

Finally Fanny thought it best for Minnie that her girls should have their own governess. A Miss Gardiner responded to the advertisement and was duly appointed. For Minnie it was one of the best decisions her mother ever made. She loved Miss Gardiner from the first evening she swept into the schoolroom behind Fanny in a trailing silk gown. But it took the governess rather longer to settle in her unusual environment.

It was a wet January evening when I wended my way to Harley House. I had been accustomed to the country and shed some tears as I passed through the dismal, crowded streets in the dull, old-fashioned cab, wondering what lay before me. But I soon passed out of gloom into brightness, for the house was lighted up and I found that a visitor was expected to dinner in the person of Harry's headmaster. How well I remember that evening and the kindness with which Mrs Guinness drew me into the conversation and made me feel at home![6]

But the feeling of being "at home" only survived until breakfast the following morning, when the sheltered Miss Gardiner was totally perplexed by the presence of two swarthy Syrians sharing her breakfast table, one of whom was totally blind.

All the children warmed to the new governess with her "dark eyes full of merriment", and her ability to make the dullest lessons interesting. In the summer the sun streamed into the little schoolroom above Fanny's study. On cold, foggy winter afternoons it was a cosy refuge and the children would huddle around their governess' knee, close to the fire while she recounted stories as a reward for work well done in the morning.

Miss Gardiner for her part felt very drawn to the whole family. She remembered Minnie as a loving child, a second mother to Phoebe and Agnes. Lucy was frail and brilliant, Gershom a rosy-cheeked little seven-year-old, full of mischief and the darling of the students. He carried his violin around with him everywhere. When, during one of the lessons, Minnie first showed him a map of London, he studied it for some time, asked where it was that they lived, then said, "But why are all the parks at one end and the docks at the other?" It was a question even Miss Gardiner was hard-pressed to answer.[7]

At mealtimes the parents emerged from their respective studies to hear about their children's progress, Henry Grattan, according to Miss Gardiner, "radiant with the light of heaven, absorbed in some fresh thought connected with the Second Advent". He was still writing *The Approaching End of the Age*, and Mrs Guinness was "putting it into more simple, popular form".

Eventually Miss Gardiner so acclimatised to life in the Guinness household that she became indispensable and ready for anything. She helped Fanny with her correspondence, the students with their English, presided at meals if necessary and supervised the endless toffee-making which the children insisted was a vital part of an English education, both for themselves and the students. Whenever any of the Bryant and May match girls popped in on their way home from work, as Fanny encouraged them to do in ever-increasing numbers, poor Miss Gardiner was all but turned to toffee and Henry Grattan could not hear himself meditate for the delighted shouts and laughter coming from the kitchen.

No joy compared with the summer holidays. That was the best time of all, when the sun always seemed to shine and the boughs of the old pear tree hung low under the burden of the new fruit. The children spent as much time as possible in the garden and paddock. Harry taught Gershom to ride a one-wheeled bicycle, so that they could follow each other, playing their violins in harmony. He also decided that five times round the garden was a mile and challenged Bertie and Howard Taylor to a fifty-mile run. The four girls and Gershom were loud and admiring spectators all day, until Fanny, summoned at last from her desk by the continual din, stopped Harry just as he completed "forty-eight miles". To his chagrin the Taylor brothers managed the full fifty miles.

In 1875 Henry Grattan was given a gift which was to change summer holidays for evermore, his own stately home. In North Derbyshire there lived a couple by the name of Hulme. They owned an extensive property consisting of a large country house, a farm, many outbuildings and a small chapel, all in several acres of beautiful Derbyshire countryside. The entire estate suffered from sad neglect. The Hulmes were elderly and it had become too much for them. Nor had they children to inherit the home they loved so much. Yet they felt that someone must have a positive use for it.

Driving home one day in their carriage from the station, Mr Hulme watched the house come into view in the distance, turned to his wife and said quite suddenly, "I think I have it now! Yes, I am sure this is the right thing." He went on to explain to her that he felt convinced Cliff House should become some sort of training place for lay people in missionary work at home and abroad. He had no idea how that might be possible and died before any steps could be taken.

Not long after her bereavement Mrs Hulme was in London and she happened to visit Harley House. The moment she saw the college she knew she had found the fulfilment of her late husband's vision.

Cliff House, by then in the hands of a group of trustees, was offered to Henry Grattan Guinness as a "northern branch" of the Institute.

If Fanny groaned at the thought of the extra work and cost involved in taking on a "white elephant", it had little effect on Henry. They could hardly personally supervise a college at such a distance, that much he was forced to admit. They would have to find a principal and a principal's salary, but otherwise, he assured her, Cliff College would be utterly self-supporting. He had long dreamed of such a place. An increasing number of students were becoming enthralled by recent exploration in Africa. Life was utterly primitive there. If they were serious about the possibility of going, they would need to be completely self-sufficient, having learnt the basics of subsistence farming. Once renovated, the property would be ideal.

Cliff finally passed into the Guinnesses' hands in December 1875 and Henry Grattan set off at once with a working party of students, blessing the Almighty for having given him in that year's intake several carpenters, joiners, painters and glaziers. In near freezing temperatures they camped in the empty shell of the house, working from first thing in the morning to last thing at night, only breaking for chapel services. There was a great deal to be done for the floors were riddled with dry rot, almost all the windows had to be re-hung, pipes and gutters were blocked, roofs needed mending. Once the basic repairs were complete the students started on the necessary alterations, converting barns into dormitories, building doors and staircases, adding baths and windows, and a large number of lavatories; then the painting, papering and whitewashing had to be done. The local people came out to stare. Never before had the quiet rural village of Calver experienced such an invasion. Word got round that they were theological students, some of them foreign, and it caused great interest, especially in the local chapels. "The people expected us to be great guns, coming from a college in London and having attended Moody's meetings," one of the students said. "So we tried not to disappoint them!" That sometimes meant sitting up half the night after a day of hard physical work, to put a decent sermon together for Sunday morning. "We kept ourselves fresh by singing many of the new 'Sankey' hymns."[8]

One day a local deacon arrived at Cliff looking for a preacher for some special services he had arranged at his chapel. The students were in the process of demolishing an old building and for overalls were wearing sacks with holes cut out for their heads and arms. The worthy deacon approached one young man, who was covered from head to foot in dust, muck and debris, and asked if he might speak to one of the students from London. The young man informed him that he was doing so already.

113

"What, you a student?" the deacon exclaimed incredulously, then seeing an acquaintance working in the farmyard, found an excuse to slip across and verify that these really were the students from Harley House.

While Henry acted as supervisor of works, the task of justifying the time and money spent on Cliff to the Institute supporters fell to Fanny. Funds were needed urgently. Her problem was compounded by the fact that the Institute was branching out in other expensive directions all at once. They had bought two more houses in the East End of London to serve as dormitories. More important, Henry and Fanny were becoming increasingly concerned by the number of established churches, Anglican and even Methodist, which were leaving the slums and rebuilding in more salubrious neighbourhoods. Apart from nonconformists like William Booth and George Holland, and committed individuals like the Pennefathers of Mildmay and the Charlesworths of Limehouse, establishment Christianity appeared to have no desire to identify with the drink-sodden, starving poor. Such snobbery infuriated Fanny, especially when the population of the East End was increasing all the time and hundreds were prepared to turn out every night in the pouring rain to hear the students preach.

But if the establishment did not want the poor, nor did the poor want respectable, "churchy" religion. In imitation of the pubs and concert halls, the age of the mission hall had dawned. Henry and Fanny resolved to establish ten of them in the most needy areas in the district. Wealthy churches which turned their backs on their financial responsibilities, as well as their spiritual and practical responsibilities, received the full force of her tongue, even if her forthrightness meant alienating the respectable and forfeiting the support she so badly needed.

For weeks while Henry was at Cliff she trailed the streets of London, examining old, abandoned churches and chapels:

> large, cheerless, desolate, dirty-looking structures, the very aspect of them, with their high-backed pews, and their formal religious associations, would be sure most effectually to repel the very class we wanted to attract . . . It is vain to expect that services conducted in such dismal sepulchral places should rival the attractions of the brilliant and beautiful gin-palaces by which they are surrounded.

Eventually she found a sign-painter's shed in Old Ford, a little disused chapel in Bow and an ex-Presbyterian iron church which she had uprooted and moved to Stratford. She also arranged to rent a school on Sunday evenings as a Sunday school for the hundreds of destitute children walking the streets with nowhere to go. Desperate for warmth, many of them poured into the established churches for the evening service, only to be ejected on the spot. How could anyone blame the congregation, Fanny admitted. Three hundred rough, uneducated children could be disruptive, but what a challenge for the Harley House students!

It was not always easy to hold a child's attention, so two oxy-hydrogen lanterns were purchased and proved extremely useful. "Dissolving views" were a colourful means of illustrating a talk, Fanny wrote, explaining the purchase to her supporters. "Our men make the oxygen gas and work the apparatus themselves, so the expense of such exhibitions is trifling, while the benefit and enjoyment they afford is great."

The Guinnesses' resourcefulness did not end here. One student, a former sailor who wanted to work among seamen, succeeded in convincing them that one of their mission halls should be afloat. It could sail up and down the Thames or round the coast among British and foreign shipping, and in the summer anchor at the seaside resorts. A thirteen-ton cutter came on to the market early in 1876 at the incredibly low price of £120 and was bought with the help of a single donation. The students repaired and painted her with loving care, renamed her the *Evangelist* and launched her in the spring, with three students and a captain on board.

But how, with all these added pressures, with their commitment to the poor, could Fanny justify running a college, not in squalid Bow, but in beautiful Derbyshire, with its hills and tors, woods and caverns, rushing rivers, moorlands and picturesque valleys? First of all, she said, those who did not live in the East End could not imagine what a relief it was to get away for a while. Gazing at a sky unobscured by a leaden pall of smoke, hearing birdsong instead of the clanging of trams and shriek of the train, seeing hills and fields instead of filthy alley-ways, give a sense of exhilaration. "Night brings real silence," Fanny wrote wistfully. "Your whole being seems to expand with a sense of relief."

An additional advantage was that while Cliff had little to offer students preparing for town-life in China or India, apart from an occasional holiday, those hoping to go to the interior of Africa could be better trained to cope with a rural existence. Experimental farming would also provide employment for some of Barnardo's destitute boys. Altogether, Fanny concluded, despite her original misgivings, it seemed a perfect arrangement. "Therefore, as in the Providence of God, it was offered to us, we did not feel justified in turning from it."

The children first saw Cliff in the summer of 1876 and could hardly believe their eyes. Miss Gardiner was in charge, for Fanny was suffering from exhaustion and stayed at Harley House. With the children away she could at least recuperate, moving her couch out into the garden to her favourite spot underneath the shady old pear tree.

After the East End of London, the fresh air and open spaces of Derbyshire were a taste of heaven. There had been country holidays before, occasional visits to their uncle Wyndham Guinness, who was vicar of Rathdrum near the east coast of Ireland, but this was different. It was theirs! Built on a terrace one hundred feet above the Derwent, Cliff House commanded a breathtaking view of the river and distant hills. Behind the house the farm stretched out into moors of rock and heather, grass and bracken, climbing up to the limestone cliffs and beyond, as far as the eye could see. There was so much to explore. When they were finished with the house there were the mushroom and calf-houses, the pigsties and storerooms, a higgledy-piggledy, rambling group of structures linked by quaint winding stone steps, which lent themselves to games of hide-and-seek. And then there was the excitement of living on a farm. For little Phoebe and Agnes milking-time twice daily was an endless source of delight.

From that first summer Cliff was not only home, it was a paradise, associated for ever in the children's minds with many idyllic summer memories. They were blissfully ignorant of the tensions it caused their mother, driving her to her couch under the pear tree. Nothing marred their enjoyment and Fanny was determined to keep it that way as long as she possibly could.

4

From that first summer, Henry Grattan realised that in Cliff he had found the refuge he so desperately needed. For some months he had been engaged in a particularly heavy preaching schedule, speaking up and down the country on the Bulgarian atrocities. Where, he wanted to know, was the voice of protest at the barbaric cruelty with which the Muslim Turks and Bulgars had crushed the uprising of Bosnia? All the Christian people wanted was their political and religious freedom. Why could no one understand the significance of such an event? Like a rotten fruit, decayed at the very centre, the Ottoman Empire was manifesting the external signs of its corruption. Its barbarism was a death rattle, the panic tactics of a tyrant who knows its days are numbered. All was exactly as the Bible predicted. Whenever any subject caught Henry's imagination it absorbed him completely, until all his emotional energy was expended. It was at Cliff that he relaxed, unwound and restocked.

But for all the pleasure Cliff afforded, the expenditure exceeded

Fanny's worst fears. Having swallowed up a fortune in renovation it was still barely presentable. There were no curtains at the windows, no coverings on the floors. Since the latter were full of crevices, "giving a peep of the regions below", something would have to be done before the really cold weather set in. "It will afford great pleasure to the students when we can cover them with impervious and ornamental kamptulicon, which we will do as soon as some kind friend will send us £50 for the purpose."

Some rather less unusual yet useful gifts did come in, such as £15 worth of iron bedsteads and bedding for the Barnardo boys' dormitories, or home-made knitted quilts. But they represented a drop in the ocean. The new principal, Mr Dening, whose elegant wife Geraldine had been a celebrated speaker and close friend of Fanny's before her early death, submitted a long list of urgent necessities. He must have a cart, another force-pump, a couple more cows and "half a horse", half a horse because some kind supporter had sold his pony and sent the money, which represented half the price of the new horse.

Begging lowered Fanny's spirits dreadfully. Morally she did not see why she should have to, when some £250 million, which could have been put to better use, lay untouched in the Bank of England. For her 1876 and 1877 were years of "almost unbroken financial pressure in consequence of the rather too rapid extension of our undertakings last year". The situation was so desperate that at times she resolved to get rid of Cliff altogether. Yet how could she? Every available space was filled with industrious students. Mr Hulme would have been thrilled to see it.

She kept a painfully honest account of her struggles and anxieties in her diary:

March 21st, 1876. Received this morning two SMALL donations and two LARGE bills, one for books, £50 and the other for building and plumbing work, £75. Expenses are great!

April 28th. No money came in today; we have not a week's expenses in hand, with a hundred people dependent, in a sense, on us.

April 29th. £12 from two donors today is a help towards present necessities and a cause for thankfulness. We were considering last night on how little it would be possible to keep the men for a week should it be needfull to come down to dry bread!

May 1st. No funds came in today, only bills. We have never been so low before.

May 2nd. Nothing again this morning, save tidings that they have the measles at Cliff!

The situation eased a little over the summer, but by December things were so desperate once again that Fanny "resolved to stop the butcher's bill at any rate, by dispensing with meat; told the students so, and was pleased with their readiness to make needful sacrifices: told them the Director wrote from Cornwall that he too was fasting . . . and that he had written to the household at Cliff to turn vegetarian, pro tem."

Christmas was at hand and she so badly wanted to treat the children of the Sunday school to the Christmas Day dinner and party they had never had before. "Feeling cast-down and tried," she noted in her diary. Miraculously the money arrived just in time, one cheque for £50 being delivered late on Christmas Eve. There was not only enough to feed the children, but also to provide a Christmas tea for the mothers' meeting and a Christmas dinner for all the students.

Despite constant financial worries, by the summer there was talk of building a brand new college. Harley House was a family home and too small. Fanny admitted at last that the dormitory accommodation at Stepney Green was inadequate. It was not really acceptable to expect grown men to forgo the privacy of their own bedroom. Of course the idea was out of the question, until it occurred to them that if they built a college on the paddock beyond their own back garden there would be no land to buy. The house on Stepney Green could be sold for about five hundred pounds. Then a generous supporter offered them £1000, over a third of the cost of a new college. A Purchase and Building Fund was set up, which, Fanny reminded her supporters, was in addition to, not in place of the General Fund. She was also at pains to assure them that her own family expenses did not come out of the Institute's funds. "We labour otherwise in order to meet them." They came presumably from Henry's writings and preaching engagements. "We feel, therefore, all the more free to urge on others the claims of a work to which we give – all that we have to give – OURSELVES, and to which in due time we hope to give our children also."

For Minnie life already was the Institute. She had no ambition to be anywhere else. The first awareness that she could not always live a secluded, protected life, came in 1878, shortly after her fifteenth birthday. Miss Gardiner had felt for some time that there was no more she could teach her. Knowing how attached Minnie was to her home and that the break would have to come one day, she suggested that Fanny should send her to school.

For Minnie the thought was unbearable, but none of her pleading was to any avail. Her parents chose a boarding school in Weston-super-Mare, where the staff were prepared to go to any lengths to make her happy, even to giving her her own room in the headmistress' private house. But it was no use. Minnie pined day and night for her two little sisters, until her eyes were so swollen with crying she could hardly see. After six weeks she became ill and Fanny was summoned in a hurry to take her home. Minnie was too relieved to be rid of the torture of separation to feel any sense of failure, and neither of her parents ever reproached her for what had happened. The school informed them that she could not spell. If she was backward at some of her lessons, then so be it, her mother said. Spelling was not everything and Minnie was mature in other areas. Time proved Fanny right. Spelling would be a weakness all Minnie's life, even after she became a well-known writer, touring the world. No longer did her parents try and force her out of her reclusive tendencies. Wisely they realised that there was a time for everything.

When Minnie came home the new college was well under way. Fanny's description of the progress, or lack of it, sounds strangely contemporary. The cost of bricks went up by a third. Builders seemed to demand very high wages for very short hours. Despite her frustrations she organised a large supper party for all the bricklayers when the walls had almost reached their destined height. Having watched the men from his study window, balancing precariously so many feet above ground level, Henry felt inclined to pray publicly for their safety.

Some days later a sudden, almost tropical, thunderstorm broke over London. It was six in the morning and the men had just started work. One clap of thunder, followed instantaneously by a vivid flash of lightning, was so deafening that Fanny was convinced something or someone must have been struck. Within minutes Henry was summoned to the building site. One of the labourers standing on the very top of the scaffolding had reached out an arm at just that moment and it had been struck by lightning. For an awful moment the labourer thought his arm had been torn off altogether. It was completely numb. Henry rushed him to the local hospital where it became obvious that he was suffering more from shock than any physical damage.

"If you 'adn't said that prayer, sir . . ." he said to Henry.

Henry asked him if he knew how to pray himself.

"Oh yes," he said. "I can say 'Our Father charten 'evn, allord be thy name' and 'Matthew, Mark, look on John.'"

To Henry's amusement and despair, he realised that the man attached no meaning whatsoever to the sounds he was making, but he obviously thought he had impressed because he added, "My little boy can say these prayers as good as I can, sir; that's just what I was teached, and I try to teach 'im the same."[9]

Harley College, the East London Institute for Home and Foreign Missions, was opened without debt on a biting autumnal day in 1878. It was an imposing red-brick building with a grey roof and large sash windows. The Venetian blinds were Fanny's pride and joy.

Minnie revelled in being part of the buzzing life of Harley again, to serve teas and share in her parents' excitement, but most important of all, to be able to care for her two little sisters. Every night she supervised bathtime, then led them down to Fanny's study where they would sit on the sofa playing chess, as quiet as two mice, lest they should disturb their mother's concentration. It was Minnie who took them up to bed and she resented any engagement which took her away from them. Nothing prepared her or any of the family for the cruel blow to come.

5

The missionary zeal of the nineteenth century grew out of the religious nature of the era. The Victorians were a self-confident race of people, resolute, convinced and determined, not yet too disturbed by Darwinism nor plagued by the theological uncertainties spawned by two world wars and the threat of a nuclear holocaust. It was the age for great and stirring preachers, huge meetings, sentimentalism and a revivalist zeal which affected every level of society.

In recent years the missionary ideal has been criticised for confusing Christianity with imperialism. Civilising the savages meant importing a British Christian culture which was not as superior as the Victorians believed. For some, particularly the early Catholic and Anglican missionaries, this was undoubtedly true, but it is a sweeping generalisation. Britain's colonialising tendencies wreaked havoc long before most missionaries arrived in India, China or Africa. Adventurers, traders, soldiers and government representatives imported alcohol, drugs and guns, in a deliberate effort at subjugation.

Hudson Taylor deplored the colonial attitudes he had witnessed in China and felt committed to undoing the harm already done, particularly by the opium trade. His missionaries were to live simply, serving the people. To identify completely they must adopt the national costume, the men shaving their heads and wearing pigtails, the women observing the cultural traditions in all but binding their feet. His society was interdenominational, so that there would be no cathedrals or vast monuments out of keeping with the local surroundings. It accepted working-class men and women with no formal academic education or training other than what they received at Harley College.

The late nineteenth century saw a sudden burst of geographical exploration. Maps continued to alter. Missionary magazines, with their engravings of hitherto unexplored regions and their inhabitants, filled readers with awe and excitement. Wherever he went Hudson Taylor's descriptions of China had an enormous impact. When he spoke of the countless souls without Christ, men and women wept. When he described the way the British had imported opium, slowly poisoning the Chinese people for material gain, they hung their heads in shame. The urge to go, to give oneself, to die for the cause if necessary, was strong. It was the age of the Salvation Army and of hymns like "Rescue the perishing". It was the age of Amy Carmichael and her vision of countless people hurling themselves over a cliff to endless damnation, while some sat on the grass making daisy-chains. The end-of-the-world age was near. Christ's return was imminent. The time had come to throw down the daisy-chains.

The Guinnesses shared Hudson Taylor's ideals entirely. In 1875 the first twelve students went out from Harley House, Joshua Chowriappah back to India, Ruben Saillens back to France, where he eventually founded a similar college to Harley in Nogent, just outside Paris, still in existence over a hundred years later. The two Kaffirs went back to South Africa. Four young men set off for China, one of them, Arthur Douthwaite, leaving his fiancée behind because he felt he could be more useful without a wife. One student went to Japan and one to Burma.

On the day of their departure the "Mother of Harley" brought them a few last words. "Feeling the solemnity of the occasion," one of the students wrote later:

> I sharpened a pencil and took a notebook to record her farewell advice. Presently she said, "I have one piece of advice to give you which I hope you will remember all your life." I felt for the pencil; it was all ready. I listened eagerly. "Whatever part of the Mission field you may be in," she said, "always be sure to keep your hair tidy."[10]

Practical, capable, no-nonsense as Fanny may have been, the student discerned an unmistakable twinkle in her eye on this occasion. It masked the terrible wrench she felt at their parting. All the students were "her children", but "our first twelve" always had a special place in her affections. She hung their photographs over the chimney piece in the dining-room and at mealtimes allowed her vivid imagination to carry her to the countries they represented. When letters arrived she read them aloud to the children. The descriptions of lively Japanese towns, junk-traversed Chinese waters, the scorching plains of India or Burma and work on the West Indian plantations held them enthralled. But most thrilling of all were the descriptions in the newspapers of Stanley's discoveries in the hitherto unexplored continent of Africa.

For some years Africa had exerted a magnetic charm for a succession of explorers, commissioned by the Royal Geographical Society to discover the sources of the Nile. The early pioneers, Speke, Burton and Baker, had no real love of the African and thought him too savage to civilise. That did not prevent Speke from bartering with guns. "There is no such thing as love in these countries," Baker wrote. "Everything is practical, without a particle of romance. Women are so far appreciated as they are valuable animals . . . I am afraid this practical state of affairs will be a strong barrier to missionary enterprise."[11]

What they discovered was the existence of a Stone Age system of life, cruel and brutal, yet valid in its own way. But even without the arrival of Western explorers it could not have survived. The Arab traders were already there, plundering and pillaging, taking huge human booty of slaves, setting an appalling example of debauchery and savagery, enforcing Islam in the process. Britain, as a civilised government, felt a moral obligation to destroy the slave trade, but how was it to impose such standards without resorting to force? To the African the British ultimately appeared to be another kind of trader, arousing suspicion and hostility. Yet Baker insisted that unless Britain stepped in, this promising wilderness would be utterly despoiled by the slave traders and lost for ever to Christianity.

In response the Royal Geographical Society sent out David Livingstone. His aim was not to save individual souls but to suppress the slave trade and open up the country so that Christianity could follow in his wake. The gracious, gentle Livingstone, who refused to use a gun, soon became known by the Africans as "a white man who treated black men as his brothers". He had a genuine love for Africa and wrote, "The strangest disease I have seen in this country seems really to be broken-heartedness and it attacks free men who have been captured and made slaves."[12]

When Livingstone disappeared it was the American adventurer Stanley who found him. Two years later, in 1873, Livingstone died. The natives carried his body overland and it was shipped home for burial in Westminster Abbey. Stanley went back to Africa, determined to continue where the doctor had left off. He managed to reach the mouth of the Congo and in 1875 his dispatches appeared in the London *Daily Telegraph*. His book, *Through the Dark Continent*, describing his extraordinary adventures, was published in 1877. Stanley was a journalist and an accomplished writer. As a real-life adventure story his book made compelling reading. Small wonder Lucy Guinness described it as a miniature version of Hans Andersen.

Both the dispatches and the book contained emotional appeals, calling on men and women to go as missionaries to the lost continent. Stanley was profoundly influenced by Livingstone, who just before he died had written: "All I can add in my solitude is may Heaven's richest blessings come down on everyone, American, English or Turk, who will help to heal this open sore of the world." Dying on his knees, stretched out across his bed in prayer for Africa, the great, godly man had thrown down the gauntlet to the students of the Harley Institute.

"The 'dark continent' that was a mere blank mass to our fathers, has become to us a most deeply, painfully interesting quarter of the globe," Fanny wrote. "Why has God in these last days permitted the covering veil to be removed from this immense unevangelised division of our world? What is His voice to His Church on earth by means of these great discoveries?" The answer was clear. "The end of all things is at hand, and the Gospel must first be preached among all nations before the end come!"[13]

By the middle of 1878 the Livingstone Inland Mission had been set up, with Henry and Fanny as founder committee members. In June Henry Craven, a Harley student, led a pioneer party out to the Congo, with the intention of sending the committee a detailed report. By November one of the party was dead. But that did not deter several other Harley students from pledging their lives to Africa too. Livingstone had so loved the African people that he had been ready to die for them. It was not simply a romantic notion. They knew what was involved. The idea was to establish missionary stations all the way down the swift-flowing Congo to Stanley Pool, where the river contracted to an unnavigable torrent, hurtling its way down in a series of cataracts to the lower Congo and Atlantic. Stanley had made it quite clear that the waterways of Africa were treacherous, the climate unbearable at times, and the natives suspicious, violent and cannibalistic. Disease was rife and untreatable. Hardly any of the men in his or Livingstone's party had survived to tell the tale. To go to Africa with the intention of settling there was certain death.

Among the students at Harley was one who had become the Guinness children's hero with stories of his travels in Africa. Adam M'Call had spent seven years in government service, big-game hunting on the Upper Zambesi. He was the ideal leader of another little group that was preparing to go. But Fanny, for all her yearning for the tribes of Africa, felt a deep uneasiness that she seemed to be encouraging her "children" to make sacrifices which she, safe and secure in England, would never know herself. But before the second group sailed an event occurred which was to change all that.

As Easter 1879 and Harry's school holidays approached, Fanny planned to take the whole family to their uncle Wyndham's in Rathdrum, Ireland. Both Henry Grattan's brothers had become clergymen. Frederick, the youngest, had an incumbency in Manchester and was single, but Wyndham, the favourite, had married an Irish girl, Dora Boxwell, and with their three small children lived in a wonderful rambling old vicarage in a glorious setting overlooking the sea.

Some ten days before Easter Henry set off to speak at a series of meetings in Torquay. With him went Gershom, who had been invited to stay with Fanny's cousin. Fanny was loath to let him go just before the holidays, but he had always been a frail child and she felt that at nine his health and strength were more important than his amount of knowledge. The whole family stood on the porch of Harley House to see them off, Phoebe and Agnes waving and laughing until the carriage was out of sight.

The following morning, Wednesday, Agnes complained of a headache. Fanny thought little of it and made her stay in bed. But she got up and played as usual in the afternoon, saying she felt much better. By late afternoon however, Agnes was feeling very unwell. She had a pain in her neck and ear and it hurt when she moved her mouth. Fanny, who was about to go out to speak at a meeting, thought she must have caught a cold and told Minnie to make sure Agnes went to bed early.

In the middle of the night Fanny was awakened by the creak of her bedroom door. It was Agnes.

"Only me, mother dear," she said, "I want to come to you because I can't sleep, and I've disturbed Minnie once or twice, and I am so hot, I don't know what's the matter with me."

Fanny lifted her into her bed and discovered she had a high fever. She slept there fitfully and in the morning Fanny sent for Dr Dixon. He diagnosed tonsillitis, a condition Fanny had not heard of but apparently not serious. Fanny tried hard to believe him but as the next two endless days went by and Agnes showed no sign of improvement, a terrible, sickening fear took hold of her, sitting on her stomach like a lump of lead. What if Agnes had diphtheria? Where could it have come from? And she suddenly remembered the meeting for their hundred and fifty Sunday school teachers the evening before Henry had left for Torquay, and Agnes helping to hand out the tea and cake. What if her friends and relatives, so critical of her taking her children into the disease-ridden East End, were right? Someone could so easily have brought the infection into their home.

By Saturday Agnes' throat was so sore that it took her ten minutes to screw up enough courage to swallow her medicine and there was no longer any doubt as to the nature of the disease. Dr Dixon sent for a throat specialist called Mackenzie who managed to remove some of the membrane from Agnes' throat, but it left her feeling very drowsy. Fanny held her and sang to her and when she slept, scribbled a note to Henry, begging him to leave Gershom in Torquay and come home.

From the moment the diagnosis was made, Dr Dixon told Fanny not to panic as yet about the students, but to get the other children out of the house as soon as possible. On Sunday, before she had time to make the necessary arrangements, it became clear that Phoebe was very ill too.

That was a night to end all nights. Agnes was desperately ill, Phoebe was violently and incessantly sick, and Minnie, just beginning to develop symptoms of the dreaded disease too, was too unwell to help. Fanny struggled on as best as she could, but by Monday morning her own throat was beginning to feel very sore. She telegraphed again to Henry, telling herself she was simply suffering from strain and tiredness, but by the time he arrived home on Monday evening Dr Dixon had seen the characteristic membrane across her throat and sent her to bed.

It was a relief to have Henry in the house, even though she was not allowed to see him. He was kept downstairs with the students in quarantine. Lucy had been sent to stay with relatives.

On Tuesday, communicating by a series of notes, Henry and Fanny decided to send the students away for an early vacation. Minnie, at seventeen, was strong enough to fight the disease, Agnes was a little improved and Phoebe seemed to be holding her own. Fanny began to feel that the worst had passed.

By Wednesday however Phoebe's condition had deteriorated so rapidly that the two doctors held out little hope for her. Fanny begged them to let her get up and go to her children, but they refused. By the evening she could bear it no longer and dragged herself to the nursery. Phoebe held out a hand to her and it was cold and clammy. She was labouring for breath. Fanny sat on the edge of her bed, sponging her brow, when she suddenly looked at her and said, "Mother, dear, you shouldn't take that trouble, you'll make yourself worse."

The following morning Dr Dixon performed an emergency tracheotomy, opening the windpipe and inserting a tube just below the disease. The relief was instantaneous and Phoebe began to breathe freely. Fanny sent a message to Henry to say that she had regained consciousness and he came and stood in her room just inside the door. It was the first time he and Fanny had seen each other since his return from Torquay and they knew they must not touch or even go near each other. Within a few minutes Phoebe died peacefully with Fanny beside her, her father watching from the doorway. Fanny sat very still for a while, too stunned even to cry. Then, remembering Agnes, she bent down to give Phoebe one last kiss, and went to see to her youngest daughter.

Agnes and Phoebe were inseparable. It seemed impossible to think of Agnes living without her sister. Dr Mackenzie was with her and Fanny had to take one look at his face to know that there was nothing more to be done. A tracheotomy was pointless. The disease had spread to her chest. For several hours Fanny fought on, filling Agnes with the medicines, willing her to live. If only she could save her little Agnes, her bright, giggly little six-year-old who was like a sunbeam dancing round the house. But by late evening her breathing slowed and pulse weakened. Henry came and stood in the room again. Agnes could not see him, but recognised his voice. She died at ten o'clock, ten hours after her sister.

Fanny was numb with grief and shock and weakened by the disease. She longed for Henry, to feel the comfort of his arms, but knew it would be madness to take such a risk. The house reeked of carbolic and disinfectants but they were no preventatives. Instead she went to Minnie and they cried the night away together, wondering how they were going to break the news to Harry, Lucy and Gershom.

By the weekend she felt a little better physically and sat down to write to Wyndham and Dora. For the last years, she said, work at the Institute had left her little time for relaxation or recreation. Her only real rest and refreshment had been the company of her two little girls at brief, snatched moments of leisure. They were so merry, so vivacious, such good, considerate children. "But remember," she wrote, children are "winged joys, ready at a moment's notice to take their flight". Even now she could hardly believe that Phoebe and Agnes would not come running in. The tears came every time she thought of all the treats she would never give them. Her only comfort was that there were far better treats in heaven. She thanked God for all they had meant to her, for all they were now in his presence, and, hardest of all for the temporary separation. "But oh! dear brother and sister, need I say, for the present, it is not joyous, but very, very grievous."

The funeral took place the following Wednesday, April 2nd at Abney Hall Cemetery, Stoke Newington, where Fanny's eldest sister Madeline and her four children were buried. Neither Fanny nor Minnie was allowed to go. At home Fanny wondered why it was that she and Minnie should be spared and the two little ones taken. Why were Lucy and Gershom providentially out of the way?

Perhaps it meant that God still had some special work for them to do. The thought was a tiny ray of hope piercing the pain. Perhaps it was possible that out of this apparently pointless bereavement would come some kind of meaning. But for the moment it was a case of surviving one day at a time, for every ounce of her being seemed to scream out, "How can I ever go on without them?"

7

1880–1882

A New Generation Grows Up

1

For months after Phoebe and Agnes died, Minnie cried herself to sleep at night. It was as if she had lost her own children. Henry and Fanny, struggling to come to terms with their own grief, submerged it in their work, and seemed largely unaware of how deeply she was affected. Minnie had always been the strong one, a source of support to others. She herself felt she had to be brave. There were Lucy and Gershom to consider. Since everyone else relied on her for comfort, she kept her feelings to herself and cried in secret.

For Fanny, the relief of having a purpose-built college with properly equipped classrooms and dormitory accommodation, was offset by the anxiety of running such a venture. The college housed a hundred people, seventy students and thirty staff. The budget of £1500 in 1873 had leapt dramatically to over £11,000 by 1878, and it was still not enough. There were building and maintenance costs for Harley, Cliff and the mission halls, and salaries to be found for teaching staff and the mission-hall pastors, before she even considered how to feed the students. The college was still non-fee-paying and applications poured in, over a thousand in the first six years. Fanny found it hard to turn anyone down.

During the 1870s the first Jewish immigrants began to arrive in the East End. Their poverty made the English East Enders seem rich. One day in 1879 a minister from the Mildmay complex turned up at Harley with five young Jewish men, all recently converted to Christianity, all destitute and alone, but determined to study with Grattan Guinness, whose interest in the Jewish people and biblical justification for the Zionist cause was becoming well known. There was really no room, but Fanny took them in. One of them, David

Baron, would later play an important part in the first international Zionist Congress.

Since the publication of his book, *The Approaching End of the Age*, at the end of 1878 Henry Grattan was once more in great demand as a preacher. By the beginning of 1880 it had been reprinted five times and acclaimed by theologians of the calibre of Professor T. R. Birks of Cambridge University. Lord Shaftesbury said publicly that he was "so struck and moved by its contents . . . that I cannot resist the desire I feel to bring it under the immediate and serious attention of the public."[1]

There had been books on prophecy and world history before, but this one was distinctive and original, thanks to Henry Grattan's recently acquired passion for astronomy. It was sparked by a book by Professor Birks which set out hitherto unknown discoveries made in 1754 by a Swiss astronomer called Jean Philippe Loys de Cheseaux. Up to that time medieval astronomers had always maintained that there was no way of detecting any kind of harmony in the different revolutions of the earth, the sun and the moon. It was too hard to establish a cycle. De Cheseaux, who had been trying to establish the date of the crucifixion, fell upon the fact that 315 years constituted such a soli-lunar cycle, the sun and moon coming to within three hours, twenty four seconds of absolute agreement. No sooner had he discovered that cycle than, to his excitement, he realised that 315 was a quarter of 1260, the number of "days" mentioned in the book of Revelation as having significance for the end of the age. Therefore 1260 years, as a multiple of 315, was itself a soli-lunar cycle. But even more extraordinary, when he examined it closely he discovered that 1260 years was the time it took for the sun and moon to move into conjunction within an hour of each other. He had found the key: 1260 years was a complete cycle of time, bringing the lunar and solar calendars into almost total harmony.

Henry Grattan was so enthralled by de Cheseaux's findings that he acquired an enormous eight-inch telescope so that he could continue the astronomer's studies himself. It was to be a lifetime's occupation which would eventually earn him honorary fellowships of the Royal Geological Society and the Royal Astronomical Society, and a doctorate. The telescope commanded pride of place in the Guinness overcrowded dining-room at Harley, until it was equatorially mounted in a purpose-built observatory at Cliff. It was Henry's only valuable and most treasured possession. Most of the students at one time or another were invited to admire it and to hear of Henry's most recent research. For David Baron it was an unforgettable experience. He went back to the observatory on his own some days later and noticed that on the side of the telescope were scratched in Hebrew the words "Holiness unto the Lord".

As he continued his studies Henry began to see that just as the earth had its own cycles, the minute hand on a clock to measure an hour, the hour hand making a cycle of twelve hours, light and dark to make a day and the four seasons to measure a year, so there are cycles known to astronomers which measure very large periods of time. Most human beings are used to small cycles of time, but Henry became convinced that God used a much vaster time-scale measured by these huge astronomical clocks.

This would suggest that Daniel and Revelation, the apocalyptic books in the Bible which talked about the end times, were written in a kind of astronomical code. The books themselves made it clear that they were "sealed up", shrouded in mystery, until an appointed time. Unwittingly, in discovering the link between astronomy and the apocalyptic books, de Cheseaux had broken the code. The days, weeks, years and "times" of which they spoke were "natural astronomic cycles of singular accuracy and beauty, unknown to mankind until discovered by means of these very prophecies". The appointed time had come. The mystery of the last days was about to be revealed.

Once the code was broken it was relatively easy for Henry to establish that biblical time was often measured in lunar, not solar years like the western calendar. The key had been two apparently contradictory figures at the end of the book of Daniel. Once Henry realised that the difference between the two was the difference between 1260 solar and lunar years, all sorts of calculations became possible. Many scholars of prophecy had long since realised that a biblical "day" symbolised a year, that "a week" meant a multiple of seven, but it was only when Henry calculated Daniel's figure for the end times, the "week of years" or "seven times", in lunar years that he arrived at a figure of 2520 years, twice de Cheseaux's 1260.

There was no doubt in Henry's mind that the "end times" of the apocalyptic books was the era Christ called "The times of the Gentiles". It was the era "of Jewish degradation and dispersion", dating from the sacking of Jerusalem and the destruction of the Temple. If it was to last a period of approximately 2520 years, that was highly significant for the immediate generations, for it was fast running out.

But Henry Grattan was no crank trying to guess the end of the world or the second coming of Christ. What he said was that just as there are cycles in nature which reveal God's careful planning, so there are cycles in history which demonstrate his total control. Exact dates were out of the question, but there were signs, certain indications and very definite patterns for those who chose to see them. For example both apocalyptic books divided the end times into two periods of three and a half times de Cheseaux's 1260 years. Daniel, in his futuristic vision, saw the world controlled for "a time, two times and a half a time", by four terrible beasts. According to Henry and many earlier theologians, these beasts, which would dominate the first half of the end times, were the four great pagan empires of antiquity, Babylon, Persia, Greece and Rome. From the accession of Nabonassar, the first king of Babylon, to the fall of Romulus Augustus, last emperor of Rome, there elapsed an interval of exactly 1260 lunar years.

Daniel also said that the fourth beast had ten horns and once they were destroyed the "beast" would produce another, very different from the last. This last, sprouting from the head of Rome, was believed to be the political power of the Vatican. From the moment it began to control European history to its startling demise, which Henry and Fanny witnessed in 1870, was another period of 1260 years. This could only mean that 1870 had been a vital turning point in world history. The great "seven times", the cycle of the "times of the Gentiles", was slowly drawing to a close.

If this were so, Henry said, then the main implication was that the time of Jewish degradation must soon be over. The Jewish people would return to their homeland. That had never been even a vague possibility until the present time. For hundreds of years Palestine had been controlled by the all-powerful Ottoman Empire. No one had managed to loosen its stranglehold. But by the 1870s it had been weakened to such an extent that a power vacuum was left in the Middle East, involving the major European countries in a series of political games known as the "Eastern Question". The cycle of 1260 years of Muslim occupation of the holy city of Jerusalem would soon be complete.

Henry was by no means the only one who thought that the solution to the "Eastern Question" was a Jewish restoration. Lord Shaftesbury and others had long since said so. Even George Eliot in her novel *Daniel Deronda* maintained that "The regeneration of the Jewish people is the great divine mystery of world history." It was the Jewish people themselves who appeared uninterested, living in relative tranquillity throughout the Diaspora, until one fateful day. On March 1st, 1881 Tsar Alexander II was assassinated. The Jews became the scapegoats. Jewish villages were rased to the ground. The pogroms had begun and Jewish refugees in their thousands fled across eastern Europe, some to Palestine, many to the East End of London. Only then did Henry Grattan's expectations take on an immediate significance, and even he would not live to see their fulfilment.

At the back of *The Approaching End of the Age* were Henry's meticulous astronomical and historical charts, which even Fanny, in her popular précis of the book, had to admit had deterred some from reading it. But, she said, though it appeared daunting, they showed how every important world event fitted into an astronomical cycle in a way that "Any person of ordinary education and intelligence, reading it with attention will find no difficulty whatever in understanding and following its statements." Now, she concluded, with undisguised triumph, the Christian student had found "a new weapon wherewith to defend the Book of God against the oppositions of science falsely so called – a weapon with which, indeed, he may assume the aggressive, and challenge opposers to account for a fact which nothing but the Divine inspiration of the Bible can account for."

While Henry and Fanny were absorbed in the interest stirred by Henry's book and the demands of running a conglomerate of colleges and mission halls, Minnie went on brooding. Nothing amused her. She refused to socialise. She seemed old before her time and began to complain of pain in her back. Part of each day was spent lying on a spinal board on a couch between the windows of the empty schoolroom, filled with so many aching memories. The combination of physical and emotional pain was almost too much for her to bear. If only God would let her die. Since her little ones could not come back to her, she would go to them. Seriously concerned at last that her daughter was becoming morbid, Fanny insisted that she should socialise a little and accept a kind invitation to visit her Guinness cousins in the West End.

Although Edward Cecil Guinness was now head of the brewery, Sir Arthur Ernest was the undisputed head of the family. He and Lady Olive were shocked and saddened by the death of their cousin's two little girls. The two families had stayed in touch, but they had little in common and it was only now that Lady Olive felt she might be of some service to the four remaining children. Childless herself, and given to aristocratic, charitable gestures she felt her poor cousins were a worthy object of her attentions. After all, from their Fitzgerald mother, the true blue blood of Irish nobility flowed through their veins. How could Fanny bring them up in the dreadful East End?

Olive was very taken with the children. Harry had dash and character. Minnie was tall and slender, pretty in a quiet, demure, appropriate sort of way, like a little kitten needing to be coaxed. Lucy's facial features were too strong to create an impression of beauty, but she had another quality altogether. When she sat at the piano and played her face became radiant, her large eyes iridescent like two deep, dark pools in her pale face. Lady Olive was captivated. She was too keen a connoisseur of the arts not to recognise musical brilliance when she found it.

The children were introduced to Sir Arthur's brother Edward Cecil and his wife. Dodo agreed with her sister-in-law, that the young cousins ought to be groomed, polished and introduced to the right people. Though well-meaning she was not naturally maternal. The birth of her first son in 1874 at Berkeley Square was noted in her diary in an offhand manner: "Baby born at quarter to six. Boy. Christened Edward Cecil Lee Rupert at Ascot 30th April".[2] Two more boys followed, Arthur Ernest in 1876 and the new baby, Walter Edward, the future Lord Moyne, in March 1880. Her own children were obviously far too young for their teenage Grattan cousins. Minnie would have liked to have played with the children, but Adelaide insisted they needed company their own age. It so happened that her full cousin, Richard Seymour Guinness, had recently moved to London to expand the Guinness Mahon banking business. He had taken up residence in St George's Square, and established himself at the City Carlton Club in St Swithin's Lane where he carried on business without a clerk or account books. Richard Seymour had ten children, several of whom were in their teenage years. And so the Grattan and Rundell banking branches of the family were introduced for the first time, went on boating expeditions and played tennis together throughout the summer.

The one social invitation Harry and Minnie continually declined, unlike their Rundell cousins, was to the many magnificent balls arranged by Edward and Adelaide. Not to be invited was regarded as a social slight in London society and Dodo hated leaving anybody out. A society journal described her as a curious contrast of the "Puritan and the Plutocrat".[3] She was small and slight, with dark hair drawn neatly back. She dressed simply and spoke in a low voice. She was very devout and strongly high church. Everyone was impressed by her quiet, dignified manner. She was kind, yet distant, for there was something about her which was very much the "grande dame". Edward Cecil was more gregarious. Lively and witty, small in height, though muscular, with strong, even features, he possessed a charm which put his guests at ease. Small wonder the couple had become popular company for the Prince of Wales.

All of their homes were luxurious but when Dodo threw a ball the decorations were breathtaking. She liked to weave a world of fantasy and magic around her guests. Sometimes her themes were oriental, at other times they were simply exotic. Money was no object. Augustus J. C. Hare, a professional socialite who one day shocked polite Victorian society by publishing his diary, which contained startling revelations about their intimate lives, noted on June 18th, 1879: "In the evening I was with the Prince at Mrs E. Guinness' ball, on which £6000 are said to have been wasted. It was a perfect fairy-land, ice pillars up to the ceiling, an avenue of palms, a veil of stephanotis from the staircase, and you pushed your way through a brake of papyrus to the cloakroom."[4] But none of the Grattan Guinness children ever beheld the sight. Their evangelical piety forbade dancing.

Both Dodo and Olive were rather austere, frightening figures, but the children warmed at once to their kindly uncles, particularly the gentlemanly Sir Arthur, who seemed to have a permanent twinkle in his eye, except when he was discussing Irish politics with their father. Harry, Minnie, and Lucy had all grown up with a strong sense of their Irish identity, but it was Sir Arthur, with his determined opposition to the increasingly violent demands for Home Rule, who rekindled their interest in the political situation there and taught them to mistrust the leader of the Land League and instigator of all trouble, Charles Stewart Parnell.

Since his retirement from brewing Sir Arthur had devoted his life to munificent spending. Like his father and grandfather he chose his projects carefully and sensibly for their long-term benefits to the people of Ireland. He financed the rebuilding of Archbishop Marsh's library in Dublin and the Coombe lying-in hospital. But the gift which earned him gratitude in Dublin in spite of the unpopularity of his politics, was the lovely St Stephen's Green Park. From local householders he bought the twenty-two acres of land overlooked by the town house where he and Edward Cecil had grown up. The land had always been a private park, fenced off from the public. He had it landscaped with walks, flower-beds and an ornamental lake, then presented it to the city. In 1880, in gratitude for his many services, he was created Lord Ardilaun of Ashford, the first Guinness peer. He had proved that a confirmed Unionist could still serve his country. Even his outspoken political stance earned him a grudging respect from the Nationalists. After all if it was popularity he craved he could have disguised his views. But like his grandfather, the second Arthur, integrity would not allow him to please any except his own conscience.

The Ardilauns so established themselves as the arbiters of elegance and good taste that when any of the rest of the family committed a social gaffe, they would exclaim with mock horror, "What would the Ardilauns say?"[5] Lady Olive continued her attempts to polish the Grattan children and tried to persuade Fanny to let her present them at Court. Fanny referred her back to the children. In this, as in most other matters, the ultimate decision was theirs. She would not stand in their way. Unlike many Victorian parents, she and Henry did not believe in burdening their children with endless restrictions. Some were inherent within their religious tradition, like the prohibition on dancing, but parents could be too extreme:

It is folly continually to harass children with prohibitions [Henry preached]. There are parents who, in their desire to keep their children right are perpetually forbidding this and that. The word most commonly on the lips of those who have to do with children is DON'T . . . They are constantly repressing, forbidding, prohibiting. Now there is another, far better, more useful word – that is DO.

There is a certain irony about Henry's words in the light of the fact that one of his respected friends, a referee and committee member of the Institute, was a naturalist by the name of Philip Henry Gosse, a fervent member of the Brethren, had married late. His wife had died leaving him with a young son, Edmund. He had no idea how to care for the child and certainly never followed Henry's advice, for years later, in a classic book called *Father and Son*, which shocked devout Edwardian society, Edmund Gosse described in meticulous, heart-rending detail the suffocating repressiveness of his religious upbringing.

As far as the Grattan children were concerned Lady Olive's offer did not necessitate any serious consideration. Harry had just won a much-coveted scholarship to the London Hospital to study medicine. Lucy was only fifteen and about to go to boarding-school for the first time. Minnie felt painfully out of her depth in such company. She was only too aware of the lifestyle of her wealthy cousins, shooting parties on their estates, the Dublin horse show, the Punchestown Races and all the other leading events in the Irish social calendar, London for the season, Cowes, Scotland. It was another world, one which she dismissed with her usual earnestness as "an unsatisfying round of amusements". The death of Phoebe and Agnes had cast a gloom over her which had made her more sensitive than ever to the pain and sorrow of the poverty-ridden East End. She felt it her lot to carry that pain, and alleviate it in some small way if she could. Daydreaming of meeting Queen Victoria and the Prince and Princess of Wales was one thing, the reality another. The Court was no place for her. She had begun to give classes to factory girls, teaching them to read and write. That was where she belonged, where she felt really useful. "Society" by comparison was brash and superficial.

Lady Olive and her sister-in-law, inevitably targets for sycophantic poor relatives and friends demanding money and introductions, must have been amazed by their rejection. Yet Minnie had one satisfaction. Looking back at those days in years to come, she would tell the younger generations with a twinkle in her eye that she could have "come out", and been quite a society belle, had she wanted.

Howard Taylor entered the London Hospital College at the same time as Harry. It was the place to study medicine. Sir Frederick Treves held the chair and he was one of the foremost physicians of his time. In later years his reputation was established as the kindly doctor who gave sanctuary to London's famous "elephant man", protecting him from exploitation and the lurid fascination of the British public. Harry and Howard felt privileged to have the opportunity to sit at his feet.

While Howard was a gentle, rather retiring young man, Harry dazzled with his enormous charm and *joie de vivre*. He was a born leader, tall, athletic and handsome, with stunning blue eyes and a hearty, ringing laugh. He seemed to radiate vigorous physical and moral health. His energy was boundless. He founded the Hospital Athletic Club and on June 10th, 1881 at the Crystal Palace, cheered on by Minnie and a huge crowd of fellow students, secured the world record for slow bicycling on the old high bicycle then in fashion, which was almost impossible to ride other than at full speed. Cycling was to remain an abiding passion for the rest of his life.

As far as he was concerned the most important incident of his college career occurred on the first day. In an effort to be friendly a fellow student invited him to the Debating Society, known as the Clinical Society.

"When is it?" Harry asked.

"Tonight, and we like to get new men," the student said, then added, "You needn't be a bit afraid – there is nothing religious about it. In fact one of our rules is that no one is allowed to allude to a religious thing."

Harry was amused at the student's attempts to reassure him and wondered how he would have reacted had he known his background. At a bit of a loose end as most freshers are, he decided to go to the debate. Sir Frederick Treves himself was in the chair. The subject was some medical matter about which Harry as yet knew nothing. He understood little of what was said until one of the speakers for no apparent reason suddenly became offensive about Jesus Christ. "I wondered what ought to be done," Harry said, "I think, as far as I know, that my brain had not made up its mind, but my legs had automatically made up their mind, and I found myself standing on my feet."

As he was standing up, Harry realised everyone was waiting for him to speak, so he took a deep breath and said, "Mr President and gentlemen, I do not know whether you would like a First Year man to speak."

"Hear, hear," they said, "we shall be glad to hear you."

"Well," Harry said, "I may be out of order, but I was informed when I came up here by the gentleman who invited me, that it is against the laws of your society to allude to religious matters. Is that so?"

"Quite right."

"If that be so, Mr President – if we be not allowed to allude to religious matters, then I beg to protest against the words of the gentleman who has just sat down. He has spoken against one who is my Lord, my Saviour, my King, in a way that has made my blood boil and I beg to protest against it."

Harry sat down and silence fell. He waited for the hisses, jeers and laughter, then to his astonishment there came a thunder of applause.

As he was leaving the hall he felt a hand on his shoulder. He turned and there with his hand stretched out to him was Sir Frederick Treves. He asked him his name then said, "Now, look here, Guinness, I'm glad to know you. You come back to these meetings, and if ever a man does what that man did tonight, you do exactly what you did. I'm very glad to meet you."

From that day on Treves became one of Harry's personal friends and Harry had learnt a lesson he never forgot. What were all his sporting achievements, his popularity and physical prowess if he had no moral fibre? A real man would stand up for what he believed, would "run his flag up to the masthead", as Harry called it.

In any free moments left after his medical duties and sporting activities Harry rushed home to Harley College to help in whatever way he could. The population of the East End was growing all the time, spreading rapidly out from Bow, north, south and east, to Hackney, Limehouse and Stratford. What few support agencies there were could not keep pace with the expansion. There was as yet no "Factory Helper's Union", no amusement or entertainment other than the few gin palaces, no schools or educational facilities other than the few Ragged Schools set up by charities and mission halls for small children. But there was always something happening in or around Harley College: night schools of one kind or another, lantern lectures on winter evenings for women and children, garden parties in the grounds on summer afternoons for cabmen, policemen and their families. Harry was in great demand as an entertainer. He could play the piano and the cornet, sing, organise games, and do a very passable ventriloquist and conjuring act. And when he was not providing a cabaret he ran his own men's evening class, teaching them to read and write.

Howard Taylor often went home with him, partly to help, partly to be near Minnie. He was a quiet, fair-haired young man of medium height, with a small fair moustache and striking blue eyes. His manner made him a favourite with Henry and Fanny,

and the family servants, who did their best to support his cause.
Despite her painful back, Minnie spent hours out riding on her own.
Howard would find some excuse to turn up and usually managed to
discover from the maids which direction she had taken, so that he
could meet her "accidentally" as she was riding home. But Minnie
took no notice of him. She was totally absorbed in her evening classes
for the factory girls. The classes were her way of sublimating her grief
for her two little sisters.

A night school had been Fanny's vision from the moment she
moved to Bow. A few social pioneers in the East End, like the
Rev. Samuel Barnett who set up the Toynbee Hall, believed in the
ability of education and culture to satisfy the mind and broaden the
horizons. Fanny was one of them. She and her children would watch
from the schoolroom window as the girls poured out of Bryant and
May's at six or seven o'clock in the evening, dressed in long dark
skirts, hugging their dark shawls around their shoulders, the only
splash of colour the plumage in their hats, so that they looked for
all the world "like birds let loose from the cage". Their bodies
may well have been tired, but their minds were active, hungering
for interest and amusement, anything to deaden the monotony of
the day's work, which would start again at six in the morning.
"Their often wretched homes afford nothing," Fanny wrote to
their financial supporters. She had just bought the little chapel in
Bow, down the road from Harley House and right next to Bryant
and May's. She had recognised its potential, but it was in desperate
need of renovation. "They cannot get a country walk, or a stroll on
the sea-shore; they are shut up to crowded, noisy streets, all aglow
with gin-palaces, and thronged with young men who are only too
glad to take them into these hell-traps, or into the penny gaffs and
dancing-saloons, or even to the cheap theatres." Small wonder, she
went on, that so many are led astray or end up on the streets. It was
futile for "respectable" people to suggest they should go to chapel or
to the mission hall. Why should they be so inclined? A link between
the two totally opposing worlds was called for, something "partaking
more of the nature of recreation and rest".

For several years the children had been running down to the gate
of Harley House at factory closing time to invite some of the girls
in for a cosy time round the fire, drinking tea, listening to a book,
or making toffee. By December 1876 the renovation of the chapel,
called Harley Hall, was complete. The old pepper-box pulpit was
replaced with a pretty little platform, the pews thrown open and
lowered, and the schoolroom brightly painted and fitted out with
schoolboard-desks, forms and cupboards and "apparatus for giving
tea"; bearing in mind that the girls would be coming from work.
By way of invitation a letter was distributed among the girls

offering them classes to help them become useful and sensible mothers and wives. As well as lessons in reading and writing, there would be dressmaking, book-keeping and music. As long as they behaved nicely, were quiet, gentle and polite, they might laugh, talk and ask questions, for, "We quite understand that what you want, after a hard day's work, is a pleasant evening, 'a good time' (as the girls in America say), and that is what we will try and give you." There was no fee. All they had to do to become a member of the Working Girls' Self-Improvement Association was to report to Harley Hall on a Tuesday evening.

From the first Harley Hall was packed to capacity. Two evenings a week was quite obviously insufficient to cope with the demand, but it was not until Minnie started to help Mrs Cole, the teacher, that they managed to hold the class every night of the week. By 1880 Harley Hall had become too small, and the classes were moved into the brand new Berger Hall, called after one of the Institute's most generous patrons.

The classes were a revelation to Minnie. Growing up in the East End she thought she knew the people, but she soon discovered how much she still had to learn. The evening began at six or seven with tea and bread and butter, which cost a penny, then the girls settled down at their desks to learn to write. One of Minnie's first pupils was Matilda, a fourteen-year-old from Bryant and May's match factory. The girl who sat next to Matilda already knew how to write and constantly distracted her.

One day Matilda arrived at the class with a black eye which she tried in vain to hide.

"Why, what's the matter, Matilda?" Minnie asked her.

"I knocked it," she said, without looking up.

"It's a lie, Miss Guinness," her neighbour shouted. "Her father give 'er it."

Minnie asked her to come out and sat with her for some time, listening appalled to details of the girl's home life.

An admiring Matilda turned up at Minnie's Sunday afternoon Bible class, which she proceeded to disrupt completely, winking at her friends and making faces behind Minnie's back.

"Close your Bible, Matilda," Minnie commanded.

Matilda did as she was told, but also decided to make a quick get-away at the end of the class. She had heard how obstreperous members were invited to take a walk round the gardens of Harley House, where Miss Guinness would pick them a buttonhole and "get us a bit civilised". She slipped downstairs when she thought the teacher was not looking, and was amazed to find Minnie waiting for her in the street. So Matilda ended up taking the inevitable turn around the garden. Minnie asked her why she had been so difficult.

"Well, you know, Miss, that I can't read," Matilda said.

"I am sorry, Matilda," Minnie said, "I hadn't thought of that."

By way of apology she leant forward to kiss Matilda on the cheek, but the girl shrank back.

"Why do you draw yourself away?" Minnie asked.

"Because I thought you were going to hit me or something," Matilda said. No one had ever kissed her before.

The incident left a deep impression on Minnie and she asked Matilda if she would like to go into service in the country.

"No one would have me," Matilda said.

Minnie insisted she should ask her mother's permission, though Matilda said it was not necessary, she knew already what she would say.

"She said I could go to hell for all she cared," Matilda reported a few days later.

"Well you can tell her that's just where you're not going," Minnie replied.

So Matilda and two of her friends were sent to an acquaintance of the Guinnesses, who had a lovely home in the country and a large heart.

The classes were by no means Minnie's only commitment. To free her mother, who was increasingly absorbed in stirring up support for the Congo Mission, Minnie took over the domestic reins of Harley House and found herself acting as hostess to a number of important, influential guests. The "society" which she had declined began to come to her. Lord Shaftesbury was a regular visitor. If the weather was fine he loved to sit out in the rambling garden, on the bench beneath the beloved old pear tree, sharing his hopes and plans for the poor with Fanny and Henry. Lord Polwarth, a member of the Congo Committee, would stay for a few days whenever he came to London from his stately home on the Tweed. Other visitors included Lord Radstock, Lady Louisa Asburton and Dr Karl Baedeker, the celebrated traveller and writer. Charles Spurgeon brought the students of his Pastor's College over for an athletics competition with the Harley men. Harry was in his element.

In December 1880 Spurgeon's College returned the invitation and the Harley men went there for a pre-Christmas dinner. Lucy noted in her diary with great glee that Mr Spurgeon had stipulated that Mama should be the only female member of the Harley party, but Mama, who was not daunted by anyone, even the most famous preacher in England, took five female friends with her including her two daughters. Never in her life, Lucy claimed, had she heard such a deafening noise as the sound of all those young men eating and talking!

There was never any privacy for the Guinnesses at Harley, but then privacy was not a Victorian expectation. All sorts of strange people from all over the world were made welcome by Fanny and the children never knew who they might find in their beds, but at least they were together and that made home a haven. That Christmas, the last before Gershom was sent to school, Lucy and Minnie went with their parents to Whiteley's Universal Emporium, the first department store in London, to do their Christmas shopping. They emerged laden with presents, beautifully wrapped and tied up with ribbon. The girls decided to paint their own cards. On Christmas Day "after tea, Papa brought down some of his experiments, microscopes and electric machines, besides lots of others . . . It was great fun watching some of the students trying to get a sixpence out of the water, of course none of them could." Harry then amused everyone with his conjuring tricks, Lucy organised charades and Henry Grattan read from Byron, Cowper and Milton. An almost-perfect day was spoiled only because darling Mother was "in bed all day with a very bad headache, brought on by riding in an omnibus".[6]

3

I think this diary must be a very stupid one . . . I wonder how most people write their diaries, not like mine I am sure. Gracie's is the only one I ever saw, and that was all like prayers and pieces of sermons, and holy thoughts. Mine is not like that at all, because I am very afraid of anyones seeing it. Harry for instance!! How terribly fearful that would be.

Lucy's diaries, which she began to write in 1880 when she was fifteen, are an extraordinary record of the emotional development of a young girl, through adolescence into maturity. Gifted artistically in every way, her writing is expressive and imaginative, and her observations make a fascinating commentary on the age in which she lived. Yet her feelings are strangely contemporary. For a teenager she was uncannily perceptive, though often self-indulgent. For someone brought up in a Victorian, religious environment, there is a distinct lack of piety. Her "dy", as she started to address it, was a friend. To be less than real would be to betray a friendship.

The first diary was a record of her time at boarding-school in Hastings, though there was much more to report when she was at home, where the situation in Ireland was a constant topic of conversation and concern. At school no one showed any interest.

January 30th, 1881. Ever since I came away I have not heard anything about the disturbed state of Ireland; no one seems to

know anything about it here, Miss Byam did not even know what
Boycotting meant!!!

It was indeed amazing that Miss Byam did not know what boycotting
was, as it was headline news in all the papers. The foundation of the
practice was laid at Ennis in September 1880 in a historic speech
which Parnell delivered to his supporters. The Land League, of
which he was the leader, had been campaigning vigorously for
radical reforms which would protect tenant farmers from being
evicted from their land without any compensation. The economic
climate in Ireland had been poor for some months and tenants
often fell into arrears with their rents through no fault of their
own. Eviction meant utter destitution. Pressure must be brought
on the government to introduce far-reaching reforms. "Depend on
it," Parnell said to the crowd, "the measure of the land bill of the
next session, will be the measure of your activity and energy this
winter." What he suggested was this:

> When a man takes a farm from which another has been evicted
> you must shun him on the roadside when you meet him, you
> must shun him on the streets of the town, you must shun him in
> the shop, you must shun him in the fair green and in the market
> place, and even in the place of worship. By leaving him severely
> alone, by putting him into a moral convent, by isolating him from
> the rest of his countrymen as if he were a leper of old, you must
> show him your detestation of the crime he has committed.[7]

The first victim of such a policy was not an Irish farmer at all, but
an English land agent called Captain Boycott. The plan was more
effective than Parnell could have dreamed. Boycott's ostracism was
total. His labourers refused to harvest his crops, his blacksmith and
laundress refused to shoe his horse or do his washing, his servants
walked out, his mail was not delivered, the shops would not serve
him and wherever he went he was booed and jeered.

For a while the world was ignorant of his plight, but in October
1880 the story broke in the London *Daily News*. Righteous British
citizens were indignant and made Boycott their cause, but too late;
he was forced out of Ireland. The Irish peasants had discovered a
passive weapon, and they began to use it freely. All over Ireland
tenants rose up against their landlords, refusing to harvest their
crops, ship their cattle or buy their goods, and the forces of law
and order were helpless. Despite his position and popularity Lord
Ardilaun was at risk. Lucy's diary continues:

> I wonder really what has happened there since I left home, and
> how Sir Arthur has been, and if his tenants have risen against

him as they were expected to do; and if Parnell is imprisoned or punished in any way for rousing the people as he has, but no one can tell me.

Papa is coming down soon to take some meetings, one on prophecy and some on the Congo; I wish he would come down soon and then I will ask him all these things and he will tell me, because he always knows.

Parnell was imprisoned for a time, but there were no charges and he was released in order to take his seat in the House of Commons. Nor did Lord Ardilaun's tenants rise against him. It would have been strange if they had, because he was by no means a hard landlord. On the contrary he was one of the few enlightened landlords in the country, treating his tenants well. Evictions were unnecessary as he had the means to provide plenty of work for them to do. His schemes of vast afforestation brought prosperity to one of the poorest and most beautiful parts of Connemara. He stimulated the tourist industry there by introducing a steamer service on Lough Corrib between the large, baronial-style castle he had built at Ashford, and Galway City.

Lucy was no doubt relieved to hear that all was well with her uncle, but school continued to be a trial. She was often homesick and very conscious of not being pretty, though, when she was inundated with presents on her birthday, even she had to admit, "I allmost think that it isn't allways the pretty people who are liked the most."

The redeeming feature was the chance to improve her music, and shine before her teachers, fellow-pupils and their parents in the end of term concert. She was not so modest that she could not see, "though it is very horrid of me to say so, that I could beat any of the girls at this school". Her assessment was gratified when, at the end of her first term, she was invited to play two pieces in the concert instead of the usual one, replacing her cousins Edith and Dora Fookes, whose duet was not good enough to inflict on the public. The applause rang in her ears for days, silenced only when she was awarded the drawing prize, which she felt she did not deserve, and denied the music prize, which she knew she did. To make things worse Julia won it. Julia, "who plays like a machine". Life was not fair.

When she went back to Hastings in January 1881, she noted, "I shall make them give me the music prize which I deserved last time." As it happened it was a bitterly cold winter and for several weeks the school was so cold that Lucy's fingers were too numb to perform. But spring eventually came and with it the exciting news that Fanny had agreed to her coming home for a few days for Florrie Charlesworth's wedding. When Florrie got engaged to her father's curate, Mama had said that Florrie was far too young for such a thing, but Lucy wrote: "She is only a little older than Minnie and I should laugh if Minnie were engaged." Ten years later, in a red pen, Lucy added the following sentence to her diary: "Minnie is engaged nowadays, and I don't laugh, but cry."

The wedding almost lived up to Lucy's dreams. It was a great occasion. The streets of poverty-stricken Limehouse were lined with cheering crowds, all anxious to catch a glimpse of the vicar's daughter. The church was packed. Florrie looked beautiful: "The one and only thing that spoiled her was that she was laced most dreadfully tightly, which made her look like a doll. She is short and the tight-lacing did not at all become her figure which was never slight."

The wedding breakfast was disappointing. Lucy, just awakening to the charms of the opposite sex, was escorted in by a certain Sidney Beddome, who turned out to be desperately dull. "He asked me amongst other things if I went to Belstead. It seems to be the correct thing for all young ladies to do in their part of the world!" Across the table Sidney's sister had Harry as her partner and from her laughter was evidently having a great deal more fun. As far as Minnie and Lucy were concerned any potential suitor must at least have the charms of their much-admired elder brother. Their escorts would always have a great deal to live up to.

Henry and Fanny had chosen the few days that Lucy was at home for yet another great occasion, the launching of the first steamer for the Congo. It was to accompany M'Call's expedition, in the faith that he would somehow manage to climb the 230 miles of treacherous cataracts in the lower Congo and reach Stanley Pool. From there on was a thousand miles of navigable river into the heart of Africa. A steamer would be vital, if only they could get there. No one had managed it so far. Craven's party had been in Africa for two years and were still struggling in appalling conditions in the lower Congo region. But nothing could dampen the excitement and enthusiasm of the Harley students, most of it aroused by Fanny.

On March 8th a huge crowd gathered for the launching ceremony at Forrest's shipbuilding yard. Back at Harley there had been arguments over the naming of the boat. Some students, who were vociferous in their feelings, wanted it to be called the *Fanny Guinness*, but Henry felt the *Livingstone* was more appropriate. It was Minnie who decided things and knowing her father's wishes, her decision was inevitable:

Minnie and I stood up on a sort of wooden stand and Minnie named the boat by saying with a loud voice, "God speed the

Livingstone!" then there were great cheers and the boat was pushed into the water. This part of the performance was rather ignominious because the tide was too low for her to slide off gracefully in the correct manner and it took rather a long time to shove her into the water.

A great cheer went up as Fanny got on board, but she was terrified and would have climbed straight off when they put up the sails if her hardy, seafaring husband had let her. "There was really nothing to be frightened at," Lucy noted, "because there was not wind enough to make her go along, nor would there have been room amongst the torpedoes, barges, boats, steam-launches and cutters in process of construction that filled the cutting where we were."

Two days later Lucy and Minnie accompanied their father and several of the students for a trial run of the *Livingstone* up the river Lea into several rather dangerous and exciting locks. There were so many low bridges and other vessels that artful manoeuvring was required and Henry Grattan commented, "If they can steer on this crowded and narrow river they can steer on the Congo."

It was at this point that a gentleman called Murray seemed to enter Lucy's life. Just before she went back to school he took her to the Saturday evening concert at the Bow and Bromley. "It was nice indeed!" she commented in her diary, "I like concerts." In another red-pen addendum made ten years later, she wrote, "And nice boys! I meant to write in, I remember, but never had the pluck till now."

Back at Hastings Lucy's first letter from her mother was sadder than usual.

March 28th. Harley House
My darling child
You will I am sure have remembered today the sorrowful events of this day two years ago.

Hour by hour as it has passed they have been present to me! It is now 5 p.m. – just the time I crept up to the schoolroom for my last sad watch by our precious little Agnes' couch!

God be praised they can never die again, and that the time of our separation grows shorter day by day! Oh the joy of meeting them once more! The exquisite joy of again holding them in my arms and hearing their sweet voices call me "Mother".

You are spared to me my darling child, the only one out of the pretty little trio constantly before me in this room! God preserve and bless you and spare you still if he so pleases.

As she studied the photograph of the three little girls which she kept in front of her on her desk, Fanny had just cause for concern. Her children were not always as strong as she would have wished. Lucy was often frail with mysterious complaints. Adolescence was a trial to her. She often felt too lethargic to study. Gershom was having constant trouble with his tonsils and the doctor threatened to remove them. It was a barbaric piece of surgery at the time, occasionally fatal and usually performed on the kitchen table. Fortunately he was granted a reprieve at the last moment. Minnie, the strongest of her children apart from the spartan Harry, suddenly acquired a septic finger and had to have it lanced. She fainted and in retrospect felt quite proud of herself. At least she received some of the attention for a while.

In the summer of 1881 Lucy came home from Hastings for good, still without the coveted music prize, but with the satisfaction of having caused quite a stir once again at the end of term concert. The applause made her purr with pleasure: "I never played better in my life which is I think saying a good deal for me. I am afraid what I write in this journal sounds vain, but it is all strictly true."

Lady Olive Guinness managed to persuade Fanny that a finishing school abroad would be the ideal experience for her youngest daughter. It would broaden her horizons, polish her, give her a good command of a foreign language, and, most important, give her the opportunity to study the piano with a better class of music teacher. Fanny had her hesitations, but could see the wisdom of it none the less. It was Lucy herself who finally convinced her, though Lucy was not above having second thoughts in the endless weeks of waiting, particularly when she realised that she would be away from home at Christmas.

How dreadful to think of going so far from home, and for such a long time too . . . I suppose everyone will be changed when I come back again, perhaps Harry will have a beard! What a salubrious thought! . . . Perhaps too I shall have an illness and die before I come back, though that doesn't seem very likely; and then someone might read this journal, just fancy how dreadful – I could not bear anyone to read all these things. I don't think they could understand like I do, and it would seem different to them.

Just before she left, the news reached England of the death of Mary Richards, the first woman missionary on the Congo. Recently married, she was buried by her husband. Mary had spent a lot of time at Harley House and had seemed like one of the family. She had married one of the students. Lucy was devastated by her death. It drove home the inescapable reality than anyone choosing to go to the Congo was throwing away their life. It puzzled her that anyone could want to do such a thing. In her diary, beside a picture of Mary Richards' grave, she wrote simply, "How could M'Call?"

4

The Miss Ellerbys' Finishing School for Young Ladies was situated on the top two floors of an imposing six-storey building in the elegant Boulevard Malesherbes. Henry Grattan Guinness delivered his youngest daughter there at the end of December 1881.

It was a pale creature the Miss Ellerbys welcomed and they must have assumed that there was much "finishing" to be done. Lucy, always violently ill in anything which moved, had been so sea-sick on the crossing that she could still barely stand without wobbling. All had been wonderful at first. It was a real adventure sitting on the deck with dear Papa all to herself, watching the "silver moon rise up from behind a dark cloud, making a silvery pathway across the blue, rippling water". Then suddenly she noticed that in the light of the moon, some of the passengers looked decidedly pale:

> Were they moonstruck, I wondered, that they got up so suddenly some of them and disappeared below? If so perhaps I was moon-struck too . . . for I was obliged to follow somewhat hurriedly in their wake. Oh wretched me! I can never remember being in a more pitiable state than I was in those hours, or years as they seemed to me.

By the time the boat docked at Boulogne Lucy could barely walk or speak. Henry Grattan almost carried her into the nearest restaurant where, to his daughter's disgust, he ate a hearty meal and drank coffee. A sailor to the marrow, he insisted it had been a quiet crossing. "How could he?"

Although Lucy fell in love with Paris, its pretty shops, so neat and attractive, demonstrating admirable "French taste and tact", the school was disappointingly dreary. Its elegant exterior masked a penny-pinching drabness and a rigid regimentation which lacked real warmth and imagination. Christmas Day was deadly dull. No letters from home were to be opened before the evening. Lucy waited in an agony of anticipation and when she finally unwrapped her one and only parcel, discovered that the charming china flower brooch had been smashed to pieces in the post. The pretty leaves were still intact and she wore it none the less. Minnie's hilarious letter made up for everything, but Lucy stifled her laughter. Young ladies did not laugh out loud. The warning pokes in the back from her neighbours reminded her that they did not wish to be disciplined on account of her, not today of all days!

It was being allowed one candle in every five days which Lucy found the hardest to bear. How could she read at night, or write in her diary? She became a scavenger of "stumps", hiding them in her neighbours' washing-stand drawers without their knowing. They scoffed at her for keeping a diary and wanted to know her secrets, so she waited until they were asleep then wrote by the light of a last spluttering piece of wax:

January 1st, 1882. How strange it seems to put 1882 as date, here, for the first time in my diary . . . How very funny it would be to put 2000 [she meant 1900] and something on one's letters! I wonder very much whether the world will last so long – I shouldn't think so – let me see how old I should be then – about 48! I can't imagine myself 48! What should I ever be like? Frightfully ugly and fat – I should think, with a nose something like Miss Ellaby's only worse, a great deal worse, I daresay, so there!

Murray was still very much on the horizon. He had asked her to write to him, and she did, wondering whether Papa would think it "inadvertent". Yet despite his attentions, and particularly in Paris, where she felt surrounded by so many chic and pretty girls, Lucy began to despair of her appearance. The opposite sex was increasingly enticing and she very much wanted to please. In her dreams she charmed and dazzled, but like many teenagers she felt unattractive and gauche. This was the portrait she painted of herself, as she thought others saw her:

A little, pale, slight, thin, girl, apparently about 14 years of age – with a great quantity of untidy, curly, hair, tied behind and straggling short and loose round a pale, oval face, whose chief default is that its features are much too large – big, greyish, eyes; frightful teeth which happily are not much to be seen – a high white forehead – ugly pale mouth – and a nose!! of which the less said the better . . . she plays the violin a little, the piano a good deal, though not in a satisfactory fashion – draws and paints pretty well seeing she had never learned till she came to Paris last December, and is generally "good all round". She is dressed in a very neglected manner being by far too unobservant to see that her garments are in need of mending, until one of the girls tells her of the stringless shoe & holey stocking when she is very much surprised & makes all sorts of good resolutions to mend her ways, takes a fit of darning and then forgets again . . .

She is very sensitive and rather quiet than otherwise as she does not find it very easy to talk with her elders & betters in French.

She is, I believe, rather selfish, though this quality generally arises more from thoughtless, dreamy ways, than anything else.

For Lucy the months in Paris represented that strange adolescent no man's land between childhood and maturity when the former slips sadly out of our grasp and the latter seems too frightening a substitute. Her "bodily troubles" caused her some embarrassment. Womanhood beckoned and repelled.

Oh! What do you, do you think, dear old diary! Florrie has got a little baby!!!!! A baby! . . . A BABY!! A little daughter just ten days old! Florrie too? Who used to do lessons with Minnie and me only yesterday as it seems! though I suppose it must be almost 8 years ago now!! How dreadfully old I must be getting! How happy Florrie must be! to have a baby all of her own! But How CAN people do such things!
I can't understand!

When yet another of her friends became engaged, Lucy noted tartly, "it seems to me that people are getting very unprincipaled". Fortunately for her own peace of mind she was not aware that her own sister was on the verge of becoming "unprincipled".

Though Howard Taylor was always at Harley, happy just to live in Minnie's presence like a perpetual shadow, he was not her only admirer. He began to notice with feelings close to despair how positively she responded to a young doctor who had suddenly started to show her attention. The new suitor was handsome and accomplished, with a brilliant medical career ahead of him. Howard felt inadequate in the face of such competition. It became obvious to him that Minnie had fallen in love.

However exciting this new experience, Minnie was too serious a young woman to allow her head to be completely governed by her heart. She had work to do, by day the supervision of the domestic details of the family home, by night, her classes. But she would not have been a woman if the attention had not brought a bloom to her cheeks.

Fanny watched with interest and eventually decided that Minnie was hardly being fair to her suitor. A letter had come with a proposal months ago and she could not make him wait for a reply indefinitely, while she was sorting out the problems of the East End. The heartache for Minnie was that she knew he was not the man for her. Professional success appeared to be his only goal. Their aspirations were different, their lives destined to go in opposite directions. It was a terrible decision to make. That was why she had postponed it so often.

Being of a practical turn of mind, Fanny felt that Minnie needed a break and asked her if she would like to go to Paris to bring Lucy home? Minnie was thrilled. She missed Lucy and it was ten years since she had been to Paris. She wanted to see if it was still how she remembered it.

Lucy was just as excited, though she had her reservations. Minnie had a way of making her feel very giddy and immature.

I wonder very much whether Minnie will come here? I am not at all sure if it would be good for her, for she is so different to other girls of her age, so much nicer and with quite different ways and thoughts so that I don't know whether she would like being here at school with these silly, merry, girlish girls.

When Minnie reached the elegant house in the Boulevard Malesherbes, Lucy came running out to meet her in a new emerald green Parisian dress, looking so chic that with a sinking heart Minnie felt she was almost a stranger. As they climbed the stairs Lucy chattered on with all her news. On the ground floor lived a colonel in the French army, a quiet, gracious man by the name of Dreyfus. She did not see him very often, but his two sisters took lessons with her at the school and were among her dearest friends. The name, which meant little to Minnie then, would within a decade be emblazoned on the front of every English and French newspaper, as the "Dreyfus affair" became one of the most celebrated scandals in Europe. Then Lucy would see the strange irony that she, the daughter of a leading Zionist thinker, had known the man court-martialled for treason on no other grounds than that he was a Jew.

But Lucy was right in her assessment of her sister. Bypassed by adolescence herself, Minnie found Lucy and her friends too superficial. She disliked their backbiting and cattiness. Being a rather sanctimonious young woman she proceeded to lecture her younger sister on the negative effects the school had exerted on her character. Lucy felt it a just criticism and was mortified.

Intense though Minnie may have been, she was never sour. Lucy described her in Paris as being quite merry and coquettish, "coiffing herself with a little bow of bright red ribbon in the middle of her arrangement behind!" singing "Suppose, & suppose that your highland etc." in such a loud, dolorous voice that Lucy could no longer concentrate or write anything.

The next time Lucy wrote her diary in Paris was the last time, and she wrote, "Plus jamais de ma vie", never again in my life! How many times would she have to say those words and how she wished they did not exist. Life at the Miss Ellerbys had not been all she might have wished. Her French had improved but not her character, at least in her perception of things. Her music had not progressed satisfactorily, and yet she was sad to leave. Another episode of her life, another new experience, was over for ever. She had an overwhelming, frightening sense of the passage of time and the vanishing of youth. She wanted to capture each sensation, carry it with her into the future, so that she could relive it whenever she wanted. Perhaps that was why she wrote a diary. And yet by July, writing at the round table by the window of her old bedroom at Harley, Paris already seemed like a dream.

5

July 11th, 1882, Harley House. Oh! My home! My home! How I love you!

It is just home and nothing else that gives me this feeling of happy content I suppose. For this is what I feel sitting here trying in vain to write evenly and keep my eyes from wandering out to the dear old fashioned garden below – just contented – so nice it is! – I can hear Papa and Mamma's voices as they pace the corridor in earnest and grave consultation about some weighty matter; and Minnie, Dora & Maria chatting in the dining room at the large door window, while Polly – laying supper – jangles about the spoons and some train whistles in the distance to the accompaniment of a ringing bell.

Wherever any of the children went, they were always glad to be home and part of an ever-extending family. When Fanny's two teenage nieces Edith and Dora Fookes, who had been at school in Hastings with Lucy, lost their mother Fanny took them in.

Whatever Lucy felt about herself, to her family the transformation was obvious. She spent more time over her appearance, was more polished and ladylike. Instead of chasing like a hoyden round the garden after Harry and Gershom, she was happy to sit at her window as the evening shadows began to lengthen, watching her younger brother and a little foster-child called Ada swinging in the hammock: "I wish I could take it down, just as it stands – this sweet scene before me . . . I wish I could perpetuate it till I am old and all the bright warm young life of today has passed away for ever!"

No summer was complete without at least a month at Cliff. For the upper classes house parties were the tradition of the time. Just as Lord Ardilaun and Edward Cecil entertained royalty on their estates, Henry Grattan liked to share his "estate" with a number of families and friends who returned year after year. That was part of the fun.

To Minnie fell the responsibility of supervising the transformation of the college into a comfortable holiday home. It was a mammoth task. The main classroom became a drawing-room to which the piano was brought from the other end of the house and the desks removed to make way for summer furniture and flowers. There were all the bedding and catering arrangements to see to. In the summer of 1882 all the forty bedrooms were in use. Although people came and went it was hard to keep up with the arrivals and departures. One evening Lucy counted fifty-three visitors sitting down to dinner: "I like having many visitors on the whole I think, the more the merrier – c'est à dire, if they are select (which unhappily they are not allways!)"

Henry Grattan would have brought the whole world to Cliff if he could. He never ceased to marvel that he should own such a place. He was too generous-hearted to keep it to himself. For all who came, Cliff was an escape from the tensions of life, an absolute, total rest, a rare experience of the peace and purity of rural life. For the Grattan Guinnesses, especially Henry and his overworked, overwrought wife, it was a lifeline:

Is there a pleasanter, sweeter spot in all England than Hulme Cliff? Behind it rises to a height of 800 feet a heathery upland moor. Before it winds a narrow, verdant valley. Up the moors the hills rise to perpendicular sandstone cliffs, with miles of moorland stretching from their summits, north, south, and east. Down in the valley rushes the glittering Derwent, filling the air with the sound of ever-falling waters. Hill rises beyond hill all round and clefts open to narrow valleys and rocky gullies, with lovely, undulating country here and there. Close around are clustering trees, and beyond them cultivated fields and waving woods, but we see no roads, no dusty highways, and hear no sound of traffic. The woods are green with summer foliage, the far-off hills grey with mist and distance; the air is fresh and cool, for there seems always a breeze stirring here, and the voice of the waters, breeze, and birds, mingle from morn to night. As I write, the latter are singing as though there were no sin and no sorrow in the world. No other sound reaches me except these tranquilising voices.

We call this OUR GALILEE – our refuge from close, crowded, noisy, dusty, ill-savoured, enormous London.

Unlike his Guinness cousins at Farmleigh and Ashford, Henry Grattan may not have offered a decent shoot or entertained royalty, but his house parties were as much fun. Every summer there were tennis and chess competitions, picnics to Haddon Hall in Castleton with its famous caves, boating on the river and hikes up the Eagle Rock led by Henry himself, who, hammer in hand, went in search of interesting fossils. Few there were, even among the young, who could keep up with him or match his energy.

The evenings were a feast of music. Most years they could almost manage a full orchestra. In that summer of 1882, there were eight violins. As an alternative to a concert there might be a lecture from Fanny on Central Africa or from Henry on prophecy and the Jews. If he happened to choose astronomy as his subject, it was to the despair of the older members of the party for he would march the young people out to the observatory for half a night with the telescope. Harry later claimed that he grew up knowing more about the mountains in the moon than the geography of his native land.

"What a happy month we had at Cliff," Minnie wrote in her diary at the end of August 1882:

Oh the pleasant mornings at tennis, the afternoon walks and splendid rows, the evening games, and then sometimes the moonlight strolls up to the observatory, where, in the darkness, Harry would tell some thrilling tale! Often, especially toward the end of summer, we would lie for an hour at a time in the shade under the bank just at the bend of the river with as many as twenty in the boat, while someone told a story and the others listened, watching the swiftly flowing water. How sweet it looked – up toward the bathing-house and pier, with the wooded hills behind, the Middleton Valley on the right, and the old cotton-mill among the trees by Duke's Drive!

It was always exciting to boat on the Derwent because of its speed. At Cliff even Minnie relaxed and joined five others in one boat attempting to row up the mill stream where the water was running at full force. They were capsized before they got very far and while the girls lay dripping on the bank the boys retrieved the boat.

Howard Taylor then decided if he could not row up the rapids he would navigate them in a canoe. Not to be left out Gershom offered to accompany him, standing in the prow. Howard paddled expertly and they had made it to the last plunge when Gershom got completely carried away with excitement and dived in with a whoop. Somehow, against all the odds, Howard kept his balance and was the hero of the holiday.

Lucy stayed on at Cliff that year long after everyone else had gone. It was there, shortly before leaving for a few months in Ireland, that she came to the end of her first diary:

October 9th, Cliff. Goodbye – Goodbye, dy; I have written and kept you these two long happy years. Very happy years they have been – childish – thoughtless – happy years!

I feel older now; I am beginning to see that life is real and earnest work, so it is fit that I should close your records.

The trauma Lucy experienced in growing up did not disappear overnight. Her descriptions of her inner conflict continued well into her second diary:

Killarney Wood, Bray, Co. Wicklow. November 17th, 1882. I don't want to be a young lady – I mean grown-up and charming and dangerous – like Minnie. Not that there is any need for me to be afraid of being charming – unhappily!

Then she discovered she was wrong. It was not only Minnie who possessed certain dangerous charms! The son of the house was evidently susceptible to hers and took her out riding. His gentle, considerate qualities however were not enough for Lucy. She wanted someone dashing and masterful, like Harry. Besides she had no time for her would-be suitor's attitude to Darwinism, nor his dismissal of her intellectual powers simply because she was a woman:

Oh! surely, men with great minds, powers of thought (and of expressing that thought) & who are also gifted with education and leisure – might, in these last days which are (& who knows how swiftly) drawing to a close find some better means of employing their time than in speculating whether or no we are descended from monkeys, tadpoles & minute specs of protoplasm . . . I wish now that I had said so . . . who am not, being a girl – supposed – at Bray at least – to think on such matters.

Back at Harley in the spring, Lucy found her mother confined to her room with a bad headache, "brought on by certain anxieties and troubles with regard to the students – Creatures that they were – !" But what shocked her most was her own reaction to being back in the East End of London. In some extraordinary way, and for a reason she could not explain, it was as if she were seeing it for the first time:

I could find no words fitting to describe my sensations that night, driving home with Papa . . . along Whitechapel and Mile End Waste. Oh, it was too dreadful – terrible. The degradation; dirt; defilement; noise; glare; atmosphere; people; houses; sights; and sounds; all, everything combined to horrify and amaze me . . . How was it that I had never noticed it to be so before?

The seeds of her future life's work were here in the emotions she felt that night, but it was too soon for germination. Her parents had

Arthur Lee Guinness, an aesthete and lyrical poet

Elizabeth (Bessie) Guinness, wife of Sir Benjamin Lee Guinness, with her two eldest sons, Arthur and Benjamin

Jane Lucretia D'Esterre, the
'beautiful Miss Cramer of
Dublin' who married Captain
John Grattan Guinness in
1829

Captain John Grattan
Guinness of the 12th
regiment native infantry,
Madras Army

Henry and Fanny Guinness in
1861, the year after they were
married

Fanny Guinness and her children, Harry, Minnie, Lucy, Phoebe, Agnes and Gershom

Harley College in Bow Road

Sir Edward Cecil Guinness,
the first Earl of Iveagh,
brewer and philanthropist

Lucy Guinness (seated) as
'only a factory girl', with
Sarah, the maid

Cliff College, Derbyshire, summer home of the Grattan Guinnesses

Henry Grattan Guinness in
1886, aged 51, at the height of
his popularity as a writer

Gershom and Janie Guinness
in Chinese dress

missionary farewell at Harley House, centred around the famous 'waterspout'

Henry Grattan Guinness and Grace Hurditch on their wedding day, July 7th 1903. She was forty one years his junior

Annie Reed Guinness, at her desk at Harley College

Dr Harry Guinness

Henry Grattan Guinness' favourite photograph of his second wife, Grace. He took it with him everywhere

Olive, daughter of the 3rd Earl of Bantry, the formidable Lady Ardilaun

Walter Edward Guinness, D.S.O., the first Baron Moyne, assassinated November 6th 1944

Dr Harry Guinness' three youngest children, all of whom became clergymen: Howard, Desmond and Gordon

Sir Rupert and Lady Gwendolen Guinness, 2nd Lord and Lady Iveagh

Father Jack Guinness, CR, a monk and a quintessential Guinness

never sought to spare her the first-hand experience of the pain and despair of poverty, but somehow, though it was all around her, it had never really reached her in her sanctuary at Harley. Minnie could have told her, but that would never have had the impact of seeing for herself. That night her eyes were opened, but it would be a long while before she felt ready to do anything about it. Her immediate reaction was to escape, to run away to Derbyshire, where her eyes and emotions need no longer be assaulted: "I was sick – as usual – in the train! It would probably have been much worse, only just as the train was leaving St Pancras, Papa – that darling – Sweet Papa! – appeared with a glass of port wine, which I drank only too thankfully and which did me much good." Henry Grattan's teetotalism was evidently waived when health indications made it necessary.

For the first time Lucy enjoyed the luxury of a winter at Cliff, experiencing "a calm that enters my very soul". She revelled in "the short cold winter days – the afternoon teas by the firelight – the long winter evenings and terribly windy nights when I used to get so frightened – the snow and snowballing! – the pinching cold windy walks – bare countryside . . ."

Spring melted away the ice and frosts and slowly gave way to another hot summer. Lucy counted over sixty visitors that year. Among them was a rather commanding, regal-looking lady she had never met before by the name of Mrs Reed. Mrs Henry Reed and her children were from Tasmania and she had a suggestion to make which opened up a whole new life for Lucy and Gershom:

August 14th, Cliff. My diary yes, For – shall I tell you? Well this is it. The great it that fills all my thoughts – since yesterday. Gershom and I are returning to Tasmania with the Henry Reeds.
  What do you think? What shall I say? . . . Can it be true? Only yesterday proposed – imagined – thought of. But oh! How far away from home – what a long time. Certainly my life is a curious one! I suppose I shall be changed when I come home, perhaps never, for who can tell? And if I go to Tasmania, why it will be to be a blessing I hope, a comfort and help to dear Mrs Reed, a sister to Annie, to take care of darling Gershom, to gain health, strength, information, self-reliance, a knowledge of the world . . . above all to be as my name says, "a Light".

On the evening of Saturday, September 8th Lucy made a last sad entry in her diary before saying goodbye to another long, happy summer at Cliff:

Good-night, dy, I would like to tell you more, but must refrain just now – only this one thing – one person never came this

155

summer. On the whole it was best I think – but tell me only – will they come again?

There comes no answer to me – only the flickering of the firelight, and the deepening blue darkness outside – perhaps a little murmur from the river – shall I tell you what I think?

8

1882–1885

The Tasmanian Adventure

1

Meanwhile at the brewery Edward and Dodo's three boys were growing up. The earliest memories of Rupert, their eldest son, were of endless journeys from house to house accompanied by a retinue of nannies and governesses. He saw little of his mother. Dodo was distant and reserved and very definitely of the opinion that children should be neither seen nor heard. Edward Cecil took more interest in his children, noting the smallest details of their progress in his pocket-book. He was meticulous about writing everything down, even the penny he spent on a newspaper. But he was often too busy to pay his sons much attention.

For the aristocracy the 1880s were the most glittering years in Ireland's history and the Guinnesses were not only part of the high life, they were the leaders of fashion. The glamour of their social life often hid the amount of hard work Edward Cecil put into the brewery. He was determined it should expand from a national to an internationally respected company. At the same time he had set his heart on a peerage. To that end, from 1880 he considered a political career, even against his will hoping for some sign of gratitude from the Tory Party. Truthfully he preferred being at the brewery and when invited to stand for Dublin said, "to sit would be most distasteful to me in every way, the unpleasantness of it would be very great, for I was always to be found by anyone at St James' Gate."[1] He did not win the seat, and there was no hint of a peerage. Nevertheless just as the Viceroy's railway carriage was distinguished by an X, Edward Cecil had XX inscribed on his.

Winston Churchill's grandfather was Viceroy for a time. Rupert and Winston were almost the same age and when they were five years old they shared the same governess for a time. Their relationship

157

was uneasy. On one occasion they were given a toy harness and coachman's whip and told to go and play together. "You be the horse," said Winston. The idea did not appeal to Rupert at all. Winston, who was holding the whip, lashed Rupert across the face and caught his eye. A leading Dublin eye specialist was called in. He applied ice, then a caustic solution which burned Rupert's eyelashes and brows and left permanent scarring.

Years later, when the two men, then in their eighties, met again at a rehearsal for the new Knights of the Garter at St James's Palace, Winston turned to the second Earl of Iveagh and said, "I say, Rupert, do you remember that fight we had in Dublin?"[2]

From early on Rupert's academic ability was a source of bitter disappointment to his parents. He attended various prep schools, according to whether his family was in London or Ireland, and despite extra coaching seemed unable to grasp how to read or write. At first everyone thought he was backward. Then they suspected he had eye trouble and he was taken round a host of eye specialists, who could find no problem. Unfortunately dyslexia was not a known condition at the time. If they had thought about it carefully his parents would have realised that their eldest son was not educationally subnormal. When Rupert was seven Edward Cecil acquired a microscope. While Henry Grattan, his cousin, was gazing at the stars, Edward wanted to examine the as yet unknown effects of the yeast culture on the brewing process. Rupert begged his father for a microscope of his own. It became his favourite toy in the nursery, and was the beginning of a fruitful and lifelong fascination with the sciences. But meanwhile his parents showed more interest in Ernest, who was obviously bright, while Walter, the youngest, was their favourite. For Rupert growing up was a hard and painful process, but in the end it revealed the true mettle in the man.

Even with attentive parents, Lucy found adolescence difficult. The HMS *Ballarat* of the P&O line bound for Tasmania was the right environment to force the butterfly from its chrysalis. For the first time in her life she had to rely completely on her own resources. By the time the six-week voyage half-way round the world was over, Lucy knew that she had made the more significant inner passage to womanhood, but the transition cost her many tears.

Neither she nor Gershom had been exposed before to anything like shipboard life. Home and school were sheltered environments. Even in Paris Lucy had never gone out without a chaperone. She had never lived in a world where people drank, danced, smoked, played cards, flirted, gossiped and fell out. Gershom had a companion his own age in Henry, Mrs Reed's youngest child, and like teenage boys they fished and played, oblivious of the complex and tangled social intricacies woven around them, which Lucy found a revelation.

Mrs Reed took her responsibilities to shield her young charges seriously. She was an austere, autocratic old woman who, without any explanation of her motives, demanded total obedience. She rarely got it. Lucy, who was used to Fanny's sensible reasoning, was not surprised that two of the Reed daughters, Maggie and Mary, became quite a handful, flirting with every officer on board. Mrs Reed's suspicious mind seemed to drive them to it and they had almost daily "rowings-up" with her.

Mrs Reed had been a widow for three years. Her late husband, Henry Reed, had been one of the founding fathers of Tasmania. An early settler in Victoria, the story of his shrewd business sense and rapid rise to enormous wealth almost paralleled the first Arthur Guinness. Henry Reed was also an extremely religious man, a preacher and supporter of many worthy causes. Ruthlessly honest, unswerving in integrity, he was totally inflexible. When, on one of his many trips to England, he met the powerful William Booth it was potentially a clash of the Titans. Somehow the two men developed an understanding, and despite his reservations Henry Reed became the foremost financial supporter of the newly formed Salvation Army.

He married Margaret Frith when he was fifty-seven. She was thirty-five, the daughter of a well-to-do Anglo-Irish family, and combined aristocratic elegance with evangelical piety, both qualities inherent in her pedigree. One of her ancestors, a certain John Frith, had been betrayed by Sir Thomas More for distributing Tyndale's Bible and was burnt at the stake at Smithfield in 1533. Margaret Reed was proud of her family's pioneering and spiritual tradition.

Despite their maturity the Reeds produced three daughters and a son. They bought a holiday home in England, Dunorlan in Tunbridge Wells, and met the Grattan Guinnesses who became their close friends. They had many interests in common and their children were of a similar age.

When her husband died in 1880 Margaret Reed continued to make generous gifts to the causes of her choice, her first being the presentation to the Livingstone Inland Mission of a second steamer for use in the Upper Congo. It was to be called the *Henry Reed* in memory of her late husband.

Early in 1883 Margaret Reed's eldest daughter Annie persuaded her mother to let her go to Paris. William Booth's daughter Katie, known as the "Maréchale", was trying to establish the Salvation Army there. It was the perfect opportunity to see Paris, yet be of some use. She volunteered for service and though no beauty was an immediate sensation. The maiden "Maréchale" was as tough as her nickname suggested and quite used to handling crowds of cut-throats. Annie was rather more naïve and blissfully unaware of which of her particular attractions was drawing such large crowds of men. News of the escapade reached Mrs Reed at Dunorlan and she set off for Paris immediately, bringing Annie back to England forthwith.

Hearing about the saga, Fanny sympathised with the widow and invited her and her children to join them for their annual month at Cliff. It was there that Mrs Reed decided Lucy and Gershom should return with her to Tasmania. Fanny was opposed to the idea. After all she had her children's education to consider. But Mrs Reed was adamant. One by one she dismissed all Fanny's arguments. Lucy could go to school with her daughter Mary, and Gershom with her son Henry. The experience alone would broaden their minds and the climate work wonders for their constitution. All was settled so quickly and in such a flurry of excitement and packing that Fanny barely had time to realise how much of a wrench it would be to say goodbye to her youngest son.

A trip around the world was a great adventure in those days. The Reed children had done it several times and were a little blasé, but for Lucy and Gershom it was a new experience. They were very homesick at first. Everything seemed alien. But gradually, as they crossed the Mediterranean and steamed down the African coast, the long, lazy tropical days in the sun and the warm evenings watching the moonlight sparkling on the water worked their magic spell. Gershom sometimes played his violin for the guests in the music saloon and the sound of it would echo all around the deck. Gazing out to sea, Lucy could just discern the coastline of Africa and felt her stomach churn with excitement. "And shall I ever be nearer it than I am now?" she asked her diary, sensing perhaps that her destiny was there, somewhere beyond the black horizon.

Occasionally the ship berthed and there were opportunities for sightseeing. "What a mummery the Roman Catholic religion really is – what a pretence – and system of man's invention!" Lucy wrote after a visit to a Capuchin monastery in Malta. As the daughter of an Irish Protestant she was far harder on Catholicism than on the Buddhism she saw later on. The crime of the Catholic Church was that it ought to know better. "How these Catholics seem bowed down," she wrote some months later, "yet they have Jesus!" It was the apparent misrepresentation of Christianity she could not bear. She was just as intolerant of the boring, miserable weekly Anglican service with its "weary, meaningless hymns and prayers", which took place in the captain's cabin.

The tour of the Maltese monastery would have been a ghoulish and harrowing experience even for those of a less susceptible disposition. She was led down a long, dark flight of stone steps into a cold underground hall. As her eyes became accustomed to the eerie flickering torchlight, she beheld the most ghastly sight she had ever seen. From niches all around the walls:

the skeletons of decaying withering corpses of dead monks are gazing, staring stonily at you, dressed still in their same brown monkish garb, cassock and cord, hanging limp around them, clinging to the skeleton within; propped up by a board in front of them, they stand, what once were men! Some with bare skulls, some – oh horrible – how can I write it – with the flesh still on them – with tongues – yes – eyes – still glaring at you. They stared there all round that chamber of death, some of them have stood there a century – with bony hands clasped as if in prayer, or leaning forward over the bar – stretching out an arm – pointing – entreating – still standing – silent – dead.

For Lucy, often frail herself, unhealthily conscious of the brevity of life since the death of her two little sisters, coming face to face with man's mortality was a traumatic experience. "Are these grey, lifeless, decaying, powerless, mouldering corpses all that we are? Is there no soul in man, nothing unseen, enduring?" In theory she was totally convinced of the eternity of the human spirit, but no matter how hard she tried, she could not drive an overpowering sense of the horror of death and decay from her mind. It only seemed to emphasise the pettiness of human relationships on board ship. If the little, carping community on the *Ballarat*, with its pointless pleasures and petty agitations, was a microcosm of society, what hope was there for mankind?

At first Lucy set out to reform it. A certain Mr Holliday, who approached her, cigarette in hand, was her first victim:

Poor fellow, he wants to smoke very much I expect, but then it's his own fault. Why did he promise me he wouldn't? And when men promise they must perform. They don't always I am afraid. He does, I am glad. It is only till next Saturday he has promised, and this is Tuesday. He gives me the cigarette and I have the pleasure of throwing it overboard into the blue Red Sea. He is a strange sort of creature, quite worldly, but somehow in spite of things, he apparently likes talking to me – and I lecture him about drinking and smoking . . .

It never entered Lucy's head that Mr Holliday's intentions were anything but honest. Who could possibly want to flirt with her? She was not a "fine" girl, like Maggie or Mary. "They have had very dreadful 'rows up' these last few days, on account of the fifth officer – little Mr Arnold . . . I am just glad I am not inexperienced like they are! For I do not think my nature is at all different, probably worse, only somehow I am different from them."

Smugness soon gave way to disillusion when Mr Holliday failed all her high expectations and broke his promise. "What a weak will!" Lucy fumed. "I never knew people didn't speak the truth before – it is very sad – I can't bear to think of it."

The ship continued uneventfully on its course until it reached the Suez Canal. On the evening of October 9th most people, except Lucy and the Reeds, were dancing as usual. As ever, dancing was strictly forbidden. Lucy was inclined to agree with the prohibition, though at the back of her mind was a certain reservation, which developed as the weeks passed by into an ethical struggle. "The girls don't know how and I would not like," she said primly, then added hesitantly:

Is there any wrong in dancing? Any harm? I see none. The thing itself is delightful, motion in rhythm and time and swing with music. I like it very much – with girls, like we used to do at school, but here it is quite different, and though my feet keep time and long to go, I would hate to dance as they dance here – with these men – it is not good.

Most nights, instead of attending the concerts, theatricals or "worldly entertainments", Mrs Reed made all her charges sit in the stern, singing hymns, "in opposition", Lucy said wryly, adding hesitantly, "Well, perhaps it was naughty to say that."

One particular evening Mrs Reed had been too tired to sing and Lucy and Maggie were taking advantage of the situation by strolling amidships in the alluring company of Mr Arnold. He was suddenly and mysteriously called away, then a great commotion broke out. The ship appeared to be on fire, sheets of flame and clouds of smoke billowing out from somewhere near the engine room. The steam pumps were working as hard as they could and before long the fire had been put out. "The Captain was very cool," Gershom wrote home to his parents, "and they say that it was owing to his calmness that the ship was saved. But you should have seen men and women rushing through the smoke to get to their children!"

The ship was detained for repairs in the Suez where the heat was so intense that Lucy found it unbearable. "Oh how hot it is!" she wrote to Minnie, as she lay on the deck "melting", being served endless amounts of ices, iced water, iced fruits and jellies by the overworked crew. "Why must people wear clothes? The lightest things are almost unbearable. Mrs Reed and Annie dispense with the most necessary articles of clothing but I don't like doing this — it feels too shameful."

Despite her lethargy Lucy could not help but be entranced by the parakeet colours of the Egyptian and Arab boats, laden with their cargoes of beads, corals, muslins, shawls and other mysterious Eastern curiosities.

But nothing she had seen so far compared with Ceylon, which they crossed by train to Kandy. Lucy thought it the most beautiful place in the world. She was captivated by the exquisite shifting lights and shadows made by the sun streaming through the lush palms and ferns. Even the train was "all green with green shades standing out from the roof".

Back on the *Ballarat* there was a much more interesting preoccupation, the first shipboard romance. To Lucy's bewilderment Mr Arnold had become engaged to a Miss Dixon:

What a creature she is! Atrocious. How can he, what can he see to admire in her, short, pale, thin, ugly, badly-dressed, gawky, ungraceful in her manner and gait, chattering, gossiping, flirting, unaccomplished, unladylike, apparently uneducated. How can he or anyone like or admire her in any way? If she were pretty now, one could understand, or even if she could talk sensibly. But as it is, it is simply unaccountable and marvellous! However, I suppose there must be something in her which I have not found out as yet. But I hope, for Mr Arnold's sake, that they may as Maggie gracefully expresses it, "chuck each other up". Still, men are geese.

2

Without warning Lucy's halo slipped, if not in her own eyes, then in the eyes of the other passengers. One of the young women accused her of blatantly stealing her young man. "Had I ever tried to take away her dear Haythorne? Had I ever wanted to have anything to do with him?" Lucy demanded with indignation, to no avail. Gossip was rife all around the ship. It was the only pestilence worse than seasickness, the favourite pastime of bored, mischievous adults. "I had no idea the world was so bad or people so foolish and wrong. I believe that girl would stop at nothing hardly to do me a harm. I have done nothing to her, nothing . . . she knows as well as I do that I am not a flirt!" If neither Mrs Reed nor her school had fully instructed her in seemly behaviour, Mama had.

But behind Lucy's self-righteous self-appraisal glowed an unmistakable spark of pleasure. She would have been neither human nor a teenager if her female vanity had not been susceptible to masculine approbation. The barriers she had built so carefully around herself began to crack and she was left vulnerable. Which of the values she had accepted before, almost unquestioning, really mattered? She longed now to dance, to dress up in beautiful clothes and shine before the world, more especially before a certain gentleman. When Mrs Reed refused to let her go to the fancy dress ball she felt angry and churlish:

October 19th. They had their ball, their fancy dress ball last night, and I expect they enjoyed it very much. It must have been amusing I should think, and – well, why wrong? Am I very bad to question? . . . I wish I had Papa and Mother here to ask about these things! I want to understand, and I can't.

What I saw last night was not so bad, but on the contrary very charming, and I do so believe, in my heart, if I could have an easy conscience, I would love to have gone! There!

It was a terrible feeling to sit in the stern watching the others going in, dressed in their beautiful costumes, Miss Wallace as Bo-Peep in short petticoats and powdered hair, Miss Martin as a fishwife, Miss Hewlett in an "exquisite" dress of the last century, Miss Dixon as a Turkish lady. Small wonder that Mary Reed had made up her mind to tear off her blue ribbons, the symbol of abstinence, at the first opportunity, that she intended going to parties, balls and the theatre as soon as she was old enough. But she did not dare tell Mrs Reed yet for fear of a "rowing-up".

Lucy's depression continued after Australia came in sight, almost a week later. She had taken to sitting alone on an isolated seat in the stern, ruminating on life and whether anyone would miss her if she fell into the sea. Presumably she was thinking of one person in particular, for suddenly two cryptic lines were scribbled alone on a single page of her diary: "What have I done? Oh God was it my fault?"

The following day was the last on board. Lucy was in a disturbed state of mind:

Was it my fault yesterday? Oh, what am I to do! What have I done – what have I done . . . what am I – where am I – how can it be true? . . . I have no one to go to, no one to tell me what to do. Why was I ever made to bring such trouble to people? What can I do to make it right again? And he – Poor fellow – poor fellow.

She never referred to the gentleman in question by name, except to call him "H" later on. Presumably it was the mysterious

"Haythorne", the subject of all the gossip, who had made his feelings clear to her. It was in keeping with Lucy's naïvety to reject what was apparent to everyone else. Her guilt was due to the fact that in her heart she knew she had encouraged him. There is no doubt his feelings were reciprocated:

You are on board this ship – and so am I – and yet I cannot see you – cannot speak to you nor tell you what I want – nor say goodbye this last time – and forever!

Have I done right? Yes, yes, I know I have – but it is hard – Oh it is very hard!

How have I born this day – I cannot tell – shall I ever have a harder one to live? But it is over now.

I have gone through it. One look from me would have made all right tonight.

All right? Perhaps all wrong.

Now I have done it! Well – "fast asleep"!

All over now – all done – goodbye – goodbye.

In the morning they berthed at Melbourne and transferred to the *Flinders* which was to take them the last stretch to Tasmania. It was the roughest part of the journey. Lucy was too busy fighting her usual battle with seasickness to indulge in self-pity. Her letter home to Minnie was light and cheerful, giving no hint of her real emotional state. She expressed her amusement at the way the passengers were suddenly divested of their Victorian dignity every time the boat lurched. "An old gentleman will skim gracefully along on his back, or a lady will make a bow and then lie extended on the deck."

Gershom was sad to leave the *Ballarat* too, but his regrets vanished as he caught his first glimpse of Mount Pleasant, the gracious Reed family home. It stood in a perfect setting against the Blue Mountains, high above the town of Launceston, commanding a magnificent view of the Esk Valley. In the late Australian spring the great house was in its glory, the gardens a riot of colourful flowers, the cherries and luscious strawberries waiting to be picked, to be followed by apricots and peaches.

It was a beautiful, if isolated, spot and Gershom entered with gusto into the Reeds' quasi-colonial life in the rough-and-ready outback. He learned to ride, pole-vault, shoot and drive the light pony and trap bought especially to take him and Henry to school in Launceston. During his first week at school he had an encounter with the local tough, who thought the white-skinned English boy with the plummy accent was fair game. Unknown to him, in England Gershom had been having lessons in ju-jitsu. With a quick flick of his wrist he tossed the bully over his shoulder, to the cheers of a large group of spectators.

But if Gershom revelled in the arduous station life, Lucy found it a strain, particularly after the sophistication of Paris and the *Ballarat*. She conquered her fear of horses and rode passably well, but cows were another matter. When a whole herd advanced across the paddock where they were all out riding, she was paralysed with fear and begged the others to encircle her until the danger had passed.

"And what if we are gored to death?" Mary Reed asked, but that made no difference to Lucy.

For a long time she felt lonely and ill at ease. The experience on the ship continued to trouble and unsettle her.

Mount Pleasant, Launceston
November 1st, 1883. Seven weeks ago today – Thursday – we left England . . . were they weeks or years? Am I the same girl now as then?

If I wrote that letter – but I shall not – I might tell you one thing – you have opened my eyes – for better or worse? You would say for better I know – is it for better? perhaps so – one cannot live in this world and do it good without understanding some of its evil – but – oh – I would like again to be as trustful and pure and innocent as I was before I came on shipboard . . .

I hope I shall never see you again, never see nor hear of you – no, I will not say that. I hope I shall hear of you – that you are doing well – well in the best sense, that you have found the truth and are making some use of your life.

Maggie and Mary knew nothing of Lucy's romance and hurt her deeply when they teasingly prophesied that she would never marry.

Gradually the peace of Mount Pleasant, nestling at the foot of an unbroken view of undulating hills, entered her soul. As the days turned into weeks she discovered a sense of calm and serenity she had not known before, a peace born of the inner integration which comes with the acceptance of the new adult. Farewell to her lover had been a farewell to childhood:

November 26th, 1883. And now I have come to the last page of this diary – what an important and eventful period of my life it has recorded! I do not want to live it again – it was happy, very sometimes; sorrowful sometimes, very; but it has come and gone and I trust taught me its lesson. A lesson I shall never forget. And though sometimes like last night, I long and ache and thrill with wanting – wanting – wanting – yet I know it is best as it is.

Lucy went on hungering for affection and suffered when she did not receive it. Gershom was busy climbing, sheep-shearing and shooting rabbits. Tasmania had awakened his dormant pioneer spirit. Lucy's intentions of taking care of him were superfluous. He did not need looking after. Reed family life was spartan in the emotional, as well as the physical sense. Mrs Reed was unable to show any affection. Mary was often selfish and bad-tempered, Maggie was flighty and temperamental, and Annie, the eldest Reed sister, nicknamed "Cull" by Lucy, and the only one to show her any attention, was totally matter of fact and devoid of sentimentality. It was a relief when the time came for her to accompany Mary across the Straits to the Presbyterian Ladies'. College in Melbourne. There at least she could find consolation in her music, for the college, which had trained the future Dame Nellie Melba, had an outstanding musical reputation.

At college Lucy was regarded as a character. So hopeless at arithmetic that they nicknamed her "cypher", she still managed to persuade the other girls to do her maths homework for her. In English and composition she eclipsed everyone else. But it was her musical brilliance which attracted the most attention.

Great store was put by the school's Senior Pianoforte scholarship which Lucy won easily. Even Gershom was proud of his sister's triumph. "It is a fine thing to get it," he wrote to his parents, "they have to play before a lot of swell Melbourne musicians."

The scholarship earned Lucy an invitation to play in a concert at the Athenaeum. The school sang Tennyson's "Break, Break, Break", a part-song which she had set to music. The music critic of the *Age* was present and in an article for the following week's magazine said that here was a talent which presaged a great future in the front rank of musicians: "Miss Guinness' tempo was at times a little faulty, no doubt owing to nervousness in the young performer." Mary Reed laughed loudly when she re-read the magazine cutting years later. "Lucy Guinness was never nervous," she said. "Lucy's tempo was often faulty, but it was just because she preferred her own tempo to that of the composer! She was after all a great-granddaughter of Cramer the composer, the first pianist of his day."[3]

The music critic was not the only expert to notice Lucy's talent. The great violinist Remenyi paid a visit to the college and at the request of the musical director heard her play. He was amazed. She was, he said, "on the very threshold of the inner temple of classical music," and if she so desired a serious career as a concert pianist was quite possible.

"Was she pretty?" Mary Reed was asked years later. "Pretty? No! She was more than pretty, she was interesting to the last degree.

She was small and dark with a clear, pale face, and with something vivid about her. She had a way of getting herself up in the evening – a rose in her hair – a scrap of lace, maybe – and the result would be charming." Her fondest memory was the sight of Lucy on cold, dark wintry mornings, up long before the bell, sitting by the window huddled up in rugs, reading her Bible, as the dawn spread its first eerie light across the dormitory.

Lucy's piety did not prevent her breaking any school rule she thought extraneous. She simply knew how to carry it off. One such rule, which owed its existence to some high-spirited prank instigated by Nellie Melba, was that girls were not allowed to return to their dormitories before five o'clock in the evening. Everything needed for the day had to be collected straight after breakfast. Lucy thought this ridiculous and went up and down whenever she felt like it. "One day," remembered Mary Reed, "she encountered the lady superintendent on the stairs. With perfect calm, she engaged her in conversation, so interesting, so vital, that the lady was simply held and fascinated. At its conclusion they parted pleasantly, Lucy coolly continuing her way on forbidden ground. The rule was never mentioned." The conversational gifts which Fanny Guinness had instilled in her children stood her daughter in good stead. Before the world Lucy was poised, controlled, sociable. It was at night, overwhelmed with loneliness and homesickness, that she would cry herself to sleep.

After only a year at college Mrs Reed decided that the girls should stay at home, where two marriageable young women could learn more about domesticity.

3

While Mary spent her time flirting and sulking, Lucy was frustrated and bored. She tried hard to develop her domestic skills, making jam and poultices, baking bread and saffroning lace, but she showed no great talent in that direction. She promised herself she would be diligent in piano practice instead, but too much free time made her lethargic despite all her good intentions.

At last the news arrived that instead of their father, Harry was coming to take them home. That was January 1885, but it was March before Harry sailed in the *Lusitania*. The invincible Fanny gave her family a shock by suffering a sudden attack of Bell's palsy. The stroke was minor but left her with a permanent, disfiguring facial paralysis, distressing for everyone concerned.

When Harry finally arrived in April there was little time for the shooting Gershom hoped they could do together. Mrs Reed quickly discovered that here was a budding preacher with all the charisma and promise of his father and she set him to work. Soon he was in demand all over Tasmania. To Lucy's despair he consented to stay in Tasmania for another few months.

It soon emerged that Mrs Reed's intentions for Harry were by no means disinterested. Since his coming, relationships at Mount Pleasant had been a little less strained and more in keeping with the house's name. Mary now tried to keep her temper under control and both she and Maggie dressed immaculately. "Well no wonder! They have twice as much money as I, so they dress twice as well, natural consequence," Lucy wrote in her diary with a sourness unusual for her. The tense atmosphere within the house had oppressed her, but now she had her Harry. "Harry is a splendour of glory! I told him last night about Charles H. I did not tell him all. I could not tell anyone all." And Harry confided in her. There had been someone at home who had fallen in love with him, a daughter of the eminent evangelical Bewes family. They had made a dreadful fuss when it was discovered that her feelings were not reciprocated. But despite their confessions to each other, neither brother nor sister perceived what was happening under their very noses.

On July 23rd Lucy noted in her diary with undisguised horror:

And now I must tell you how my eyes have been opened. Who would have dreamt of such things?

Well – the long and short of it is simply this – Mrs Reed wants Harry for a son-in-law! And he – is thereby perplexed!

How very awkward to be sure!

Harry doesn't want to marry anyone just at present, much less one of these girls. But Mrs Reed has given him to understand that poor Mag cares for him and that it is his fault, and that he can have her if he likes — terrible —!

I never imagined Mrs Reed could be driving at such a thing . . . the only sensible thing is to let things take their course as before, allowing the matter to drop entirely – at least Mrs Reed, Mag, Harry and myself can never feel as simple and natural as before this matter arose . . .

The only fortunate thing about the affair, as far as Lucy could see, was that Mary knew nothing about it, and Cull said she did not even like him. "*Tant mieux* if it be true."

But Mrs Reed's favourite game of "throwing her daughters at his head" was suddenly disrupted, as was a projected sightseeing trip to Sydney, when she was forced to retire to her bed with congestion of the lungs, liver and stomach. "She doesn't seem so ill," Lucy commented a little ungraciously, but understandably in the circumstances. Cull and Mag nursed their mother day and night, applying hot poultices to the offending organs, and Lucy had a lonely, uneventful twentieth birthday. "I dreamed the other night a terrible dream," she wrote, "I dreamed that Father was dead. And that night I woke up crying bitterly."

Mrs Reed soon made a total recovery and everyone set off for mainland Australia. Harry's reputation as a preacher had gone before him and requests poured in from Sydney, Brisbane, Adelaide and Melbourne. Wherever he went, according to his fond sister, he took the hearts of the people by storm. In particular demand were his talks for men only, entitled "Social Purity" or "The Temptations of Men in the City". As a newly qualified doctor he was concerned by masculine ignorance on sexual matters. Many men seemed largely unaware of how their own body functioned, let alone the workings of the female anatomy. Ignorance led to fear and fear tempted a man to underhand, illicit sexual activity. It was senseless to maintain a polite silence, pretending these things did not exist.

No one had talked publicly about sex before. In England men had fainted as he spoke and had to be carried out of his lectures. The Australians maintained they were of tougher stuff, but that did not prevent them being both shocked and intrigued. "He has the look of a thoroughbred," wrote one daily Melbourne newspaper:[4]

Dr Guinness is one of the highly favoured, richly endowed sons of Adam, who can command success in almost any calling . . . The Admirable Crichton must have been such a man.

Truly, if there be soul in a man, Dr Guinness will find it; there is a soul in him and it looks out at every avenue. It is easy to see that it is a real soul, a fiery soul, a soul that means to carry all before it, and put wrongs right; it is a combative soul, a soul ready to singe, scorch, lash, burn, destroy evil in whatever form he meets it . . . He has revelation in his right hand and science in his left, and can use both weapons freely.

In the light of Harry's later social crusades the portrait has a strangely prophetic ring.

Despite the luxury of the hotels in which they stayed, Lucy found the trip a bitter disappointment. "The men wear the same ugly coats and stiffest of collars and hats, the women have the same pretty faces and foolish fashions as they do at home," she wrote to Minnie, who at Mrs Reed's insistence had decided it was time to revert to her real name, Geraldine:

I always am at the bottom of the wave, just as surely as Henry is always at the top and Harry and Cull mostly there . . . Is it my

fault I wonder? What can I do? I cannot be natural with dear
Mrs Reed; I feel she does not like me; it shrivels me up; I am
constrained and cold and dull. It is a wretched state. I wonder
if when I am liberated and get back home again I shall be once
more my old natural self? I think it has not been wholly good
my coming out here; it has transformed me; and I would rather
be like Mother than Mrs Reed . . . these two loveless years have
changed me from a merry, happy child into a small, dull, slow,
pale, little woman.

By the end of 1886 Harry was still in such demand that Mrs Reed
would not hear of his leaving for England. Gershom, who had been
promised a sledging-trip in America on the way home to his parents,
felt as desperate about the situation as Lucy. The only solution was
that they should go on ahead with Annie and Henry Reed for
company, leaving Harry behind. If Mrs Reed did not "effectually
catch him now, she ought to!" Lucy noted cryptically.

One evening she wrote a long, philosophical letter to Geraldine
to try and prepare her for the inevitable. Nothing ever stayed
the same, even home. Though they were a close family, one day
someone must come between them and after all:

Margaret is a nice girl: a very, very nice girl. She is a Christian,
and well-educated; a lady and rich; with excellent abilities along
certain lines, such as for instance mathematics, nursing, and
household matters [every area Lucy disliked]. I never met any
girl that sewed on buttons better than Margaret does, or that
worked a sum in algebra with more swiftness and exactitude . . .
It is a pity that she cannot write or play (hymns even at prayers are
beyond her . . .), but then she is gentle and affectionate and useful
and bright and further – a great matter as regards the impression
she makes, she is tall and well-dressed.

But then after all, "perhaps Harry will prove himself to be a wiser
boy than I think he is and manage to escape the snares of Mount
Pleasant without committing himself in any way! I only hope it may
be so, but fear it may not."

For some reason Lucy showed the letter to Harry, and he, hardly
surprisingly, urged her not to send it. She ought to be careful.
Even if she put "Private" on the envelope the chances were that
someone other than Geraldine would read it. Lucy believed him.
Harry always knew best, and she never questioned his motivation
or wondered why he was so content to stay behind in Tasmania.
Nor, despite her own "affaire du coeur", could she understand why
Maggie Reed was always in the dumps these days. Not until Friday,

January 29th 1886. That night Harry announced his engagement –
to Annie Reed.

Of the three sisters Annie was the most devout and the least
pretty. Her features were heavy, her chin long. In fact she was
rather plain. But she was sensible, practical and thoroughly down
to earth, very like Fanny Guinness in many ways. Unknown to
everyone it was Annie who had caught Harry's eye from the first.
"Annie is just splendid!" he had written to his parents after he had
watched her organise tea for 1500 people without the slightest sign
of fatigue or strain. Harry, the charmer, the incurable romantic, who
could have chosen any one of the dozens of beautiful young women
in England or Australia who swooned at his feet, had enough
commonsense to see that this woman, plain as she was, had all the
qualities he needed in a wife.

Lucy was stunned. Her departure for England with Annie was
less than a fortnight away. How had she been so blind? Even young
Gershom had wondered whether Annie had not always been "the
real nugget". But once her initial shock had worn off she could see
the positive side of the situation. If Harry had to marry one of the
Reed girls, "Cull" was her favourite:

Cull – dear, good, hardworking, unselfish, simple, humble, sober,
practical, useful, devoted, brave, strong, kindly Cull — and
HARRY! Who would have thought it!

Ah well, they are emminently suited for each other – and she
loves him – and he loves her.

Harry a talker & speaker – Cull rather slow of speech.

Harry a writer – Cull not!

Harry extravagant – Cull careful.

Harry well fitted to shine in society – Cull not – as yet!

Harry broad – Cull narrow.

Harry musical – Cull unmusical.

Harry poetically inclined – Cull absolutely matter-of-fact.

Cull a mathematician – Harry not.

Cull a businesswoman – Harry not very practical.

Both earnest – Both deeply loving.

Both consecrated and with one aim.

Both full of life, health and vigour.

Both young. Neither very handsome.

Both tall and both true-hearted.

Both just as affectionate and happy as they can be.

On January 31st Lucy spent a long, last evening with her diary.
Her wonder and amazement at the sight of a romance blossoming
under her nose was too novel and fascinating an experience for her

to ignore any detail. Harry was excited and joyful, "the marks of the tears of gladness still plain on his dear face". He seemed "suddenly grown, altered, completed somehow". Cull, "beaming and blissful", sat next to him "with her hand nearly always in his". Mrs Reed was "overflowing with delight and satisfaction, unable to settle to anything, watching the two with glad eyes and laughing to herself, often right out at them". Gershom was triumphant, "the bull's eye having at last been fairly hit!" Mary was "astounded, half-pleased, half-vexed". And as for Mag:

poor Mag . . . She worked hard all yesterday, sewing, marking, mending, packing – always away by herself, and was hard too in her demeanour, almost cross; and then in the evening so bitterly weeping, alone in the dark drawing-room, and would not be comforted but sent me away, and then came and lay on my bed and talked till 11 o'clock, but not about anything in particular. Poor Mag! Could she have loved him I wonder?

It seems extraordinary that Lucy should still have had any doubt, but her assessment of others was often as naïve as that of herself.

When everyone else went out to the mission meeting Lucy stayed at home, complaining of a sore throat. It was a perfect opportunity to recount the whole story.

It had happened late that Friday night. Everyone had been to a church meeting and did not get back until nearly eleven. They had had supper, then went to bed – all except Harry and Annie. Annie went upstairs to fetch Harry's nightshirt, which her mother had been mending, and he asked her if she was coming down again:

She came into the dining-room and Harry evidently wanted to say something to her but could not. So they two stood there (Harry describes his own experience at that moment as that of having his "tongue glued to the roof of his mouth" – unusual for him!) and at last Harry said "Cull, I want a great many things – " and she answered "So do we all" (in her blunt tone!) and Harry said nothing more, so she said goodnight and went out into the hall and had got up two of the stairs when she turned round and Harry was behind her. So they two stood again and then he said "You will soon be leaving the old home, Cull," to which she answered "Yes – it was very soon," and he said "I should like to make a home for you in the old country, Cull, if you will let me" – and Cull stood still feeling like a stone, and knowing now, until she said, "I will – if Mother will". And they two turned and went into the little room and — I don't know what happened there exactly . . .

This is a faithful record according to Cull's own account. (I think they did it very badly myself!)

Lucy was in bed when Harry rushed into her room to tell her the news, Annie close on his heels. Roused by the noise Gershom soon arrived, followed by Mary and an agitated Maggie, and there was much general crying, joy and congratulations, all in the darkness.

"Diary, it was very very queer," yet, Lucy admitted, it was a fitting end both of a diary and a chapter in her life. Soon, after more than two years, she would be home again, bringing a new sister with her. "When I began you a year ago, I never expected your contents to have been what they are, I thought you would have brought me home to England – my new diary must do that; but you have brought me in a good way, the best way, the shining upward way – and so I thank you."

But there never was a new diary.

4

While Lucy and Gershom were in Tasmania Henry, Fanny and Geraldine, like everyone else at Harley, were following M'Call's party step by impossible step up the 230 miles of cataracts in the lower Congo. A huge map of Africa as it was presumed to be at the time, hung on a wall at Harley and every time news of the little party reached London their progress was recorded with tiny markers. If only they could reach Stanley Pool and the thousand miles of navigable river flowing into the heart of Africa. The gateway to a vast, unexplored continent lay just beyond their reach. On and on they struggled in desperate conditions, with inadequate supplies, no map or guide except Stanley's diagrams, no drugs, no understanding of the causes of malaria, dysentery or the fatal Blackwater fever.

The arrival of the steamer *Livingstone* in 1881 enabled M'Call to press on up the cataracts as never before, establishing stations all the way, Banana, Mattadi Minkanda, Pallaballa, Banza Manteki, Bembi and Manyenga. Each station was consecrated with a grave. As one after another men and women went out and died, husbands burying their wives and wives their husbands, others sailed out to take their place, some dying sooner after landing than those they had gone to replace. Harley mourned and treated each loss as a personal bereavement. But still there was no shortage of volunteers.

Stanley Pool was finally reached in 1883, by which time M'Call was dead. The new steamer, the *Henry Reed*, Mrs Reed's gift to the Livingstone Inland Mission, arrived in Africa in five hundred pieces and was transported, as Stanley's boat had been, on the heads of a thousand carriers up the cataract region, to be reconstructed at Stanley Pool. Fastening the vessel's 160 plates required sixteen thousand rivets, all done beneath a blazing African sun, with no access to spare parts! More men died, many were invalided home, but at last the great day came when the *Henry Reed* could be floated on the upper river and a new adventure would begin.

Fanny had realised for some time that the administrative work of the Congo Mission was becoming too much for her. She was fifty-four, and beginning to feel increasingly tired. It took her all her time to run the Institute these days. The attack of facial palsy had been a warning. It was also an embarrassment. She no longer felt at ease travelling around speaking and raising support. Reluctantly she handed over her life's work to the American Baptist Missionary Union.

Henry was too absorbed in teaching and his travels to notice the decline in his wife's energy and she would not tell him. Her facial disfigurement pained him because of the distress it caused her, but as far as he was concerned she appeared to manage the Institute as well as ever. Geraldine felt uneasy, but dismissed her anxiety. After all her mother was no longer as young as she once was. Rest from the responsibilities of the Congo Mission was all she required.

But Fanny could not rest while she was needed. One day she received a letter from an elderly bachelor friend of the family, asking for advice in an embarrassing predicament. A friend of his had died recently leaving her only child, an eleven-year-old girl, in his care. What should he do? Fanny had no hesitation. She would adopt the child. So Leila Dennison came to live at Harley and once again the schoolroom resounded with childish laughter. Geraldine took over the care of the beautiful little girl, sewing a dress and cape for her in soft blue while Leila did her lessons.

For some months before he left for Tasmania Harry had been begging Geraldine to take over the men's night school. With his medical studies and preaching he was too busy to run it any longer. Geraldine refused point blank. She was not capable of coping with a classful of loud, rough working men, many of them the worse for drink. And she was annoyed that Harry should even expect it of her. Madcap and fun-loving as he was, he could also be exceedingly irresponsible at times.

One Sunday afternoon he sent word to the Berger Hall that he was "unavoidably detained" at the hospital. There was nothing for it. The men were waiting and could not be disappointed. With her heart pounding, Geraldine marched into the class and an hour later decided that perhaps it was not such a bad experience after all. The men were stunned into perfect behaviour when a woman walked into the room. "I can see her now, standing on the platform at

Berger Hall, with her white handkerchief, on the rostrum," one of them said later. "She was like an angel." None of them knew how frightened she was.

That was the start of a new venture. Edith Fookes, three years younger than Geraldine, yet more developed intellectually, took the advanced class at the men's night school, teaching Latin, logic and mathematics. Geraldine's special responsibility was the beginners' class and the drunks. Howard Taylor supplied her with some medicine, which, when administered with strong black coffee, effectually sobered any miscreant she had dragged into the back room for causing a disruption.

Henry Grattan was seriously concerned for his niece and daughter's well-being. However competently they ran the night school, walking home at night unaccompanied through the streets of the East End was another matter. One night Geraldine was feverish and Edith had to go to the Berger Hall alone. Before she left Harley House Henry asked her what time the class ended and despite her protestations insisted he would be there to meet her and escort her home. At the appointed hour Edith sat waiting at the Berger Hall but there was no sign of her uncle. She waited until it was very late indeed, then set off on her own. As she was walking down Devons Road she noticed a small crowd gathered underneath the flaring lights of a public house. Intrigued she went to have a look at the source of the curiosity and standing on tiptoes saw her uncle, diligently scribbling astronomical notes, unaware that he was the centre of attention. Edith pushed her way through the crowd and touched his arm, before he came back to earth, apologising profusely for his remiss behaviour. He was in the process of writing *Light for the Last Days* and it had so absorbed him that he could not think of anything else. Edith forgave him, but never again waited for him to collect her. Like the rest of the family she had learned to respect the fact that "sustained reflection on high themes was to him a necessity of life", as Harry later put it. Harry knew from experience. He had once sat opposite his father in a tramcar from Bromley to Bow without Henry Grattan noticing him.

Strong-willed, widely read and an independent thinker, Edith Fookes had a profound influence on Geraldine. In Edith she discovered certain aspects of the adolescence she had missed. Edith encouraged her to explore her own repressed romantic instincts. They swooned together over the poetry of "our friend" Robert Browning, went to concerts and art galleries and discussed books. Edith insisted that they must take an evening off every week, so that they could leave off their deaconess uniform, "feel normal", and go to some distinguished lecture in the city.

But even Edith, for all the stimulation and encouragement she provided, could not save Geraldine from the bouts of prolonged depression which afflicted her with increasing frequency. She seemed to have inherited her father's intensity without his Irish expansiveness. Unlike Harry she could not relax. Instinctively she felt the blackness of any situation without being able to see its humour. Lucy found it hard to laugh too, but Lucy had charm.

There were times when Geraldine felt the pain of the East End to such a degree that it was almost unbearable. She drove herself day after day until the inner pain became acute back pain once again. Fanny sent for a specialist, and Geraldine was ordered to wear a surgical appliance to strengthen the spine and to rest for several hours every day. When there was still no sign of an improvement she was sent to Redhill to recuperate.

Henry Grattan wrote to her there. It was a wise, loving letter. She wrote on the envelope, "Father – to go with me wherever I go," and carried it with her for the rest of her life. He more than anyone else in the family understood what she was going through. She was so like him: "You have been brought face to face with sorrow, poverty, pain, death, miseries of many kinds. You see the world full of them. The problem presses upon your thoughts, it is too much for weary nerves and heart." He himself had once teetered on the brink of a breakdown. That was why he felt so sad, that he of all people should have relied on her strength so much and understood her sensitive nature so little. But now it was time for her to have a complete change. "Give the brain a rest, give it sleep, give it fresh subjects. Read about other things, about natural history, and whatever interests and pleases you. Go out; let the sweet influences of Nature refresh your tired physical frame and mental nature too. Let sunshine and breezes, singing of birds, flowers and springtime do their work."

It was the perfect prescription. Geraldine returned to Harley House in the summer of 1886, just in time to help Fanny with the exciting preparations for the arrival of Gershom, Lucy, Henry Reed and their new sister-to-be. For a while she was preoccupied and happy. It was lovely having the house full of family again; but it gradually became apparent that Annie Reed was at least as competent as she was in supervising the domestic routine. Geraldine felt no bitterness. It was not in her nature. Her own insecurity did not make her critical of others. Besides she had only run the house to help Fanny. She did not particularly enjoy it and that Annie did was a source of relief.

In the autumn Gershom and Henry Reed set off for the Leys School in Cambridge, and Lucy accompanied her parents to Cliff, where Henry continued his writing. At Harley Geraldine was left to her own devices. The only place she felt really useful was at the night school. She happened to come across a pamphlet called, *The Bitter Cry of Outcast London,* written by a pioneer of social reform. Shaftesbury had died the previous October, but others were taking up the causes for which he had fought so hard. The descriptions in the pamphlet of the slums of South London affected her deeply. She thought she knew how hard conditions in the East End were, but the pamphlet made her realise that it was one thing to see them from the safe confines of Harley, or even to hear about them from the men and girls at her classes; it was quite another to experience them first-hand. How could she begin to understand what it was like to be destitute when her life had always been so sheltered and comfortable? Gradually the idea took root that there was only one way for her to get inside the skin of the poor and deprived. To know them intimately she must live in the same conditions, dress as they did and work where they worked. To identify completely she must become a factory girl.

5

Geraldine saw no necessity to consult her parents. They were at Cliff and what they did not know would not worry them. Besides she was twenty-three and knew her own mind. But she did need an ally. Annie Reed was the obvious choice. As a Tasmanian Annie was free from English reserve and caution. To her it seemed a natural and sensible thing to do.

Annie remembered that the kitchen maid, Sarah, had once been a factory girl, one of the wildest and roughest at that. Pledging the maid to absolute secrecy, they told her the plan and asked about suitable clothing and accommodation. Sarah thought the idea sheer lunacy. Miss Geraldine must have taken leave of her senses! Her posh accent would give her away at once. Factory girls had ways and means of dealing with people who tried to ape them, like stripping to the waist and giving them a good hiding with their fists. With no disrespect, Miss Guinness was such a frail-looking little thing that they could blow her over in one puff. But nothing Sarah said would deter her and eventually the girl agreed to help, on one condition – that she went too. Geraldine consented. She was not as brave as she tried to pretend.

In a pawn shop Sarah found clothes for both of them, then she was sent to Colliers Rents, a turning off Long Lane, just south of London Bridge, to hire a furnished room. Geraldine could hardly preserve her incognito in the East End where everyone knew her and her family. South London was unfamiliar territory and Colliers Rents the very street mentioned by name in the pamphlet she had read. A triumphant Sarah returned with the news that she had managed to rent a room with a bed, table and a chair.

Factory hours were seven in the morning until seven at night, so Geraldine decided to move to Bermondsey on a Saturday evening. That would give her all day Sunday to get used to her new surroundings before she started work on Monday morning.

As the appointed Saturday drew near she was filled with an increasing sense of dread. She kept handling the strange, rough clothes, wondering why on earth she was taking such a step, yet at the same time convinced it was something she had to do. Finally the moment came for her to go up to the schoolroom and put the clothes on. She had never felt so nervous in her life as she buttoned up the drab skirt, wrapped the ticklish woollen cross-over round her shoulders, then pinned on her apron. For some time she stood looking in the mirror at the transformation. Tentatively she lifted up the hat with its large gaudy, trailing feathers and put it on her head. The sight shocked her and she took it off quickly. Slipping a fur cloak round her shoulders, she ran downstairs, holding the awful hat in her hand. She had not the heart to put it on until the last possible moment.

Annie was waiting in the hall. For a moment their eyes met, Geraldine's as grave as ever, Annie's twinkling with unsuppressed amusement. Annie had to fight hard to stifle her laughter all the way out to the pony chaise. She was to drive Geraldine to London Bridge where Sarah would be waiting for her under a lamp by the church. They drove in heavy silence. When they reached the bridge Annie slowed the chaise. With a rather desperate-sounding "Goodbye", Geraldine dropped the fur cloak on to the seat, slapped the hat on her head and stepped down. Annie shook the reins and Geraldine watched the chaise speed away, fading quickly out of sight in the murky October dusk.

Sarah was waiting and together they walked down Long Lane. The frenetic activity and constant noise assaulted Geraldine's senses. She felt in the midst of pandemonium as she wove her way in and out of the stalls and barrows manned by yelling costermongers. The countless public houses looked increasingly inviting as the dank chill of night began to enter into her bones. She was pushed, shoved and jostled by swarming humanity out for a good time and reeking of drink. It was a relief to reach the comparative quiet of Colliers Rents.

The door of their lodgings was locked and there was no sign of the landlady. A woman poked her head out of the next door window and said that she had just gone round to the "public" and would be straight back. They sat on the doorstep for what seemed an age. Mrs Tester appeared at last, considerably the worse for drink yet kindly none the less. She showed them in and they climbed up a ladder to get to their room. Geraldine could hardly believe her eyes when she saw it. It was far worse than anything she had seen in the East End. Sarah had tried to clean it up a bit, but the dirt had defied all her attempts.

That night was the most frightening of Geraldine's life. There were drunken brawls in the street until the small hours of the morning. A whole lodging-house of seventy men was involved in a fight outside their window. Geraldine trembled so much that the bed shook. That was no sooner over when a window was flung open nearby and a woman started screaming, "Murder! Murder!" The police came and took her away.

As dawn cast a grey light over the drab little lane a sort of uneasy, exhausted silence reigned at last. Lying next to her, Sarah had managed to doze off. Geraldine lay awake listening to the sound of the heavy snoring coming from Mrs Tester downstairs. She got up to think and pray, sorely tempted to give up the whole idea. Then she remembered it was Sunday. She would have to find a church. Looking at her skirt and apron it suddenly occurred to her that she had no choice in the matter. Her presence would not be acceptable in a "respectable" place of worship. The boundaries created by class division were rigid. In her factory dress only a mission hall would welcome her. It was this sudden awareness of how pernicious the class system really was, how alien from true Christianity, which made up her mind. She would stick it out.

On Monday morning they started work at the match factory. Sarah introduced Geraldine to the other girls as her mate from the country, which was half true as Geraldine had only recently come back from a holiday at Cliff. Her silence was because life was so strange down here and she was shy. The explanation was accepted. These country bumpkins did find city life hard at first.

Geraldine was torn apart by her experience in the factory. She was terrified of opening her mouth, yet longed to get close to the girls. She was appalled by their conditions of work and angered by the way they were treated. Her heart went out to them. So this was what it was really like. She suddenly felt of no more value than an animal. And for what feeble returns. At the end of the week she and Sarah counted their earnings, a mere four shillings and fourpence-halfpenny between them! It had been a slack week and they had done piece work. On a good week they could have earned eight shillings.

By the end of the second week Geraldine began to feel unwell. The pastor of the mission church she had attended at the weekend urged her to go home and reluctantly she allowed him to send for Annie. It was a dejected-looking Geraldine who climbed into the pony chaise for the return journey. She felt a failure. Those girls had to put up with their lot for ever and she could barely cope with two weeks. And yet, in years to come, when she looked back at those two weeks she was to see how formative they had been. The experience taught her that if necessary she could adapt to a totally alien culture. There could be no better preparation for the unknown future which lay ahead.

She recounted every detail of the adventure to an enthralled Lucy, who was just back from Cliff. Lucy had been feeling at a loose end since she came home from Tasmania, wondering what she should do with her life. Unlike most well-raised young women of their time both sisters intended to be more useful than ornamental. There was no further talk about her becoming a concert pianist and she had to admit that in her circumstances it was hardly realistic. There were more important things in life. Geraldine's adventure in Bermondsey confirmed it. The idea of writing had always appealed to her. She had a natural flair for using the appropriate word, which made even her conversation compelling. Unlike music, writing could be really useful. It could inform, move men and women, and stir them to action. The popularity of Dickens proved it.

She decided to write up Geraldine's experiences. She also felt that to write honestly and realistically she could not simply rely on her sister's account. She must experience the life of a factory girl for herself. Poor Sarah was requisitioned again and repeated the whole process, this time with a determined, persevering Lucy, who in her quest for authenticity was prepared to go to greater lengths than her sister.

In *Only a Factory Girl* Lucy powerfully conveyed the sights and sounds of deprived London, the narrow streets piled high with refuse, "rags and bones, piles of decayed vegetables, bits of paper and scraps of food, bunches of straw, oyster-shells, rotten eggs, fish bones etc., shot off the costermongers' barrows"; the overpowering "exhalations from the steaming fish-shops", the middle-aged woman in shabby, torn clothing with a red and bloated face, dancing about with a drunken man to the sound of a black minstrel band, while the children look on and laugh "at the pitiful spectacle of degraded womanhood".

The door of a public house swings to and fro and a rough working lad inside, seeing Lucy standing outside in the shadows, puts his head out and says kindly, "'E ain't 'ere, old gal! 'E's gorn home, 'e is." Seeing that she still hesitates, he adds, "Never you mind 'im, 'e ain't comin' back 'ere agen tonight. You jest come into the warm, ole gal, you an' yer mate!" And Lucy takes her first faltering steps into a public house.

Inside, dozens of factory girls with pretty faces, half-stupid with drink, allow themselves to be fondled by countless men. "We have often wondered at the language and uncontrollable wildness of factory girls. After tonight's experience, we shall never wonder again, but rather marvel that, seeing their lives are such, and that such places are open to them nightly, they should ever be content to come to our evening classes and sit and sew and spell!"

Out in the street large gangs of girls and lads lark about under the archways, shouting, swearing and singing music-hall songs. What is there to go home to? A wretched tumble-down tenement, cold, damp and overcrowded? Who is there to go home to?

Lucy had never felt so invisible in her life. No one noticed her. As a factory girl she simply did not exist. No one cared that she was cold and wet through with the rain beating down on her bare head. There was one way of keeping warm, the girls told her! "If we listen to their suggestions, we shall never go home again – ! Pardon, gentle reader! We did not mean to shock you. We only wanted to tell you of things as they are."

The booklet did shock its polite readership, and for all the reasons Lucy hoped it would. Its immense popularity led to the formation of the Shaftesbury Society, an organisation still trying to improve conditions among the poor a hundred years later. It was Lucy's first opportunity to test the power of her pen and ensured that she would never again be less than outspoken. She had enabled some to see that the working classes were not inherently different from everyone else, a race apart. There was no such thing as inbred respectability. All men were the same before God, sharing the same dreams and longings. The difference was that by birth some had the means to fulfil them and others did not. This was where Lucy was a radical for her time, why no one could accuse her of patronising the poor. She did not believe they were inferior. Behind her well-fed, well-heeled exterior, she was as much a factory girl as they were:

All the day long, all the year round, from early morning, standing ten hours a day, with weary feet and aching limbs, we work in the din of the busy factory. Often hungry – so hungry – even for a bit of bread! Often tired; always ill-clad; always poor; always tempted to sin; always outcast and despised, for no fault of our own, but that we were born to it – never at peace, and never satisfied; intensely affectionate, yet unloved, except by those who would injure us; unloved by those who would aid us if they would.

THIS is how we live . . .

THOUSANDS OF US LIVE THAT WAY!

"Only a factory girl" people say when they see us misbehave. "Only a factory girl" and they pass on.

ONLY A FACTORY GIRL – But that means SOMETHING!

6

It was in 1886, while Geraldine and Lucy were working in the match factory, that the news broke in the city that Arthur Guinness and Son was to go public. Two-thirds of the shares were to be sold, the rest, worth about £6 million, kept by the Chairman, Sir Edward Cecil Guinness, for his family. The title was bestowed upon him by Gladstone the previous year, "in recognition of your high position in Ireland", and in gratitude for services rendered as High Sheriff for the County of Dublin. Sir Edward, on his own initiative, had personally supervised the warm reception extended to the Prince and Princess of Wales on their visit to Ireland. Given the political tension in the country, the visit could well have been anything but successful. When the great moment came for Edward Cecil to step forward to receive his honour from Queen Victoria, he was perturbed to discover that he had not been informed of the proper etiquette. He was supposed to wait for Prime Minister Gladstone to present him.

Excitement in the city over Guinness shares rose to fever pitch. In an article entitled "The boom in the city", published by the *Daily News* on October 26th, "A Disappointed Applicant" noted that "nothing within the memory of living man had been quite like it". The offices of Baring Brothers and Co. who were handling the sales were besieged. Police tried in vain to hold back the jostling crowds, but Barings' door was still broken. The list of applicants was closed within an hour of opening. Only six thousand of the thirteen thousand who applied for shares were successful. *The Times* was inundated with letters from frustrated correspondents making allegations of dishonesty. It was true that Baring Brothers, not anticipating the demand, mishandled the situation, but there was no question of malpractice on Guinness' part. Bequests to the managerial staff were small and Sir Edward had said all along that he intended to maintain ultimate control.

It was hardly surprising that the demand for shares far out-weighed their availability. The firm was one of the most thriving, well-managed companies in the British Isles. If the workforce had been well treated under the régime of Benjamin Lee Guinness, that was nothing compared to the improvements in conditions made by his son. The *London Gazette* reported, "Sir Edward Cecil Guinness is anything but an ostentatious man. Perhaps his failing is that he leans too much the other way – that he is rather retiring – if not timid. His wealth is boundless, and his enterprise is not less so . . ." He had 5000 men in his employ, whom he treated in a "princely" way:

Emigration allowances, where men are silly, or wise enough (as fortune decides) to leave, are fixed on a large scale, widows are provided for, orphan children educated, and trained for business, and the whole order of things has reached such a pitch of princely generosity as well in the housing and care of the ordinary working man as in the upper commercial grades, that it is probably not exceeded in Europe.[5]

After their experiences in the Bryant and May match factory, Geraldine and Lucy would have approved their cousin's benevolence. A worker at the Guinness Brewery certainly counted as a "someone". He was one of the "aristocracy of the Dublin working classes". There was security of employment, rare in those days. For misdemeanours such as drunkenness, smoking on duty, late attendance, carelessness and wilful neglect, a labourer would be fined but not dismissed. Wages were higher than anywhere else in Ireland. Edward Cecil is supposed to have said, "You can't expect to make money out of people unless you are prepared to let them make money out of you," a radical statement coming from any Victorian employer, let alone an Irish Protestant with a largely Catholic workforce. There had been pensions and occasional holidays with pay since 1860. 1869 saw the appointment of a medical officer, a free dispensary and the free services of a midwife. The medical officer was also a welfare officer, checking out the living conditions of the workforce. This was one of the earliest pilot schemes of industrial medicine. Employees received full pay when they were ill and two-thirds when they were in hospital.

A report from the two medical officers to John Tertius Purser in 1881 stated that in 1880 they had had nineteen thousand attendances at their clinic and had made 2260 home visits. They had prescribed as medicine 764 bottles of wine, 535 bottles of whiskey, and 213 bottles of brandy. What Purser, a Moravian and abstainer from spirits, thought of their treatment is not known, but sixty years later the chief medical officer, commenting on the report, said, "Today, none of such are ever prescribed, but only Guinness, which, it has been found in the process of time, is much better."[6]

In 1872 Sir Edward began his housing programme with the Belview Buildings. Like his Grattan cousins in Bow, Sir Edward had been worried as a young man by the slum dwellings of Dublin, which he saw as the greatest social evil of his age. He was committed to their clearance and began by trying to improve the lot of his own employees. By the time he funded the Rialto Buildings, built in 1882, he had provided housing for a seventh of his workforce. In a report of 1884 he wrote: "A man living in a well-ventilated clean and sanitary dwelling is healthier, happier and capable of performing double the work of one who resides in an over-crowded house, not to mention the liability of the latter to contract disease, draw sick money, or perhaps die prematurely, leaving a widow and family to be supported by the firm."

In 1885 Sir Edward gave evidence to the Royal Commission on the Housing of the Working Classes, saying he had provided 180 dwellings, mostly one- or two-bedroom flats, with living-room, running water, lavatory and scullery. Tenants were regularly inspected and forced to comply with the regulations regarding cleanliness.

Some members of the committee commented that Sir Edward had been too good. His houses were too well-built and their cost excessive. Being too benevolent to one's workforce might not encourage personal effort and thrift. Sir Edward disagreed. He had not done enough. "I have some thoughts of erecting cottages perhaps outside the city boundary in the country and bringing my people in by train if I could see my way to do it, but I have not yet matured my point."[7]

Sadly none of Sir Edward's further building schemes for the brewery materialised. The Belview and Rialto Buildings were not an unqualified success. Many of the flats remained empty, the workers complaining that rents were too high, the coal range too extravagant, the shops too far away and the regulations too restrictive. The latter was a constant matter for discussion. A succession of medical officers demanded penalties for failing to report infectious illnesses and dismissal for those whose homes remained unsanitary. But the management committee recognised that to enforce cleanliness was an unthinkable violation of human rights and privacy.

Because one of his schemes appeared unsuccessful Sir Edward did not give up. He never asked for gratitude and was prepared to learn from his mistakes. A shopping co-operative was established in the Rialto Buildings. The firm subsidised allotments, classes in cookery for employees' wives, and classes in gymnastics for their children. And Sir Edward continued his grandiose building schemes, outside the brewery. Like his forebears he believed in fulfilling his duty once he had discovered it. Some words of Thomas De Quincey describing another well-to-do Irish merchant could equally apply to him: "Protestantism it is that has invested him with these unbounded privileges of private judgement, giving him in one moment the sublime powers of the autocrat within one solitary conscience; but Protestantism it is that has introduced him to the most dreadful responsibilities."

Though he had rebelled against the narrow nonconformist teaching he had received at his mother's insistence at Bethesda Chapel and had read Darwin with an open mind, Edward Cecil's religion was a guiding force in his life and he expressed it in terms of his duty to humanity. The Purser family, partners in the brewery for three generations until it went public, were originally Moravians and John Tertius Purser had a profound influence on Edward

Cecil's attitude to religion and good works. Any man working for the firm who did not wish to take the daily ration of stout to which he was entitled was given a monetary substitute. But Edward Cecil was not the only benevolent employer of his time. Quaker firms such as Rowntree and Cadbury were equally progressive in their thinking. The Guinness Brewery was however unique in the scale and scope of the welfare provided.

It was their outstanding generosity which ensured the family a personal popularity far outweighing their unpopular political stance, as they swam against the strong nationalistic current. Civic gratitude was expressed in a growing number of statues. Sir Benjamin Lee gazed benevolently down on the city from outside St Patrick's Cathedral. Lord Ardilaun's statue graced St Stephen's Park. The people understood their absolute commitment to the economic and intellectual advancement of their country. When the brewery went public Sir Edward gave a gift of three months' wages to all the employees in the commercial department and one month's wages to all the other manual workers. He paid out about £60 thousand but the returns in loyalty and respect were inestimable, particularly at a time of growing trade unionism.

For four years Sir Edward Cecil remained as Chairman of the Board, then in 1890 he decided to devote himself to his many public duties. The sale of the business had increased his disposable wealth. Now all he needed was the leisure to use it, which, after all, was a gentleman's prerogative. After a trip to America he had commented that it was a fine country, but it was no place for a gentleman to live as everyone worked![8] He was only forty-three but his health had not been good. He was subject to the continuous colds and sinus troubles which had afflicted his mother. But there was a problem. Who could take his place? Rupert was only sixteen and along with his younger brother Ernest was still at Eton. Edward Cecil felt it should be a member of his side of the family, a direct descendant of the first Arthur Guinness, founder of the brewery. But he had no full cousins. All five sons of his father's only brother, the Rev. William Smythe Lee Grattan Guinness, had died without issue. One of them, Frederick Darley Guinness, had taken "poison by accident" in 1869, making him the first member of the family to die in mysterious circumstances. Sir Edward Cecil would have to look further afield.

The first Arthur Guinness' eldest son Hosea, the clergyman, had had thirteen children but only two of his sons produced issue. The younger of the two, Francis Hart Vicesimus, had emigrated to New Zealand and started a branch of the family there, one of whom had entered upon a brilliant political career and was soon to become Speaker in the New Zealand parliament. Hosea's elder son Arthur was a clergyman. He had sons, one of whom lived in Tibradden near Dublin. They were keenly aware of their seniority in the family pedigree, but Sir Edward Cecil decided not to approach them. Benjamin Lee had endeavoured to train the Rev. Arthur's eldest son, Arthur Hart Guinness, as a future partner, but the relationship had not been a success.

Of the first Arthur Guinness' other sons, both Edward and Benjamin had daughters. William Lunell's only son, the Rev. William Newton Guinness, had two sons, one of whom was carving out an outstanding career in the army, but Sir Edward was not in touch with them.

The only branch of his side of the family with which he had any real contact was the Grattan Guinness line, descended from Captain John. But their teetotalism made them unlikely candidates for the board of the brewery. Although Henry Grattan was responsible for what was becoming in effect a large international company revolving around the East London Institute, he had little practical business sense and left the details to Fanny. His mind was totally absorbed with treasure of the heavenly rather than earthly variety.

As for Harry, Geraldine, Lucy and Gershom, they stood on the threshold of their own most fruitful years and had already decided upon their goals. With Lord Ardilaun and Sir Edward Cecil they had inherited the Guinness drive and determination, intending to put it to a similarly philanthropic, yet dissimilar purpose. They believed implicitly that not only wealth changed the world. God could do it with only man or woman willing to take the risk. They determined to be that man or woman.

Eventually Sir Edward Cecil turned to his wife's side of the family. In 1881 he had brought in Adelaide's youngest brother Claude, to prepare him to succeed an elderly John Tertius Purser as chief brewer and General Manager. Managers were usually recruited from the ranks of the apprentice-brewers, but when it came to the General Manager Edward Cecil realised how vital it was to find someone as loyal to the firm and the family as the Pursers had been. Claude Guinness was an exceptionally astute man whose standards matched exactly those of his brother-in-law. But General Manager was one thing, Chairman of the Board another. Faced with so few possibilities on his own side of the family Sir Edward was forced once again to turn to his wife's relatives and he invited her brother Reginald to be the new Chairman. And so the banking descendants of Samuel the goldbeater were firmly established on the board of the brewery. The Grattan Guinnesses had had their chance and made their choice. Their vision was too wide and too other-worldly to be contained within the brewing industry.

9

The Building of International Empires

1

Some weeks before Harry was due to sail for England at the end of 1886, he received a letter from his mother which made his heart sink. She was missing him terribly and longed for him to come home. "How glad I shall be to have you to talk to! A man of action, of sociable disposition and popular sympathies." Marriage to Henry Grattan who lived as much in heaven as he did on earth could be a lonely experience. He was not given to chit-chat about the mundane things of life. "Darling Father, you inherit from him all your best gifts, but you also have a touch of your mother in you that will make you doubly useful, I hope!" That was the prelude to the suggestion that he might take over her work when he came home. It would mean shouldering all responsibility for Harley College and Cliff, Doric Lodge, the new training college for deaconesses, and the Berger Mission Hall with its night school. The other mission halls were now independent.

It was the last thing Harry wanted to do. Treves had predicted a brilliant medical career. His success in Australia had made him wonder whether he should not be an itinerant preacher as his father had been. He was essentially gregarious and adventurous by nature. To be stuck behind a desk with mounds of paperwork played no part in his dream. Yet he was the obvious choice. Marriage into the Reed family meant that he would never have to worry about earning his living. How could he refuse? His mother was no longer fit and had overworked for years. Now she wanted to be free to help Father with his writing. Henry struggled without her. The great concepts were there in his head, but he needed Fanny to convert them into readable form.

Reluctantly Harry conceded. He had never admitted it before, but it worried him that his father's preaching was not what it had been. If preaching was an art, then Henry Grattan Guinness had been a great artist, but like any artist he relied on a spark of inspiration to kindle the dry wood of the discipline of his craft. As he grew older that inspiration seemed to escape him at times. At some insignificant gathering he could enthral his audience. But when it was vital to deliver a memorable address, he could be a bitter disappointment. One Sunday Harry had accompanied him to a small church near Victoria Park, where he had preached a marvellous sermon to a sparse congregation. The same evening he had repeated it to a packed East London Tabernacle eagerly anticipating gems of wisdom. By then the inspiration had passed and he stood in the pulpit labouring his way through, stuttering and stammering, an acute embarrassment to everyone present. As he remembered it Harry could still feel the sweat break out on his brow. Yes, it was better that Father should devote himself to his writing, and that Fanny should be by his side to keep his feet on the ground, as she always did. Running the Institute might not be such a deadly experience. It was time there were changes. Fresh vision was required. The idea slowly took hold of him.

Fanny was relieved. She recognised that it was not an easy step for Harry to take but urged him to understand that nothing was for ever.

Dear Father's EARLY experiences were your present ones, and even more marked. Then came a change and for many years his work was that of a teacher rather than a preacher – and then came the Institute. You know what practical work that has meant, but you do not yet fully know how completely dear father is now incapacitated by an overwhelming sense of the call of God in other directions for the management of the Institute.

We are writing again even now! and in these days of infidelity, not only in the lower, but in the upper classes, we feel it laid on us to contend for the faith by writing as well as speaking . . . A widespread and deep awakening is taking place all over England, on the subject of Missions. The Institute OUGHT to be enlarged, extended, improved . . .

Harry had discovered that his life was as hidebound as that of his brewing cousins, his future as predictable. It was the duty of a son to run the family business, and expand it. Fanny had sacrificed all for the work and her husband. That she expected the same dedication of her children was her greatest weakness.

Seeing his mother again after nearly two years was a shock. She seemed smaller, tired, grey-haired and shrunken. He realised then that there had been no choice. She could not carry on any longer. He was also thrilled to see the way his Annie had become a daughter to her, taking as many burdens as she could on her capable shoulders. She was like her future mother-in-law, a deal more practical than any of Fanny's own children. He had chosen the right woman.

He married Annie on March 17th, 1887 at Charrington's Great Assembly Hall, the only hall in the East End large enough to seat all the guests. A formal announcement appeared in *The Times*. "The best wedding that ever was in every way," was how Harry described it in his diary. It was certainly unusual. The congregation was the oddest mixture of London's rich and poor. The Guinnesses' wealthy friends and supporters were there. So were the men and women of the night school. Nobility and rank, elegantly and tastefully dressed, rubbed shoulders with barrow boys, labourers and factory girls in their gaudiest array.

The honeymoon was a trip to Egypt and the Holy Land. Annie's father had left her an allowance which would ensure the couple a comfortable lifestyle, if they so desired. Harry, who had never had access to much money before, suddenly discovered the joy of lavishing expensive presents on the woman he loved. Annie, who possessed neither sentimentality nor a love of trinkets, whatever their value, began a practice she maintained throughout their married life. She sold the jewellery and china behind his back and gave the money to missionary work. Since Harry never remembered what he had given he remained none the wiser.[1]

That was only one of many areas where Annie had to fight to contain, or at least channel, her husband's impetuosity. On the first day of their marriage he left her in London at the Metropole Hotel while he went off to conduct "business". She had no idea where he was or what he was doing, though it was probably something to do with funds for the Institute. He disappeared the following morning too on a sudden impulse and they only just caught the eleven o'clock train from Victoria to Paris. Life with Harry would never be boring.

They journeyed through Lucerne and Milan to Ancona and stayed at the Hôtel de la Paix. "Bad," Harry noted, "fraud wood fire! Men chopping wood for it. Inexpressible odours!" They arrived at their hotel in Brundisi in an omnibus "with about six red 'Indians' hanging on behind". In Brundisi they boarded the SS *Siam*, "a capital and commodious vessel", and had the first opportunity to weigh up their fellow "pilgrims". Harry was much impressed with a loquacious American lady who monopolised the conversation at dinner; then there was the double-chinned ship's surgeon who regaled them with unintelligible Mark Twain jokes; and Mr Hocking, the Eyam curate, who attached himself to them and might have made good company were he not so small "in every way!" When, on the dusty, hot train to Cairo Mr Hocking put his feet up on the seat, "his dusty boots almost reaching Mrs Kimble's shoulder", it was the limit.

Cairo, the journey by steamer up the Nile, the donkey ride to the pyramids, the bazaars where they bought carpets, all seemed unreal, like something out of *A Thousand and One Nights*. Harry thought that the sound of Muslim prayers ascending to heaven as the sun set was like "the wailing of a city dirge, a requiem of days gone by".

They travelled on to Jerusalem via Port Said and Jaffa, touring throughout the Holy Land. Harry bought a difficult horse from a "scamp of an Arab". Hocking, he noted, had the sense to walk! With few regrets they parted company with the tour and went to Damascus to see Dora Fookes who was working there as a missionary. From Beirut they steamed up the Turkish coast towards Greece. Then Harry's diary came to a sudden stop.

Back in Hampstead, where she had settled in a large house since her daughter's wedding, Mrs Reed received a desperate letter. Annie had contracted typhoid fever and was dangerously ill. She had been carried ashore at Smyrna and taken to the Jews' Hospital. Harry was doing what little he could without nursing assistance, because relatives were supposed to take care of their own sick. Mrs Reed packed her bags and set off immediately with Mary.

Before she left she offered the use of her home to Geraldine, who was ill again and needed rest. The publicity surrounding Lucy's *Only a Factory Girl* had turned her into something of a local heroine. She could not cope with the acclaim, and the pressures it provoked. The pain in her back was unbearable.

This time Howard Taylor insisted on a specialist and brought Dr Anderson, one of the best surgeons of the London Hospital, to see her. Anderson was a shrewd and kindly Scotsman from Aberdeen. He knew her symptoms were psychosomatic, but did not dismiss them. His prescription was a total change of environment. That was why she moved into the Reed House in Hampstead. Anderson visited her there every day. As he sat with her he explained gently but firmly that she must learn to conquer her pain. The doctor who had prescribed a spinal board had made her feel sorry for herself. She had a choice. She could either learn the dignity of self-control or give in to self-pity and be a self-made invalid for the rest of her life. Geraldine was shaken. She struggled with Anderson's words for days, and it was a measure of her inner resources that when she returned to Harley to face the family six weeks later, still feeling unwell, she had made up her mind to fight.

Howard had watched her suffer from a distance for years and grieved at his inability to do anything to help. His aunt, Mrs Broomhall, saw how distressed he was and suggested that Geraldine was pining because he had not declared his love. Howard was unsure. She seemed so broken, so unlike herself. It was hardly the best time to receive a proposal. Still, his aunt was wise and a woman. He knew so little about the female emotions. He would trust her judgment.

It was a beautiful June day with the sun streaming into the familiar dining-room at Harley House when Howard found Geraldine there alone. He told her quite simply that he loved her, that he had always loved her since he was a boy, and could not imagine any other woman sharing his life. Geraldine was dismayed. She loved Howard as a brother. She had never thought of him in a romantic light. The pain in his eyes as she declined his offer distressed her unutterably. The last thing she wanted was to hurt this gentle, sensitive man who had always been such a dear and loyal friend. She tried to soften the blow by explaining that she and Edith had decided they were not going to marry, but would devote their lives to serving the poor. That suggested an absolute finality to Howard, which left him in near despair. He apologised for having embarrassed her and let himself out of the house.

Meanwhile in Smyrna Annie made a slow, but complete recovery. She and Harry returned to London and moved into Harley House. Once they were settled Geraldine went to Cliff to see how her parents were coping. Fanny seemed better than she had been for years, alert, interested and a great deal more tyrannical, a discovery Geraldine made to her cost.

One morning a letter arrived from Edith recounting her rejection of an eminently eligible suitor. Without thinking Geraldine read it out loud to her mother. Fanny was outraged. How could the girl be so stupid? What did she mean when she said the life of self-sacrifice they had chosen was far more exciting than "the poetry of romance and the prose of the married estate"? What could be more exciting than marriage?

Geraldine was forced to tell her mother about Howard Taylor's proposal and Fanny was doubly aggravated. Drastic action was called for, action she suddenly realised she should have taken years ago. The girls were too pious for their own good. They had to be separated. Edith was dispatched forthwith to friends of the Guinnesses in Berlin and Geraldine was sent to Ireland, to build up her strength in the invigorating atmosphere of her uncle Wyndham's vicarage in Rathdrum.

It was a difficult parting. She and Edith had been very close friends for five years. Harry and Annie had taken her place at Harley. Lucy was totally absorbed in her writing and Leila had become like a daughter to Fanny. Geraldine was no longer needed at home. What should she do with her life? A holiday in the beautiful Irish countryside would at least give her time to think.

2

The tranquil atmosphere of Rathdrum Rectory always had a soothing effect on Geraldine's uneasy spirit. She accompanied the family on their annual August holiday to Courtown Harbour. Daily rides on the long stretch of firm, white sand, the sea air filling her lungs and stinging her skin, made her feel more alive and at one with her true self than she had done for years.

One morning she rose before dawn and went down to the beach to await the sunrise. A strange orange glow gradually appeared on the horizon, melting the eerie grey light of early morning. As she sat and watched she slowly became aware of another light, this time an inner light, penetrating the dark confusion of her mind. In a flash she knew with absolute certainty that she was to go to China. On the distant horizon a blazing red ball rose silently and majestically out of the sea, illuminating everything around. Day had dawned.

She wrote to tell her parents of her decision. Fanny responded with warmth. It was all she had ever desired for her children. Henry was less happy. Letting go of his daughter was a much harder struggle than he had anticipated. They had been close, especially in recent years. She was a soul-mate. She entered into his dreams and visions in a way Fanny never could. Of all his children it was she who was most fearful of launching out alone.

Since he had a preaching engagement in Ireland shortly after receiving her letter, he went on to Courtown Harbour to satisfy himself that Geraldine knew exactly what she was doing. They spent two days together, talking and walking up and down the beach, and at the end of it Henry gave his reluctant consent. As he had done so many times before, he found an outlet for his anguish in writing a poem, which began, "I give thee up to God, his hands shall keep my Geraldine".

The Victorians were fond of sentimental occasions. Missionary farewells, with their familiar twist of the heart strings, were becoming quite a popular source of entertainment, particularly after 1885 when the departure of the "Cambridge Seven" for China captured the imagination of the public. The "seven" were all Cambridge graduates, and included C. T. Studd, captain of the Cambridge cricket eleven, Stanley Smith, stroke of the Cambridge eight, Montagu Beauchamp, Lord Radstock's nephew, and two officers of the British army. This was no common or garden missionary departure. The cream of England's manhood, its glorious potential, had opted to put God before country. Such self-sacrifice caused an enormous stir.

Geraldine's public farewell took place in a crowded Exeter Hall on January 23rd, 1888. Every eye was fastened on the slim, pale, serious young woman. Her simple close-fitting black dress enhanced her neat figure and clear complexion. She wore a black bonnet on her fair, waving hair, which was parted in the middle and drawn neatly back across her broad forehead. Dr Barnardo spoke about how he had followed her progress since she was a babe in arms.

Then Henry Grattan rose to his feet and said that this was the "gladdest and saddest" gathering he had ever attended. "It is one thing to send out other people's children, but quite another to send out your own," he said, turning to look at her. There was hardly a dry eye in the hall.

Outside in the cold winter rain some of the men and women of the night school were waiting to say goodbye. When Geraldine emerged one man, a tall, rough-looking old pedlar, was so overcome that words failed him. Unafraid of what his mates would say, he took her hands in his, work-toughened and calloused as they were, and with as much dignity as a prince, stooped and kissed them, tenderly and reverently, sobbing all the while. The control which Geraldine had maintained for so long broke at last and she allowed herself a few tears.

On her last morning the family gathered in the dining-room at Harley house. Henry read Psalm 121 from his large, familiar Bible, his deep voice resonant with the emotion of the words: " 'The Lord shall preserve thy going out and thy coming in from this day forth, and even for ever more.' " Lucy noticed the wintry sunshine playing on the coloured glass of the window, painting patches of beautiful light on the floor. But then, she noted later, "details are noticed in the presence of a great, overwhelming pain."

A huge crowd gathered at the docks to wave Geraldine off. There were family, friends, factory girls and students, joined by some of the dockworkers. She could still catch the strains of their singing floating after her down the Thames long after the ship had set sail. In many ways it was a relief to be at last alone.

Naples was the first port of call. Passengers were allowed to go ashore to visit Pozzuoli. It was there that an event occurred which Geraldine endeavoured to dismiss as an amusing, but insignificant coincidence. One of the stately homes had a visitors' book, which was handed to her to sign first. As she put her pen to the paper she suddenly noticed the name of the last entry: F. Howard Taylor. Howard had been to Pozzuoli the previous summer and no one had signed the book after him, until she came. She made no mention of the incident in her letters home.

It was evening when the ship left the lovely Bay of Naples. Geraldine stood alone on the deck waiting to say goodbye to "old Europe", the homeland she had never left before. As the sailors pulled up anchor a voice rang out through the night air, "The chain's short now, sir."

"Heave right up," the Captain called back.

As the ship glided swiftly and silently out of the bay, the sailor's voice called out again, "All's clear now, sir, all's clear."

"All's clear now," Geraldine reiterated to herself quietly and thankfully as the lights of Naples dwindled into distant stars and she set her sights on the new world ahead.

At Penang a crowd of Chinese came on board and installed themselves on the deck with boxes, bedding, household goods and bundles. Their sudden appearance took Geraldine by surprise. It was her first encounter with the people of her adoption and she felt excited and nervous all at once: "Real Chinese they are, with shaven heads, long pigtails and yellow skins – so strange! They chatter away to one another and look kind and friendly, smiling at us – and we do want to love them from the first."

The ship sailed round the Malay Peninsula to the beautiful tropical island of Singapore. A short call there had to be extended when the HMS *Deccan* became ungracefully stuck in the mud when the tide went out. Geraldine and two of her companions could not resist the opportunity of going ashore. It was her first experience of oriental life and she was enchanted. Everything was green and luxuriant, just like the pictures she had seen in the missionary books, and yet so different first-hand. She found it hard to believe that here she was wandering around a silent, moonlit tropical jungle, far from "the pressure of nineteenth-century life in the great world's metropolis".

Singapore town was five miles from the shore. Their only possible method of transport was a jinricksha, "the hansom cab of China": "The nearest approach to it that I can think of is a baby's single perambulator, or the seat and hood of a very light bathchair, perched on two high, slight wheels, and having long, narrow shafts joined in front in a half-circle."

When Geraldine first saw a jinricksha darting about, pulled by a "human Chinese pony", as she called the coolie, she made up her mind that nothing would induce her to ride in one. But if she wanted to see Singapore town there was really no alternative. A jinricksha came to a standstill beside them. The coolie lowered the shafts and she and her companion stepped gingerly inside, convinced the thing was going to tip them out backwards the moment they sat down. To their surprise they stayed upright – until he lifted the shafts and flung them backwards with their legs in the air in a most undecorous manner. Helpless with laughter they clung to each other as the coolie tore off at a terrific pace through a banana forest. There would be many times in the future, when, crossing China in the inferior wheelbarrow, she would long for the comfort of a jinricksha.

The whole adventure seemed totally incongruous to Geraldine, so unlike anything she had ever imagined herself doing – or enjoying. All primness was gone, all the reserve which had been such an impediment. She felt ready for anything by the time she arrived at the China Inland Mission Home in Shanghai. It was there that she put on Chinese dress, a prerequisite of every missionary in

Hudson Taylor's Mission, representing a total identification with the people. Some of the new missionaries obviously found the procedure amusing. Geraldine regarded it as "a sacred and serious exchange . . . a sacrament". But still it was a relief to her that it was dark when she went out in her strange new robe for the first time.

That night she took the steamer to the language school at Yang-chou, a two and a half days' journey up the Yangtze river, travelling second class with the Chinese unlike the rest of the Europeans who paid six times as much for a first-class ticket. It was the principle not the money that mattered. It was there she saw for the first time the prevalence of opium. Drowsy and apathetic, the Chinese women sat in the hot sun smoking all day. But her distress at the sight could not quench the excitement which bubbled up inside her as they travelled on into the heart of the great Chinese Empire.

Acquiring a grasp of the Chinese language was to be a much harder battle than Geraldine had ever imagined. She arrived at the language school to find that it was greatly overcrowded. She would have to wait for a bed and make do with a table meanwhile. She did not have long to wait. That first night she sat by the bed of a young woman dying of typhoid fever. The woman had been in China only five weeks, but her radiant acceptance of God's will left an indelible impression. Whatever she had to face, however uncomfortable or difficult, how could there be room for self-pity now?

It was difficult however to put theory into practice, when no matter how hard she tried, the Chinese language escaped her. She had never learnt the discipline of schoolwork and study, and ended up crying, as she had as a teenager at Weston-super-Mare. She cried so much that her eyes began to trouble her. It was not only the language study which upset her. She was coming face to face with the poverty, suffering and despair of the Chinese people, and, as in the East End, her hyper-sensitive nature refused to let her distance the pain of others. The continual sobbing and wailing of beggars in the narrow street below her window disturbed her beyond measure. "I scarcely know how to write, these sounds of grief so rend my heart. None of the passers-by seem to take any notice, or care at all!" She felt utterly helpless, unable to communicate with them or give them the money they demanded. She had already discovered that the results could be catastrophic.

One afternoon at four o'clock as she was about to go to her language class there had been a loud hammering at the front door; yet another urgent demand for the missionaries to come and save an opium suicide. There were four or five suicide attempts a week, usually women determined to escape their miserable lot. They belonged body, soul and spirit to the man who owned them. Their happiness depended on his mood and treatment. If he died their lives were about as much value as the refuse on the streets.

On this particular occasion the members of the household most experienced with dealing with opium overdoses had just dealt with two cases and were tired out. Geraldine would have to go. Swallowing her sense of panic, she enlisted another missionary called Lottie McFarlane and a local guide and set off through the maze of narrow streets. The guide led them to a respectable-looking house in a quiet courtyard. The living-room was crammed with women, all shouting at the tops of their voices in a state of great excitement. Above the din, Geraldine could just about make out the sound of moaning and confused struggling coming from an inner apartment off to the right. She went quickly into the smaller room and as her eyes became accustomed to the darkness, saw that the creature held down on the bed and struggling like a tormented animal was a child of about fourteen.

Before she could do anything the women dragged the girl into the living-room. Geraldine and Lottie tried to calm her a little but it was impossible in the circumstances. They prepared a strong emetic, but the girl refused to take it, screaming that she would throw herself down the well if the poison did not work.

The onlookers crowded round, amused, indifferent, children playing at their feet, totally unconcerned. Geraldine was loath to ask them to go or to take the girl back to the smaller room as there was such suspicion of foreigners. But eventually, when she realised that the child would certainly die if she did not take drastic action, she led her into the inner room, closed the door and managed to soothe her into swallowing the medicine.

In between vomiting the girl recounted her sad story. She had been sold at the age of six to a cruel family, to be the wife of one of the sons. Her mother-in-law, whose house this was, treated her badly, beating her regularly. The mother-in-law was not there. She had only sent for the missionaries because if the girl died she would have to buy another wife for her son. Nor did she wish to be haunted by the girl's dead spirit.

But the child was not yet married. Whenever a man's face appeared at the window or in the doorway she shrank away in terror. Geraldine tried to cover up the window with a paper curtain, but the men tore it away and continued to leer and giggle.

Exhausted by her ordeal the girl eventually lay quiet, her face a picture of utter despair. Geraldine left her, wondering with a heavy heart what she had actually achieved. Lottie was in the living-room, trying to talk to the crowds of women about the one great God who made and loved human beings. When the men of the house arrived home the missionaries were sent on their way.

Geraldine recounted the child's story to Lottie and was appalled to discover that it was repeated thousands of times throughout the empire. She went up to her room, threw herself across her bed and wept as she had never done before. The culture was beyond her comprehension. "Oh, God – China, China! The whole vast empire, million-peopled – all its suffering, sinning, anguished hearts; its women, its little children! The long years of darkness, the few to bring them light!"

3

After only a few weeks at Yang-chou it became apparent to Geraldine's tutors that the only way she would learn the Chinese language was from the Chinese themselves. She would make herself ill if they did not let her go. With three other young women she travelled in a Chinese river-boat down the Grand Imperial Canal to a mission station at Tsingkiangpu, scribbling down her impressions all the way. The sheer beauty of all she saw took her breath away. Lush green trees fringed the tow-path which ran alongside the vast expanse of pale grey-blue water. Wide water-covered rice-fields, which stretched as far as the eye could see, were intersected in regular squares and strips by raised brown paths. But such apparent serenity only seemed to highlight the terrible poverty and wretched living conditions of the Chinese labourers. Geraldine's descriptions were becoming more reflective and less spontaneous. She knew by now that Lucy was publishing excerpts from her letters in the Institute's magazine, *The Regions Beyond*, but did not know that in pouring out her ever-increasing passion for China, she had started on what was to become her life's work.

Life at Tsingkiangpu did not satisfy Geraldine for long. There were already Chinese Christians there. Brought up with the ideal of reaching the "regions beyond", she wanted to go where no missionary had gone before. An isolated town called Antung aroused her interest and she persuaded a Chinese man to arrange a stay for her on a farm there. Since Lottie McFarlane spoke fluent Chinese she was the obvious choice of a companion. "As Lottie and I are going to live in a real Chinese home," she wrote home with great excitement, "and in all ways possible to conform to Chinese customs and manners, we thought we had better begin at once by taking into use Chinese chopsticks and dining in Chinese fashion."

The reality was less fun than Geraldine had anticipated. Antung was only twenty-five miles from Tsingkiangpu, but the journey took ten hours by wheelbarrow. The Chinese wheelbarrow consisted of a single large wheel, with a seat on either side of a horizontal crossbar. Geraldine and Lottie sat there with their belongings while the coolie pushed. After ten minutes, let alone hours, Geraldine felt she never wanted to sit down again. They stopped frequently at the many villages along the way and crowds came out to gape and chatter and demand treatment from the magic medical case.

It was late evening when they arrived at the farmhouse. The daughter of the house, a pleasant young girl of twenty-one, her mother and sister-in-law with a baby in arms, showed them into the dreariest, filthiest room Geraldine had ever seen. The women were desperately anxious to please but manifestly overawed by the company. After everyone had sat in an uneasy silence for what seemed an age, their hostess asked if they would like to retire. She led the way to one of two apartments partitioned off the living-room by an old blue curtain. The apartment was so dark that Geraldine could see nothing at first, but her sense of smell had not been impaired. As moonlight struggled through a tiny barred window, so high she had not noticed it before, she became aware of a large double bed "of very questionable appearance". At the head of the bed was the retiring place for all the women of the house, hence the putrid odour.

All that first evening they were watched in total silence. Lottie made several valiant attempts at conversation, but eventually gave up. They ate a tea of rice and hard-boiled eggs in silence. Several pairs of wide, searching eyes followed their every movement, even when they got ready for bed. Eventually Geraldine begged them to put their candle out. Despite the nausea caused by the stench and filthy bedclothes, Lottie quickly fell into a deep sleep. Geraldine waited until she heard the women retire, then balancing a lamp on Lottie's lifeless form, with her journal on her knee wrote, "A painful misgiving for a moment crosses my mind as to the advisability of a prolonged residence in such a place!" Her misgivings proved correct. The bed was alive with non-human activity. But neither woman was prepared to give up.

Their determination gradually paid off. Fear of the strangers diminished and they were soon accepted in the town, and in great demand. Geraldine, with her limited medical knowledge, found herself forced to treat cases which would have stretched the skills of many a qualified doctor. It tested her faith to the limits. She learned Chinese quickly.

May 26th, the anniversary of the sailing of the first missionaries to China, was designated a day of prayer by the China Inland Mission. Geraldine rose early and went to a barn to be alone. She rededicated her life to God, reminding him that she would do anything, go anywhere he asked. The young woman who as a child could not cope with six weeks at boarding school now asked if she might not be sent through the closed doors of Tibet where no missionary had ever been before.

In the all-enveloping silence which followed she slowly became aware of an inner voice, speaking quite clearly. "Go anywhere? Do anything? Even marry Howard Taylor?" She was stunned. It was the last thing she wanted to hear. The idea repelled her. But then, as she thought about it, she began to wonder whether she was not in fact in love with her own romantic notion of the devoted life. Marriage would not be so terrible if it was meant to be. She had said "anything" and anything it would be.

For the time being she shelved the idea. There was nothing she could do about it and there was much else to occupy her mind. The hot season had arrived and she was ordered back to Yang-chou. Submitting to discipline was never easy, but there was wisdom in the instruction. The temperature rose to a steaming 106 degrees and life at Yang-chou was a little more bearable. "We have WATER to drink (just think of it!) and a little milk sometimes, and feel ourselves rich in comforts."

A month later she boarded another Chinese river steamer, bound for the P'o-yang Lake in the great province of Kiangsi. A number of Chinese passengers were very taken with her and invited her to sit and picnic with them on their little piece of carpet on the deck. It would have been rude to refuse, but Geraldine had not bargained for what followed:

> Next came tea, of course politely offered, and I was nothing loathe to accept, but what was my surprise when the elder woman handed me the large teapot bodily, and seeing my momentary hesitation, went on to put the spout to my lips . . . But they seemed so pleased when I drank it, and took the teapot myself to facilitate the process, that I really enjoyed it, in spite of the consciousness that we were being watched by at least a hundred curious eyes.

Among the amused spectators were not only Geraldine's fellow missionaries, but also a dignified, aristocratic-looking gentleman, who turned out to be Grand Duke Alexander of Russia, full cousin and ambassador to the Tsar. For a time Geraldine wondered what she would have done if she had known, and then decided with satisfaction that she would have done exactly the same. After all, she was ambassador to a far grander king than the Tsar!

It was at Kiangsi, sitting on the shores of Lake P'o-yang, that an announcement in *The Regions Beyond* magazine caught her attention:

> Dr Howard Taylor, MB Lond., FRCS, has been assisting his father, the Rev. J. Hudson Taylor, in his present lecturing tour in the United States and Canada. We heartily congratulate both

father and son on the entrance of the latter on that co-operation in the China Inland Mission for which he has been so long and so thoroughly preparing, and to which he so unhesitatingly devotes the superior talents, high qualifications and bright young energies which could easily raise him to eminence and fortune at home.

So, he was coming. What would it mean? She tried not to think about it.

As it happened Howard's elder brother Herbert, his wife and little boy were taking a few weeks leave at Lake P'o-yang too. She got on well with them and they invited her to accompany them back to the province of Honan. All Harley people knew the name of Honan, the "unreached" centre of the empire, fifteen million people without medical, social or spiritual help of any kind. Geraldine jumped at the opportunity.

Christmas Day, her twenty-sixth birthday, was spent en route for Honan in a cold Chinese junk, moored to the sandy bank of the Han river. Christmas dinner consisted of rice, potatoes, cabbage, carrots, tea and bread. "We have salt too, and sugar and condensed milk, so what more can we desire?" But the apparent cheerfulness disguised the desperate loneliness she felt at being so far from home at Christmas and on her birthday.

The journey across Honan to She-ki-chen, their destination, was the most difficult of any she had ever known. Snow fell making the roads almost impassable. It was bitterly cold and the wind howled across the exposed fields, making the hours being carried by chair a miserable experience, especially for the Taylors' little boy. In addition no foreign woman had been to the region before, so that when they stopped at an inn crowds pressed in upon them, wanting to see their unbound feet. On one occasion the crowds were so frightening that the landlord begged them to leave. Before they could escape they were surrounded by hundreds of leering, shouting men and were forced to submit to the examination of scores of hands wanting to ascertain that they were really women and not men in disguise, as their unbound feet suggested.

At She-ki-chen life was no easier. Once it was known that Geraldine had some medical knowledge she was in constant demand. Apart from the steady stream of opium suicides, there were countless cases of mumps, measles and whooping cough, often fatal because of ignorance. The commonest treatment in Honan for illness of any kind was the administration of long, red-hot needles. Few babies or small children survived such treatment.

At first people came to her, but she wanted to do more. To visit local homes was a major breach of local etiquette, but after several weeks of being shut up within four walls she felt she would go mad if she stayed indoors any longer. Everywhere she went, she was followed by huge crowds of men, poked and prodded, leered at and jeered. Frustrated and exhausted she persevered, preaching to groups of women, whenever possible, before the men drove them away. There was little sign of success.

Looking back on the year Geraldine described it as one of the hardest, most difficult years of her life. Her eyes were giving her trouble, probably because she was crying so much again. She resented having her liberty curtailed just because she was a woman. But this was not Africa, amenable to Western influence. The ancient Chinese culture was strong and well-established. Ultimately there was no choice but to submit.

More than anything else one memory filled her with searing pain and would haunt her for the rest of her life. Herbert Taylor's wife gave birth to a baby girl. It was not easy in their cramped quarters in She-ki-chen with little privacy or comfort, but a trained nurse had come from another station and all had gone well. Although the baby was strong and healthy, the mother took a long while to recover. This put great strain on Geraldine, who ended up running the house, caring for the Taylors' little boy, and responding to the constant stream of callers. To make matters worse the baby became ill with dysentery. It was then, at near exhaustion-point, that Geraldine made a fatal mistake. The nurse asked her to pour out a dose of medicine for the baby. Under pressure she took the wrong bottle. The medicine was administered and the little one quickly lost consciousness and died.

It was the most appalling shock. A funeral was out of the question. In China a dead baby girl was of no value whatsoever. Herbert Taylor carried his little daughter out to some quiet spot in the Honan countryside and buried her there.

Geraldine was utterly devastated, the more so because Herbert Taylor and his wife made it clear that they bore her no bitterness. She wrote home to Hudson Taylor, telling him everything, asking him whether death might not have been due to the baby's illness. She longed for comfort, for some sort of reassurance from the head of the Mission, who also happened to be the baby's grandfather. Not being a medical man himself Hudson Taylor wisely passed the letter on to Howard.

That was the start of a new, intimate correspondence between the two. Only Howard knew the guilty secret which gave her no respite day and night. There was no one else with whom she could share her despair. She had forgotten what a dear friend he had been, how strong and sane he was, how much she had relied on his brotherly comfort in times past.

When, some months later, she went to Shanghai, badly in need of rest and treatment for her eyes, Howard was standing on the shore of the river waiting for her. He had just arrived from England. One look at his face told her that his feelings had not altered with the passage of time. His attentive behaviour so embarrassed her that she could hardly hold his gaze. In his usual way he took over and she was in no mood to resist. She was tired of being independent, strong and brave, to the point of a foolhardiness which led her into all kinds of catastrophic situations.

Howard prescribed for her eyes and they responded to treatment. He left for language school almost at once, but since he was the only doctor in the area and had to travel to the coast a great deal, he managed to fit in regular visits to his eye-patient in Shanghai.

Meanwhile, without telling her sister, Lucy had illustrated and edited Geraldine's letters home and published them in a book called *In the Far East*. A first print run of five thousand was sold out within weeks. It was to run to several editions, and was translated into French and Swedish.

The importance of the book was in its open expression of Geraldine's outrage at the results of the opium war at a time when the British government was coming under increasing pressure to ban its export. The harrowing stories she told of opium suicides armed the crusaders in their struggle. The government, determined to subdue and control the rebellious Chinese in the interests of expansionism, and the dealers, equally determined to hold on to an exceedingly lucrative market, were highly embarrassed by the publicity.

She told of one occasion in She-ki-chen when she was called to the bedside of a dying sixteen-year-old. She cradled the girl in her arms, while the girl's two distressed little sisters, aged ten and eight, clung to her hand. In the next room their mother smoked herself senseless: "Heartsick and overwhelmed with grief and shame, I bowed my head beside that dying child. There swept over me an awful realisation of the part England has played in this devil's triumph – the heavy curse of my adopted people."

Barely a house in China had not known some death because of opium. Was it any wonder, Geraldine asked, that one Chinese actually said to a missionary, "I don't know about heaven, but I know there is a HELL, for China has been a hell ever since you brought the opium to us."

The whole empire was saturated with deadly poison, rammed down their throats at the point of a bayonet. Having administered the killer-drug by force, England must now find the antidote and put right the dreadful wrong she had done. As far as Geraldine was concerned there was only one way to do that. "We have given them our OPIUM; can we refuse them our BIBLE?"

What Geraldine never understood was that her letters had a contradictory effect. In her vivid descriptions of China, fired by indignation, she unwittingly conveyed her frustration with the Chinese culture, caricaturing its people in the eyes of the British public as slant-eyed, sly and untrustworthy.

Hudson Taylor, recognising the powerful influence of Geraldine's writings, also missed their potentially negative effect and asked Geraldine to write a history of the Mission. She agreed, though reluctantly, finding the thought of staying in Shanghai, and the discipline needed for research and writing irksome. But the idea of conveying the atmosphere and needs of China to the people at home was very attractive.

In May 1890 Howard came to Shanghai for a few days before setting off for Honan. It was there that once again he asked her to be his wife. Inevitable as she knew it was, she had dreaded the moment. She had made up her mind in the barn nearly two years earlier that if he proposed she would accept, but she never anticipated how numb she would feel. Howard was almost beside himself with joy and cabled the news home. Both sets of parents were thrilled. Everyone was excited, except Geraldine. She had presumed that somehow, when the moment came, she would suddenly fall in love, but in fact she felt nothing. She could not face the congratulations and begged Howard to keep their engagement a secret. He was a little puzzled, but since he was about to go to Honan it did not seem too unreasonable a request.

Barely had he reached his destination when a letter arrived from his betrothed begging him to release her. She loved him as a sister, not as a wife. She needed time. Would he please write to her as he always had, as a friend, not a lover? Howard was devastated, yet he would not force her hand. He was not that sort of man. He would wait.

But he could not have known how long that wait would be, for in March 1892 a cable arrived in Shanghai asking Geraldine to return to England at once. Her mother had had a stroke. This time it seemed it might be fatal.

4

In the four years Geraldine was in China life for the family at home had not stood still. The publication of *Light For the Last Days* at the end of 1887 and *The Divine Programme of the World's History* in 1888, established Henry Grattan Guinness as one of the foremost authorities in the world on history, astronomy and biblical prophecy. It was in *Light for the Last Days* that he first suggested that the evidence seemed to point to 1917 as a crucial year for Jewish restoration. In 1889 status was at last added to reputation when he was awarded an honorary doctorate in divinity. Next came the singular honour of a fellowship of the Royal Astronomical Society, hardly surprising considering that his astronomical tables were a standard reference in many observatories throughout the world.

Dr Dreyer, FRAS, in charge of the Armagh observatory, verified their accuracy and added:

The tables will be of great practical value to chronologists and historians, who can find from them the day of the week, and the age of the moon corresponding to any date. Particularly to students of oriental history they will be invaluable, as the noon is the clock-hand of Eastern nations. But they will also in many cases be of great use to astronomers as a ready means of finding by a mere glance the whereabouts of the moon in the sky at any time during the last three thousand years.[2]

The books were published in the United States to great acclaim. The hostility of nearly thirty years ago was long forgotten. A new generation had arisen, deeply devout, raised on the preaching of D. L. Moody, the most popular American evangelist of the nineteenth century. Moody had stirred up a fascination for biblical prophecy and a missionary fervour more powerful than in Britain. Guinness was a personal friend of Moody. The name opened doors all over the land and Henry Grattan spent almost the whole of 1889 and most of 1890 touring America and Mexico. Men such as John R. Mott, the founding father of the World Council of Churches, would later say that it was to Henry Grattan that he owed the inspiration for his own world-wide travels.

Fanny stayed quietly at Cliff and Gershom went up to Caius College, Cambridge, the science college known affectionately as "stinks", to study medicine. "Mother is writing another missionary book about the Upper Congo region," he wrote to Geraldine. "How she does work! As far back as I can remember, it is always Mother writing away late at night, by the light of a green-shaded candle-lamp. Darling Mother, may God keep her still strong and well!"

At the Harley Institute Harry indulged his ever-widening vision to the full and, following a well-established pattern, left the practicalities and consequences to his capable wife. He studied for his MD degree, supervised the intake of new students, dealt with the mass of correspondence, and fulfilled an endless stream of preaching engagements. Annie, who gave birth to their first child, Annie Geraldine, known as Gene, in 1888, and a second, John Frith Grattan in 1889, administered a business which rapidly expanded into soup kitchens, medical mission and dispensary, midwifery school, maternity hospital and children's home. Lucy went to live at Harley House to help, taking full responsibility for the night school, but more important, editing a monthly magazine, so that supporters could be kept up to date on the industry's ever-increasing ramifications.

At first she simply intended to inform her readers, to touch their hearts and their purses, but gradually, as her writing gift became obvious and the circulation of *The Regions Beyond* increased, she became bolder, adopting a more crusading, political tone.[3] Her passionate nature and ruthless honesty would not let her keep silent in the face of gross social injustice. It appalled her that the miners' strike of the early 1890s could leave thousands homeless "under pitiless wintry skies", without anyone raising a voice of protest; that fifty thousand men and women in London alone were suffering unemployment and no one seemed to care; that alcohol was claiming the lives of a hundred and fifty people a day but no one did anything to stop it. "Is there no mutter of a pent-up storm in the social atmosphere?" It amazed her that the working classes had not risen to throw off the shackles of the miserable oppression they were forced to endure. Yet comfortable England lived in blissful ignorance of the fact that she teetered on the very brink of revolution.

According to Lucy it was not only the gross injustices on her own doorstep which the vast majority of England's complacent citizens chose to ignore: "In the 'free ports' of China, day by day, the officials of the Imperial Customs are dealing with our Indian opium to an extent that makes Queen Victoria the greatest poison-seller the world has ever seen." Was it not enough, she demanded, that fifty years earlier we had bombarded a helpless, defenceless people with our British shells until the gutters of Canton ran with blood, that we should now bombard them with a substance yet more destructive? Not satisfied with that, we were now on the point of wreaking the same damnable destruction in Burma and in India. "Jesus-opium", the Asian people called it, because it came to them from a so-called "Christian" civilisation.

Lucy's anger burned with such indignation that her outspoken accusations might have earned her a libel suit in a later age. She had no qualms about naming names. If Queen Victoria was a "poison-seller", than Her Majesty's government was little better. The Commission of Inquiry appointed to look into the opium trade was a farce. The Chairman, Lord Brassey, KCB, was the director of a company that made its enormous profits from opium. Its parliamentary representative, Mr Robert Mowbray MP, had voted in favour of the traffic. Its Indian representative was the Maharaja of Darbhanga, one of the largest poppy-growers in the country. Other names were listed as evidence that the commission could hardly be unbiased.

But God saw it all – that was Lucy's comfort: "He sees the English

Government supporting and continuing this work, its mouth full of loud futilities and arguments to prove the excellence of its system; and in its heart the blackest misgiving, a desperate half-consciousness that its excellent system is INDEFENSIBLE." By the early 1890s the nation was paying for its sin, in the Indian Mutiny and Afghan war, costing the country millions of pounds and the annihilation of our troops, in the desperate financial crisis caused by the collapse of several building societies, which swept away about £50 million sterling of national wealth, in the social unrest of the dockers' strike and miners' strike. Britain deserved to lose her ill-gotten revenue. It was not an acceptable argument that if we did not ruin China someone else would. One day we would reap the rewards of our murderous behaviour. It was as well that Lucy had no idea how prophetic her words were, or of the tragic consequences their fulfilment would one day bring to her sister's fellow missionaries.

However much she believed in divine retribution Lucy never sat back passively. As long as there was breath in her body she would rally support from an indifferent "Christian" British public for the poor and downtrodden, for the prohibition of opium, for action against the Arab slave trade in Africa, flourishing right under the noses of the British gunboats. The only cry for justice Lucy appears to have ignored came from Ireland. Home Rule was not a cause she supported. Not a hint of criticism of the British government's handling of the Irish problem appeared in her writings. Perhaps one blind spot was inevitable. But she did what little she could to resolve the problem on her own doorstep. So did Harry. Their motto, the principle upon which they built their lives and the whole Harley industry was: "'Inasmuch as ye did it unto one of the least of these . . . ye did it unto me.'"

The sight of human suffering never left them untouched and the suffering of the East End seemed to increase as the years went by. By 1890 life there reached an all-time low. Jack the Ripper prowled the streets, terrifying factory girls. Poverty increased. The arrival of thousands of immigrant Jews, ready to work for a pittance, had meant a radical reduction in the average wage and massive unemployment.

One December day Lucy came upon a group of powerfully-built, honest-looking young men singing on a street corner. They were dressed in the rough corduroy of working men, and had the familiar "toil-worn" look which she had come to know so well. "The grey, hungry look of want and hopelessness", on their faces, though equally familiar, pained her terribly and she stood for a while in the biting cold listening to the words of their song. She had heard it before. It was a new popular song, called, "Git it to do", but somehow the words had never affected her so deeply before:

Thousands in England is starving,
> it's all through no fault of their own;

The troubles of poverty sharing,
> and only to them it is known!

It's 'ard when the cupboard is empty,
> and through the streets poor men must roam,

All the week through no work to do,
> with poor 'ungry children at 'ome.

Then pity the unemployed workman,
Starvin' all the week through;
They don't want to shirk any kind of 'ard work,
But, kind friends, they can't git it to do!

That experience convinced her of the need to provide meals for the unemployed. They became a regular feature of life at Berger Hall and she could hardly believe the rush which ensued the moment the doors were opened. The men ate ravenously. Some had not had a square meal for months. Whatever money they had fed their wives and children. Lucy never forgot the sight of one dispirited, middle-aged man with barely the strength to walk the length of the hall to collect his food, holding his basin with trembling hands and eating as though the rest of the world had ceased to exist. It never failed to move her how steaming hot soup and meat pudding could effect such a radical change in people. "An altered look – a human look – comes over the men."

It was this belief in the innate dignity of mankind hidden behind the degrading effects of poverty which motivated the establishment of a medical mission and a midwifery service. There were few progressive firms like the Guinness Brewery in the East End.[4] Most families depended for their support on dockers and labourers, whose work was casual. A doctor's visit cost a shilling, a small fortune for most people. The London Hospital offered free medical help, but it was three miles away, too far for a mother with small children and no means of transport, and for a worker it would mean the loss of a day's work.

At two thirty every Tuesday and Thursday afternoon the doors of Berger Hall opens to admit a stream of people, pushing and shoving their way up the stone stairs to get an early place in the queue. A Harley student is waiting to take their particulars and ensure that they really cannot contribute towards their treatment.

"What's your father's occupation?" he asks a young girl.

"A bricklayer."

"Bricklayer, or bricklayer's man?" asks the student, trying to assess the probable income.

"I couldn't say which, sir. I never sees 'im lay the bricks!"

The girl gets the coveted blue ticket which says, "Patients must attend on Tuesdays at half past two o'clock, and bring a bottle and galley pot." The ticket entitles her father to see the doctor for two months for the sum of a penny. A white ticket would mean a charge of twopence. The small charge is a vain attempt to cover the costs of the vast quantities of medicine needing to be dispensed, about seven to eight gallons a surgery. The bottle and galley pot, carried by every prospective patient, are the means whereby the miracle cure is carried home.

By 2.45 the chapel, converted into a waiting-room, is packed to the doors. The people are still coming and there is half an hour before the doctor arrives. A student takes his place at the harmonium and leads half an hour's hymn singing. The deaconesses move among the female patients, sympathising with the elderly, offering child-care advice to the young mothers and spiritual counsel wherever it is needed.

At 3.15 the doctor arrives and patient number one disappears inside the makeshift surgery. In three hours he sees between seventy-five and a hundred patients. The most common complaints are arthritis and rheumatism, fevers, asthma and bronchitis, but often a more sinister disease, consumption or cancer, is present too.

Every week Harley students helped the doctor and under close supervision manned the dispensary, learning as they went. Handling vast quantities of strychnine, arsenic, prussic acid and opium was frightening at first, but they recognised that as future missionaries they might have had to do the same thing without experience or training.

The midwifery course for the deaconesses took only three months, but such was their wealth of experience in that short time that most of them passed with ease at the London Obstetrical Society's examination. Harley's maternity department was opened in 1890. In 1894 the Bromley Mission Hall was converted into a nursing home, but most of the maternity and post-natal care still involved visiting women in their homes. Many a woman in labour had cause to bless "them 'eternity nurses", as they were called. Of all the social work undertaken by the Harley Institute, this was the most heart-rending. The conditions the deaconesses saw and the pathetic stories they heard were a real test of their suitability for work overseas. In many homes they found women lying in indescribably filthy conditions, on beds of dirty rags with no blanket to cover them, in damp, freezing houses with no money for food or coal. They were often so worn down by malnutrition or consumption that they either produced a stillborn baby or did not survive the birth themselves.

Harry and Annie recognised that the deaconesses could not simply hand motherless children and babies over to the workhouse and in 1895 they opened their first children's home. It was Annie's special love and interest for many years.

The work of the Harley Institute among London's poor was by no means unique. It was one of many Christian charitable organisations whose work was a striking feature of the East End of the 1880s and 1890s and formed part of its colour and character. Political socialists have accused them of dealing with the symptoms rather than the disease. When the Earl of Shaftesbury died they lost their political voice. But on the whole they were more interested in changing the individual than the system. They did what they could within the realms of their own calling. They did it with an earnestness and a single-mindedness which cost them their own comfort. And though at times they may have patronised, may have been a little too earnest, love covered a multitude of sins and earned an abiding respect.

Where the Harley Institute was different was in the breadth and scope of its undertaking. The Guinnesses were not satisfied with doing, they trained others to do and taught them by example. The East End was merely one of many fronts on which they were working. Injustice must be fought throughout the world and as Harry would soon discover, there were times when the cause demanded aggressive political activity.

5

Throughout the 1890s, while the Grattan "empire" expanded in the East End, social concerns preoccupied Sir Edward Cecil Guinness too. In many ways, faced with widespread social deprivation, the Harley Institute, for all its achievements, could only stick a plaster over a gaping wound. Sir Edward had the means to deal with the festering sore itself. Once he had made up his mind to rid his two home cities of the scourge of the slums, no effort was spared to achieve his aim.

He stayed on the board of Arthur Guinness, Son and Co. as a trustee for his three sons, but to mark his retirement from active management he invested the vast sum of a quarter of a million pounds in a trust fund. The aim of the Guinness Trust was to provide decent housing for the labouring poor. Two hundred thousand pounds was to finance various building projects in London, the remaining £50 thousand in Dublin. It was an imaginative, radical idea. Low rents were to be charged for brand new dwellings. That way the fund would be kept intact, albeit by a low return of interest, new homes could be built, and the lot of the tenants would be improved "without placing them in a position of being the recipients of bounty".

The familiar Guinness Buildings began to appear all over London and Dublin. Though by today's standards some may seem grim tenements, in their time they were unique. There were community bathrooms for men and women, laundry rooms, facilities for making tea with boiling water, sheds for the costermongers' barrows and spacious yards so that the children could play safely. For what *The Times* called "the most splendid act of private munificence that had been contemplated and carried out in our time by any Englishman",[5] Sir Edward was created Baron Iveagh.

Not all of Dublin was pleased. It provoked lengthy correspondence in *Truth* and the *Dublin Evening Telegraph* about whether he had any right to assume the hereditary title of the Magennis family. Although Sir Edward had genealogists to support his claim, nothing could be proved either way and the debate was left to quieten down. Henry Seymour Guinness, eldest son of Henry Guinness and director of the Dublin branch of Guinness Mahon, was fascinated by the hullabaloo and began his own research into the family pedigree. His findings were inconclusive.

Meanwhile Ireland's only private bank and land agency prospered quietly. In 1891 Captain Willie O'Shea divorced his wife Kitty on the grounds of her adultery, citing Charles Parnell, the leader of the Irish Home Rule party, as co-respondent. The party disowned him. Lucy Guinness' adolescent wish some ten years before, that Parnell be punished for his insolence, appeared to have been fulfilled. Parnell married Kitty and died three months later, poverty-stricken and broken-hearted. All his money had gone on his political campaigns. Guinness Mahon were the receivers of the O'Byrne estate in County Wicklow, where Parnell owed £50 rent on some quarries. The company wrote to Mrs Kitty Parnell to ask whether she intended paying the rent or surrendering the quarries. It cannot have been an easy letter to send. But apart from that single contact with the famous, the directors of Guinness Mahon – Henry in Dublin and Richard Seymour in London – kept their heads firmly ensconced in the business. Their lives were pedestrian. Richard still failed to keep account books, but the brothers wrote to each other daily about business matters. There were no outstanding parliamentary careers in the banking branch, no clergymen or missionaries, no great acts of philanthropy, no peers of the realm and no mixing in high society; not yet at any rate.

For Sir Edward Cecil however it was now imperative to find a suitable country seat in England, so that he could entertain according to his new status. When Elveden Hall in Suffolk came on the market following the death of the Maharaja Duleep Singh, he recognised its potential at once. If the house appeared past its former glory, the estate was one of the best shoots in England, and that was of far greater importance. Buildings could be altered to meet requirements.

The Maharaja was an Indian Prince deported to England and given Elveden in compensation for the annexation of his territory by the British army. Although he had transformed a modest Georgian manor house into an elegant mansion, his interior design was not as tasteful as it might have been. He had tried to recreate the atmosphere of an Indian palace, covering the walls from floor to ceiling with mirrors, but the overall effect was more suggestive of a high-class music hall than an Indian palace.

The Iveaghs, who enjoyed a sense of oriental splendour, decided to develop the theme. A duplicate of the Maharaja's mansion was built nearby, then the two buildings were linked by a massive round edifice, topped with a copper dome. This central block constituted the sensational snow-white Marble Hall. It was an attempted miniature of the Taj Mahal, with pillars and galleries and Indian designs carved into the marble from the floor to the dome. Two huge Renaissance-style fireplaces dominated the room. Around the fire in the late afternoon the guests would congregate for tea, the ladies in their elegant tea-dresses, the men in their tweeds as they returned from the shoot. And in the evening everyone would gather in full evening dress before the formal procession into the dining-room, with its magnificent tapestries. The fireplaces were in fact for show; the Iveaghs had the whole house centrally heated.

A passage connected the main building to a large new servants' wing. There were seventy men employed in the game department alone. A house party of about thirty guests would require as many servants in the house, not to mention accommodation for the maids accompanying their mistresses.

The stables Sir Edward built looked from the outside almost as grand as the house itself. The invention of the motor car a few years later made them largely redundant. Sir Edward was a fervent automobilist.

The effort and energy invested by the Iveaghs in redesigning Elveden to their taste reaped rich rewards. The Prince of Wales was a regular visitor, even after he became King Edward VII. So was his son, the Duke of York, the future George V. The latter was invited on his own merits as a crack shot. His father however only appeared to take any interest in the proceedings when the ladies arrived for lunch.[6] The future Prime Minister, A. J. Balfour, was also a favourite guest.

Shooting parties usually lasted from Monday to Friday. An elaborate ritual evolved. The guests were given the time of a London train and descended with servants, trunks and innumerable round black hat boxes at Thetford Station. No lady travelled without her "dress basket", a large wicker receptacle covered with shiny black fabric, which contained the dresses she would need for five days. Ladies were expected to change regularly and never wear the same dress twice. Waiting to transport the entire party and belongings to the house would be a well-organised procession of carriages, brakes, dog-carts and traps. The Prince of Wales and the Duke of York were met by a carriage with postilions and a guard of honour supplied by the Lord Suffolk Hussars. In time, Sir Edward tried to persuade them to use his motor car, but the Prince of Wales never trusted the new-fangled invention and insisted that a second car travelled behind in case his broke down.

On November 14th, 1895 Augustus J. C. Hare recorded in his diary his impressions of a house party at Elveden. He went, he maintained, hoping to meet the Duke and Duchess of York, but to his disappointment the Duke was there alone, the Duchess awaiting "an impending event". The Duke he found "very unaffected and pleasant", good-looking and punctual, "probably due to his naval discipline". But, said Hare, how boring it must be to be a prince. There is never any real discussion as no one dares contradict him. Nevertheless the house party was lavish even by Hare's standards, and he had been a guest in the homes of all the mighty in the land.

I floated here in the luxurious saloon carriage of a special train, but felt rather shy, because whereas all the rest of the party were on terms of Christian name intimacy, I knew none of them except Lord Rowton . . . But I was interested to see those who are so frequently part of the royal circle, and liked them all, especially Lord and Lady Carrington; but then everyone does.

I wonder if you know this house of Elveden? It was Duleep Singh's and he tried to make it like an Indian Palace inside. Much of his decoration still remains, and the delicate white stucco-work has a pretty effect when mingled with groups of tall palms and flowering plants. Otherwise the house (with the kindest of hosts) is almost appallingly luxurious, such masses of orchids, electric light everywhere etc. However, a set-off the other way is an electric piano, which goes on pounding away by itself with a pertinacity which is perfectly distracting. In the evenings singing men and dancing women are brought down from London, and are supposed to enliven the royal guest.

You know, probably, how this place is the most wonderful shooting in England. The soil is so bad that it is not worth cultivating, and agriculture has been abandoned as a bad business. Game is far more profitable . . . Each day I have gone out with the luncheon party, and we have met the shooters at tents pitched at different parts of the wilderness, where boarded floors are laid down, and a luxurious banquet is prepared with plate and flowers.[7]

In lavishing their attention on Elveden the Iveaghs did not neglect their other homes. In 1899 a new ballroom, studded in onyx, was added to the house in St Stephen's Green in Dublin at a reputed cost of £30,000. A ballroom of Carrara marble was installed at Farmleigh. Despite her role as a society hostess, Dodo was old-fashioned in her attitudes. She never invited anyone to her balls whom she had not already met. The *Tatler* describes her as having "an incongruously puritanical appearance". It rebukes her for "a severe smartness and a proud reserve which can only be equalled by that of our typical grande dame, the Duchess of Buccleugh . . . Your parties, if dull, are reckoned among the most exclusive in London."[8] The truth was that Dodo had never become completely accustomed to wealth. The attitudes learned during a penny-pinching childhood remained ingrained.

Sir Edward's grandson, Lord Moyne, maintains that the grandeur of the Iveaghs' hospitality often masked the simplicity of the host and hostess.[9] There was nothing Sir Edward liked better than to spend time alone with Dodo and his family. He made a point of leading the household prayers morning and evening and enjoyed a close friendship with Mr Blundell, the rector at Elveden, whose profound sermons sometimes reduced the congregation to tears. To his staff he was always kindly and approachable. "It costs nothing to be polite," he would say.

While some have maintained that his sudden anonymous incursion into the art market between the years 1887 and 1891 was undertaken with philistine rather than aesthetic purpose, Lord Moyne remembers the quiet pleasure his grandfather displayed as they admired the paintings together when the schoolboy dropped in for lunch at 5 Grosvenor Square. Some two hundred paintings by Rembrandt, Millais, Vermeer, Gainsborough, Turner, Watteau, Van Dyck and Canaletto were later housed in Kenwood and bequeathed by Sir Edward to the nation, so that the general public could enjoy them too. In fact Lord Iveagh had the perspicacity to see that in competing for paintings with the foremost American millionaires he had effectively preserved a collection of valuable treasures for the British nation.

While the Iveaghs were entertaining royalty at Elveden, their sons were at Eton. Rupert still struggled on an academic level. His headmaster approved his behaviour, however. Rupert was, he said, "a model of good conduct and good temper to all . . . I think that his character is one of the most perfect I have ever met with in a boy here and I can hardly think it possible that he could ever do anything discreditable." He then added sadly, "I wish his ability approached his character in excellence."[10]

If Rupert's confidence was shaken by his lack of academic achievement, especially compared to that of his brother Ernest, it was restored by his prowess in rowing. He was the perfect build for a rower, small, yet stocky like his father, with broad shoulders and good strong muscles. In 1895 he beat the champion Guy Nicholls in the Diamond Sculls and became a popular hero overnight. In 1896 he went up to Cambridge and spent a year rowing. He won the Diamond Sculls again and was regarded as the undisputed amateur sculling champion of England. It was then that doctors diagnosed a weakness of the heart, wrongly as it later proved, and his father ordered him to stop. He left Cambridge too. Without rowing, there was little reason to stay on.

With his favourite pastime denied him, Rupert turned to his second love: scientific experiment. He still spent hours with his microscope and when a workman at Elveden was bitten by a rabid dog he persuaded his father to endow Lister with £250,000, leading to the establishment of the first Radium Institute. Despite the young man's obvious scientific ability, Sir Edward had a blind spot when it came to his eldest son. He could not see how Rupert could ever develop the vital cerebral qualities necessary to run a successful business. Though Rupert was made a director in 1899, the title meant little. Ernest was nearer his father in temperament. He was also a brilliant engineer. When it came to brewery matters, Rupert was usually passed over in favour of his younger brother. Of gentler stuff than Sir Edward expected, in Rupert a new breed of Guinness was born to the Lee or brewing side of the family, a Guinness more like his cousin Henry Grattan's line, in his penchant for travel, innovation, scientific discovery, and ultimately in his total identification with the poor.

10

1890–1900

Adventures Overseas

1

In 1891 Harry Guinness sailed for the Congo. It was a journey he knew he had to make despite the risks, and Annie, despite her third pregnancy, knew it was useless to argue.

The idea had first taken root in his mind in 1888 when John McKittrick came back to Harley College from the Congo with Bompole, a native boy from the Balolo tribe. Years before, when McKittrick had been a Harley student, Harry had found something immensely likable about the enthusiastic, gentle Irishman from Belfast. Both men were athletic and adventurous by nature, both filled with a deep and abiding passion for Africa. Their close friendship was almost inevitable, and it was cemented by McKittrick's engagement to Dora Fookes, Harry's cousin, who had just returned from Damascus.

McKittrick had spent four years with the Livingstone Inland Mission at its furthest outpost on the Equator, but it had become a frustrating exercise. The American Missionary Union, which had taken over when Fanny could no longer cope, did not have her pioneering vision. It had settled down in the lower cataract region, with no intention of forging on northwards into the unknown Upper Congo. McKittrick was disappointed by their attitude. Before his leave was due he asked permission to go on an exploratory journey by canoe up the river to the vast horseshoe bend between Equatorville and Stanley Falls. This was known as the Lulonga region, the home of the populous Balolo people. Permission was granted and what McKittrick saw there made the hairs on the back of his neck stand on end, and filled him with the certainty that this was where he was meant to be.

Listening to his friend's stories of the savagery of the Balolo people, and to Bompole's pleadings that the white man should come and help them, Harry became convinced that Harley College should once again be a base for pioneering work in the Congo. In 1889 he set up the Congo and Balolo Mission, later to be known as the Regions Beyond Missionary Union, to support McKittrick in this new venture.

Geographically and historically, 1889–90 was to be a memorable year as far as Africa was concerned, and the missionaries had no small part to play. The death of Mackay of Uganda re-aroused public interest in the continent. Stanley published *In Darkest Africa*. There was a conference in Brussels of the great powers, called to look into ways of curbing the slave trade there. A small yet vocal group of protesters, including Lucy Guinness, publicised the dire results of the drink traffic for Africa. The British South African Company opened up Rhodesia and the Church Missionary Society sent an expedition out to the Sudan. The exploiter and the defender of the exploited raced against each other, irresistibly drawn by the magnetic powers of that mysterious land.

In February 1889 John McKittrick had married Dora Fookes and in April they left for the Congo, heading a team of six other Harley students. Dora McKittrick sent Harry a detailed account of their arduous journey, made for the most part on foot. Sudden violent storms and torrential tributary rivers made it hazardous, especially for the ladies with their respectable Victorian skirts clinging limply around their ankles in the heat. Despite the discomfort, Africa seemed to weave its magic spell around her. Its beauty was more spectacular, more dazzling than anything she had imagined. Immense flowering shrubs, a riot of colour, wafted their perfume down-river on the breeze, so that the scent reached them long before the incredible sight met their eyes.

From the time the party boarded the *Henry Reed* at Stanley Pool and steamed into Lulonga territory, her letters took on a darker tone. "Every prospect pleases, And only man is vile," she wrote bitterly. The words of the hymn seemed to encapsulate her feelings. A corpse had floated past her down-river, its hands and feet bound to a stake. This was the work of the slavers. Then she saw them first-hand, their canoes laden with their terrible human booty.

The McKittricks and their party did not dare land, for the river bank was lined with hostile natives, who, thinking them slavers, were armed with spears and knives. They anchored midstream and tried to make friendly overtures from there, until at last the drums telegraphed their message of peace throughout the forest and they knew it was safe to go ashore.

The missionaries quickly earned a reputation for peace and fairness. Four stations were established within three years, Bonginda,

Ikau, Lulonga and Bogandanga. Dora McKittrick soon discovered that compared to reality, Bompole's account of the cruelties of his people was tame. They suffered as much from each other as at the hands of any foreign slaver. Victims of tribal warfare, or even of tribal customs, would be strung up, have their arms and legs broken and be left to die. They loved blood. Throat-cutting, knife-throwing at a human target, and feeding people to the crocodiles were commonplace. So was cannibalism. Legs, arms and hands, boiling in a pot or dry roasted, were considered great delicacies. The macabre reality of life in Lulongaland tore Dora's nerves to shreds, and reading her letters, Harry knew it. That was why he decided to go. How could he be the secretary of the Congo Mission and represent their struggles adequately, if he did not see them first-hand?

An added impetus to his decision was his interest in tropical medi-cine. In 1890 a young Congo Christian called Mandombi came to Harley College at his own expense suffering from sleeping sickness. He hoped that by studying his case the English doctors might come up with a cure. Harry never could resist a challenge and having completed his MD degree in Brussels in January 1891, specialising in tropical medicine, he decided to continue his research by sailing on to the Congo. Annie and the children were left en route in Tasmania with Annie's mother.

By July he was reunited with the McKittricks at Bonginda. He had barely arrived when he and John began to make preparations for two exploratory journeys, one north and one south, to discover the limits of the Balolo tribe and assess the feasibility of setting up new mission stations. Both regions were unexplored. The north was inhabited by the fierce N'gombe tribe, given to a particularly atrocious form of cannibalism. Inevitably the two men decided to go north first. The plan was that on their return from the second trip they would rejoin Dora and travel with her to Stanley Falls. But nothing worked out according to plan.

The journey north exposed Harry to his first experience of the barbarism of the area. Lulled into a false sense of security by the beauty and apparent tranquillity of his surroundings, he had begun to wonder whether some of the tales circulated about the natives were not a little exaggerated. One evening, putting in for wood, they found themselves in the burnt-out ruins of a village which had just been raided by the N'gombe. Harry saw both a decapitated corpse and the frightfully mutilated body of a young boy. He could not now ignore the brutal facts before his eyes. Nor would the Mission's supporters! The art of photography, still in its infancy, was one of Harry's favourite hobbies. His most treasured possessions on the expedition were his tripod and large box camera with its heavy metal plates. He took copious photographs whenever he could. No one at home would believe him unless he did.

That experience was nothing compared with what was to come. On August 22nd they arrived at a village called Bosi Dikolo, where the natives were so friendly that they pressed and crushed into the "tent", a sort of low roof supported on a few posts without walls, until the perspiration poured down Harry's face.

The following morning a great "palaver" was called. The chief's minister presented them with the ritual, placatory "dash" consisting of plantains, fowls and a goat. Then he made a formal, goodwill speech and expressed the hope that John and Harry would act as arbitrators in settling peace terms with an adjoining N'gombe village. Bateko, their spokesman, graciously replied that they would be only too delighted to re-establish peace between the two villages, but that they would not accept the goat until they had succeeded. He then placed their "dash", two tin plates, two tin spoons, some blue beads, some cowries, and two pieces of cloth before the chief. The natives were delighted with the gifts, and after they had volunteered five or six guides, the party set off.

Naïvely Harry expected the same welcome at the next village, Bongwonga, but the heavy silence which greeted their arrival made them feel uneasy. The story of what happened then, recounted in a letter home, still made Harry's flesh creep to think about it.

When we reached the enclosure we found the gate shut and before we could mount a little ant-hill to gain a view of the interior, we heard the unmistakable war-cry within! McKittrick leapt on to the roof of a house, and shouted out that we were come on a peaceful errand, whilst a number of us passed through an open space that separated the house, into a kind of wide street, three hundred yards long. The moment I could take in the situation I saw it was one of critical danger. A scout had evidently warned them of our advent; the women had fled to the wood, and the men, painted in hideous guise for the battle, and armed with spears and shields, presented a horrible spectacle. Bateko and an old N'gombe man ran towards them, gesticulating wildly to show our pacific intentions, whilst McKittrick and myself advanced towards them absolutely unarmed. We made our men keep in the background and eventually, when we got to within forty yards of the spears of the dancing demons, sat down before them and awaited the issue. They were so astonished at our behaviour that they did not kill us on the spot, as they could have done with the greatest ease, but maintaining their threatening attitudes, and waving their spears with horrid cries they advanced quite close to us.

Bateko cried out, "See, I am unarmed, I come for peace, not war", whilst the old N'gombe man with equal intrepidity jumped repeatedly over his spear, which was an oath of friendliness, and then throwing it on the ground, took some leaves and stuck them on its point which was tantamount to saying, "May I be killed with this spear if we preserve not the peace."

It was a terrible moment. A bright execution knife flashed in the sunshine close by the old man's head. We thought he was wounded and that furious vengeance would be poured upon us, but we sat perfectly still, and were, thank God, absolutely composed and fearless.

Another difficulty threatened, a number of the enemy were stealing outside the houses to the upper end of the enclosure where our men were stationed. We saw that they were being surrounded and that all our pacific representations were useless. McKittrick jumped on the chair and shouted, as he pointed out in an unmistakable way their discovered strategy. After half an hour of suspense the storm began gradually to abate, and eventually some of the painted warriors came and shook hands with us, carrying however their shields and spears all the while. We established ourselves in a little house where we lunched as well as might be expected under the circumstances. Towards the close of the meal one of their most prominent men, a powerfully built fellow, with cicatrices the size of a Calabar-bean in front of and below each ear, yelled out at the top of his voice, "They love me! Come here! Come here!" and by degrees a good many gathered round us and we did a pretty brisk trade in purchasing fowls and eggs. At length when we thought that peace was fairly established, we were suddenly surprised, when the same man gave a shout, and all his men at once fell back into line and again grasped their spears and shields. What had taken place? One of the N'gombe with us had said some unadvised word, and the storm was round us once more. There was nothing for it but to face it. McKittrick and I put our chairs in the open in front of the house and sat down as before. It was a trying time, far more than I can tell, or you understand. A cruel death threatened us at every instant.

The problem was that the natives thought the white men were representatives of the Belgian state authorities and were terrified of them. Though Harry and McKittrick carried guns, they had already decided only to use them as protection against wild animals, never against human beings, not even in self defence.

A respite came once more. The warriors held a private palaver to which they summoned the old N'gombe man from Bosi Dikolo.

Satisfied with what he had to say, a peremptory "dash" was offered of fowls, plantains and an antelope and a big palaver about the peace proposals was promised for the next day.

Night fell and Harry began to feel ill with a fever. He only wanted to sleep, but McKittrick, sensing that all was not well, stayed awake by the camp fire. One of their men had disappeared. An uneasy, tense sort of truce reigned all night, everyone jumping at the slightest sound, until five in the morning, when the old N'gombe man, who had gone to sleep in the chief's tent as a sign of goodwill, suddenly returned to tell them that the enemy had decided to kill them all. It would be madness to stay.

Reluctantly they fled into the forest, the enemy in hot pursuit. McKittrick fired into the air to frighten them. Harry was so weak he could hardly hold his rifle. Not until they saw Bosi Dikolo in the distance did they realise with immense relief that the ordeal was over and they were safe at last.

The upshot of the story was that the missing man, who had fled in terror, also found his way back to Bosi Dikolo. He so stirred up the people with his story that they went out and killed sixteen Bongwonga men who were out hunting, and carried off their heads, which were subsequently eaten. So much for the peace terms which Harry and McKittrick had hoped to arrange. The state finally decided that enough was enough and sent officer Mr Peters and his men into Bongwonga with their own solution to the problem. Thirty-four of the N'gombe died at the muzzle of a gun. State officer or slaver, superiority belonged to him who wielded the magic weapon.

Harry meanwhile gave up any idea of making a second journey south. The tribes there were at war, making it a pointless exercise, and he was still suffering from recurrent bouts of fever. He stayed instead at Bonginda, witnessing the work there. Dora had learnt the language from Bompole and had started a simple school.

In November he took a trip down-river with the McKittricks, John entering with boyish delight into his role as captain of the SS *Pioneer*, the new steamer, a gift from the Irish YMCA. He was brimming over with life, full of his usual Irish banter, which made the sudden attack of blackwater fever all the more stunning. It was a sinister disease. No one knew its cause or its treatment, but its dire effect on the red blood corpuscles left its victims completely anaemic.

By the time Dora got him home to Bonginda the fever had abated and he seemed much better, though very unlike himself. He would not let her out of his sight. He tried to get dressed, but was too weak and had to go back to bed. Within two days of their return she noticed a sudden change come over him and sent for Harry at once. Harry took one look at the comatose figure and fell to his knees by the bed. "Be with our brother in the hour of his death," he whispered and only then did Dora grasp what was happening. She was utterly devastated. Before she even had time to collect her emotions, her husband was dead. "Africa kills all her lovers," one of the missionaries wrote home to England. Few had loved Africa as devotedly as John McKittrick.

Harry stayed on to baptise the first five Balolo converts, then set off for home, taking Dora and another Harley missionary called Luff with him. All three went down with the blackwater fever on the way and Dora nearly died herself.

On January 29th, 1892 the family in England were stunned to receive a telegram which read, "John McKittrick died November 22nd. Luff died December 19th. Dora and self returning. Guinness." Exactly one month later Fanny had a stroke and her life hung in the balance. Despite the shock of the telegram's terrible news, the family were immensely relieved that Harry was on his way. They wired Geraldine in China, asking her to come home at once.

By the time they arrived it was evident that Fanny would live. Though still paralysed down one side, she was beginning to regain some feeling and a little speech. Harry was too ill to be of much help to her, or to enjoy his new baby son, Henry Reed Guinness, whom he saw for the first time, or to enter into the family reunion, with Geraldine back from China, Annie from Tasmania and Lucy from a successful speaking tour of the United States.

He did however manage to send off a detailed report on the sleeping sickness to Dr Sir Patrick Manson. Its value was inestimable in their research into the disease, Manson wrote to Fanny, so that even if her son had not come back alive, his journey would not have been in vain.

2

Geraldine was never entirely sure of the exact moment during those two years in England that she knew she was in love with Howard Taylor. She only knew that some time before she went back to China she was ready to fix the date of their wedding.

When she first arrived home the girls of the night school had heard the news of her engagement and bombarded her with questions about her intended. Was he handsome? Was he kind? And all Geraldine said was, "You would love him."

"You'd be jealous if we did, Miss," Matilda replied and the girls shrieked with laughter. But not Geraldine. Not a flicker of a smile crossed her face. It was far too serious a matter.

With Fanny still paralysed, unable to say very much, but in Leila's tender care, Geraldine travelled extensively, researching her history of the China Inland Mission. She was in England long enough to see the book's immense success. Its sentimentality gave it an instant appeal. Geraldine's contemporaries were fond of heart-rending deathbed scenes. But if sentimentality sold the book, there was no denying the self-sacrificial existence of the early missionaries to China.

As a wedding present her future parents-in-law invited her to accompany them on a tour of the United States en route for China. Leaving her mother to her twilight existence at Cliff was a terrible wrench. To see what had once been a fine, active, competent woman reduced to a helpless, dribbling invalid was hard to bear. So was her father's distress. But if she had stayed it would have pained them more. At least Fanny had the satisfaction of knowing that her children were living out her dreams. Harry was fit again and his family continued to expand at a steady rate. Lucy had her writing and was becoming a popular speaker at the large new conventions at Keswick in England, and at Northfield, Moody's conference centre in the United States. Gershom was practising medicine at the London Hospital with a view to leaving for China himself, following long conversations with his elder sister.

It was April 1894 when Geraldine eventually docked at Shanghai. This time she allowed her eyes to meet Howard's as he stood waiting for her on the quay. She walked off the boat and he longed to touch her hand, to enfold her in his arms, but Chinese propriety would not permit it. Instead the expression on his face said it all. It was over seven years since he had first proposed. She was now thirty-one, but he had loved her ever since in pinafore and pigtails she had opened the door for him twenty years before.

They were married by Bishop Cassels on April 24th in a crowded Shanghai Cathedral, both in Chinese dress. The cathedral was a mass of flowers. Geraldine wore pale grey, white being a sign of mourning in China. Her two bridesmaids were in mauve silk with real flowers in their hair. As she walked slowly down the red-carpeted aisle the organ played "Oh rest in the Lord, wait patiently for him, and he will give thee thy heart's desires", from Mendelssohn's *Elijah*. These words had sustained Howard through the long years of waiting when he doubted that this day would ever come.

That night they set off on a three-week wedding trip by houseboat up the Imperial Grand Canal. They boarded the ordinary-looking junk to find that friends had draped their little cabin with red cloth. When they pulled the cloth back they discovered that there were huge cracks in the woodwork separating them from the boatmen's living quarters. Their friends' forethought protected them from prying eyes and converted the cabin into an attractive, cosy little home. A lamp had been lit and yet another wedding present, a pretty, toy-like china teaset had been laid out on the table. It was an idyllic honeymoon. The canal banks were a mass of spring flowers and Geraldine felt as if she were playing at married life. It was over all too soon.

Back in Shanghai they discovered that Howard's parents had set off for Honan in a very agitated state. A crisis had arisen which threatened the resignation of about fifty missionaries. Howard and Geraldine thought their father far too old to be making such a punishing journey and rushed after him to stop him. But neither Hudson Taylor's sense of responsibility nor his determination had diminished with age. If they could not stop him there was only one alternative, to join him.

The journey was a mixture of adventure and misfortune. In eleven days they covered 1280 miles, travelling for the most part by wheelbarrow. One day they arrived at such a steep hill that Geraldine was determined the coolies should not push them. To their utter astonishment she and Howard leapt out and raced each other to the top. For a few moments of glorious abandon they shook off the restraints of an alien culture, revelling in the exhilarating view, the softness of the air and the sweet scent of some wild shrub which covered the hillside. "Oh, China, China!" lamented Geraldine. "We could not stand near together, or sit down side by side and enjoy the beauty and the stillness. Very stiffly and properly, we had to make our way down the hill again, at a little distance apart. Was there ever such a country for a wedding tour?"

If the inns in which they stayed were not quite up to Geraldine's usual standard of hygiene, experience had taught her to cope – or so she thought – until the day the landlord sprinkled sugar over her rice ball with the filthiest fingers she had ever seen.

"Oh Howard, how can I eat it now?" she asked.

"Don't tell him they're dirty," Howard replied cheerfully. "No doubt he thinks they're cleaner than most people's and quite fit for use as sugar tongs."

Geraldine looked up doubtfully at her landlord and this time caught him licking the offending fingers with relish! The dismay on her face made Howard roar with laughter. No wonder his father nicknamed him, "The Lifeboat". He was unsinkable.

Howard's indomitable spirit stood them in good stead over the weeks of torrential rain, continual drenchings and hold-ups due to flooding. Howard's inner strength carried her through the heart-break of her first miscarriage. She would have only one more chance of motherhood and again the bumpy roads, continual joltings and miserable conditions of barrow travel ensured the termination of her pregnancy. Ever after she would be subject to bouts of longing for the two children she never bore, until the day when unexpected circumstances gave her back the joy she thought she had forfeited.

By the summer Hudson Taylor had completed his mission successfully and it was time to escort him back to Shanghai. In the carts the temperature rose to an unbearable 140 degrees and they decided to travel by night.

One night on a forsaken country road two mysterious gentlemen suddenly materialised out of the shadows. Geraldine nearly died of fright. The howling of wolves had set her nerves on edge and she thought the two men were brigands. One of them was Mr Hoste, a missionary, and the other the legendary Pastor Hsi, who had come to escort them safely to the next town.

Pastor Hsi, whose life story Geraldine would one day write, was one of the foremost leaders of China's indigenous church. Given the mistrust of the imperialist tendencies of the foreigner, the missionaries had long since recognised the importance of handing over all responsibility for small new churches to the Chinese themselves. "We have to be most particular not to give anything to the Christians or enquirers, which would attach them to us," Geraldine wrote. Where there were men like Pastor Hsi, there was no problem.

Mr Hoste had an ulterior motive in coming to meet them. In a country where men were not allowed to look at a woman, let alone speak to her, he needed them to help him propose to Gertie Broomhall, Hudson Taylor's niece. It was a novel experience for Geraldine to act as a go-between in such romantic circumstances. Fortunately Mr Hoste was accepted and the couple joined the party so that they could be married as soon as possible. Geraldine hated waving goodbye to Pastor Hsi. She had loved him like a daughter from the moment they first met.

Gertie only just survived to see her wedding day. She and Geraldine were enjoying the luxury of travelling in an enclosed mule-cart. As they were crossing a ford much deeper than anticipated, the mules panicked and broke free. To their horror the two women found they were completely trapped and had started to float down-river. The more they struggled the faster the litter sank. Mr Hoste and Howard suddenly noticed their plight, dived in and swam after them. It was quite a struggle and Mr Hoste was white-faced when he eventually managed to open the litter door, lift his slight young fiancée out and carry her to safety. The litter had sunk too far for Howard to reach Geraldine, but the muleteers arrived in the nick of time and hauled her to the shore with ropes. She was badly shaken.

It was with little regret that they came to the end of the journey, left their parents in Shanghai and set off back to Honan. In the three years before their marriage Howard had been the only doctor in a province the size of England and Wales with a population of thirty-five million. He now wanted to explore Cheng-chou, a town no missionaries had ever visited before.

Cheng-chou was an ancient prefectural town, so exclusive in its traditions and fixed in its ways that the inhabitants had given even Confucius a hard time. Howard found a little house to rent and rushed back to Geraldine to tell her how beautiful it was. The walls had been covered with fresh mud and the windows freshly papered. Geraldine was thrilled with the prospect – until she saw it, an old, dirty little cart-inn consisting of four rooms, a dilapidated roof which leaked, and a dark prison-like courtyard enclosed by four high walls. But she had to admit with the irrepressible Howard that after their recent travels any home would be beautiful!

Geraldine worked hard to make the shabby little house with its sparse furniture feel like home and it soon became a refuge, not only for them, but for the masses who flocked to Howard day and night for treatment, and for many a stray, homeless animal. One dog became Geraldine's special friend. When he came to them he had been a nervous, cowering creature, but before long his tail came out from between his legs and curled right over his back. He would run in to greet her wagging it furiously. Geraldine rejoiced in his new confidence. It symbolised all her dreams for the Chinese women.

But one day her dog crept in shivering and yelping and in a terrible state. Some boys had poured boiling water all over him and he had come home to die in the only place where he had known real love and peace. Geraldine wept bitterly for her faithful old friend.

Though a warm, tender-hearted man, Howard was often puzzled by his wife's emotionalism. Their relationship was not always easy. They were dependent for all their resources, emotional, spiritual and intellectual, on each other and they were very different. She was excitable and impulsive. He was much more rational and sensible. She was given to great swings of mood, whereas he was even and steady. His methodical reasoning often grated on her nerves. He was just too calm, too considerate and concerned for her well-being. It stifled her sense of freedom and independence. Marriage, she realised, could be an asphyxiating experience if she let it, or it could be enriching if she submitted to its discipline. She opted for the latter. Howard, she decided, had the nicer temperament. She would give way to him as often and as generously as she could. Over the years they did learn to complement each other, but that meant sacrifice for both and it never came naturally to Geraldine.

While maintaining a base at Cheng-chou they also hired rooms at Kai-feng, gravitating between the two and leaving the latter station in the hands of two missionaries, Ruth Brook and Mary Hodgson, while they were away. It was at Kai-feng that they had what was probably their most traumatic experience in China, and a taste of the horrors to come to that turbulent empire.

The city was in a state of distress caused by the worst drought for many years. A Buddhist nun, jealous of the missionaries, spread the rumour that they had large sums of relief money to give away and every person who called at their house would receive a generous hand-out.

On the appointed day barrows, carts and crowds arrived in their masses, all demanding the money which they thought was theirs by right. Howard and Geraldine spent the day apologising and explaining politely that there had been a mistake. Disgruntled and disappointed the crowds dispersed, but suspicion and rumour in the town soon grew into a desperate howl for revenge.

The single women were upstairs, Howard in the courtroom and Geraldine in the guest-hall when a vast mob arrived, poured over the walls and invaded the entire house, smashing whatever they could get their hands on and carrying off whatever they fancied. They forced their way upstairs. Mary Hodgson managed to slip away to a neighbour's house, but Ruth Brook was beaten and her clothes violently stripped off her back. Geraldine tried to help her and was attacked by the crowd and treated in the same way. A woman with a hoe hacked at her and split her head open. The blood poured down her face and neck. Holding her torn clothing around her, she was standing waiting to be hit again, marvelling at her own sense of calm, when her attackers suddenly froze. A commanding Chinese gentleman, whom Geraldine had never seen before, had pushed his way to the front and his presence seemed to have a sobering effect on the mob.

"My name is Wang," he said to her.

"I hope, sir, that you will stay with us until help comes," Geraldine whispered, allowing herself to take a quick look at her rescuer, which was improper conduct for a woman. In the circumstances propriety was the last thing she was worried about. She suddenly wondered what had happened to Howard.

"I will not leave you," Mr Wang replied reassuringly.

Within minutes they heard another commotion. The Mandarin had arrived in full attire. Grabbing four of the perpetrators by their pigtails, two in each hand, he shook them until they quaked. Most of the mob fled. Twenty-four were arrested. The Mandarin was a fine young Manchu, very zealous in observing law and order and very apologetic for what had happened. Howard had been tied up to a post in the courtyard and his arrival had only just saved him from being stoned.

That evening they bathed their wounds and, sitting amidst the dereliction which had been their home, ate the hot meal which the

Mandarin had had sent. The next morning he sent clothes, a cart and mules so that they could travel back to Cheng-chou in relative comfort.

One month later, when things had quietened down, the Mandarin invited them back to the town and they were received with full civic ceremony, bands, banners and a triumphal procession worthy of royalty. At the city gate they passed the twenty-four culprits kneeling in chains by the roadway.

Howard went straight to the Mandarin's residence and as a favour, begged for their release. The Mandarin, who had intended making a great example of them, said that Howard might make any request he wished, anything but that. Howard insisted that he had no other request and eventually the twenty-four men were led under armed escort to the mission courtyard and made to kneel down. They thought their last moment had come. So did Howard. Suddenly the Mandarin presented him with the key to their padlocks. As they cowered in front of him Howard walked slowly over, unfastened their chains one by one and lifted them to their feet. The men were beside themselves with disbelief and joy.

But most important for Geraldine, Mr Wang, their mysterious protector, who had carefully watched the proceedings from beginning to end, decided that if this was Christianity, this strength and dignity which he had witnessed, then it was a noble and worthy calling for his own life.

3

The photographs of the Congo which Harry published aroused considerable public interest. No one had seen anything like them before. There were Stanley's vivid descriptions, but they still left a great deal to the imagination.

It was the missionaries who acted as the nearest thing to a television in their day. Their revelations were the first step in the shrinking of the boundaries of the world. They disclosed the mysteries of unknown empires and godforsaken continents. They turned legend and fairy-tale into reality with their descriptions and photographs of strange tribes and peoples. The Grattan Guinnesses played a part, not because they were more committed or self-sacrificial, but because, as part of their Guinness heritage, they possessed the drive and breadth of vision necessary to propel them further than other missionaries before them, to the "regions beyond". They were often criticised for it, accused of individualism, of preferring to set up their own societies rather than work with anyone else. Visionaries rarely fit into a team well.

Nor was their crusading passion for social justice, with its implicit and sometimes explicit, criticism of their great homeland, always regarded with sympathy by their contemporaries. Like their ancestors, the first and second Arthur Guinnesses, with their abiding distaste of bigotry towards the Irish Catholic community, the Grattan Guinnesses acted according to the dictates of their conscience, exposing the exploiter and defending the exploited. Maintaining the balance was a fine art. How to deliver the opium eater from his deadly habit without making him a European, how to save the African tribesman from the slavers and turn him into a law-abiding citizen without destroying his tribal individuality, these were the constant dilemmas. The Guinnesses may not have always got the delicate equilibrium between religion and culture right, but unlike the state authorities, the British army and many denominational missionaries, they tried. The rigours of life at Harley College in the poverty-stricken East End of London kept its students earthed in reality.

When Gershom arrived in China he found wearing Chinese dress a trial. The cumbersome shoes and long gown cramped his athletic style. He hated shaving his head and wearing a pigtail, but his vocation required it. Wherever the Harley missionaries went, they lived as simply as possible, identifying with the people as fully as they could, laying down their lives when called upon to do so. They were the "guerrilla" priests of their day, siding with the people against the tactics of the British government in China and particularly in Africa, where the Europeans walked in and took control.

In 1884, having manipulated Stanley for his own ends, by a series of deft political moves King Leopold of the Belgians annexed the Congo as a Belgian colony. He sold himself to the European powers as a benevolent philanthropist anxious to preserve the rights and liberty of the Congolese people. His promotional campaign was so convincing that even Fanny had been totally taken in. When Harry left for his visit to the Congo she warned him to be "broad-minded". Any abuse he might see was probably due to the corruption of local officials, and not the intention of the king. Harry believed her at first, but gradually, as evidence poured in from his workers of atrocities against the defenceless natives, carried out by the rubber plantation owners, supported and encouraged by the European authorities, he could no longer deny them. He became involved in a crucial humanitarian battle in the Congo, launching a campaign which in 1896 took him into the presence of King Leopold.

Meanwhile, of the thirty-five missionaries who followed McKittrick out to the Congo, only six lived to see the new century. Edgar Wallace, the writer and journalist, attested to their achievement. Wallace was not a religious man and had little sympathy with the missionary cause until he took a trip to the Congo and saw the work of Harry's Congo Mission for himself:

> For me, Bongandanga represents the end of a long and trying journey, a journey that has left me heartsick and bewildered . . . What the State has done for the Congo and its people, posterity shall judge. What the missionaries have done, I am seeing with my own eyes, and seeing, I am prouder of my fellow countrymen and women than I have ever been before . . . Every work the Congo has seen has owed its inception to, and has been brought to fruition by, these fine people. If from the depths into which the natives have sunk through oppression and neglect, men and women have been brought to the level of good citizens, the missionaries have done it. All that is best in this land is the work of missionaries. Already the Congo is to me a dreadful nightmare, a bad dream of death and suffering . . . when every law of man and nature is revolted and the very laws of life are outraged. A bad dream, save only this, that mingled with the bad delirium of lawlessness comes a brighter theme. It is of men and women living their lives and dying their deaths at humanity's need; who are creating a manhood from a degraded race. Hard, bitterly hard is the work . . . Somebody down river told me it was difficult to get men and women for missionary work in the Congo. I wouldn't be a missionary in the Congo for £5000 a year. I am grateful to the missionaries for this, that they have made me ashamed of my futile life.

By the time Edgar Wallace wrote those words the interests and influence of the Regions Beyond Mission had spread way beyond the Congo. "Guinness" was truly encompassing the globe. The brewing Guinnesses had expanded their enterprise to the West Indies, the banking Guinnesses were beginning to be involved in financial investments overseas; but for breadth of vision and spirit of adventure, neither branch could match their Grattan cousins.

For a while South America and its denial of human rights had absorbed Lucy's attention. In 1894 she published *South America, the Neglected Continent*. Since Pizarro the Spanish conquistador ravaged the fabulous Inca Empire almost four hundred years previously, Peru had been dominated by the Roman Catholic authorities, to the extent that its constitution forbade religious liberty. Several Harley students had gone there none the less, in the only capacity a Protestant missionary could, as shopkeepers. The local priests informed the authorities and they were thrown out of Lima and Cuzco, even though they had kept strictly within the law. The government offered to pay them two hundred pounds in compensation. That admission of guilt earned them the support and sympathy of many of the more intelligent Peruvians who deeply resented the activities of an oppressive régime. They wanted the missionaries to stay, but with no organisation behind them and no means of earning their living it hardly seemed possible.

Lucy's book aroused fresh interest in their plight and in 1897, travelling at his own expense, as he always did, Harry set out for Peru to see if it was possible to link up the missionaries there with other independent Harley men in Brazil and Argentina, providing them all with the necessary help and support. The visit took all the energy and magnetic charm he possessed, but he managed to resettle the men in the same old shop in Cuzco. That was the first step towards the passing of a bill which in the new century would give Peru its religious freedom.

As Harry reached Peru, Lucy was touring India with her father. Henry Grattan decided to go on to China to see Howard and Geraldine and left her there, revelling in a totally new experience. It was hard to keep up with Lucy and her "causes". Her soul was like a butterfly, elusive in its constant motion. But India trapped and held it for some months. India was "ours", part of the British Empire, and Kipling had made the English very empire-conscious. It hardly seemed possible that parts of India had escaped Christian influence. But Lucy found them. In *Across India at the Dawn of the 20th Century*, published in 1898, she brought the continent alive for her readers. They could experience with her the majesty of the Himalayas, the sweltering plains of Madras with its luxurious vegetation, the crowded streets of Poona, the Hindu temples, thronging bazaars and dusty streets, the wretched poverty of the people. A newspaper review called it "A most useful and instructive volume, beautifully illustrated . . . one of the best Christmas gift-books we have seen." As ever it ended with a challenge. Workers were urgently needed for the neglected Bihar region, a call which led to the founding of the Bihar and Orissa Mission in 1899. Despite Fanny's attempts to marry her off, Edith Fookes, still single, was one of the first volunteers.

Fanny did not live to see her departure. She spent six years at Cliff, sitting quietly by the fireside, enjoying from the window the view of her beloved Derbyshire hills, the beauty of the sunsets and the brightness of the evening stars. Though life had become a burden to her she never complained, but with the help of an amanuensis wrote long, loving letters to her children, wherever they were. She insisted on being kept up to date with every new development of the work at Harley. In thirty years she had watched the tiny acorn of a mission house at Stepney Green grow into an enormous oak, its branches stretching way beyond her dreams. For the sake of those dreams, she had given all, even her children. When Gershom, her youngest, said goodbye to her in 1897 it was the hardest parting. She knew she would never see him again. She died on November 3rd, 1898, and was buried in the peaceful cemetery of Baslow Church.

Of her four children only two were present at her funeral. It took months for news to get through to China. Lucy stayed on for a while in Derbyshire. She could hardly believe her mother was not there. Fanny had become an institution. Her presence seemed to fill the place. As Lucy wandered around Cliff trying to take it in, a thousand memories floated back from childhood. The summer-house was still there by the river, where they used to have tea with her, the music of the water playing in the background. So was the observatory with its equatorially mounted telescope, where her parents would hold them enthralled with the secrets of the stars and the burnt-out craters of the moon.

> All is the same there today in the falling of the year. The flaming tints of autumn, the silent drop of yellow leaves, the terraced shrubberies, the lingering flowers, the ridge of purple moorland, the red sun westering over the hills – all unchanged. But the dear heart that knew and loved it all so well has passed from the old places to Jesus' other side.

Henry was devastated by Fanny's death. Over the past six years his extensive travels had been a kind of escape from seeing her as she became. Yet though she was not the Fanny he had married, and not the wife his passionate nature needed, he had relied on her presence and advice. Lucy knew there was only one way to distract him from his grief, to take him on his travels again, this time to the Holy Land. He had not been there since his honeymoon.

Lucy had an added reason for wanting to escape. Inevitably, given her passion for worthy causes, she was in demand as a public speaker. The gift seemed to run in the family. Only Gershom was bypassed. In his recollections Eugene Stock, the ecclesiastical historian, remembered that when Lucy rose to her feet she turned a deadly dull meeting of the Leicester YMCA into a memorable evening. He also remembered what a treat it was to sit in the evening twilight and "hear her pour out, as it seemed, mind and heart through her fingers on the piano". The intensity of her speaking and playing surrounded her in a romantic aura and wherever she went young men fell in love with her. But for her part she was convinced that Mary and Mag's prophecy had come true. At thirty-three, though she did not look her age, she thought herself an old maid. The proposals were no consolation. Her suitors were so young and immature that they were totally unsuitable; usually she managed to fix them up with more sensible relationships. But the inevitable happened. She found herself irresistibly drawn towards one of them. Flight was the solution.

As she and her father travelled across Europe an invitation came to visit Prince Bernadotte of Sweden. The gracious regent showed them round his palace and a large portrait of a lovely young woman caught Henry's eye. He asked the Prince who she was, and he replied that she was the daughter of very close friends, so close that he regarded her as a niece. Her name was Jane af Sandeburg. Despite every opportunity to move in Sweden's best social circles she had chosen to be a missionary in China. "My youngest son is a missionary in China," Henry said. He decided that Jane af Sandeburg would make Gershom the perfect wife, and made a mental note to write and ask him and Geraldine whether they had met the lady in question.

Three months in Palestine, galloping on a fleet Arab horse across the wide Plain of Esdraelon or on the breezy heights of Mount Carmel, enabled Lucy to blow away the remnants of her unfortunate emotional attachment. "If you come and go in a sandstorm like the Kaiser, whirling through a sirocco and grudgingly bestowing the blink of a dusty eye on the Shrine of the Universe," Lucy wrote home disparagingly, "you needn't expect to enjoy Palestine." With her usual passion for the strange and foreign, she loved it.

While Lucy rode and explored, Henry Grattan gave countless addresses, including one to the delegates of the Zionist Conference in Jerusalem. Such was its impact that ten years later David Baron, one of his Harley students, who attended the first eight Zionist congresses, said, "In Jerusalem I met Jews who were much impressed by listening to Dr Guinness during his stay here with his daughter."

On May 12th, 1899 Lucy wrote to Geraldine:

In a quiet evening light, we are travelling south through Egypt once more, Father and I together. We left Alexandria this morning and after a very busy week there, are going for a few days to see "the Garden of Egypt", an oasis called Fayoom, on the edge of the Sahara. Mr Kumm, one of the North African Mission workers is with us. He is the only one of their men in Egypt who has worked in the Fayoom and comes as guide and interpreter and general protector.

We are flying down the Delta in a quiet dreamy light, half grey, half green, half misty blue; the sky lies all around us, for in this level land, one scarcely sees the country unless one looks for it out of a railway window.

Geraldine, who knew only too well Lucy's meticulous attention to detail, would have been somewhat amused by her reference to three halves. Did she suspect that the aberration and the "dreamy light" had something to do with the mysterious new protector? If so, she would have been right. From behind the flowing veils attached to her wide-brimmed hat Lucy had plenty of opportunities to observe their guide as, seated on camels, they explored the mysteries of the pyramids together. And the petite, dark-haired Englishwoman soon fell under the spell of the blond giant from Osterode in the Harz Mountains of Germany. Although several years her junior, Karl Kumm was mature, sensible and charming. He was studying for a doctorate in Egyptology and she was deeply impressed with his learning. He also had a passionate love of music and travel, Lucy's two favourite occupations.

He for his part was captivated from the first. Everyone found Lucy interesting, but he revered her. She was so contained, yet there was some mystery about her he longed to possess. He was strong and masterful and Lucy had been waiting for someone to sweep her off her feet. By the time he escorted them back to Cairo they were deeply in love.

In Cairo, Henry and Lucy stayed at the same hotel as Lord Kitchener and Henry watched him with acute interest from a nearby table. But the main object of Lucy's attention was the handsome young man at her side, who was about to take his leave of her to make a voyage of exploration up the Nile valley. Before they parted they made a trysting place. If in the next months her feelings for him remained unchanged he would be waiting for her at Luxor in the first month of the new century.

Lucy returned to England and continued the romance by letter. Unlike many of their female contemporaries, neither of the Grattan Guinness women was squeamish when it came to expressing emotions. Geraldine and Lucy may have been intense but they were also highly articulate and that was their safety valve. "Where is my wandering boy tonight?" she wrote to him, ". . . I wish I were in his arms."

Karl felt that honesty was more important than passion at this stage and warned her of what their life would be like if she married him. "I must be true to God and conscience all my life. Are you willing to bear separation if the Lord shall cause it? If I have to work night and day you will not think me selfish? There will be very little 'drawing-room time' in my life."

In January 1900 he made his way back down the Nile to Luxor, wondering how Lucy had responded to his letter, but she was waiting for him just as she promised. They were formally betrothed at Aswân in the traditional Sudanese way, joining their hands over the joined dark-skinned hands of two native Bischareens, from whom Karl was learning the language and grammar.

They were married at Cairo a month later in a civic ceremony at the German Consulate, followed by a service taken by Henry Grattan at the American Mission Church. The wedding breakfast was a tea-party for three hundred soldiers, to whom Karl had been acting as chaplain. The honeymoon was the return journey to Aswân in one of Thomas Cook's discarded Nile steamers. Domesticity still did not come easily to Lucy, but she "learned to cook potatoes splendidly, and to make the most delicious soups (out of tins)". At first, while she and Karl were together, she was resilient and resourceful, but all too soon the realisation dawned that she had not fully taken in the implications of his last letter. When she married Karl Kumm, she also married the Sudan.

4

While Lucy and Karl were enjoying the first months of marriage, the longest stretch they would ever spend together, political tension in China rose to a crescendo. With the encouragement of an enlightened group of reformers, the young Emperor Kuang Hsu had endeavoured to bring the provincial Mandarins to heel, transforming China into a modern constitutional monarchy. The dowager Empress Tzu Hsi, undisputed leader of the powerful reactionary party, organised a coup, placed the emperor under house arrest, and took over the ruling of the country. The detested foreigner was her scapegoat. In November 1899 she issued an edict instructing her supporters, the "Boxers", to rid themselves of the foreign influence in their midst.

Gershom had by then settled in She-ki-chen in Honan. He had come to China two years earlier in time for an unexpected family reunion. Henry Grattan had stopped off on his way home from India, and Geraldine and Howard had come to Shanghai to see him. The strained relations between China and the European powers were already apparent. Henry Grattan felt ashamed of his nation's unwarranted aggression in its own commercial interest.

After his return to England he wrote to Geraldine:

I suppose you see by the newspapers what is going on in what they call "the scramble for China" . . . Germany seems bent on making acquisitions in the East, and Russia has practically taken over the control of Corea, and has ensconced her fleet at Port Arthur . . . There are probably great changes pending. The victory gained by Japan in her struggle with China has proved to Europe the weakness of the great Chinese Empire to resist the forces of civilisation . . .

The German Emperor's brother is on his way out to the province along whose coast we sailed together on our way to Chefoo. He has not arrived yet, but has reached Colombo en route. The Chinese authorities must be perplexed at times by the contending interests and conflicting proposals of the "barbarians", whose naval and military power make them so formidable, and who will have their own way and pay no attention to long-cherished usages.

Geraldine was disturbed by the political situation but put it out of her mind. For the time being she had an exciting distraction, escorting Gershom to Honan. "I brought him up, you know," she would say proudly to everyone they met. She was thrilled to be able to introduce the little brother she had often mothered to the language and customs of the people she loved. A newcomer to a missionary station was a source of some interest to the Chinese Christians and a feast was organised in his honour by "Ch'en of the Pearly Wave", a retired Mandarin and distinguished scholar. It was a trial to Gershom. He did his best to comply with local custom, but that he did not quite succeed was clear a year later, when the hospitality was repeated and Mr Ch'en was overheard to say:

Now that Dr Guinness, it is really wonderful how he has improved since last coming to Honan! Last year, when he dined with me, he was gauche in the extreme. He hardly knew how to make himself presentable (in Chinese dress); he could not handle chopsticks properly and was unable to reply to a polite remark. But now, in a little more than a year, he is becoming quite a gentleman!

If his reputation as a gentleman took time to establish, his fame as a doctor spread faster, thanks to an unusual incident. One day a huge crowd arrived at his door, dragging a poor creature who seemed to be half-dead. It transpired that he was a tailor who had swallowed the needle he was holding in his mouth. A long piece of thread was attached to the eye, but as the needle had gone down first, attempts to pull on the thread had only driven the needle deeper into the poor man's gullet. His employer was irate. His would be the responsibility of the funeral expenses, not to mention ridding the workplace of the man's ghost.

By the time Gershom examined the tailor's throat it was raw, swollen and bleeding. Not having seen such a case before, he was perplexed about what to do. Suddenly inspiration came. Someone was sent for an india-rubber tube. When it arrived he threaded a piece of strong silk through it, which was then attached to the thread in the man's mouth. He slid the tube gently over it and down the swollen throat until it reached the needle. With a little pressure the needle was dislodged and passed into the stomach where there was room for it to dangle vertically down. Then, to the incredulous gasps of his admiring audience, Gershom pulled on the thread and drew the needle safely out.

It was an immense relief to Geraldine and Howard to have another doctor in the province. For some time Howard had been prone to prolonged bouts of fever and dysentery. Sometimes he was too weak to sit up and had to be carried into the courtyard across three forms, where he would see his patients lying down. A holiday was imperative. Now that Gershom was in Honan they could set off for Mount Pleasant with an easy mind. En route for Tasmania they stopped in Adelaide, where Geraldine, the more gifted speaker, had several engagements. On the first evening after her talk, she was approached by an elderly gentleman who said, "I'm so sorry to hear of your recent bereavement."

"Thank you," she said lightly, "but my dear mother is getting on quite nicely, in spite of the paralysis."

The stranger stared at her, nonplussed, then finally muttered, "Haven't you heard? Your mother died over a month ago."

Stunned by the sudden shock, Geraldine broke down.

Despite the ominous political rumblings and increased resentment of the foreigner, Gershom enjoyed life at the station in She-ki-chen, which he shared with another couple, the Conways, and Miss Watson, a single missionary. His bicycle arrived and was a source of fascination to the Chinese people who had never seen one before. Their final judgment was that since it offered no shelter and sometimes instead of carrying its rider, had to be carried itself, it was not nearly as practical as a mule and cart.

The main problems which everyone in China had to face were drought and famine. By the turn of the century the situation was so severe that the Boxers easily stirred up hatred for their scapegoat. In June 1900 the Dowager Empress decreed that all foreigners should be destroyed. It was on a sweltering July day that word came to the little party in She-ki-chen that their lives were in danger and they must fly. It was easier said than done. Where could they go? The waterway to the sea was dried up. It was pointless to travel overland. A thousand miles of Boxer-infested country separated them from the coast. In addition the Conways had a six-week-old baby, Nora.

But the baby's nurse was already prepared for an emergency. She had persuaded their neighbour, Li Ch'uen-rong, whom Gershom had attended in a near-fatal illness, that as he owed his life to the missionaries he must offer them his protection in the event of a riot.

It was five o'clock in the morning when the rioters arrived. As they began to break down the barricades Gershom, the Conways and Miss Watson slipped out of the back door, up a ladder and over a ten-foot wall, across their neighbour's courtyard, and up another ladder into the relative safety of his attic. There they hid, listening to the crash of falling masonry and timber and the murderous shouts of the mob. The crackling sound of flames left them in no doubt as to the fate of their home.

After several hours Mr Li's house was overrun by hysterical crowds screaming, "We must kill them! We must kill them!"

The nurse shouted back, "Kill them? Kill me first!" and both she and Mr Li blocked the trapdoor.

Sulkily the mob retired and as the sounds died away in the distance, the little group in the attic heaved a sigh of relief.

The respite was short-lived. Within a short while the trapdoor was pushed up and Mr Li appeared pale and trembling. "You can't stay here," he said. "This is the room where my servants sleep. They will soon be coming up and I daren't rely on their secrecy."

He could not think where to hide them when Mrs Conway asked him about a deserted-looking building in his back courtyard, adjoining the mission-house. That, he said, was his haunted loft. They were welcome to it.

"The more haunted the better!" Gershom said, and under cover of darkness they ran across the courtyard into what appeared to be a granary. Balancing a ladder on wooden boards placed across mounds of wheat, which were held in place by strong cocoa-matting, they managed to heave their way up to the tiny, filthy loft. It was haunted all right, but by armies of insects rather than a ghost.

Within minutes the trapdoor was pushed up and some tea and bread appeared. After twenty-four hours of heat and high humidity with nothing to eat or drink it seemed a feast. They had barely finished when a stranger climbed into the loft and urged them to follow him. He had come to escort them safely out of the city. They followed him and were almost out of the courtyard when Mr Li came rushing after them. The man was the leader of the rioters, come to decoy them out of hiding. If that was not enough, the chief of police was on his way. "Quick, quick," he shouted, "back into the loft!"

They were just in time. When the officer and his men arrived the granary was ransacked. Then the officer ordered a search of the loft.

"It's haunted," the men quivered.

"Nonsense!" the officer said.

One soldier fetched a beam and began to ram the trapdoor.

"Rigidly fixed!" the soldier shouted, with relief. "Quite immovable!"

Gershom, who was sitting on the trapdoor, resting his full weight on it, felt it move beneath him. Mrs Conway held her baby tight. One cry was all it would take to seal their fate. The sweat dripped from Gershom's and Mr Conway's faces. But after a while all went silent. The officer and his men had abandoned their search.

Tuesday, July 10th was the worst day. The rioters set to work early, smashing everything in their wake. They poured on to the granary roof, peering in the window. Gershom, fortunately, had discovered that a tiny corner of the loft was invisible from outside and they crouched there against the wall while the uproar went on around them. And baby Nora still did not cry.

From their corner they noticed men in the courtyard below gathering wood and grass and bundles of straw, and piling it up high around the granary. There was no mistaking their intention. Just as they were about to set it alight Mr Li's farm-workers arrived and stopped them. The labourers were not going to stand by and see the results of their hard work destroyed. Disgruntled, one of the mob went and fetched a ladder instead and the party in the loft heard his footsteps climbing steadily higher towards their window. Any minute now and they would be face to face with their assassin. But the ladder was too short. The man could only reach the window by pulling himself up by his hands for a moment. He quickly scanned the room, and though Conway felt his breath on his cheek, he never saw who was hiding in the corner right next to him.

The missionaries hid in the loft for six days with little food or drink. Every time the trapdoor opened their hearts stood still. One day, to their amazement, two packets of post were shoved through. Postman Lu, grateful for the treatment he had received for a boil on his foot, had helped in the only way he could.

With the post came newspapers carrying stories of the Dowager Empress' edict and the terrible realisation that the Boxer uprising was so widespread that to stay in hiding was their only hope. Gershom managed to write home on a scrap of paper:

It is the sixth day of the riot, and we still lie on a dirty floor. The ladies are worn and sick; Conway done. I am well enough, thank God, but don't see quite how we are to get away. Clouds lend a hope of rain. If it fell, it would make all the difference. Continual firing against thieves and plunderers goes on. We have no change of clothing; and day by day, living in a temperature of 90–100 you may imagine our condition – all four in one room with a baby. The Lord grant it may be soon over.

That night they heard a pitter-pattering on the roof. It grew louder and louder until a torrential downpour drowned every other sound and they were able to leap around for joy. The trapdoor opened and

Mr Li's head appeared. "Truly," he said, "your God is wonderful. Only this night I have made terms with Mr Wang, and now under cover of this rain and darkness, I will get you to his house."

Mr Wang was a leading businessman in the city. If anyone could get them safely away he could. But to lessen the danger of being seen the party had to split up. Old clothes and blankets were wrapped around their heads and the baby taken from them. It was so slippery Mrs Conway kept falling in the mud.

Three of them arrived at last at their destination, but no Miss Watson and no baby Nora. Mrs Conway was almost beside herself when one of Mr Li's farm labourers struggled up the ladder to their new attic with a bundle in his arms. "Truly this baby is good," he muttered. "Had it cried when I was in clerk's office, all would have been spoiled by me!"

Apparently the labourer had blundered by mistake into one of Mr Wang's offices.

Miss Watson arrived some hours later. She had lost her shoe in the mud and had looked for it in vain. That turned out for the best, for when the Boxers found it they were convinced that the foreigners had escaped from the city.

To their immense disappointment the rainfall was insufficient to fill up the waterway so no escape was possible. On their eleventh day in Mr Wang's attic Conway heard excited shouts below. "Ai-ya! Ho-li-kan, fah shui liao! Amazing! The dried-up river fills with water!" They could hardly believe their ears. How could the river rise when there had been no rain? They waited in an agony of expectation. Two hours later Postman Lu climbed up to their attic shouting, "Have you heard the news? The river has actually risen to half its banks! Far back in the hills, rain must have fallen."

But danger was far from over. That night they crept stealthily out of hiding, climbing over soldiers lying asleep on mats in the courtyard. The baby started to be uneasy, but Mrs Conway managed to quieten her. Wang had arranged for a cart to take them to the river where a boat was waiting. But first they had to pass the city's iron gates with its guards. Lying in the cart covered with old blankets and matting, they held their breath while the driver made negotiations. At last a bribe made the gates swing open and soon they were steaming on their way towards freedom.

The five-day journey took ten days. They spent hours shut up in the cabin in the heat lest they be seen from the land. Every province had its own bureaucracy and officials and there were Customs after Customs to pass. Each border encounter was potentially disastrous. The women covered their feet and hair and they all pretended to be asleep. "Your travellers are very silent," one officer said to their escort, poking and prodding them, but he let them through none the less.

At last the foreign settlement of Han-k'ou came into view. Keeping low, they glided rapidly downstream past the final Customs depot, until they were out of Boxer territory at last. Gownless, dirty and unshaven, Gershom went on ahead by ricksha to the China Inland Mission-house to inform them of the arrival of a Honan party, thirty days after the riot.

Only then did he discover that seventy-five of their fellow missionaries including twenty-two children had perished. Why they died and he was spared, he would never know.

It was a short while later in Shanghai, where he was recovering from his ordeal, that he first noticed a lovely young woman, tall and slender, a mass of fair curls caught at the back of her neck. Both were struggling to come to terms with the terrible events of the last months. They felt drawn to each other and spent hours talking about their experiences. But the budding relationship had to be curtailed. She decided to go home to Sweden. Her name was Jane af Sandeburg.

5

While Gershom was caught up in the Boxer uprising, the twenty-five-year-old Rupert Lee Guinness was experiencing his own first adventure. In 1899 Britain was once again at war against the Dutch Afrikaners in South Africa, known as the Boers. Sir Edward Guinness endowed a field hospital, which was known as the Irish Hospital, and Rupert persuaded his father to let him accompany it as chief-of-staff to the commanding officer, Sir William Thomson, past president of the Royal College of Surgeons. Rupert had no medical knowledge. His job was to supervise the moving of the hospital – which was no mean feat as it consisted of seventy-five staff, eight tents with eight beds apiece and twenty small tents for stores and supplies, all of which was drawn by twenty-one wagons and mules.

From a diary Rupert kept in shorthand and inadvertently left behind at Norham Castle, it appears that his war was a lot of fun at first. He served his country as Treasurer of the Entertainments Committee, which organised dances and a fancy dress competition. Rupert went as a baby. The social life was an opportunity to try out his charms on the ladies, whom he had began to find quite "agreeable". Some predicted he would not marry until he was forty-five. With one lady he spent a "very odd evening". She felt ill, and "we consoled her. I am glad there were no witnesses!"[1]

He was in Cape Town when the news arrived that Kimberley was relieved. The Mount Nelson Hotel was so full of "old Etonians" that Rupert had to sleep in a camp bed in Sir William's room.

Gradually conditions deteriorated and Rupert began to experience the horror and misery of war. In March 1900 his was the only field hospital to go with Kitchener to Prieska. From there he travelled on to Bloemfontein. It was backbreaking work. The wagons were continually stuck in the mud and Rupert had to heave them out. Supplies were inadequate for hundreds of wounded men, not to mention the thousands suffering from dysentery or enteric fever. It was not long before Rupert succumbed to the fever himself, but he refused to give in. By June the hospital had a more permanent base in the Palace of Justice in Pretoria, and Rupert went home to receive the Companionship of the Order of St Michael and St George, for services to his country.

That same summer of 1900 the news of the Boxer massacres reached Hudson Taylor in London where he was recovering from a slight stroke. It broke upon him like a tidal wave on a tired swimmer. His devastation was total. Fearing for his sanity, his wife took him straight to Davos high in the Swiss mountains. Howard and Geraldine, numb with shock and desperate for news of Gershom, joined them there.

The telegram telling of Gershom's escape brought Geraldine only momentary relief. As the full total of their losses became apparent it seemed like some impossible nightmare. Hudson Taylor, feeling personally responsible for every death, paced the floor of his room, hour after hour, day after day, tears pouring down his face, saying nothing. His agony was too deep for words. He had believed implicitly in some special protection for every one of his workers. They had sacrificed so much already. Why had God taken his hand away? And even if the missionaries had to die, why should innocent children suffer?

Geraldine, who was writing a biography of Pastor Hsi, would work in his room while he paced up and down like a demented, caged animal. One day he walked over to the table where she was writing and said to her, "I cannot read. I cannot think . . . I cannot even pray." She looked up at him with deep sympathy in her eyes and after a long pause, he said quietly, "But I can trust."

By the end of the year news came from Gershom that he was going to Chefoo, four days north of Shanghai, where there was a school for missionary children. Many of them had been bereaved. In addition hundreds of refugees were pouring in daily from the interior, many needing medical help. The resident doctor had suffered a complete breakdown, and Gershom's help was urgently needed.

Hudson Taylor's health, though not fully restored, was sufficiently improved that Howard and Geraldine could leave him for a speaking tour of the United States. Wherever they went Geraldine, rather than Howard, was the centre of attention. He was shy to the point of self-effacement. She exerted an unmistakable magnetism. Though not overpowering, she none the less had presence. People noticed her.

This then was the future pattern of their lives, Geraldine in the limelight speaking and writing, Howard in the background looking after her. Every book she wrote was an instant success. Though formal and by modern standards a little stilted they captured the exotic atmosphere of the missionary adventure of her day. Her heroes and heroines were beautiful, selfless and flawless. The Victorian reader demanded idols worthy of his adulation. Nothing less than perfection would do. Blemishes had no place in Geraldine's portraits, partly because she thought it uncharitable to dwell on the weaknesses of another, partly because she happened to be blessed with a generosity of spirit which saw only the good in others.

One of Harry and Annie's boys remembered years later that as a child he once told his Auntie Geraldine that a master at his school suffered from asthma. "I hope the boys are kind to him," Geraldine said earnestly. To which Annie laughed uproariously and said in her matter-of-fact way, "Don't make the boy tell lies, Geraldine dear."

At a time when the suffragette movement created a vogue for unusual women speakers, and there was a certain intellectual snobbery attached to being part of a following, Geraldine established a reputation in America and Canada. Her beautifully modulated English voice and refined English-rose appearance made her a favourite. Hundreds of young women volunteered for missionary service. "I met Geraldine in Montreal in my early teens," one of her young admirers wrote. "Even at that age she was my model because of what I knew from her book, *In the Far East*. She so fulfilled my highest ideals, I longed to be like her, so much so that, having seen her, I attempted for some time, by standing before a mirror, to make my mouth to the expression of hers."

The tendency to lionise Geraldine continued throughout her life and was often counter-productive, both for the imitator and the imitated. Such was the power of her personality that living up to her proved an impossible strain for those who tried. Nor could Geraldine cope with the limitless demands which the image of perfect Christian womanhood thrust upon her. Howard alone knew her through and through, knew that the real woman was often tired and weary, could be petulant and difficult, and struggled with the disappointment of childlessness and the sense of inadequacy which had dogged her from childhood. Without a question or a word of complaint he gave up a career in medicine to care for her. He saw to it that she took daily exercise, went to bed early, ate properly and regularly. She was not allowed to decide these things for herself. Like a child she depended on him, but sometimes she exerted her independence and with a mischievous twinkle broke free and played truant. When she was wilful Howard was hurt. "Darling," he once said to her after a particularly fierce quarrel over something he refused to let her do, "where would you have been by now if I hadn't been taking care of you?"

"In my grave long ago," she admitted ruefully.

While Howard Taylor was nurturing and encouraging his wife's vocation at the cost of his own, Karl Kumm sent his wife to Davos so that he could get on with his pioneer work in the Sudan. Lucy was pregnant and desperately sick. Thirty-five was old to be having a first baby, especially for someone who had always been frail. She hated separation from her beloved Karl and though they were to be constantly apart, it never became any easier. "I do love you so, and long to creep into your arms . . . Come back soon to both of us," she wrote. But when he failed to appear her letters took on a chiding, petulant tone. The foetus she carried began to move inside her and she wrote to Karl, "He's a nice little darling to come and cheer me when naughty Husbie keeps so far away! Naughtie Husbie said he was coming on the 10th and now today is the 11th and never a word to say when he will come or how, at all, and yesterday no letter! Naughty, naughty, naughty, naughty." In a more rational frame of mind she remembered the promise she had made before they were married: "Now, I know you understood, when we first talked of working hand in hand and I told you I never would hinder but always set you free to serve." But as the separation continued Lucy's sense of duty was in ever-increasing conflict with her sense of need.

Their first son, Henry, was born at Wiesbaden, Karl's home, at the end of February 1901. Karl was in Wiesbaden for the birth but set off on a fact-finding mission to Wadi Halfa before the baby was a month old. There was a single-mindedness about him which precluded normal domestic life. He had the whole-hearted devotion to Africa of Livingstone, his hero. There was an urgency in his task. The Arabs were bringing Islam to the tribes of the Sudan. He must reach them with Christianity first. All must be sacrificed to winning the race before it was too late. Rather than stay on her own among strangers, Lucy went back to her father at Cliff, in theory to regain her strength, in practice to raise support for the new pioneer mission she and Karl had in mind.

Apart from a few servants, Henry Grattan had been living alone in his apartment at Cliff since Fanny's death. Leila Dennison had long since married Henry Reed and returned with him to Tasmania.

It was a lonely existence for the elderly man, who still possessed the energy and intellectual powers of someone half his age. He was glad of Lucy's company, all the more so because he was facing a crisis and needed her support.

The Boer War had severely depleted the Harley Institute's volunteers and funds. Then in 1901 Queen Victoria died. Times were changing. Her passing marked the end of an era and the entry of a new age. King Edward VII had a reputation for joviality and affability rather than religious devotion. There was almost instant reaction against the sobriety and strictness of his mother's reign. The people threw off their restraints. The Edwardian age, epitomised by the golden lifestyle of Elveden, was gracious and carefree. Interest in missionary work, hitherto most acceptable among society's well-to-do, died overnight.

Henry Grattan insisted that the only option was to close down the college at Cliff. Harry was horrified at the suggestion. What would his mother have said? For thirty years Cliff had played such a vital part in their lives. But during a preaching tour of Ireland he contracted typhoid and the recurrent bouts of fever left him severely weakened. Heart-breaking though it was, closing Cliff College now seemed unavoidable. The next sensible step was to sell it. Much as he loved it, it was far too big for Henry Grattan to justify living there alone.

To his disgust the first bid came from the Jesuits. It became imperative to save Cliff from the clutches of Rome, the Scarlet Woman of the apocalyptic books. He begged Lucy to persuade Karl to take over the property as a potential centre for their new mission. The idea appealed to Lucy. Her heart was at Cliff. She felt tranquil there, at peace among happy memories. But Karl was dubious. It was impractical. They had no money. It would be a burden. And besides, Karl knew from experience how easily people were dominated by the powerful personalities of his wife's relatives, and he feared it. Cliff was Henry Grattan's throne. Would he really abdicate or would Karl have to submit to a benevolent autocracy? The latter was unthinkable to his proud Germanic spirit. But in the end he could not resist his wife's insistence. She was pregnant again and had to live somewhere when he was away. They would take over Cliff, but only on a temporary basis.

It was there that little Karl was born in 1902. Separated from the husband she adored, Lucy lavished all her affection on her two babies. They were a precious gift she had thought would never be hers. Feeding them was one of the satisfactions of her life. As a teenager bound for Tasmania she had turned up her nose at the "fits, convulsions, teething or one of the many mysterious maladies to which I understand all babies everywhere are subject." Motherhood changed all that. Now she sat for hours with them in her arms, marvelling at the exquisite workmanship of their tiny features, startled by the penetrating gaze of the large trusting eyes fastened upon her. The belated blossoming of her mothering instincts produced poems and prose celebrating the almost indescribable wonder of this unexpected, new sensation.

As long as there are babies in the world the age of miracles will never cease.

All mothers know this.

To look at the dainty, breathing, moving creature lying in its curtained cot with its own energy and volition, its own world and life, its private joys and sorrows, pains and satisfaction – to look at it and think that a few months ago it had no existence and that to you and another its presence on earth is due, is to realise yourself in the presence of a miracle compared with which all but one other pale. For this to which you have given birth is a life which will go on. How far? How long? And whither?

The poems, "long withheld as too sacred for publication", did not reach the general public until 1929. Though steeped in Victorian sentimentalism they none the less touch something of the wonder and mystery of life itself. Reading them is like barging into a shrine without removing one's shoes, for in them Lucy pours out her inner soul, her love for her children. As if she sensed she had found a treasure too precious to keep, Lucy wrote of the immediacy of death and separation. Perhaps it was born out of her experience of marital love, a great passion granted, only to evade her possession continually. Or perhaps she had some inner premonition of what was to come and thought that writing about it would exorcise its ghost.

To Karl's immense relief in 1903 the Wesleyan Methodists made an offer for Cliff. They wanted to create a training college for Methodist ministers. As for Henry Grattan, the Wesleyans were not as sound in their interpretation of biblical prophecy as he might have hoped, but compared to the Jesuits they were angels of light. And Cliff would still be training men for the ministry. The Guinnesses had until the end of the year to vacate the premises and find new accommodation. Lucy found a small cottage to rent in Castleton in the Derbyshire hills, near enough to Sheffield where Karl had set up his British headquarters. But where was Henry Grattan to live? She wrote to Geraldine, who replied, "I know how perplexing the question seems about Father's future home. We cannot fully see how the needs are to be met."

But Henry, to his children's surprise, found a most ingenious way of solving the problem.

11

1900–1908

The Dawn of the Edwardian Age

1

On August 14th, 1900 Henry Grattan had scribbled the following words on a piece of paper, which he then kept folded in his wallet.

> After a quiet day of prayer in the woods at Eisenach, had a very vivid dream in the night. I had prayed that God would bring me a wife suitable for me and had endeavoured to trust him to do so. Dreamed she came to me in the night, and sat on my knee and kissed me – with a bright smile, her own act. Not given to dreams! Will wait, and wait on God. Through his grace.

Three years later the following postscript was added in a woman's hand: ". . . and Grace came and sat on his knee and kissed him! My own act. 11th June 1903."

For a respectable young woman to sit on a strange man's knee was remarkable by the standards of propriety of Victorian England. That Henry Grattan was sixty-seven and she twenty-six makes the event extraordinary by any standards.

It was at Wilton House in St Leonards that Henry's dream was fulfilled. He was house-hunting in the area and the House of Rest for Christian Workers, belonging to his old friend Charles Hurditch, was the ideal place to stay. On the morning of Wednesday, June 11th he called to book a room. Grace Hurditch went to deal with his request. As she walked down the staircase into the hall where he was waiting their eyes met and there was instant, mutual attraction.

Grace was the seventh and youngest child of Charles Russell Hurditch, a leading light in the Plymouth Brethren, who had made a career out of supporting worthy causes. Grace wrote later:

247

My parents were born in the great revival of 1858. In point of fact this was their Second Birth, but it was an event in their lives of such unparalleled importance that they hardly ever troubled to mention the first, and we children might have been forgiven for imagining that they had leapt into existence Athene-like in that fervid hour, full-grown and spiritually armed, had it not been for a list of dates in the large family Bible, and a small collection of miniatures, oils and daguerrotypes scattered over the walls of our home.[1]

Although, in true Brethren fashion, life was rather serious and austere at home, none the less hers was a warm and loving family and the Hurditch children found ways and means of indulging their high spirits. Since only games of a religious nature were allowed, they held mock adult baptisms. By suspending sheets from the bedsteads a four-poster bed was converted into a baptistry, into which the candidate was "plunged" by an "elder", balanced precariously on a bedside table. "I must confess that somewhat unholy mirth accompanied the proceedings when occasionally elder and candidate together suffered total immersion."

Since their father was much too preoccupied with his philanthropy to supervise his children, and their mother was a sweet, shy woman with an implicit trust in her children's predilection for righteousness, they were left to their own devices. Musical evenings, the only entertainment they were permitted, rapidly expanded into full-blown music hall and Grace's exceptional talent for mimicry earned her pride of place on the billing. The victims of her impersonations were usually revivalist preachers or members of their mission hall congregation, whose idiosyncrasies she had plenty of time to observe during the long Sunday services. Her reputation soon spread and she was offered an opening on the stage at a starting salary of fifty pounds. It was a fortune for those days. "I'd rather see her in her grave," was her father's stern response.

But Grace grew up to exercise a freedom of choice and independence of mind unusual in a woman of her background and generation. At twenty-six she had evaded all attempts to marry her off and had chosen a career in nursing. Shocked by the ignorance of her contemporaries in the basic workings of the human body, and equipped with specimens of animal viscera obtained from the local butcher, she delivered a series of lectures in elementary human anatomy:

I would then proceed to demonstrate the fascinating action of the valves of the heart by pouring water into the auricles and ventricles, and show the workings of the lungs, which I inflated by means of my bicycle pump; when suddenly there would be a thud, thud, thud, as one after another of my audience fainted away at these "ghastly sights".

Having nursed for several months in the poverty-stricken East End of London, Grace had to abandon her work when her father bought Wilton House at St Leonard's, Sussex, with a legacy bequeathed him for missionary purposes, and turned it into a "rest home" for Christian workers. In all his philanthropic schemes Charles Hurditch expected the support of his two unmarried daughters, Grace and Beatrice.

Grace loved Wilton House with its heavy Victorian furnishings and gracious air of comfortable solidity. Mr Hurditch would permit no rules or regulations to mar its home-like atmosphere. Massive gilt-framed pictures hung on the walls, lending an air of quality and richness. They were painted by an artist of repute, a Fellow of the Royal Water-Colour Society, whose chief merit in the eyes of the Hurditch family was his membership of the Plymouth Brethren.

When Beatrice sustained a serious injury as the result of a riding accident, Grace ran the house on her own, experimenting with new management principles. Ruth, her favourite sister, was a missionary in Africa and on May 11th Grace wrote to her with the news.

Amidst the many reforms the entire domestic staff were swept off the premises! The new lot were not brought in until the following day. Well, my dear, for twenty four hours we were domesticless and you never in your life heard such peals of laughter as emanated from these premises in that twenty four hours. All the visitors helped. There were twenty six of us.

Of the twenty-six several, it appears, were men who took advantage of the occasion to flirt with the vivacious Grace. Intelligent and teasing, exceptionally pretty with an oval face, large, luminous eyes and a mass of light brown curls, held against their will in a bun at the nape of a long and graceful neck, she was never short of admirers. But, she went on to tell Ruth, she had no time for suitors or people who said stupid things to her about "ought to be married". Not until a fortnight later when Henry Grattan Guinness walked into her life.

Her next letter to Ruth, dated Sunday, June 27th, 1903 was radically different in tone.

My Ruth, my darling Sister
At last! The awakening has come, and your little Grace is transformed, and she is really in love. Oh my darling Sister, how I have longed to cable this to you, or at any rate the date of our

wedding, July 7th, and yet I dare not for fear it would come as too much of a shock to you just now. But the relief to sit down and talk to you about it, knowing that you and Bee will at least understand it all, and so what do I care for all the other criticisms. Fancy, Ruth, that Dr Grattan Guinness (he is 67 darling!) has been the one to break down the barriers I was building round my little life, barriers I thought unsurmountable until I met him here just 2 weeks ago.

Henry Grattan Guinness was not a total stranger to Ruth. Ironically it was under Geraldine Guinness' influence, at her farewell in 1887, that Ruth, a teenager at the time, felt the call to be a missionary herself. In time the formidable Ruth was to prove more intrepid than her heroine, becoming the first white woman to climb Mount Kilimanjaro, delivering all five of her babies herself and confronting the legendary Tippu Tib over his slaving activities.[2] But as Grace knew only too well, admiration and respect for the Grattan Guinnesses was one thing, marriage to the elderly patriarch another. Some detailed explanation of her extraordinary choice of fiancé was required. "I must tell you all about it," she wrote:

Well, his magnificent presence appealed to me very strongly, his clean-shaven face and white hair brushed back off that great forehead of his. He tells me his first impressions of me were, "What a sweet girl", and from that moment we felt most strongly drawn to each other. He watched me a great deal at lunch. Harvey Harte was sitting next to me and noticed it. Edith Greenhill sat at the head and of course she noticed it.

Well after lunch we had tea as usual, and everyone went out but the doctor and me, and strange to say I did not feel in the least afraid of him as the great Dr Guinness, as everyone else seemed to be. And then he took my hand and asked me a little about myself and what I was doing here, after which he gave me a kiss – such a kiss – and I loved him and felt I never wanted to leave him, but never for a moment thought that he would care for me like that. Such a thought never crossed my mind. I only knew that it was an exquisite day to be with him then and the future never occurred to me.

The next day he was with me a great deal, coming to meet me as I came from dressing a wound of one of Dr Berry's patients and taking my hand and walking up and down with me and talking all about his travels, and how he would love me to see these places and how it would develop me. Then Friday night, darling, he asked me to come and have a talk with him in the office and he drew me to him and told me how he loved me right from the first, and how for five years he had prayed God to bring him this love, which I had awakened in him, love he tells me such as he has never known before.

If Grace was not afraid of the great Dr Guinness, she was none the less overwhelmed to have a man of his reputation and standing declaring love to her:

Really, darling, I could not have thought it possible to be so happy, yet so humbled, for Ruth I cannot understand why he loves me. Such intellect, and such a soul. I tried to tell him of all my faults, but he only kisses me and says he has never known such love before . . . Now, my darling, how I shall need your prayers, for I long to be worthy of my high calling, and he wants to teach me so much . . . He is just now completing a marvellous book on the historical sequence of the Apocalypse (and I don't even know how to spell it!) . . . I think I must give you a most exquisite little poem he wrote me just before he went away after our engagement. Somehow I don't like that word and I wouldn't allow him even to give me a ring, for we were so completely one, and from the very first he called me his little wife and there was nothing for us to wait for, and so you see that is why we arranged to be married so soon.

The immediacy of their wedding day, less than a month from their first meeting, meant that Henry had to return to Cliff to sort out his affairs and make the necessary arrangements. Saying goodbye to Grace, even for a few weeks, was a wrench, but under the inspiration of her love he wrote a poem, which he left with her:

She has come to my arms, she has come to my heart,
And the dream of my soul is fulfilled,
And the love that unites us shall never depart,
Nor the love that our union has willed.

O thanks to the Giver, O thanks for the gift,
From the gift to the Giver we turn;
From the bliss he bestows to Himself we uplift
The hearts which with gratitude burn.

There is heaven below, there is heaven above,
And they answer like ocean and sky;
For heaven is found in the bosom of love,
In spirit to spirit made nigh.

In his absence a present arrived at Wilton House almost every day, a compressed cane travelling trunk, a canteen of cutlery, two buckles

251

for waist belts, a long string of pearls and a purse with silver corners. "I have told him I don't care a bit about these sort of things but he loves me to look pretty fancy." As the prestige of marrying a famous man began to dawn on Grace she allowed herself a little coquettish pride in her conquest. After all her Henry was even in communication with the Prime Minister. "Balfour has written to me," Henry told her, "to say that he is so interested in my books, and has studied them closely." The full significance of these words did not strike Grace in that summer of 1903, nor could it for another fourteen years. The growing Zionist interest within government circles was not uppermost in Henry's mind just then either. He wrote to Grace from Cliff on June 17th:

My own darling Grace, my very own
I have read and re-read your last letters which I found on my arrival here last night, with such love and joy, answering to your own – my wife, my life – in anticipation, and in heart, intention, spirit, in reality, how wonderful is the relation – love's secret, hidden for a season in the heart, and then, slowly or suddenly, bursting into bloom!

Lucy rejoiced when I told her of my appreciation of my darling. She will leave her two babes here, and come to our wedding, so all my children will be there . . . How soon they will know that you have ceased to be Miss Hurditch! Changed your name, while remaining yourself, will you know yourself my darling? When your pure, sweet life is blended with the riper life of the one you love? . . .

I write from my quiet study at Cliff, with beautiful memories. I was in the garden this morning and the park, and wanted to gather the best of all the flowers and send them to you. I plucked the leaves of fragrant thyme, or rather lavender and roses and wanted you to have them all. You must come here with me after Switzerland, to see the place where we have lived for so long.

I hope you will have a happy Sunday at your father and mother's house, I will not say your home, for your home, darling, is with me.

I am your own loving husband that is to be. Henry.

Although it was a fairly accepted convention for a young woman to marry a much older man, the age difference of forty-one years caused quite a sensation, judging by Grace's reference to criticisms. But whatever the judgment of the bulwark of evangelical piety, the two families were genuinely pleased. Geraldine wrote from Switzerland to the future step-mother who was fifteen years her junior:

Gracie dear
How can I write to you from so full a heart? Though we have

never met, I love you dearly because of your love to him. And I long to make you feel how real is our joy in the thought that so soon you will be ours!

Only this morning father's letter reached me bringing the first news of this happy event. Of course it is a great surprise, but most welcome! And Father tells me that all is arranged and even the day decided upon . . . . It is very good and sweet of you to consent to its being so soon. I am glad on dear Father's account.

For he loves you Gracie! I wish you could see his letter to me about it. He has so much to give. The wealth of his great soul and tender heart. And it is yours, all yours. Oh such a heart Gracie! You will explore your treasures as the days go on. And you have much to give dear, your fresh young life and love. But he is worth it all. How did you find out so soon?

You will tell me all you can when we meet next week – DV. Meanwhile, with deep thankfulness to God and warm, welcoming love,

I am your own Geraldine.

It took Charles Hurditch and his wife some time to overcome their initial shock. "The events of the past few days have fairly taken the wind out of our sails whilst your craft seems to be sailing over calm and sunny seas," he wrote to Grace. But once they had recovered they began to find the whole thing perfectly natural and "too romantic", but not so romantic that they neglected their parental duty. "In spite of all the criticisms that may be passed, and under the special circumstances these may be expected," Hurditch said, he gave his willing consent to the match, with prayers that God would preserve his future son-in-law for many years yet. Then he wrote to Henry Grattan reminding him to adjust his will.

It was decided in the circumstances to keep the engagement as quiet as possible, but somehow the news travelled. When at the end of June Henry kept a prior appointment to speak at a public meeting at Harley College, the gardens were packed to capacity. Everyone thought Grace would be there and were dying to catch a glimpse of her. But she never appeared, no announcement was made and the disappointed crowds had to be satisfied with excited chatter and speculation.

2

Hastings Observer, July 7th, 1903:

A wedding of considerable interest to Nonconformists took place on Tuesday at the Robertson Street Congregational Church, the contracting parties being Miss Grace Russell Hurditch, daughter of Mr Russell Hurditch (founder and director of the Evangelical Mission, London), and the Rev. Grattan Guinness DD (founder of the East London Training Institution, Harley St, Bow).

The marriage service was conducted by the Rev. Charles New.

After the ceremony luncheon was partaken of at the Queen's Hotel, at which attended only the immediate relatives of the bride and bridegroom. Afterwards the happy couple left by train for Folkestone, en route for the continent, where the honeymoon is being spent.

Mr Dick Russell supplied the carriages.

From Brussels Grace wrote to Ruth filling in the details of her wedding day. It was a rather more traditional affair than Henry's Quaker marriage to Fanny forty-three years earlier.

Such a wedding darling, simple and quiet, just the plain marriage service read by Mr New, with Harry and his eldest child, Gershom, Geraldine and Howard Taylor and Lucy on one side, and Mother, Phil, Harry, Lil and Auntie Maud on the other in the choir stalls at Robertson St. The whole service was over in half an hour and finished with his giving me a lovely embrace. There were a few outsiders there, who managed to find out where the wedding was, in spite of our endeavours to keep it quiet. We then drove to the Queen's Hotel, where a lovely lunch was provided, with white flowers all down the table.

In case no one tells you what I wore, here goes. The palest dove grey gossamer voile dress made over silk, with a real lace berthe, a black velvet bonnet, with white net strings, and long pale grey gossamer veil down the back. Everyone said, darling, that I looked rather sweet. My beautiful bouquet was composed of tiger lilies and lilies of the valley. After a bright, happy cheerful time at luncheon we drove off to Westons to be photographed, sweet Geraldine and her husband coming too, in order to pose us (both are very artistic), then we went back to the hotel where Mother and Edith were waiting to get me into a Bolton-tailor-made pale grey coat and skirt. (I am sticking to a bonnet. It becomes me as Mrs Grattan Guinness!)

Then off we went to the station and had a loving send-off from Geraldine, Howard and Lucy. The two families had stayed at the Queen's the previous evening with their father and did a hundred and one little nice things for me, finishing touches to his toilet. He looked perfectly exquisite in frock coat and white tie and waistcoat and top hat, so absolutely aristocratic with his magnificent face and white hair and upright figure. Really it's not surprising that people stare at us both. We are a little out of the ordinary! And whenever we go into a shop he manages to say something about his "petite femme" so as to see the looks of approval!

The only cloud to cast a shadow across an otherwise perfect day was poor Bee, still lying in bed after her riding accident. Some months earlier Beatrice had been jilted at the altar. Like Dickens' Miss Haversham she kept her precious lace wedding-dress in a box, taking it out occasionally to caress its limp folds. Dr Berry felt that Grace's wedding would be too much for her and kept her sedated at home. Grace popped in and out of her room at each stage of her wardrobe and marvelled at Bee's unselfish enthusiasm and excitement.

The early days of her marriage were more wonderful than Grace had ever dared to hope. In a letter to Ruth dated July 11th, with a rapture unfettered by the normal prudery of her generation, she wrote passionately about their relationship:

How can I write to you old girl of all my happiness – this wonderful new life – isn't the love, protection, guardianship, sympathy, affection of a good man the greatest blessing that can come with a woman's life? My beloved husband has opened up a new world to me. His love has just touched the spring of that secret chamber which I never knew existed and my happiness is complete.

Ruth you don't know how humbled I feel when I think of the way God has honoured me, for my darling is so good and clever and wonderful and his marvellous intellect! He reads to me and is educating me all day, but at numerous intervals, whether in the "Grand Parc de Bruxelles" or under the palms on the Hotel verandah, impresses his ideas on me with a kiss, such a kiss, followed by some exquisite expression of his love . . .

I remember old girl, the first letter you wrote to me after your marriage you said it was all so natural and no wonderful changes had come. Well, darling, that is just about the truth of it. It is just the most natural thing in the world to be with our kindred spirit, and I'm sure you would have thought that no change had come to me, if you had seen me this afternoon in a marionette tea gown reciting to my dear Grattan, who greatly appreciates all my little funs and frivolities. Don't be afraid of his converting me into some sedate little saint, for he loves me just as I am, at least so he says!

I am keeping a short diary, just writing down the places we

visit, because we hope to travel much and it is bound to be an interesting record . . . While I am writing this there are about a dozen Americans twanging away nineteen to the dozen, they are talking such a lot of nonsense and in such loud tones, evidently wealthy people by the way they are talking about their travels. How trivial even travel becomes when done in this way, whereas with my Grattan it becomes an education, creates an interest and leaves a lasting impression.

In the four weeks prior to their wedding, Grace, aware that marriage to Henry Grattan would require more than the usual domestic skills, had taught herself photography and typing, so that she could help him as best she could. From a letter to his mother-in-law, dated July 23rd from Aix-la-Chapelle, it would appear that he appreciated her endeavours:

Dear Mrs Hurditch
You ask me in your letter to Grace what I think about your darling child now! Well I could write eloquently on the theme, if I could only trust myself to speak out all my appreciation, I fear I should seem extravagant! We are more happy together and more united to each other than I could have conceived we should be.

She is bright as sunshine, and sweet as a spring day, practical, energetic, clever and deft in her ways, and helps me marvellously well! writes for me, reads to me (and I to her) took down an article for me today for the press on "The Holy Roman Empire" and its connection with Aix-la-Chapelle – looks after my things! and is the most loving companion that could possibly be . . . I will not add, but only say my heart overflows with gratitude to God and I am doing all I can to care for my sweet treasure, your dear child, and make her life happy.

Give my love to your dear husband and believe me, dear Mrs Hurditch
Yours affectionately, H. Grattan Guinness.

As Grace had imagined, they travelled much, more than she anticipated. With his new young wife at his side, filling him with fresh energy and vigour, Henry decided to fulfil his ambition to visit former Harley and Cliff students all over the world. Now that Cliff was sold there was nothing to keep him rooted in England. After a short stay in Switzerland with Howard and Geraldine so that Henry could work on his next book, *History Unveiling Prophecy*, they set off for the United States. The honeymoon became a world tour. It would be five years before Grace saw her parents again.

Forty-five years had passed since Henry Grattan was last in

Philadelphia. In the great revival of 1859 thousands had flocked to hear him. He found it strange to preach from the same pulpits, to meet the children and grandchildren of those converted through his preaching so long ago.

For several months they toured the United States, Henry maintaining an exhausting preaching schedule. He was more popular than ever, and they were fêted wherever they went. His books sold in their thousands. *Light for the Last Days* was reprinted over and over again. Rest became imperative and a few days recuperation at the Moody Bible Institute in Chicago were exceedingly welcome. D. L. Moody had long ago encouraged Henry to regard the Institute as his American home, but this was the first chance he had had to take him up on his offer.

Under Grace's influence Henry was at last beginning to accept the limitations of his mind and body. That was obvious from a letter he wrote at the time to Geraldine. Like her father she was constantly pushing herself further than she could go. Her biography of Pastor Hsi appeared to have been a success and had already been translated into six languages, but writing it under pressure, living up to so many other expectations had worn her out completely. Full of loving concern, Henry could be quite sharp when his children's sanity demanded it. He understood their tendency to over-intensity too well.

How well I understand that nervous breaking down from which you have suffered. Let it be a warning. There is a limit you should not attempt to pass in exhausting labours. It is not easy to fix it, but experience shows pretty clearly where it is. I have been beyond it at times, when all the foundations of life seemed gone. I cannot express what that means, and hope you will never know. Most people have no conception how thin the foundations are which keep them above the abyss, where the interests of life exist no more. I tell you this, for you need to be warned. Learn to say "No" to invitations or calls or labour which destroy the power to labour and the possibility of service. I do think Howard, as your husband — and doctor — should say "No" for you, and forbid suicidal toils absolutely, firmly, finally. Tell him that with my sincere love.

From the United States Henry and Grace went on to Australia where news reached them of the death of Tom Barnardo. It was a blow to Henry. Unable to relax and share the mundane things of life with a soul-mate, he had made few intimate friends in his lifetime. Barnardo was one of the few. The importance of the relationship to Barnardo is clear from his letter to Lord Radstock, dated August 20th, 1893:

I feel dreadfully alone so far as human friendship is concerned; all my old friends and counsellors have passed away; hardly one is left; one dear old man who lives abroad is my only link with days gone by. His love seems quenchless and my own gratitude to him is the answering tie. Of those my own age who have survived, almost all have either withdrawn their friendship or are so absorbed, I suppose, in other matters that old friendships seem to have died out. Dear Grattan Guinness is the one surviving link at home with days gone by, whose human love, brotherly kindness and personal devotion to Christ are to me a source of refreshment and blessing.

In appreciation of his old friend, Henry Grattan sent a letter of condolence to his widow Syrie:

Beloved Dr Barnardo with his beaming face, cheery voice, broad brow, big brain, glowing heart, indomitable courage, tender sympathy, intense philanthropy, unwearied activity, and marvellous practical ability – when shall we see his like again?

. . . The memory of our friendship is sweet and fragrant now, a friendship never overshadowed by even a passing cloud. My only regret is that I did not see more of him in later years, but our absorbing occupations stood in the way of this. Now that he is gone, I feel that I have lost a dear, personal friend, and a precious link with the past which none can replace. And the world is the poorer for his absence; a beautiful life is ended, a fair and shining light has been extinguished, and I mingle my tears with those of the children, the thousands of rescued children, who have lost by his removal a father and a friend. Earth is poorer, heaven is richer!

In September 1905 Henry and Grace arrived in Japan. For Grace it was like entering a magic world. "The sun was setting as we entered the bay of Yokohama," she noted in her diary:

We had seen the snow-capped peak of Fuji-san towering high above a hundred lesser peaks, whose wooded slopes ran down precipitously to the water's edge. All around were fishing boats with large square sails of yellowish tint, and at anchor, numbers of warships, among which could be seen a recently captured Russian prize.

We stepped ashore and made our first acquaintance with the people – bowing, smiling, and enthusiastic – the more so because we were English, and there had just been celebrated, with great rejoicing, the English-Japanese Alliance.

They did not stay there, but went on to China. Later they returned to Japan for four months, when Henry Grattan preached at Tokyo University.

In the early hours of a chilly November morning they caught sight of the outlines of Shanghai. Streams of muddy brown water intermingled with ocean-green indicated that they had entered the great Yangtze River. Passengers and baggage were transferred to a river steamer for the remainder of the journey and before long Gershom's familiar face materialised on the quay. With him was his wife Jane. After waiting five years for her return she had come back to him and they were married almost at once.

As an interval in an almost unbroken preaching schedule Henry Grattan made one trip of particular personal importance. He visited the cemetery where Hudson Taylor's remains lay. Only a few months before Howard and Geraldine had brought him back to die in his beloved China, so that he could rest for ever beneath its soil.

But this appeared to be China's only peaceful spot. In a letter home Henry spoke of:

> Meetings, meetings, walks through the malodorous Chinese cities, walks among the graves (graves everywhere), outside the city, sedan chair rides in and out, in and out, round impossible corners, between high blank walls, opium shops, dust heaps, courtyards, with Chinese eyes scrutinising, speculating, admiring, scorning, suspecting, pursuing, all round – pigtails swinging, clothes flapping, signs swinging, cries ringing, odours pervading, poverty pleading, idolatry repelling, necessity calling – voices, voices, multitudinous, like the sound of many waters – waves which have been rolling and breaking since far distant times, anteceding all European civilisations and almost all memories of mankind . . .

The highlight of their visit to China was an invitation for Henry to speak to the Shanghai Zionist Association in the Royal Asiatic Hall. The excitement of the occasion restored his sparkle. A large number of influential Chinese Jews were present, complete with pigtail, and for over an hour he held them spellbound with one of his most eloquent addresses on "Zionism from a Christian standpoint". The entire text appeared verbatim in a local Jewish newspaper.

Their stay in the East drew to a close all too soon. At 9.15 p.m. on the day of their departure, perhaps sensing what was to come, Henry noted sadly in his diary: "Said 'Goodnight' to Gershom and Janie." Some years later Grace wrote underneath, "It was their last 'Goodnight'."

By the time they travelled back to Australia in March 1906 Grace was five months pregnant. She decided to stay in Sydney while he travelled on alone. It was their first time apart and an experience he did not enjoy.

Newcastle, New South Wales. 26th May
My darling
I am lonely – no one I care for near me – none to go to – none to talk to – no face to smile on me with love – no echo to my heart – because you are not with me – but more than 100 miles away, and I am among uninteresting strangers, kind in a way, but with no heart for anything that stirs the soul within me. Why should I write all this? Well, I want you to know how I feel when days away from you. If you were not with me, I should not stop long in Australia, but with you I could stay as long as I wanted. Strange is it not? But such is the heart.

I feel fresher today – I rose at half past five, and watched the day dawn, and had a walk since, and now am writing on the verandah of the house – the children playing about – and there's the sound of a distant train, and I wonder whether it is going to Sidney and you, and how I should feel if I was going on it!

Monday morning and I'm off from Newcastle with pleasant prospects in view. This is not an interesting place, but somehow Sidney is, especially the top storey of No 1 Glen St!

Well – farewell – it is no use to say come and kiss me – for you are too far off.

God keep you – my pet wife, and bless you.
Ever your loving husband.

Henry was back in Sydney in time for the birth of John Christopher who weighed nine pounds. The Australian midwife had never seen such an enormous baby. The labour lasted only six hours, and by the time Henry was informing the world, Grace, looking radiant, was feeding their infant son. Henry was seventy and as excited as if he had been a father for the first time. He took endless pleasure in the baby, noting every development with enormous pride and tenderness. "He would delight to carry him out into the warm Australian sunshine, and to pick the flowers from our garden, and see the child's appreciation of beautiful things," Grace noted in her diary. "It was a wonderful preparation for the heavy blow that was so soon to fall."

3

1903 was a bumper year for Guinness weddings. Lord and Lady Iveagh's three sons all married into the British aristocracy and delighted the public with three grand society occasions. In June the Hon. Walter Edward, twenty-three and the youngest, married Lady Evelyn Erskine, third daughter of the fourteenth Earl of Buchan. Walter, more military-minded than his eldest brother Rupert, had been wounded in the Boer War and mentioned in dispatches.

In July, twelve days after his cousin Henry Grattan created a stir by marrying a woman forty years his junior, the Hon. Arthur Ernest married Marie Clothilde Russell, daughter of Sir George Russell, Bart. And in October, the Hon. Rupert Edward Cecil Lee married Lady Gwendolin Onslow, eldest daughter of the fourth Earl of Onslow.

Since his return from South Africa Rupert had devoted most of his time to sailing and military service. Sailing was an abiding passion in his life. In 1901 he built a 90ft, 98 ton racing yacht and called it the *Leander*. It won the King's Cup, beating Sir Reginald Bulkeley's *Britannia* and the Kaiser's *Meteor*. "Will you ever forgive me?" Bulkeley is supposed to have said to his wife. "Never," the lady replied.[3] The *Leander* went on to win several more prizes, including the Vasco da Gama Challenge Cup, but crashed during the Kaiser's Cup in 1902, necessitating Rupert's ignominious rescue.

His commitment to voluntary soldiering was not merely a rich man's pastime. At a time when even the Admiralty seemed unaware of the growing German naval challenge, Rupert saw the vital potential of a well-trained regiment. For a while he was captain of the London Rifle Volunteers. Then in 1903 he was appointed lieutenant of the Royal Naval Volunteer Regiment. It was his enthusiasm and dedication to training which earned the regiment its eventual acceptance into the Royal Navy in the crucial year of 1913.

Lady Gwendolin Onslow had been interested in the Guinness family for some time before she and Rupert were formally introduced. As the daughter of the Minister of Agriculture she had imbibed a passion for social politics early in childhood. Because of his reputation as a philanthropist Lord Iveagh, whom she met in 1896, had earned her adolescent admiration. "Being at that time very full of ideas about social reform and having consumed much literature on the subject," she noted in her diary, she was "impressed by the great gulf between the rich and the poor and the misery and squalor of the slums".[4] Sir Edward Cecil appeared to be the living expression of her ideals. On acquaintance she found the Iveaghs rather formidable. Some years passed before they invited her to Elveden.

The house, she noted, was "luxurious beyond any dream". Of the sons of the house it was Rupert who caught her attention. Walter, she felt, was too mature for his years. His experiences in

South Africa and his scar had aged him. Rupert was acting as his father's secretary, and though courted by ambitious mamas with marriageable daughters, was unlike any other débutantes' delights she had met. He had lost none of the gentle, thoughtful qualities lauded by his headmaster in his schooldays. He was quiet and unassuming, devout in accordance with his mother's high church influence. His tastes were simple and unsophisticated. He enjoyed walking and could talk sensibly and seriously about the issues Gwendolin thought really mattered. "We had a long and enjoyable discussion on mentally defective and crippled children," she noted, accompanied by the strains of the electric piano, evidently still a trial to visitors. Ernest appears to have been the exception, for after his marriage he installed a mechanical electric organ at his house at Glenmaroon.

Rupert and Gwendolin met again at shooting parties and the relationship deepened. It was made clear to Gwendolin that she was welcome at any time to lunch at the Iveagh's London house in Grosvenor Place. But to be received at Elveden or Farmleigh or St Stephen's Green she must await an invitation. Small wonder that she felt more in awe of her suitor's parents. Lord Iveagh, often described as scholarly, Gwendolin found rather dapper, though modest and reserved. As for Lady Iveagh, it appeared she was continually recovering from ill health. Despite being "well-corseted" and not very fashionable, she played and sang charmingly. For their part the Iveaghs approved of Gwendolin thoroughly. "I consider you a very nice girl, my dear," Adelaide said to her, "and I only like to have nice girls here."

The Iveaghs were not alone in their approval. Society gossip magazines such as *Vanity Fair* and the *Pall Mall Gazette* commented favourably on the marriage, which was celebrated in a crowded St Margaret's, Westminster. The future George V sent the groom a tie-pin. For their honeymoon the couple travelled abroad – by car, not carriage. No one could accuse them of lacking a spirit of adventure.

This spirit manifested itself to the full when, immediately after his marriage and contrary to the better judgment of both sets of parents, Rupert chose Haggerston in Shoreditch as the place to launch his political career. It was an area of poverty and deprivation hardly likely to choose a Conservative as its representative in parliament. To contest the seat with integrity, despite their sheltered lives, Rupert and Gwenny chose to set up home at 266 Kingsland Road in the heart of the constituency. The Iveaghs were discovering of what mettle their eldest son was made. His father had assumed, wrongly, when he gave Rupert five million pounds on his twenty-first birthday that he would set himself up in style. Perhaps his wedding gift to the happy pair, a house in fashionable St James's Square, would change things. It did, but not as Sir Edward expected. His own son chose to live in the slums he had tried all his life to eradicate. Even the newspapers found it hard to understand: "It speaks well for disinterested public service in this country that a man whose recreations are yachting, rowing, shooting and golf, and whose clubs are the Beef-steak, Leander, Carlton, Garrick and Royal Yacht Squadron should be ready to work for the weak and needy."[5]

Rupert and Gwenny lived in Shoreditch for seven hard years. In 1906 Gwendolin was involved in a motor accident. The baby boy she was carrying was born prematurely and lived only thirty-six hours. Rupert worked hard on the London City Council, encouraging all kinds of humanitarian reforms in the treatment of backward children. Eventually their perseverance was rewarded. Rupert was voted MP for Haggerston in a by-election in 1908. Two years later at the General Election a fickle electorate abandoned him. But he had served a reasonable apprenticeship. Now the time had come to move into St James's Square and accept a safer seat.

In 1912 he was elected member for Southend-on-Sea, a seat he retained until 1927, when he succeeded to his father's peerage. As he moved into the House of Lords, so Gwendolin was elected in his place, one of the early women MPs, with a distinguished political career of her own. But in years to come when they looked back at Shoreditch they knew that those had been the formative years of their lives.

4

While Henry and Grace were touring the world and Rupert and Gwendolin living their first years in Shoreditch, Lucy made the cottage in Castleton her home. Karl appeared and vanished like a character out of *Alice in Wonderland*, and Lucy's letters followed him about with news of any support she had managed to raise for a mission to the Sudan and detailed accounts of the development of their two boys.

In one letter she told Karl she had just heard about:

a light contrivance, which costs about 2/6d and has 1000 charges. It is quite a little thing. You can carry it about in your hands and it has no outside battery connection or wires. You press a button and it shows a bright electric light, which appears as long as you keep the button pressed down and when you want to put it out, you raise your finger. I have so wished for one of these, as it would be an immense help with little Bab at nights. One need not strike a match or fumble with a candle, but one can just put a light weight on the button of the box and instantly have light enough to attend to him.

The torch was evidently an exciting new invention.

Raising support for missionary work in the Sudan was no easy task. Every existing British missionary society was fully occupied elsewhere and had no available funds. No one seemed to understand the urgency of the situation, the immediate necessity of halting the march of Islam. Lucy strained every available muscle in the cause. While Karl was learning Hausa in Tripoli, she travelled, wrote, begged, pleaded, and eventually on June 15th, 1904, managed to convene a meeting of eminent supporters in the Session Room of the Free St George's Church in Edinburgh. The elderly Dr Alexander Whyte, one of the great pioneer explorers of the Sudan, was there. On hearing him for the first time, the writer Sir James Barrie had said, "He came to announce his discoveries with a greater joy on his face than I think I have ever seen on the face of any other man. The fervour of his face, the beneficence of it, will shine on like a lamp." Dr Whyte proposed that the new initiative should be called the Sudan United Mission.

The first decision of the committee was to send Karl on a risky fact-finding expedition to the unknown Bauchi Hill Country on the Upper Benue River. In theory Lucy accepted the inevitability of another long separation. In practice her emotions were becoming severely strained. The writing and travelling continued, but at a frenetic pace. She could not relax or rest, and found it hard to sleep. Even music, usually a source of inner renewal, was pushed out. There had been many times when Henry Grattan, aware of his younger daughter's hereditary intensity, had feared for her sanity. Emotionally she was frail, like the delicate petals of some rare, exotic bloom, easily bruised or trampled underfoot. In the past he had always been there to protect her, but now he had a young wife to care for him. And Geraldine had Howard. Lucy was alone. Karl ceased to write to her regularly and she chided him gently, all petulance dissolved in pain:

> Oh my darling, why have I no letter from thee for over five weeks now again? What prevents just one post-card from reaching thy little waiting one? Maxwell actually says that you said that you couldn't write to me – you were "busy". He says you said you sent me your love. Husband! I have not missed one mail day since you left.

But Karl was too preoccupied to hear, too single-minded to understand how hurt she was, and Lucy could not tell him. She would not even admit to herself that she could not cope, let alone hold him back in any way. He was too perfect a hero to be dragged down by her inferior needs. She had constructed a pedestal for him and there he must remain, adored but unobtainable.

But she had her babies. They at least ensured her some short interludes of playfulness, though they continually asked for their father. She wrote to him:

> Bab is so sweet and funny. This morning, lying in bed, I was having little jokes with him and asked, "Who is this in Mummy's bed? A horsey?" "No", he solemnly replied in his deep voice. "A moo-cow?" I asked. "A chick-chick?" "No." "Is it a fish? A doggie?" To everything he answered, "No," till I asked, "What is it then?" and the tiny atom answered, "A MAN".

Almost at once that relaxed, unguarded moment is over and she is reading to them from the Book of Daniel, because she feels it vital they should grow up with a knowledge of biblical prophecy.

The rapid succession of the seasons as she waited for a few snatched weeks with her husband oppressed Lucy with a strong sense of the brevity of life. "Autumn weather has come today. The beautiful Indian summer has gone and the rains have broken," she wrote to him, her mood reflecting the change of weather. "The birds flew South last night . . . a great cloud of them . . . and I longed to go too – to you, to you – in the far South." The passage of time had always filled Lucy with a wistful yearning for the irretrievable. Now every fleeting moment was a sacrifice of time they could have spent together. In October she tells him the children have enticed her into the churchyard, where they play happily and she writes until, "In the still grey evening the hands of the clock in the Church tower point towards five and another day is almost gone. Sitting here, one realises that our day too must vanish. Such a beautiful day of life you have made mine, so full of unutterable beauty, wealth and joy."

Christmas approached and Lucy wrote to Karl, "In the dim faint hope that possibly you may appear, I am actually beginning to practise a piece of Chopin (his ballade No. 3) which appeals to my mind at present. Always at special seasons of life, there come to me special pieces of music, musical expressions of the thoughts of the time. The present one is very beautiful." Karl did come home for that blissful Christmas of 1905, "the people of the village coming to rejoice with us under the Christmas tree". But around the little family, revelling in moments of rare togetherness beneath the Christmas lights, the shadows were lengthening.

Within a few weeks Karl had left for the United States. It looked

as if it might be a long trip and since he knew that Lucy was feeling
a little frail he wrote asking her to join him there with the boys. He
had found a lovely little cottage for them near Moody's Northfield
Conference Centre. Moody had died but his two sons were running
the centre. It turned out to be an idyllic spot and Lucy loved it. She
wrote to Geraldine:

> Here at Northfield that you know so well, in the midst of a
> beautiful forest, with fir trees, birches and sycamores around us
> on three sides, and a lovely view of distant country stretching
> away from our hillside in front, we are living in a pretty little
> cottage or bungalow – an earthly paradise.
>
> As I write the boys are playing steam-engine, running and call-
> ing to each other round and round the house. They tremendously
> enjoy their free, open-air life up here.

Shortly before she left England Harry had told her of the recent,
shocking information he had received from the Congo of the way the
natives were being oppressed and exploited by the Belgian rubber
slavers. She was anguished by what she read and decided to use
her time at Northfield to write the strongest piece of polemic she
had ever written.

At five in the morning on July 2nd she got up early to prepare
Karl's things for a journey. He was leaving for New York and then
the Sudan, this time possibly not to return for several years. She
seemed a little stronger than usual, enthusiastic about her writing
project, and he hoped the summer at Northfield would do her good.
She and the boys went a little way into the woods with him to say
goodbye.

From that moment a sense of foreboding seemed to weigh heavily
upon her. She began to write desperately, in an agony of mind, as if
the anguish of parting from her husband, all the indignation which
she felt so keenly for the world's oppressed, were to be encapsulated
in this one book.

It was as she wrote, on July 8th, that she first felt a pain, no
longer just an inner pain, but a searing, stabbing sensation in her
lower abdomen, which doubled her up with its intensity. Her doctor
told her she needed immediate surgery, but she refused. The book
had to be finished first.

On July 22nd, by force of will, she gave an inspired, impassioned
appeal for the Sudan in the great auditorium at Northfield, but
collapsed immediately afterwards and had to be taken home in a
carriage. A second doctor begged her to have proper treatment, but
she still refused. There was too much to do. After a miscarriage the
pain disappeared and she toiled on with her writing day after day,

night after night, until on August 6th, when the pain had returned with a terrible vengeance, she scribbled the final sentence. "Now they can do what they like. It is done," she said to Alice Thompson, the children's nurse.

By the time the "curetting", a relatively new operation, was performed in the cottage on August 8th to remove the remaining afterbirth, peritonitis had set in. An ectopic pregnancy had ruptured a Fallopian tube. How she could have continued in such pain, the doctors hardly knew.

She came out of the ether after three hours. The Moodys offered her their own home, but she was too weak to be moved. The slightest noise disturbed her. The boys played outside, keeping as quiet as they possibly could. For a while she seemed to improve. "Dr Kumm has sent several cable messages and asked if he should come," Alice Thompson wrote to Geraldine. "Mrs Kumm said that was unnecessary. But I hope he does come soon."

But Karl never came. Lucy's condition suddenly deteriorated and the doctors told her she would die in twenty-four hours unless she submitted to a further operation. For the children's sake she agreed. Aware that she was probably dying, Lucy calmly set about ordering her affairs. She wrote a last love letter to her husband, a tender farewell reassuring him that she resented nothing. He had been "the light and joy and glory" of her life. In her will she left her few possessions, her journals, books, a watch, her sonnets on motherhood and a small sum of money, "enough for the journey home", to Karl and the children.

To Geraldine she bequeathed her most precious treasure, her two boys. She wrote to her sister, explaining that her own big Bible was to go to Henry, and her father's Bible, with notes in his hand, was to go to little Karl, "a Book that will give him messages from Father and from God":

I want him to study Daniel, and Revelation and the Lord's closing prophecies of the three Gospels. If he will do that for Mother's sake, when he is fifteen to sixteen, he will understand afterwards why I wanted him to do so much. When he is old enough I should like him to know all the time before he was born I had one prayer, one longing, one hunger – that he should continue Father's prophetic studies and research, and in the later days, when he lives he may perhaps see the restored Jewish state, in those unutterable days, he may understand and tell. He is only four now, but I see, I know he is a seer, a thinker. He will look more into the heart of things; will live, I hope, in those days, and he must understand. I wish he could have access to Father's library when he is old enough to hunger for it, to need to know what it contains.

Henry, my angel boy – he does seem that to me, with just an angel's heart, sympathy and devotion – will want to help the suffering, and put wrongs right. He is more called to that I think; perhaps to be a medical man. But that I do not know. Perhaps rather a preacher. Possibly both. I should like that. I must not write more. I am very restful, very happy in God. How wonderfully good He has been to us – the boys – how can I thank him? My husband, God's gift, blessed and beloved beyond words; and then you, Father, Harry, Annie, Gershom and darling Janie, whom I have never seen. My love, my heart to all of them, AND TO MY SONS – MY SOUL.

Good night, dear heart,
Without fear, yours, Lucy.

Finally she dictated to faithful Alice the following letter to her boys:

I am leaving you, darlings. I am waiting for you with Jesus – waiting till you come. Don't be lonely, darlings. You will come. It is only a little while. I want you to be brave.

I want you to have Auntie Geraldine for your Mamma. She has no little boys or girls, but she is waiting for you. She will be your mamma – only very, very much better than I have been. Ask Papa to let her be your Mamma – for a little time at least.

And now – you both belong to him. He will safely lead us home. Good-bye, darlings – heart's darlings. I am waiting for you – There.

On Saturday August 11th Lucy underwent the operation. She never fully regained conciousness. A brief memorial service was held at the cottage the following morning led by Dr Torrey and Dr Campbell Morgan, two of the most respected preachers in America. Then, on the shoulders of Moody's two sons and an ex-Harley student, her coffin was carried carefully down a winding path through the woods to the hearse which waited on the road below. It was deposited in a vault until a distraught Karl Kumm arrived ten days later. She was finally laid to rest as the sun set in the special family lot of the Moodys in the Northfield village cemetery.

Overwrought as she was, Lucy could not have carried on much longer. When the precious manuscript which had cost her so much effort was finally placed in Harry and Annie's hands, they made the painful discovery that it was virtually unpublishable. It was too subjective and emotive. Some of her descriptions were so horrendous, her accusations against the Belgian authorities and British government so outrageous, that they would have alienated any support Harry hoped to rally. For years the manuscript lay on a shelf at Harley House, untouched.

Karl Kumm's biographer Irene Cleverdon suggested that Lucy's intensity and lack of humour was no great character flaw, but rather a minor handicap such as colour-blindness, in an otherwise rich and colourful personality. It was in fact a fatal flaw which eventually cost her her life. But she died as she wished, not sitting primly on her womanly Edwardian dignity, leaving fire and courage and passion to the male of the species. She had her adventures, her causes, her dreams and many were extremely fruitful. Into her forty-one years she tried to pack another hundred, but her physical and emotional being could not cope. Like a meteor Lucy the Light, the "Brightness on the Way", burned herself out.

5

Howard and Geraldine were waiting at the Liverpool docks when Karl brought the children back to England.

Never shall I forget Karl's face [Geraldine wrote] as he came down the long flight of steps by which they had to cross from the vessel to the landing stage, carrying the little one in his arms and leading Henry by the hand. The children were pale and tired with being up so late and looked almost as pale and wan as he did and their whole dress and appearance so pitifully told the lack of a mother's care.

They all went on to Castleton to sort out the remainder of Lucy's personal belongings. It was a sudden shock when Geraldine realised Karl had no intention of leaving the children with her. It pained her that Lucy's wishes were not to be fulfilled, but Howard in his usual wise and patient way urged her to keep quiet and wait. An argument at this stage would only hurt the children. After all it was Karl's right to decide. Karl, with his usual suspicion of his wife's overpowering relatives, had sent to Germany for his sister Amanda. The Taylors bowed to his wishes and left for Switzerland, where Geraldine was writing the mammoth biography of her father-in-law.

Caring in a foreign country for two strange children who did not speak her language was quite an undertaking for Amanda Kumm. "She is going to spoil the children altogether," Karl wrote. "She simply lets them have their own sweet will in everything. Her lack of English, I am afraid, is making her lonely at times, though she is beginning to feel at home."

If he had been honest Karl would have admitted that the idea was doomed from the start. Life was miserable for them all. Amanda could not create a home. She was terribly homesick. As soon as she heard that her mother was ill she insisted that she must return to Germany at once. Karl was desperate. He was due to speak at a huge convention in the United States. There was no other alternative but to send an urgent telegram to Switzerland. Howard wired back immediately, "Send the boys to us," and set off for London to collect them.

To Geraldine it seemed that her two dream-children had materialised. Nevertheless the enormity of the responsibility, Lucy's sacred trust, made her nervous. She and Howard were approaching fifty, the boys were only four and five, how would it work out? But she discovered that her mothering instincts, so long repressed, rose naturally to the surface. "I loved them just as I had loved Phoebe and Agnes – there was something special about it," she remembered in later years. With the boys she and Howard were young again. They romped and played as they had never done before.

One day the boys arrived home full of a story they had heard about a mother who had left her baby on a bus.

"Do you think a mother could forget a baby on a bus?" she asked them, intending to teach them about God's love from the verse in the Old Testament which said, "Even a mother may forget, but I will not forget you."

Henry looked up at her, his eyes full of love and trust and said, "I don't know if a mother could, but I'm sure an auntie-mother couldn't," and somehow the moral of the story slipped out of Geraldine's mind.

She spoke to them often of Lucy, determined they would never forget her. Small as they were, they remembered her playing the piano. Everyone always did. And whenever Geraldine wanted to hold before them a model of perfect manhood she always told them to "be as considerate as Uncle Howard". Watching this sweet and courteous man, they knew she was right.

It was only a month after the birth of John Christopher that Henry Grattan received the news of the death of his beloved Lucy. "I shall never forget his tearless grief as he read the cabled message of sorrow," Grace noted in her journal. He felt he needed to be alone and went to walk along the shore of a quiet bay in New South Wales. A few Australian Aborigines lived nearby. The pain of losing Lucy was almost more than he could bear and he sat for some time on the sands listening to the mournful roar of the ocean, and burying his head in his hands he began to weep silently. Suddenly he felt a hand resting gently on his shoulder. He raised his head and turning slowly, found himself looking up into the radiant, wrinkled face of an old Aborigine woman. In a strange, halting accent she whispered, "'Let not your heart be troubled, neither let it be afraid

. . . In my father's house are many mansions.'" He turned away from her momentarily, gazing out to sea as he sought to absorb a fresh meaning from those familiar words and when he turned back she had gone. He sat for some time wondering who she was and where she had come from, and whether he had not had some angelic visitation.

The arrival of John Christopher meant that Henry and Grace's companionship could never be quite as unbroken as it once had been. Finding suitable accommodation for a wife and child was a continual problem and Henry frequently had to travel on alone, returning to visit Grace and the baby in their digs whenever he could. It was not an ideal situation. Grace was fairly resourceful, but he fretted for her and tended to overwork to avoid the loneliness. Knowing that their time together must inevitably be short made the separation even harder to bear. But what were they to do? He was much in demand and his calling must come first.

While Grace stayed in Las Palmas in the Canary Islands, Henry went on alone to South Africa, preaching to huge mixed black and white congregations, standing on the seat of an open carriage. The bills he received from Las Palmas horrified him. The expense was "ruinous". "£10 a week is frightful. £80 for 8 weeks, I hope it will not be that." But it was, and in the end they were both more than glad to be returning to England.

It was February 1908 when they finally reached home and Grace was pregnant again. Seeing England after an absence of five years was blissful. She had forgotten how ugly London could be. They steamed down the Thames on a grey, smoky, chilly winter morning:

Steamers, schooners, barges, were plying up and down the river, and then, a small boat came into view. We could scarce discern its passengers, but some strange impulse bade us respond to the waves of welcome. Yes, we were right. There were Dr and Mrs Taylor, Mrs Harry Guinness and her daughter and later on at the railway station, my dear father, mother and eldest sister.

They arrived to find the press waiting for them. Grace was by now accustomed to the fact that Henry was a source of public interest, but she would never get used to "the newspaper reporter, with his photographic apparatus, insisting on getting the travellers' impressions of the world in a ten-minute interview".

Then they were off into an exciting, frightening new world. London had changed dramatically in five years. Henry and Grace were amazed at the city's crowded streets, and "all its modern innovations of motor traffic".

They went back to St Leonards to enjoy a rest and the refreshing

271

sea breezes of the quiet coastal town where their adventure together had begun. It was there in May that Paul Ambrose, their second son, was born, "a child of energy and purpose, whose vivacious temperament helpfully balances the quiet, more meditative tendencies of his elder brother," wrote Grace with prophetic maternal insight.

At seventy-two Henry Grattan was the proud father of two small boys. His joy was complete. He bought a house in Bath and for the first time in his life settled down with his young family to a relatively tranquil domesticity. Their happiness was to be short-lived.

6

For Harry the early years of the nineteenth century were absorbed in waging war on the Belgian exploitation of natives in the Congo, that and fathering his ever-increasing family. Since the birth of his third child in Tasmania, there had been seven more, Alexander Fitzgerald in 1893, Margaret, known as Meg, in 1896, who died just before her second birthday, Victor Noel in 1898, Ruth Eileen in 1900, Gordon Meyer in 1902, and Howard Wyndham in 1903. By the time Robert Desmond appeared in 1905 his eldest sister Gene was seventeen. Two years later she accompanied her father to Peru and the book she wrote describing the trip, illustrated with her father's photographs, was an instant best-seller, making her one of Britain's most precocious travel-book writers.

But despite his many preoccupations elsewhere, Harry's heart had always been bound up in the Congo. In the early days of the Mission he had refused to believe that the reports he was receiving of atrocities carried out against the natives were not isolated incidents. During his visit there in 1891 he had seen treatment of which he strongly disapproved, for example towards the native carrier traffic, but his mother had warned him to remain open-minded. She had every confidence in King Leopold of the Belgians, but the king could not be personally responsible for every regional official.

For some time it did appear that the authorities were establishing law and order, albeit with a heavy hand. Tribal warfare had declined dramatically. Arab slave-raiding had ceased altogether. And the officials always treated the missionaries with the utmost respect and courtesy, as they would have expected of the Belgian people with their high code of honour. After all, the General Act of Berlin, the Magna Carta of the Congoland signed in 1885 by the world's super-powers, which handed authority over to the Belgians, had promised the natives total liberty. In 1890 at the Brussels Conference convened by Lord Salisbury, the anti-slavery and humanitarian aspects of the charter were reconfirmed, and in addition the sale of alcohol was banned. So were the sale of guns and gunpowder. Lucy had regarded the conference as a triumph for justice and freedom.

Although never explicitly spelt out, it was an underlying principle that commercial transactions were to be honourable on the basis that the land belonged to the African and its produce was his property. Goods were to be bartered for in the traditional way.

But the discovery of enormous quantities of rubber changed everything. The highest of principles crumbled beneath the onslaught of unbridled human avarice. Thousands of natives were driven off their territory, and their villages burned to provide the king's agents with the necessary plantations. The Africans became no better than squatters on the ground of an absentee landlord, "a landlord who has developed within sixteen years the absolutism of a ruthless despot," wrote Harry, "in place of the philanthropy of 'a material and moral regenerator'."[6]

How to force the African to collect the sticky treasure which exuded from the vines of the forest, that was the initial problem. No white man would do such a menial task in the hot and humid conditions. It was not a problem for long. The barrel of a gun soon persuaded the native to give his labour freely, willingly handing over what was rightfully his. Nearly a hundred years after Wilberforce's campaign against slavery, it was as rife as ever in the Congo.

The first authenticated stories of the outrages were brought to Harry at Harley House in 1895. They were confirmed the following year by Mr Sjoblom, a Swede and former student. Harry was so incensed by the documentation that he set off for Belgium immediately. He was interviewed by the king's personal secretary, who recognised that here was no member of a lunatic fringe. The man's accusations were so serious that he ought to lay the facts before the king himself.

King Leopold received Harry the following day. "You are an excellent young man," he said, after he had listened to Harry for some time, "but you must not believe what the natives say."

"It is not native report, Your Majesty," Harry insisted.

Then he told the king how on December 14th, 1895 a missionary called Mrs Banks had been crossing the Station Compound at Bolengi when she saw a woman being beaten by a native sentry. She asked what the problem was and the sentry said, "She has lost one!"

"One what?" Mrs Banks enquired.

"One of the hands, of course," the sentry replied.

To her horror Mrs Banks noticed that the basket on the woman's back was filled with human hands. She called her husband and Mr Sjoblom and the hands were counted in her presence. There were eighteen, some belonging to children. One was definitely missing, the sentry insisted.

"Where are you taking these?" Mr Sjoblom asked the sentry.

"To the white man to whom I have to prove that I have been diligent in pushing the rubber business, and who would punish me if I did not compel the people to bring in sufficient quantity."

Appealing to the monarch's self-interest Harry boldly suggested that exercising such methods of discipline was pure folly on the part of the Congo administration. Since only the native would be willing to collect rubber, gunning him down and chopping off his hands was destroying the proverbial goose which laid Belgium the golden egg.

The argument seemed to impress the king who asked Harry what reforms he envisaged. Harry had five suggestions. An independent enquiry should be set up at once. The natives should be paid fairly. No guns were to be employed by state agents. The police authorities were to be removed and there were to be no more murders or amputations.

To his amazement the king agreed. Looking back Harry realised that such easy compliance should have made him suspicious. The independent enquiry, the Commission for the Protection of Natives, was nothing more than a placatory gesture. Its members lived miles from the rubber plantations and met twice. All it was ever intended to do was "throw dust in the eyes of Europe", Harry maintained. One or two officials named specifically by Harry to the king were removed from their posts, only to reappear elsewhere some weeks later, more heartless than ever.

In the spring of 1897 Mr Sjoblom was back at Harley, "looking almost like a dying man". The atrocities he had seen were worse than ever. When he complained to Governor-General Wahis he was manhandled himself and threatened with five years' imprisonment if he did not stop interfering. Harry ensured that Sir Charles Dilke and other important MPs heard Sjoblom's account. He also contacted Reuters, so that the story could appear in the European press.

For several years, apart from the occasional distribution of propaganda, Harry did little more. Around the Regions Beyond mission stations some improvement was noted and Harry wanted to believe that it was due to King Leopold's direct intervention. Then in 1902 Mr H. R. Fox-Bourne of the Aborigines' Protection Society published a document called *Civilization in Congoland*, and from that moment, Harry wrote, "it became obvious that the policy of the entire State was one of rapine and cruelty, and must be publicly and determinedly exposed".

Weekly articles on the Congo in the *West African Mail* by its correspondent E. D. Morel galvanised the British parliament into action and they sent Consul Casement on a tour of investigation.

His horrendous report shocked the House of Commons and led Harry to believe that the time was ripe to set up a pressure group.

The Congo Reform Association came into being in March 1904. Of its committee members Harry alone was free to engage in full-time propaganda work, but his drive and natural charisma made him the ideal man for the job. He compiled a catalogue of the evidence of brutality. Natives were chained, beaten, mutilated, starved and arbitrarily shot. With the compliance of their white officers, native soldiers were allowed to eat their victims. For three years Harry toured the British Isles, his lectures illustrated by nauseating, heart-rending lantern slides. His most successful meeting was a public debate with a representative of the Congo government on June 8th, 1904 at the St James' Hall, chaired by Lord Kinnaird. Many present were totally unaware of the situation. As Harry persuasively delivered irrefutable proof of Belgian misadministration, he held up the chicotte, a whip of hippopotamus hide, with which a native woman had been beaten to death because her husband had not collected enough rubber. The government representative was speechless.

Convincing the British public was not enough. To accomplish reform the struggle had to continue at a diplomatic level: "Back of the ideal, which has made of the Congo a shambles – an inferno – stands a man. And that man a King!" And Harry was not afraid of confronting royalty if duty required him. He went back to Belgium twice to see King Leopold and did not mince his words. The king admitted that he did not like such straight talk but he could not help but admire the man who delivered it.

And still the king did nothing. Harry laid carefully prepared memoranda before the Foreign Secretary, Lord Lansdowne. But the British government seemed unable to exert any pressure. In 1907, on his way to Peru with Gene, in one last desperate bid to arouse international outrage he crossed the Atlantic and demanded an interview with Theodore Roosevelt, the President of the United States. It was granted. Harry reminded the President that America was the first to recognise Belgian supremacy in the Congo. The United States had supervised the signing of the Berlin Act by all the European powers. The President was therefore not only entitled to remonstrate with the head of the Congo Free State, if the constitution was not upheld, but had a responsibility to do so!

How Roosevelt reacted to being told his duty remains unknown, but since this appeal produced no obvious results Harry was forced to continue his campaign with the pen. He produced *The Congo Crisis, Rubber is Death* and *Congo Slavery*, and at last witnessed the fruits of his exhausting labours. A huge protest was organised for the evening of November 19th, 1909 in the Albert Hall, presided over by the Archbishop of Canterbury, with the Bishops of Oxford and London among the speakers.

Within a month King Leopold was dead and his successor, King Albert, bowed to the strength of public protest and instituted immediate reforms. By 1912 the reforms were complete and the Congo Reform Association had the satisfaction of dissolving itself, having achieved its aims.

After so many years of effort it was hard for Harry to believe that the struggle was over. He had to see the results for himself. The doctor warned him against it. His strength had been taxed to the full. The strong, athletic young man with the robust constitution, ready to tackle any adventure, had become rather frail and ailing in middle age, exhausted by physical and emotional strain. But he ignored the doctor's advice and went to the Congo in April 1910.

After only three months he was forced to return home, ill with the mysterious wasting disease which would in time prove fatal. But three months was long enough to see the fulfilment of all his hopes. The long campaign of nearly twenty years had not been in vain. In a circular letter to his supporters he was able to write with enormous satisfaction:

> You will be glad to hear that the conditions of slavery which characterized the old régime in the Congo are disappearing, and as far as I can judge there is a genuine desire to deal fairly by the natives. Speaking to an exceedingly intelligent native at Stanley Pool the other day, I asked him his feelings in regard to recent changes at Leopoldville. His reply was unhesitating. "The old, bad times are past, and to-day we are free!"

12

1910–1918

War and the End of an Era

1

Seventy-two though he was, the word retirement never entered Henry Grattan's vocabulary. Preachers did not retire and the demands on him were as great, if not greater than ever. Besides the new century was an exciting time in which to live. There were so many new inventions and developments, so much he wanted to do and see, so many books he intended to write.

With his thick mane of white hair swept off his high forehead, and the small moustache he had taken to wearing, he cut an impressive figure in his dark frockcoat and high winged collar. His marriage seemed to have endowed him with eternal youth. He was as adventurous and as enthusiastic as ever. His grandchildren and great-nephews and nieces found him a stimulating, charming companion and he enjoyed seeing the new world through their adolescent eyes. He always preferred younger company. On July 4th, 1908 he wrote to Grace from Harley House:

Just now is the height of the season in London. The weather is lovely, and there is much to see. I am going this afternoon with Geraldine (Junior) to see the great Missionary exhibition at the Agricultural Hall, connected with the London Missionary Society. You may judge of its magnitude from the fact that the exhibits fill that vast hall, and that there are 10,000 stewards.

Then on Saturday I have promised to take Geraldine and Dora McKenzie (my niece) to see the wonderful Franco-English Exhibition. They say it is "a perfect dream", that is – people say so – 7 miles of roads and palaces! I shall wonder if it eclipses the St Louis Exhibition.

Meanwhile I am getting on fast with my writing work, as I have

access to the books I need. It is sweet to think of you and our darling children. I long to be with you. With a thousand kisses.
Your ever loving Henry.

Every now and then Grace remonstrated with him and warned him he was overdoing things, but he was incorrigible. Judging from one letter which began, "You will see from above address that I am at Cliff," she was not always sure of his whereabouts. Henry first enthused about the wonderful improvements made to his old home by the new owners, then said he was sorry that she had waited up for him until three in the morning, apologised for the anxiety he had caused her and promised faithfully to wire her about his movements in future. "Don't be anxious about me," he underlined, and enclosed a cheque for five pounds towards her household expenses.

As a husband Henry was as impossible as ever. Grace, more than Fanny, managed to tame him. She knew how to be coquettish and winsome, and he was a much older man, more easily tired and easier to woo with the temptation of home. Aware that he needed a hobby to occupy his active mind, she encouraged him to take up painting. He had never painted before, but once started he demonstrated considerable talent both in water-colour and oils. All his life he had loved nature. Reproducing its colours, its light and shade, became a source of immense satisfaction.

If Grace worried about Henry, he was equally concerned about her whenever she was away. It was one thing for him to leave her behind, but quite another when she went away without him. It left him feeling bereft. On two occasions, when her father died and she went to clear her parental home, and then when she superintended their move to Bath, supervising the arrival of their belongings, all stored in boxes for the last five years, he wrote with the same longing and the same advice:

My darling
All goes on well and quietly here. The children are flourishing. Only I am lonely – without you – not a soul to speak to. I read and write and go out and come in and pine to have you back.
So you are at last getting on with the house at Bath, cumbered up, books and boxes up to the ceiling. But my fear, my dread, is that you should lift weights and severely injure yourself. You know how shocking this would be in its effects. So for the children's sakes, and mine, as well as your own, don't do that.
Remember!

Throughout 1909 the speaking invitations poured in. People flocked to hear the old preacher. He could still pack the St James Hall in

London and fill an overflow hall in the Polytechnic. Grace had no desire to curb Henry's active life, control his exuberant nature or inhibit him in any way, but was very aware of the strain involved. His letters began to sound weary. "London is very lonely to me – more than any other place I was ever in – such multitudes and you know nobody. Your mother seems well and contented here, and says she is never lonely. I suppose we are differently constituted."

Separation from Grace became more and more of a trial. He needed her. He had always been dreamy, but now his absent-mindedness was becoming hazardous. On one occasion, taking a train journey with a young couple with a baby, he failed to see the bundle his friends had deposited on the carriage seat. They had only just put their little daughter down, when the great man, his thoughts on higher matters than the seating arrangements, lifted his coat-tails and was about to lower himself. They caught his arm just in time. Ever after, when the mother recounted the story she would look at her daughter, sigh, and say with a twinkle in her eye, "It would have been a heavenly end for her!"[1]

Grace's anxieties proved well-founded. Following a series of Advent lectures on the Second Coming of Christ, delivered in St James' Church, Bath, which attracted great crowds and were reported in detail in the *Bath Herald*, the doctors warned Henry that his heart was severely overstrained. If he continued to tax himself as he had been doing it would prove fatal. Henry had no regrets that his public ministry had cost him his health, but realised that for Grace's sake and the boys he must cancel all engagements for the following year.

The last letter he wrote to her was on December 29th, 1909:

Darling Grace

John arrived safely with Bessie last night. I went to meet them as the night was fine. It was a great joy to get the dear boy back safe and sound. He slept in our bedroom, and today has had a good outing, and a merry evening romp and stories with me. I have seen no one else, and long to have you back, it is lonely enough now you are away.

Take care of yourself.

Karl was to have reached London today. I feared winter fogs and thought it best not to go up to town to meet him, as we may have a visit from him here.

I have been reading and writing and had a walk on the top of Coombe Down today. It was lovely up there in bright sunshine.

I think many thoughts but pen and ink are poor media of communication.

Ever darling, Your loving husband Henry.

A month later he set out on a cold, wet night to fulfil an obligation. The postman had begged him to go to his house to say a few words to his friends and relatives. Grace was loath to let him go, but he insisted. A promise was a promise, even to the postman. He caught a severe chill which quickly turned to pleurisy and pericarditis. He weakened very slowly, and though in intense pain, and unable to lie down, was as mentally alert as ever. Aware that the end was creeping up on them, in a desperate bid to catch hold of every precious moment, Grace noted down everything Henry said. He was totally unafraid. He had once written a book called *On This Rock*. "Can I sink through a rock?" he asked her.

Howard and Geraldine, Henry and little Karl, came to England to be near him, renting a house in Bath. It was to Geraldine that Henry committed the care of his beloved wife and children. "What more fitting that my only daughter should be a guardian to you and the children. You cannot find a better friend than you would have in Geraldine. She is like me. I was very like her as a younger man and I am glad she loves my darling boys, I want her to be an influence in their lives."

On the evening of June 20th, he and Geraldine had a long discussion about the World Missionary Conference meeting at that moment in Edinburgh under the leadership of his old friend and student, John R. Mott. It was the first large international, truly ecumenical conference of its kind. Both Henry and Geraldine had dreamed of such an event and were excited about its potential, rightly as it turned out, for it formed the basis of the World Council of Churches. As she was about to leave the room Geraldine turned back to look at her father and was very struck by his face. As he smiled back at her in the evening light it almost seemed transfigured.

Later that evening Grace noted:

We wheeled the invalid couch from the drawing-room, where he was during the seventeen weeks illness and as he spoke to me he was facing that lovely extensive view over the city of Bath which he loved to see from his study window. He smiled at me and said, "I am too weak to talk, but have strength enough to meditate. I think over the history of the world, the history of redemption, the progress of Christ's kingdom, the important issues of this great Missionary Conference at Edinburgh. Then of our own missionary work in the world and all that has grown out of it, work in America, on the Continent, in China, India and Africa – and I think of what my dear ones have been enabled to do, and of my own life with its shortcomings."

Someone came into the room, and he still smiled that beautiful smile, which so often illuminated his face; and throughout the day we noticed it, the light of his soul shining through. It was the last time we were alone together.

On June 21st, 1910 she wrote: "This beautiful midsummer day my precious Henry passed peacefully and quietly to rest at 10.45 this morning. I was not with him at the end, nor was Geraldine. Strange after we had been with him so constantly. It seemed as if we were not to say goodbye."

Howard had been alone with him in the room when he died. He said that his father-in-law suddenly sat bolt upright in bed and with a rapturous expression on his face raised his arms in the air. He kept them raised for some time, which was extraordinary, given the fact that he had been too weak to lift them at all the previous day. Then they dropped. He fell back on his pillow and was gone. He died, as he had been born, in the year of Halley's Comet, a happy coincidence for one who had spent so much of his life studying the signs in the heavens.

Grace wired the Edinburgh Missionary Conference with the news, and Dr Mott read the telegram to a vast audience assembled in the main auditorium. There was a moment's silence, then spontaneously everyone rose to their feet and with a noise which almost shook the building, sang, "For all the saints who from their labours rest".

Henry Grattan Guinness was buried in the Abbey Cemetery overlooking the city of Bath, his grave sheltered by a solitary copper beech tree. The service was in St James' Church, where he had recently delivered his series of Advent lectures. Like Barnardo and many of his nonconformist, evangelical contemporaries, he had returned to the bosom of the Church of England in old age.

Obituaries appeared in *The Times*, the *Daily Express*, the *Daily Telegraph*, the *Westminster Gazette*, the *Yorkshire Post* and the *Sheffield Telegraph*, as well as in many other local and religious newspapers. They referred to his distinguished career as a writer, preacher and founder of missions. Many harked back fifty years to the days when he had preached to thousands from an open carriage in Northern Ireland. Along with Spurgeon and Moody he was hailed as one of the three greatest preachers of the nineteenth century. Some referred to his brewing connections and to the old legend of his mother's first husband, killed at the hands of Daniel O'Connell. All paid tribute to his breadth of vision and achievement. The *Bath Herald* lamented:

The doctor's commanding figure will no longer be seen about Bath, which he made his residence for the last two years or more, and Bath will be the poorer, for Dr Guinness was a man of intensely human and wide sympathies, a member of all churches.

One who knew him well has described him as a great thinker, a powerful writer and forceful preacher, one who gave up his life to missionary work and found in it the greatest happiness.

The simplicity of Henry Grattan's lifestyle cannot disguise the fact that he was the quintessential Guinness. By the turn of the century certain definite family characteristics had emerged. Henry Grattan was endowed with all the drive, industry, energy, initiative and philanthropy of his cousins, not to mention the touch of austerity of his forebears too. He had the Guinness charm, the presence which made itself felt the moment he walked into a room. But there was other evidence of his genetic pedigree: his interest in archaeology, local history and scientific experiment. Some years after Henry Grattan's death, Rupert Guinness, concerned that his own passion for the sciences did not seem in keeping with the traditions of the Lee side of the family, wrote to his mentor, R. A. Fisher, asking him whether there was any evidence that his scientific bent could be a family trait. Fisher replied telling him of his cousin, the mathematician and astronomer, Henry Grattan Guinness.[2] Their love of science was not the only tie to bind the two cousins, separated in age by nearly forty years. When Rupert's mother had criticised Henry and Fanny for living in London's East End, she did not imagine that her eldest son would do the same. But while Rupert was living in Shoreditch, Henry Grattan had settled in Bath. Their paths, at this stage, do not appear to have crossed, which was a pity, for they had much in common.

From the moment he gave his legacy away, Henry Grattan's path, though in many ways parallel to that of his brewing cousins, had diverged. Almost half a century earlier, in 1868, when Sir Benjamin Lee, Henry Grattan's full cousin, died, the preacher at his funeral, the Rev. Dr Leeper, proclaimed that with "the resources of a prince, the public spirit of a true citizen and patriot, and above all, as an earnest practical Christian man, he has reared a temple on whose every stone, on whose every shaft and cornice, on whose every embellishment his nature is inscribed."

Henry Grattan may often have acted as if he had the resources of a prince, but he never renovated a cathedral or built a monument to honour his own memory. When Cliff, his "palace", became a financial burden he let it go. It had been a temporary gift, greatly valued in its time, but never truly owned as a symbol of increasing social and temporal power. His only real treasure there, the eight-inch diameter telescope, was transported back to Harley for the use of the students.

His only monument was the simple grey stone erected over his grave. On one side Grace had Fanny's name inscribed. The other side she left blank for herself. In later years, as she looked back, she saw that it was fitting that there had been no formal farewell between them. For Henry the after-life was a vivid reality, divided from this life by such a tenuous thread, that death involved no real separation for those who truly loved each other. Knowing how soon their physical relationship must come to an end, he left her a poem to comfort her when the moment came, to remind her of the eternal quality of their love:

> Love links the living with the dead,
>   The dead who only are departed;
> For lingering still when joys are fled
>   Love binds around the broken-hearted
> A sense of that which never dies
> A tie that reaches to the skies.
>
> For from beyond the shadowy veil
>   Sweet voices cry, we love you still,
> For heaven-born love can never fail,
>   Or cease the holy heart to fill,
> And souls that love are sundered never
> But one on earth are one forever.

Grace lived for fifty-seven years after Henry's death, but she did not marry again. He left her four thousand pounds, the most money he had possessed in his life but not enough to keep her and her two boys. Unlike many middle-class women of her day, she worked as a nurse and school bursar so that she could support herself and the children.

With her thick hair swept up into a bun, emphasising a long, slender neck and finely chiselled features, she attracted masculine attention, but in vain. Henry's real legacy to her was of a different kind. In seven years he had provided her with enough romance and passion to last the rest of her eighty-nine years.

In old age she would sit, ramrod straight, reading his poems and letters over and over again, the cameo he had given her fastened to the front of a ruffled collar, framing a face which still bore traces of its former beauty. As she did so that face would light up and she would be a young woman once more, deeply in love with the only man who visited her in her dreams. In many ways he had never left her. "Even now," he once wrote, "softly falls the whispers of the departed, as they stand in the cloudless light on the other side of death's dark portal, saying, 'We wait for you here – we love you still.'"

2

In the summer of 1912 the Grattan Guinnesses held a grand family reunion. A large house was rented at Newquay for the month of August. It was Harry and Geraldine's idea. Losing their father had reminded them of their idyllic childhood summers at Cliff. They wanted to recreate something of the magic of those days for the new generation of cousins, giving them a chance to get to know each other.

Everyone was there: Harry, very much the patriarch now, Annie, organising and efficient as ever, their nine children and first grandchild, Karis, daughter of Gene who was married to Ian Mackenzie, the son of her parents' close friends; Grace, the most relaxed of the party, her hair streaming down her back, her skirt caught up as she paddled with her two boys; Gershom and Janie temporarily home from China with their three children, Joy, Henry and little Mary Geraldine, known by her Chinese name, Pearl; Howard and Geraldine, with Henry and Karl; Karl Kumm himself with his new bride, a charming, petite Australian called Gertrude Cato.

For Howard and Geraldine, Karl and Gertrude, it was a tense and difficult holiday. Though made to feel at home, Karl and Gertrude were none the less outsiders. It was Gertrude's introduction to what could be an overpowering family and she was conscious of having taken Lucy's place. She was also aware that her presence meant a terrible inner struggle for Howard and Geraldine.

The news of Karl's marriage had been a sudden blow which left them winded. His original letter of explanation was delayed and the first they heard was a telegram which read, "We are to be married at once, and are coming home via the United States." They wanted the boys.

For six years Henry and little Karl had been Geraldine's life. She and Howard had moved around a great deal and the boys had gone with them, along with a governess, a secretary and the sixteen trunks of papers Geraldine needed for her biography of Hudson Taylor. She often rose and started writing long before the dawn so that she would have the best of the day free for her precious children. After six years how could she relinquish them to a complete stranger? Nevertheless she knew she would have to let go. Her only choice was whether to give them up willingly or reluctantly. The latter would only cause pain for everyone concerned, so she opted for the former on the assumption that Karl would choose a good mother for his children, and she prepared them to love and welcome her.

Within a few days the delayed letter arrived, with newspaper cuttings and photographs of the wedding. Geraldine decided they must have a wedding celebration too. Henry, who was eleven, wrote to Gertrude:

My dear new Mother

I hope you had a very nice wedding. We had a lovely wedding tea – lots of cake and jam and Devonshire cream; flowers and bouquets for each of us, and all of us made speeches in honour of the occasion. Please don't stay in America too long, because we are longing to welcome you home to England.

Please give dear father a kiss and tell him we are so glad. I send you both much love, from your little son, Henry.

[PS]We are having honey for tea tonight in a beautiful piece of honeycomb, because it is your honeymoon you know.

The letter reveals the magnanimity of Geraldine's character. She could be prim, she could be strait-laced, but she could also be generous and open-hearted. Much as she regarded the children as her own, she possessed no petty streak to make her subtly try to hold on to them, no malice which would only hurt them in the end. Her selflessness, and its resultant success, emerges again in the letter Henry wrote to his father:

My dear father

I am now looking at a little picture we have of Mother. She does look nice! I wish we had a good proper one of her as this is only one sent to us out of a Melbourne newspaper. I can quite believe she is very much like an angel and that she makes your loneliness go away. That was the piece I liked best in your letter – that part too about how you thought she was like our own Mother come back from heaven. I long with all my heart to see her and you again.

I am wondering so much what things you are bringing home, and if there is anything for my birthday . . .

Although they had booked to sail on the *Titanic*, the couple were delayed in America because Karl needed an urgent appendectomy. At last the day dawned when he and his new wife were due to arrive in Malvern, where the Taylors were living. With sinking hearts Howard and Geraldine took the two boys to the station to meet them. "You can imagine what it was like waiting for the first sight of her," Geraldine later told her niece Joy:

The boys were my very soul. The train came in, Dr Kumm jumped out, and turned to hand his wife down. As soon as I saw her I knew all our prayers were answered. I saw at once what Karl meant when he said she was like Lucy. She was small and graceful like her, but she was prettier than Lucy. She had a lovely gracious spirit and my heart went out to her.

However brave Geraldine was in public her inner pain was almost unbearable. She watched the expression on little Karl's face as he looked up into the eyes of his new mother and saw in that look that a very special bond had been made. It was all she had worked for and wanted, but it cost her more than she had ever imagined. "When I parted from them something died within me. There is a peculiar joy in having children of your own. You live outside yourself, and when it is cut off, you are very solitary. It is different to parting from anyone else." Only Howard completely understood how she felt, for he felt the same.

The pain of the final separation was postponed and prolonged by the family holiday at Newquay. Of the tensions facing the adults the children knew nothing. It rained every day but they found plenty to occupy their attention. Gordon, Harry's third-youngest son, adopted his Aunt Geraldine, went for long walks with her and decided to become a missionary. Time proved him wrong, though as a clergyman and Canon of Winchester Cathedral he would one day make his reputation, like his grandfather, as an evangelist. Desmond, the youngest brother, was half terrified by the stories of the Boxer uprising which his Uncle Gershom and Aunt Jane recounted on the long summer evenings, and decided he would never go anywhere near China. Time proved him wrong too.

But time proved Lucy right. Henry and little Karl, coyly cementing their relationship with their new mother, would grow up to fulfil Lucy's prophetic instincts, Henry as a physician specialising in the treatment of yaws disease, Karl as an episcopalian minister. What Lucy could not have foreseen was that her longing for her father's lifework in Jewish–Christian relations to continue would be fulfilled not by her son, but her posthumous half-brother Paul, Henry's own youngest son.

No one could have foreseen either that Paul's elder brother John, Grace's six-year-old son romping with his mother across the sand, would one day meet Karis, the baby in the cot, on a ship in mid-Atlantic; two strangers drawn together by chance, discovering that they were related and had met before, many years ago. They would fall in love and, in marrying, Karis would become her mother's half-aunt, one of the anomalies created when Henry Grattan Guinness sired two separate families. Although intermarriage had become a fairly regular occurrence on the brewing side of the family, this was the first opportunity for the Grattans to produce a line of double-barrelled Guinnesses.

Of the fourteen boy cousins playing together at the house party at Newquay two would become missionaries in China, and six would be ordained within the Anglican ministry. The clergyman line of the Guinness dynasty was about to be born.

That was hidden in the distant future. Before the young cousins could unfold their destiny, there came an event which would turn their lives upside down. Like a vast bulldozer, the Great War would crush and trample almost every nineteenth-century value. The world in which the new generation would make its mark would be vastly different from the secure and tranquil world of Newquay in the summer of 1912.

3

Against the odds, within the limitations imposed upon him by birth and heritage, Harry Guinness had carved out his own destiny. His larger-than-life personality had enabled him to be more than simply his father's son. Raised beneath a giant shadow, he fought his way out into the sunlight. Of Henry Grattan's four surviving children by his first marriage, he alone really knew how to laugh.

Annie, horsey at times with the heartiness of the Australian outback, prim at others with the restraints of a religious Edwardian upbringing, was often at a loss to know how to manage her adventurous, boyish husband. She alone did not succumb completely to his charm. She still sold the gifts of good china he bought her with their Reed family income and put the money to better use. Annie was above all a realist, and it was she who in the dark, disappointing days carried her whole family through.

It was as well that Harry had his triumph in the Congo to sustain him. All else was bleak. His beloved Harley College, centre of a vast empire of missionary and charitable activity, was in dire financial straits. Since the sale of Cliff at the turn of the century, the directors had been forced into a spirit of retraction. The annual income had risen steadily, but missionary work in the Congo, Peru, Behar and Argentina required an ever-increasing expenditure, which the college simply could not fund. And the deficit grew year by year.

It was the London County Council who handed over the spades with which to dig the final grave. The grounds of Harley College had been acquired years back on condition of building by the year 1908. When the council refused to sanction the existing college there seemed little choice but to rebuild. But with what? The mountain of debt grew with the new college building into menacing proportions, ready to topple at any moment. In its hopeless efforts to stem the inevitable avalanche, the committee of directors was in total disarray. The course was cut from four years to two and the much-respected Principal Jackson resigned. The charitable work in the East End dwindled to a ghost of its former days. Harley students offered themselves not to the China Inland Mission or to the Regions

Beyond Missionary Union, but to the big denominational missions who would pay them more. In 1911 the work in Peru and Argentina was handed over to another missionary society. The Congo and Behar could be kept going, but only at the expense of the college.

A friend of Harry's remembered him making the announcement that the new college would have to be sold to cover outstanding debts. He was desperately sad, heavy-hearted as she had never seen him before, because he felt he had made a dreadful mistake. "Never get into debt," he warned. He had tried to walk close to God but somewhere along the way he had overtaken him and left him behind. And the cost of it, the bitter disappointment, the strain and stresses on relationships among the committee members, many his closest friends, was hard to bear.

The new building was temporarily leased to the London Hospital as a Nurses' Home. The last few students moved into Harley House, Harry and Annie's home, but when the war broke out they volunteered and classes came to an end. Doric Lodge, the deaconesses' house, was closed too, and the maternity home at Bromley Hall.

Harry and Annie were philosophical. In the end it was the war, rather than their debts, which was the final avalanche which swept Harley away for ever, and there was little they could have done to prevent it. Besides they had other anxieties. Their two eldest boys were in the trenches. And they had begun to realise with a sickening certainty that Gene's six-year-old marriage to Ian Mackenzie was unlikely to survive. The word divorce was anathema to them. It was not acceptable in the times in which they lived. It simply did not happen in the Guinness family, particularly not in the Grattan line. How could their beloved, brilliant eldest daughter, who at nineteen had been acclaimed a writer of immense promise, bear such a stigma for the rest of her life? She was barely twenty-seven, but her future was over. Little Karis stayed with her father. The new baby stayed with Gene, and both sets of grandparents drew a veil over the whole affair.

In the early morning of May 26th, 1915 Ian's parents, the Mackenzies, arrived in London. They had been in the train all night travelling from the north of Scotland, not to see their son but because Harry had persuaded his old friend to help him administer the work in the Congo and India. They were tired and dismayed to find there was no one at the station to meet them. They had been waiting for some time when a stranger rushed up to them, took their bags and explained that all was in an upheaval at Harley House. Dr Harry had died in the night.

Harry had never been well since his return from the Congo five years earlier. His symptoms were elusive and untreatable, probably the result of some mystery virus he had picked up there. Annie nursed him devotedly but on this occasion to no avail. The doctor, a leading London consultant and close friend of the family, recommended surgery. It was in the days when most operations took place at home. Annie found temporary homes for the younger children and three operations were performed. Huge growths full of pus were removed, but it soon became apparent that there was no final cure for his condition. He was fifty-three.

When he was told he accepted it quietly. Someone asked him if he was glad. "How could I be?" he said, then after a short pause, "And how could I not be?" Then he muttered to himself, "Still young – life has been short – I might have lived another thirty years."

The children came home and each saw their father in turn to say goodbye and receive his last blessing. It was an awesome, rather than a sad occasion. Much as they revered and admired him, he had always seemed a distant figure. Their mother was the real anchor in their lives.

After the funeral she disappeared for three long, bewildering days. Then she emerged from her room in her long black widow's veils, her mourning done, ready to supervise the move to Sydenham. As she and her younger children drove away, they looked back wistfully over their shoulders. Harley House had been the home of the Grattan Guinnesses for over forty years. The college was requisitioned as a home for Belgian refugees.

Just as 1903 had been a year for Guinness weddings so 1915 was a year for their funerals. On January 20th Lord Ardilaun died, aged seventy-four. In his last years he had become more entrenched and outspoken in his opposition to Home Rule. Parnell's disgrace left a political vacuum in Ireland which was soon filled by a brilliant journalist called Arthur Griffith. It was Griffith who gave birth to the nationalist movement known as Sinn Fein.[3] In 1896 the British government, anxious to make some concessions to Irish nationalism, introduced a Local Government Act, which for the first time gave the Irish people a share in their own administration. The Land Purchase Act 1903 permitted large-scale transfers of land ownership from landlord to tenant. The intention was to kill the Home Rule movement with kindness, a policy of which Lord Iveagh thoroughly approved. But his elder brother interpreted the government's actions as weakness and spent his time in the House of Lords defending Irish landlords against the injustices of the new laws and their over-generous bias towards the peasantry. To make sure of a platform in Ireland he bought four Dublin newspapers, including the *Daily Express* and the *Evening Mail*. He was irritated beyond measure when his younger brother was made a Knight of the Order of St Patrick.

Lord Ardilaun's will, made in 1902, left most of his land to his brother, Lord Iveagh, "fearing that the care of my estates would impose too much upon my wife". But his London house in Carlton House Terrace, his Dublin house in St Stephen's Green, and St Anne's, Clontarf, were all bequeathed to Lady Olive. She promptly sold the London house to her sister-in-law's cousin Benjamin Seymour Guinness of the banking side of the family, and retired to spend the rest of her days in her beloved Ireland.

In Dublin she was regarded as a great character. St Anne's was a vast pseudo-Palladian mansion, damp and dingy inside like a mausoleum. Olive's cousin, Katherine Everett, remembered how lonely she seemed, "a tall, slight, black figure, flitting across that cavernous hall".[4] Yet Olive Ardilaun was still regal and commanding in society. Her salon at St Stephen's Green, where she entertained W. B. Yeats and no one understood a word of his poetry, became a centre for the arts. Soldiers and officers from the castle rubbed shoulders with leading figures from the Sinn Fein movement. It was the tense era between the Easter Uprising of 1916 and the civil war of 1918, but Olive Ardilaun was not one to sacrifice aesthetics for political considerations. She seemed unaware that as patron of the new Abbey Theatre there was a strange anomaly in her generosity towards a venture so manifestly nationalistic in tone. And when the British army, the notorious Black and Tans, commandeered the castle she had inherited from her father in Macroom, she was put out, to say the least. The castle was finally burnt by the Republicans. Olive despised Westminster for the timidity with which it dealt with militant Sinn Fein, but she despised the Black and Tans as much for provoking the attack on her castle.

She was most renowned for her generosity to the poor. Charity for Lady Olive implied more than a mere gesture, while Adelaide, her sister-in-law, supported the Adelaide Hospital in Dublin, named after its chief benefactress, she supported the Mercer Charity Hospital, and visited the patients regularly. There she would sit regaling them with tales of her past. It was a tradition which began when the Sinn Feiners were stealing cars. She looked out of the window of an upper ward and could not see her own.

"What should we do if it has been taken?" she asked.

"But, my lady, the tram passes your gate," said an old man from one of the beds.

"I've never been in a tram," she said. It caused a sensation on the ward.

"How would you be going then?" the patients asked, and she

told them about her coach and the head coachman, the horse and pairs, and the reserved carriages on the train for her journeys to London.

As far as the patients were concerned it seemed like a fairy story and the next time she visited they encouraged her to tell them more.

"Tell us, my lady, did you ever see the king?"

She responded with stories of garden parties and dinner parties, jubilees and coronations, all recounted with magical Irish verve and colour. The patients loathed to let her go.

"Did you ever see Queen Victoria?"

"Yes, of course, often in London; but the old Queen didn't treat Ireland too well. When she was young she and the Prince Consort came and stayed with my mother's people at Muckross, and about fifty years later she came again and paid me an afternoon visit."

"Did you give her a cup of tea?"

Olive laughed. "Yes, and a bunch of flowers."

"She'd like a cup of tea as well as any old woman, wouldn't she?"

Olive Ardilaun's rather fierce and awesome appearance was only a veneer, imposed by aristocratic breeding. After she died one old woman she visited regularly in a tenement said to her cousin, "God rest her soul, for she was good. She would sit here without a proud end on her; she was a friend to the sick and the poor."[5]

More than any other, one anecdote typifies her great ability for imaginative generosity with sensitivity, and explains the popularity of the Guinness family despite their politics and position. She once gave a party for fifty repatriated prisoners-of-war. She took great trouble over the tea, ordering her butler, with the unlikely name of Millions, to fill the prize cups on the sideboard with plenty of flowers. In the dining-room the tables were elegantly set out with plates of wafer-thin slices of bread and butter, butterfly-sized sandwiches and sugar-coated petits fours. Olive's cousin Katherine was perplexed at the sight.

"Don't you think," she said, "that the men would be happier in the servants' hall with more substantial food?"

"No!" replied Lady Ardilaun, "they are going to have our sort of tea with us, and the servants to pour it out and hand round the cream and sugar, and the best china is to be used."

Katherine later saw how right her cousin had been, for after tea one of the men stood up and said:

My lady, I speak for all present, for every one of us wants to tell you what you have done for us today. You have sat down with us, you have eaten with us, and all your servants have waited on us, and we feel you have wiped out the shame of having been spitted on in the streets of Berlin when we were handcuffed prisoners.

As the men were taking their leave, Olive took her young cousin's arm and whispered, "And you need not worry about their not eating much at tea, because I have arranged for them all to have a good, solid dinner directly they get back to Dublin."[6]

Unlike future generations of her family, Lady Ardilaun never found wealth a problem. "I should have enjoyed doing some actual work," she once said, then added as a matter of fact, "but it wasn't possible." She loved gardening but her expertise was forced to remain theoretical. "Once I pulled up a weed or two, but my dear old Head Gardener met me in the act and looked very pained and hurt, and the next day there were men and boys in every border and by-way hunting stray weeds like sleuth-hounds." Olive's strength was that she accepted the limitations of her position and used its possibilities to their fullest potential. She never had children. The Ardilaun peerage became extinct with the death of her husband.

The third member of the family to die in 1915 was eighty-nine-year-old Richard Seymour Guinness, head of the London branch of the Guinness Mahon bank, and son of its founder, Robert Rundell Guinness. Harry and Geraldine and Lucy had played tennis at his home when they were teenagers. During the years of the Great War international banking came to a standstill and Guinness Mahon in London became moribund. Nevertheless it is a token of how far this line of the family had risen in social terms that Richard Seymour's fifth son, Benjamin Seymour, was able to buy 11 Carlton House Terrace from Lady Ardilaun in 1916. From that time on the banking side of the family would be known to their brewing cousins as "the Benji Guinnesses".

The Great War had brought the Harley College and Guinness Mahon empires to a standstill, and it did not spare the gracious world of Elveden. Up to the start of the war life had continued there much as before. "It was a well-ordered, formal life, leisurely but disciplined, regulated by the shooting seasons and untroubled by any suspicion of its essential impermanence. Looking back on it now, it seems like one long summer – the last summer but endlessly drawn out."[7] The new king, George V, had visited Dublin with Queen Mary in 1911. It was Lord Iveagh who escorted them round, who showed them the progress of the Guinness Trust housing scheme and Lady Iveagh's new nursery and play centre. From then on the royal pair made an annual visit to the Iveaghs at Elveden. Edward Cecil became his sovereign's unofficial adviser in matters relating to Ireland.

But in 1914 many of the estate workers volunteered and went to the front. The big shooting parties stopped and were never revived. In 1916 the lavish entertaining came to an end when Lady Iveagh died. Lord Iveagh stayed on, a lonely man without his Dodo. Most of the rooms were closed and the furniture covered in dust sheets. Elveden, the epitome of all that was serene and self-confident about Edwardian England, had fallen asleep.

Harley House also stood silent and still. In 1918 the college was bought as a warehouse by a firm of spice merchants. The house began to gather dust. There were no more children to do their lessons in the schoolroom or run to the window to look out on the hustle and bustle of life in the Bow Road. The study where Fanny had spent hours at her desk, writing long into the night by the light of a solitary candle or turning to smile at Phoebe and Agnes as they played chess on the sofa, was musty and forgotten. The gardens where Harry and Gershom had chased each other on their bicycles, or amused the East Enders with their musical cabarets, were forlorn and uncared for. There were no leaves now on the old pear tree, under whose shade Lord Shaftesbury had once taken tea, earnestly discussing the needs of the poor. The old house, once the busy centre of a multi-national organisation, became ramshackle and dilapidated.

For all the Guinness family the self-confidence of the Edwardian age had vanished for ever. It was time to consolidate, rethink and rebuild. A new era was about to begin. The brewery never suffered any loss of trade during the war. The Guinness Mahon Bank was successfully revitalised by a cousin of Benjamin Seymour's, Howard Rundell Guinness. It was a resurrection which would take its proprietors to the dizzy heights of London society. For the Grattan line the future was not so clear. The post-war world was disillusioned, cynical and sceptical. The old religious values were under question. The Grattan Guinnesses did not forsake their vocation but its outworking was different, more in keeping with the new age in which they lived. The bank and the brewery had to adapt with the times. So did they.

The Regions Beyond Missionary Union continued and expanded, eventually under the leadership of Gordon Guinness. The Sudan United Mission founded by Lucy and Karl still operated in Africa, supporting the growth of an indigenous church there. Geraldine, with faithful Howard at her side, now completely deaf, wrote and travelled, and the books of Mrs Howard Taylor still sold in their thousands. It was partly due to her efforts that the new generation produced such a wave of prominent Anglican ministers that when confronted with the name of Guinness, anyone might be forgiven for asking, "Brewing, banking or clergyman variety?"

The Harley Institute may have gone for ever but in its time it was an exceptional venture. Harry had a favourite saying which he borrowed from Prince Albert, the Prince Consort. "Gentlemen, find out the will of God for your day and generation, and then, as quickly as possible, get into line."

It was in discovering the needs of their day and generation and in meeting them, that for a short time, in the same, if not a greater measure than their brewing and banking cousins, the Grattan Guinnesses made their mark on the world in which they lived.

13

1914–

Tragedy and Triumph

1

It was London, June 1917. General Sir Beauvoir de Lisle, KCB, KCMG, DSO, on leave for ten days, was reading *The Times* over breakfast, enjoying a return to his normal home routine, now disrupted by his command in the trenches. An announcement caught his eye. His old friend Field Marshal Sir Edmund Allenby had been appointed Commander-in-Chief of the forces in the Middle East.

This was no comfortable sinecure. The British were determined to establish their supremacy in all territories around the Suez Canal. Allenby's brief was to deliver the Holy Land from over a hundred years of domination by a now crumbling Ottoman Empire. Those who had thought it would be a relatively simple task after the conquest of the Sinai Peninsula had quickly changed their minds. With German support the Turks held on to their precious possession with the iron grip of a drowning man. The Allies under the command of Sir Archibald Murray had fought a long, bitter campaign and suffered an exceedingly painful defeat at Gaza.

Few would envy Allenby his appointment or rush to congratulate him. Beauvoir de Lisle thought differently. That was why he dressed in a hurry and with his wife went at once to the Grosvenor Hotel, where Allenby was staying. He recounted the details of their meeting in his autobiography:[1]

"No cause for congratulation," Allenby said in his gruff way. "Had to give up a jolly fine army to take over a rotten show. Archie Murray is a good man and if he could not succeed, I don't see how I can."

"My dear Allenby," I replied, "you are on velvet. You may

295

make all the mistakes in tactics or strategy, but nothing can prevent you from being in Jerusalem by the 31st December."

"How do you make that out?" he asked. I told him of the book, *Light for the Last Days* by Dr Grattan Guinness in 1886, in which he had stated that the interpretation of the three prophecies in Daniel, Ezekiel and Revelation all pointed to the same year, 1917, as the end of the Gentile Times, a period of 1260 years – Time, times and a half a time.

"At the same time," I added, "don't forget your big guns."

Beauvoir de Lisle said goodbye to Allenby and was about to go, when a sudden thought occurred to him and he turned back. "When you get to Jerusalem, Allenby, I hope you will not ride in state, for that is reserved in the future for One higher than you."

The significance of the advent of the year 1917 had not passed unnoticed. In January a correspondent in the *Daily Mail* reminded readers that Henry Grattan Guinness had said, "There can be no doubt that those who live to see this year will have reached one of the most important, perhaps the most momentous, of these terminal years of crisis."

Light for the Last Days was reissued for the sixteenth time in July and reprinted again in August. In the fourth year of a disheartening war the people needed a sense of eternal destiny, a glimmer of hope.

Arthur James Balfour, the Foreign Secretary, had in all probability been introduced to Henry Grattan Guinness' books during one of his many visits to Elveden. His host, Lord Iveagh, was the author's cousin. On November 2nd he signed his historic Declaration:

His Majesty's Government view with favour the establishment in Palestine of a National Home for the Jewish People and will use their best endeavours to facilitate the achievement of this object, it being clearly understood that nothing shall be done which may prejudice the civil and religious rights of existing non-Jewish communities in Palestine.

On December 11th Sir Edmund Allenby rode at the head of his victorious troops up to the gates of Jerusalem. Then he stopped, got down from his horse, and leading her by the bridle, walked into the Holy City.

And Geraldine Guinness Taylor opened her Bible and read to her fourteen-year-old nephew, Gordon, words he never forgot: "Therefore say to the house of Israel: Thus says the Lord God: It is not for your sake, O house of Israel, that I am about to act, but for the sake of my holy name . . . For I will take you from the nations, and gather you from all the countries, and bring you into your own land."

With her dying words, Lucy Guinness Kumm had said her boys would live to see, "those unutterable days" and she was right. But there were several more dates to which Henry Grattan Guinness had referred, the last being 1948. He had scribbled it in pencil in his large black Bible, beneath the final paragraph of the book of Ezekiel.

On May 15th, 1948 the British mandate in Palestine came to an end. The independent Jewish State of Israel was born. Geraldine Taylor, sitting in her armchair, heard the announcement on her wireless. She was eighty-five and it seemed she had waited all her life for this moment. She picked up her pen and to her niece, Joy, who was writing her biography, she wrote, "From a full heart words will hardly come this morning; yet I long to write to you. It is like trying to express the inexpressible."

The news of Israel's independence may have been the culmination of Geraldine's hopes and aspirations, the fulfilment of her father's vision, the sign that she could die in peace; for the brewing side of the family it was at best bitter-sweet. On November 6th, 1944 Walter Guinness, Lord Moyne, had been assassinated by a group of Jewish terrorists known as the Stern Gang.

The first Lord Iveagh's three sons had all developed their very different careers according to their differing personalities. They did however share a lack of emotional attachment to Elveden. They found it too grand. When their father died in 1927 it was Rupert who was burdened with the upkeep of the estate. There was no question of selling it. A thousand employees depended on him for their livelihood. And then King George himself, at his first interview with Rupert after Lord Iveagh's death, offered his condolences and said, "I hope you are going to keep up the shooting at Elveden. I shall hope to come next year and I think the Queen would like to come too."[2] The king's wish was as good as a command and Rupert's plans to transform a barren agricultural wilderness into a model of experimental farming, as he had done with his estate at Pyrford, had to wait for his monarch's demise.

While the eldest brother injected his love of science into agricultural pursuits, pioneering tuberculin-tested milk, driving round his fields in a little Citroën whose horn imitated the sound of a cow mooing to attract the other cattle,[3] while Ernest the middle brother was absorbed in the affairs of the brewery, Walter, the youngest, had successfully developed a political career of his own. Coming home from the Great War where he served as a Brigade-Major, he was appointed Under-Secretary of State for War. From 1923-4 he was Financial Secretary for the Treasury, and from 1924-5 Minister of Agriculture. In 1932 he was created a baron and took as his title Lord Moyne. Winston Churchill respected him not only as a colleague, but also as a friend, "a most agreeable, intelligent and unusual friend", according to his daughter Mary Soames.[4] In the late summer of 1934 Winston and Clementine joined him for a month's holiday in the Mediterranean on his yacht, the SS *Rosaura*.[5] They enjoyed themselves so much that both were invited to accompany Walter Guinness in *Rosaura* the following year on his world trip in search of live specimens of the giant "monitor" lizard, the "komodo dragons", for the London Zoo. The trip was to last at least four months. Such a long sea-journey did not appeal to Winston, but Clementine longed to go and eventually went without him. It turned out to be one of the most memorable experiences of her life.

In 1938, recovering from a long bout of illness, Clementine Churchill once again joined Lord Moyne on the *Rosaura* for his fact-finding mission as Chairman of the Royal Commission on the social conditions of the West Indies. She loved the Caribbean, but the cruise was a strain due to political differences among the passengers. When Lord Moyne remained silent in the face of Lady Broughton's criticism of Winston, Clementine went to her cabin, packed, and took the first ship bound for England.

But the tension between the Churchills and Lord Moyne was short-lived. Their long relationship survived intact. In 1940 when Churchill was entrusted with the leadership of a country at war, Lord Moyne was created Secretary of State for the Colonies, and from 1941–2 was Leader of the House of Lords. In 1942 Churchill invited him to join the Cabinet as Minister of State in Egypt. In 1944 he became Minister resident in the Middle East, responsible for an area stretching from Tripoli to eastern Persia. Though prestigious, it was an unenviable appointment. Palestine was under British control and tensions there were high. It was the era of the "exodus". Thousands of Jewish refugees, many fleeing Hitler's death-camps in Europe, were arriving in "coffin-boats", desperately seeking a safe haven, a land of promise. The British government was caught in an impossible dilemma. Protective of the indigenous Arab population, with whom relations were cordial, they were also appalled by the early stories of Jewish persecution which were emerging from Europe. In his memoirs Bryan Guinness, the second Lord Moyne, wrote of his father, "I have a vivid recollection of my father's intense anger once expressed to me before the war at the indignities and atrocities inflicted on the Jews in Austria after the Anschluss and before the onset of the genocide."[6] Nevertheless, in order to avoid antagonising the Arab population and to prevent conflict if possible, the British decided on a policy of limited immigration which to the Jews appeared to verge on cruelty. The existence of the concentration camps and the full extent of the Holocaust were as yet not widely known.

On November 4th, 1944 Chaim Weizmann, the future first President of Israel, then a lecturer at Manchester University, was invited to lunch with Churchill at Chequers. The Prime Minister wanted to discuss the possibility of partitioning Palestine into two independent states, Jewish and Arab, with Jerusalem as a Free City. Weizmann was delighted to hear that his dream of a Jewish homeland might yet become a reality. On hearing that his guest was intending to go to Palestine in the near future, Churchill suggested he broke his journey in Cairo and visited Lord Moyne to see for himself how the statesman had "changed and developed in the past two years".[7] Evidently Lord Moyne was not known to be in sympathy with the Jewish cause. As an amateur anthropologist he had made certain remarks regarding racial characteristics which to an exceedingly vulnerable group of people appeared anti-Semitic.

Two days after the meeting with Churchill, before Weizmann had left England, Lord Moyne was dead. He was returning home from the British Embassy to his residence on Gezira Island, separated from Cairo by the Kasr-el-Nil bridge across the Nile. The black Humber limousine drew up at the front door and the chauffeur, Corporal Fuller, got out. As he passed behind the car to open the passenger door two young men suddenly appeared from the shrubbery with revolvers in their hands. "They're going to shoot us," shouted the white-suited Lord Moyne as one of the terrorists pointed his gun through the window and fired at point-blank range. One bullet entered his neck, another his stomach. Fuller was gunned down by the other assassin. "I'm hurt", he said and died a few seconds later.

Though parliament was informed almost at once, eleven days passed before Churchill could trust himself to make an address on the subject. When he did his words were barbed. "If our dreams of Zionism are to end in the smoke of the assassins' guns and our labours for its future to produce only a new set of gangsters worthy of Nazi Germany", then he would "have to reconsider the position we have maintained so consistently and so long in the past."

It was a reflection of the patronising attitude which had given rise to Jewish terrorist groups such as the Stern Gang in the first place. However sympathetic to the Jewish cause Churchill thought he was, his imperialism was deeply ingrained and Lord Moyne was the supreme symbol of that British control in the Middle East. The assassination of no other person, in no other time or place, could have caused more embarrassment to the British, the Egyptians and the Jews alike.

Many leading Zionists, including Chaim Weizmann, publicly deplored the act. He sent a telegram of condolence to Bryan Guinness, referring to personal kindnesses he had received. Bryan

Guinness agonised over how to reply and decided in the end to ask him for his help in rounding up terrorists, because, "Without the terrorised acquiescence of the population of Palestine such crimes would not be possible."[8] It was early days as far as the rule of terrorism was concerned. In Palestine the Jewish community was stunned. The press could not find words strong enough to condemn the deed. *Haaretz*, the most influential newspaper in the country, said, "No more grievous blow has been struck to our cause."

For the Zionists Lord Moyne's death turned out to be a minor set-back. Israel's independence was declared two years later, as Henry Grattan Guinness had foreseen. For the Guinness family itself, shocked and stunned, Lord Moyne's death was only the first of a long series of tragedies.

2

Weeks before the end of the war Rupert and Gwenny's son and heir, the Hon. Arthur Onslow Edward Guinness, Viscount Elveden, was killed in action at Nijmegen. He was thirty-three. Their devastation was total. Apart from losing their only son, the family succession at the brewery was once again in jeopardy. Although Rupert was Chairman of Guinness, it was Ernest, the Vice-Chairman, who in practice ran the firm, but he had only daughters. Viscount Elveden did in fact leave three children, the eldest of whom, a son, Sir Arthur Francis Benjamin, was eight years old when his father died. Rupert appeared to solve the problem, temporarily at least, by being blessed with longevity. He lived to the age of ninety-three.

In 1967 when his grandfather died Sir Arthur Francis Benjamin became the third and present Earl of Iveagh. In the tradition of the previous earls he is a shy, retiring, gentlemanly man, deeply suspicious of publicity, with an abhorrence of scandal, a cruel irony in the light of events which have captured the press headlines since 1978.

One May afternoon Lady Henrietta Guinness, the earl's youngest sister, aged thirty-five, crossed the little Italian town of Spoleto, and went to the dentist's for a filling. She left to go home to her Italian husband and baby daughter but never arrived at the tiny, sparsely furnished council house where they had lived with his parents for the last two and a half years. Instead she stopped on the narrow passageway across the windswept Ponte della Torri aqueduct and leapt into the deep ravine. To both the family and the wider public such an act seemed incredible for an attractive, warm-hearted young woman with apparently everything to live for. But unlike many of her ancestors she was unable to appreciate the potential of her enormous wealth. "If I had been poor," she once said, "I would have been happy." Riches were a burden. She felt that it made people behave towards her in an unnatural way and there was nothing she craved so much as real affection. Growing up without a father had left a huge gap.

When she finally tried to cheat her destiny, marrying the unemployed son of a metal mechanic and a chambermaid, it was too late. Emotional scars inflicted over the years had transformed a creative, bright-eyed adolescent into a jaded, restless adult. She never recovered physically or mentally from injuries received when her lover Michael Beeby crashed his red Aston Martin in the South of France. One major source of stability in her life, Mildred Gunner, a distant aunt on the banking side of the family and known as "Aunt Gunn", died in 1975, leaving Henrietta bereft. In her vulnerable emotional state it was almost inevitable that the birth of her baby daughter should result in severe post-natal depression. The happiness she longed for appeared to have escaped her grasp and she made one final act of despair and defiance.

Throughout the years Guinness women have made their mark as politicians like Lady Gwendolin, a brilliant, outstanding speaker; as educationalists like Elizabeth Maude Guinness of the banking line, who became Vice-Principal of Cheltenham Ladies' College, and Dawn Guinness of the Grattan line, who as headmistress of Felixstowe College became the youngest ever headmistress of a girls' public school; or as wealthy society debutantes like Aileen, Maureen and Oonagh, Ernest's three glamorous daughters. Apart from Maureen, who found an outlet for her energies supporting charities for the sufferers of arthritis and sitting on the Guinness Board, the latter group appeared to become increasingly disenchanted with their lot. Unlike Olive Ardilaun they balked at the prohibitions imposed by their money, their position and their sex. Though Guinness women could sit on the Board, there was no question of their becoming managers or directors. Brewing was still a man's world. The succession required men.

There have been several Guinness women like Henrietta, intelligent, generous, yet unfulfilled. Contentment, that one gift the magic wand of wealth could not bestow, eluded them and they pursued it in a variety of ways, some in a succession of marriages, others in filling the social calendar, and others by their rebellion and unconventionalism.

Olivia Channon, the bright, attractive daughter of Paul Channon, former Secretary of State, son of Rupert and Gwendolin's eldest daughter, Lady Honor, by her marriage to Henry "Chips" Channon, was never able to fulfil her potential. In 1986 she was found dead in her bedroom at Oxford University the morning after an end-of-term party. A mixture of drugs and alcohol had cost her her life. She was not the first Guinness to dally with drugs. Seven weeks after Henrietta's death in 1978, her eighteen-year-old cousin Natalya Citkowitz, Maureen Guinness' granddaughter, was injecting herself with heroin when she slumped head-first off the toilet seat and asphyxiated herself in a bathful of water.

For some members of the family it does appear that wealth has constituted the famous "Guinness curse", the desserts of those who fought the battle between God and mammon and lost. But it is a grossly over-simplistic suggestion, a smug solution for those who cannot cope with the concept of any human beings enjoying enormous wealth without provoking the jealousy of the fates. Besides, however it may have seemed to Lady Henrietta, there is little to suggest that the poor Guinnesses always found happiness while the rich Guinnesses did not. For all their great wealth Rupert Guinness and Olivia Ardilaun lived lives that were full and satisfying, whereas Lucy Guinness was temperamentally unable to enjoy the moment. And while many members of the poor Grattan line did find fulfilment it would be highly inaccurate to suggest that it was because they had religious beliefs while the rich brewing line did not. Many members of the Lee and banking branches of the family have been devout members of their church, while not a few of the Grattans rejected the faith of their fathers. Of Henry Grattan Guinness' two sons by his marriage to Grace, Paul, the younger, became a clergyman, but John, the elder, never completed his ordination training. It was the era of liberal theology and it cost him his faith. One of his three daughters became a topless dancer in a Las Vegas nightclub. The other two followed Eastern mysticism.

The "curse" of wealth, if curse there is, is that it can inhibit drive and ambition. The Guinnesses are a family who are invincible when they find a cause worth fighting for. Nothing can impede their determination once they find their vocation. Unlike the Grattans, unlike her grandfather Rupert and great-aunt Olive, Lady Henrietta could find no cause. That was her tragedy.

Any family sprouting into the dynastic proportions of the Guinnesses, be they Smiths or Joneses, will have their share of eccentrics and drop-outs, accidents and illnesses. Unfortunately the tragedies affecting every branch of the Guinness family, rich and poor, since the fateful day its founder decided to have children, have been more publicised than the successes which have accompanied them along the way.

On the Grattan side, Gershom and Jane's little daughter Pearl died at the age of nine. Their son Henry and his wife Mary were missionaries in China, the last Europeans in Nanking when the Communists took over the city. They spent three years under threat of arrest.

At the outbreak of the Second World War they were still working at the China Inland Mission Hospital at Kai-feng, which Henry's father had founded thirty years before. The Japanese invasion of Kai-feng forced them to join the long march. In desperate conditions of flood, famine and plague they lost two of their three little boys and were forced to bury them in hastily dug graves along the way. But their third surviving child, Os Guinness, established a reputation as an academic and outstanding contemporary theologian in the hippy era of the seventies. "The vision and example of previous generations of Guinnesses is never far away from my awareness of what my wife and I are about," he wrote.[9]

That example sometimes hung heavily on the shoulders of Harry's children. While several of their seven elder brothers and sisters spurned their religious upbringing, for a time at least, the three youngest, Gordon, Howard and Desmond, all chose to become clergymen. So did one of their elder brothers, opting for the Anglo-Catholic wing of the church.

Annie had struggled to bring up her large family without the support of a husband. She was nearly fifty when he died and it was hard to be left with such young children to care for, including a granddaughter following Gene's divorce. But the indomitable Annie not only raised her family with dignity, unsentimental love and the help of a hairbrush, she also cared for the elderly throughout the neighbourhood. She was the first woman in Upper Norwood to attach a one and a quarter horsepower autocycle to the back of her bicycle so that she could deliver her home-made soup to a larger number of needy people. One day the children came home to find her stretched out in bed with a bandage soaked in blood round her head. The autocycle had caught in the tramlines and thrown her head-first into the road where she had lain unconscious until a policeman found her and brought her home. Undaunted she was back on her autocycle almost as soon as she could stand. The moral of the story, she told her boys, was to master the art, not give it up!

That four of her sons should eventually enter the ministry was a source of great joy to her. But there was a lot for them to live up to and at times, though each eventually established his own identity and reputation, living under the shadow of previous generations was oppressive as well as a challenge.

In later years most of Harry and Annie's older children returned to their religious roots. Many of Harry's grandchildren, living all over the world, carried on the evangelical tradition of the Grattan line. Unlike his father who narrowly escaped marrying one of the influential Bewes family, Canon Gordon chose one as his wife. All three of their sons became clergymen. On one occasion, Christopher, the youngest, attended the opening of a new pub in his parish. The press rapidly discovered the fact that this descendant of Arthur Guinness the brewer was teetotal. "My goodness," said the headline; "No beer for Guinness!" It echoed almost exactly what the press had said of his great-grandfather in Dublin over a hundred years before.

The banking, Rundell side of the family has had its share of trauma too, as well as moments of triumph. The British public held its breath when Jennifer, wife of John Henry Guinness, head of the Dublin branch of Guinness Mahon, was kidnapped and held for ransom, and marvelled at her spirit and courage when she was released. A few years later, in 1987, John Henry Guinness himself, out walking on Snowdonia and wearing trainers rather than proper walking shoes, slipped and fell to his death.

If the brewing side of the family reached the heights of social prestige, collecting enough titles to make the family tree look like Debrett's Peerage, it was the banking line who almost beat them to the pinnacle when James Rundell Guinness' daughter Sabrina was courted by the Prince of Wales. But the throne of England proved elusive, to the present generation of Guinnesses at least. If the Rundell family tree is not prolific in titles, names like "Rothschild" and "Niarchos" have none the less begun to appear.

A series of misfortunes, culminating in the arrest of the brewery's former Chairman has not heralded a twilight of the gods. Far from it. The brewery continues, almost as if it had a life of its own. It will weather this storm as it has weathered many others. The 1914–18 War sparked off the greatest watershed in the firm's recent experience. Both the war and the creation of an Irish Republic altered market conditions to such an extent that Guinness lost ground to its British brewing rivals. Protectionism on foreign trade destroyed its main market. Trade fell to a third of its prewar level and Guinness was in grave danger of becoming a relatively minor brewing company. To compound the problem a weak, entrenched management refused to allow the necessary change and development to enable the firm to keep up with the times. They wanted to preserve the intimate atmosphere and allowed plans to build a British brewery in Manchester to founder. Under Rupert's chairmanship the organisation proved strong enough to survive in exceptionally difficult conditions, but there was no emergence from the economic doldrums until dynamic new management took over in the 1930s. The Park Royal Brewery was built outside London. The firm began to advertise, with enormous success. It diversified, proving that the essential ingredient of any successful firm is the quality of its management.

Sir Edward Cecil spent his life resisting the idea of an Irish Republic and hardly dared to imagine what it would mean for the brewery. It was the prime reason for plans to establish a Guinness

Brewery in England, halted by the First World War. But when independence came in 1921, six years before his death, he was surprised that it was founded on the economic principles he had practised, rather than the communist ideology he had imagined. And eventually the brewery flourished in a republican Ireland, the very epitome of its national pride and glory.

The philanthropic work continues too, as vital a part of Guinness family life as it ever was. If there seem to be no more Olive Ardilauns or Annie Guinnesses, it is because the role of Lady Bountiful is no longer acceptable in society. The poor have no desire to be patronised. Today, however, a new generation of Lee Guinnesses are finding ways of skirting the problem. Simon and Alice Boyd, the Earl of Iveagh's cousins, work tirelessly for the Save the Children Fund. The Guinness Trust, the largest private housing trust in Britain along with the Peabody Trust, is now chaired by yet another cousin, Antonia, the Marchioness of Douro, and run by the members of the Guinness family alone. Guinness housing estates continue to be developed all over Britain, many providing accommodation for the elderly. Guinness-funded projects abound, including research into the causes and prevention of alcoholism.

There are no longer giants to rule over the Guinness empire. Modern society rarely produces charismatic individuals like Sir Edward Cecil, or Richard Seymour Guinness or Henry Grattan Guinness. There are few outstanding Guinness scholars or politicians today and no bishops. Pure genius is thin on the ground. Nevertheless every now and then another larger-than-life Guinness emerges from obscurity. Such was Jack Clephane Guinness, descendant of the Rev. Hosea Guinness, a great-nephew of the Speaker of the New Zealand House of Representatives, who arrived in Britain shortly after the war, knowing little of his roots. Discovering his illustrious connections was a revelation. No recent member of the family quite epitomises the delicate balance between luxury and charity, triumph and tragedy as he did. In true Guinness fashion when he found his cause he gave it his all. He hobnobbed with the wealthy, enjoyed their lavish hospitality, and lived a life of near austerity. Father Jack was a monk.

3

In 1946 Jack Clephane Guinness left his native New Zealand to join twenty other novices at the Anglican Community of the Resurrection in Mirfield, West Yorkshire. They were a spirited band, in which Jack, with his endless fund of shaggy dog stories, was a ringleader. His gift for mimicry was legendary. Within weeks he could do a perfect imitation of the Novice Guardian, touching his spectacles and raising them up his nose with a sniff. He never arrived for a meal in the austere dining-room without some new anecdote. He was always at the centre of the burst of laughter which destroyed the silence and drew stern looks of disapproval from the Superior. "Missionary Pudding again," he would sigh when the inevitable stewed prunes appeared on the table. Then leaning over to any newcomer or visitor he would explain conspiratorially that they went into all the dark places nothing had reached before and did you good! The other brothers became convinced that he not only read the *Irish Digest* which arrived for him every month, but swallowed it whole.

Jack arrived in England unaware of any close relationship to the brewers. Nevertheless, with the usual curiosity, he wrote off for a family tree and was put in touch with Brian Guinness in Frensham, Surrey, a descendant of the banking Guinnesses, whose unenviable job it was to keep up with the ever-expanding clan and compile the pedigree. When he studied the family tree, Jack could barely control his excitement. He discovered that not only was he related to the brewing Guinnesses, but that he was a member of the senior line, that his branch might have been the Earls of Iveagh had great-great-grandfather Hosea not exchanged his inheritance for the Church. He became so impassioned by all things Irish that the brothers were sure they began to detect the hint of an Irish lilt in his voice.

Brian Guinness of Frensham became a personal friend and put Jack in touch with other members of the family. Jack wrote to them and managed to secure several holiday invitations. The protected, sophisticated world of the aristocracy, with their stately homes, holiday villas and lavish lifestyles was slowly opening up before the monk. But if it bemused and fascinated him, it never turned his head. He was not a social climber and the high life had no lasting appeal. Perhaps that was why he was so unthreatening. He had no doubt of his calling and in 1951 took his final vows of poverty, chastity and obedience. What mattered to Jack was that having come to England not knowing a soul, he had found his family, and what a family!

At Mirfield, despite occasional references to his illustrious relatives, he quickly earned a reputation for a deep and gentle humility. Although a man of obvious talents he was diffident, shunning the limelight and never pushing himself forward. He was patient and sensitive, vital qualities for anyone living in an all-male community. Laughter was his safety valve.

In many ways he was an obvious choice for the community's work in South Africa. He set off for Johannesburg in 1954, travelling via

Australia, where the press showed him a great deal of interest. "A representative of the world-famous Guinness Brewery family was in the city yesterday," said a Dunedin newspaper, "but according to his own statement, 'deals in a different kind of spirits'."

In Johannesburg he joined Trevor Huddleston, whose book *Naught for Your Comfort* was having a profound effect in awakening the British conscience to the evils of the apartheid system. But the exploitation endured by the impoverished black people of Sophiatown was almost more than Jack could bear. "South Africa does something to you," he said. Apartheid in the raw was more disturbing than he had imagined. It dehumanised its supporters. "You could strike matches on their faces."

South Africa broke his heart and spirit, it broke his health too. He returned to the mother house in Mirfield and was made "custos", in charge of the grounds. It was the job and place he loved most, trundling around with his wheelbarrow after the gardener, talking incessantly, for once he discovered the Irish blarney he never lost it.

The years in England enabled Jack to make closer bonds with his family. He became warden of a Community of Sisters in Sandymount, Dublin, which meant going regularly to hear their confessions. It also meant he could visit his cousin, Major Owen Guinness of Tibradden, and strengthen his connections with the brewery at St James' Gate. He even arranged for Guinness to deliver a much-needed water-butt to the Sandymount Sisters.

One summer he was accompanied to Dublin by Brother Zachary, a tall, impressive-looking monk from South Africa. Both were invited to St James' Gate for dinner with the directors. The barman poured out a pint of stout for Father Jack and was about to do the same for Zachary when the monk said softly, "I'll have orange juice, please."

The barman stared at him speechless and eventually found enough voice to say, "Sir, this brewery has been making beer for two hundred years and never in its entire history has anyone had the gall to ask me for orange juice!"

But Brother Zachary went on drinking orange juice as he accompanied his friend on a tour of his many relatives, to stately homes in Dublin and London and luxurious villas in France. Although he had never met her, he referred to Grania, Lady Normanby, daughter of the assassinated Walter Guinness, and sister of the present Lord Moyne as "my cousin Grania". Lady Normanby was at best a seventh or eighth cousin. When Jack arrived back at Mirfield on one occasion he told the brothers that the family was desperately upset by Oonagh, Lady Oranmore's choice of third husband. Except with Major Owen, a staunch member of the Church of Ireland, religion was never discussed. "It was not that kind of environment," Zachary said.

But the family was always welcoming and generous and he was under the impression that all Jack did to gain acceptance was to point to his name on the family tree. "That he belonged to the senior branch of the family seemed to matter to him, though I never understood why."

But the happy, carefree summer holidays were almost over. The Order had a seminary for black students at Alice in South Africa and Jack was asked to take charge of the Community there. It was the hardest test of his obedience. He would have given anything never to have faced the sorrow of that land again. The Community was already subject to the watchful eye of the Special Branch because they had been involved in finding defence lawyers for young black people thrown into gaol without any charge. The monks suspected their phone was being tapped. Nor did Jack relish becoming a Prior, for he knew it would involve him in conflicts and decisions which might cause pain to others. He felt he was a pastor not a leader, better at one-to-one relationships than preaching, teaching or administration.

The seven years in Alice were hard and bitter. The political situation had deteriorated faster than he had anticipated. Of the forty African schools the Mirfield Order had established in South Africa prior to his first spell there, all had been closed down under the legislation. The atmosphere at the seminary was often charged and tense. Father Jack was appalled that the world understood so little what apartheid meant in practice, the loss of dignity, the brutality of a sophisticated secret police force, arbitrary imprisonments and deportations. An article in the *Church and People* conveyed much of his anguish. "I cannot see a peaceful solution," he said. "Eventually some kind of revolt is bound to take place – you can't treat human beings as cattle. The black man knows that time is on his side." Despite his reluctance, he was promoted to Provincial, having charge of the Order's work throughout the area, but once again his health broke down under the strain.

If Jack had dreamed of returning to his gardens at Mirfield and the quiet life he was disappointed. The Order sent him to the East End to be Master of the Royal Foundation of St Katharine, their retreat house in Stepney. It was Father Jack's moment to mix with royalty. The Queen Mother was patron of the Order and when she invited him to dine at St James's Palace he took a carefully nurtured rose with him and presented it to her, saying "From your garden in the East End, ma'am."

His health continued to deteriorate, but when the doctors finally diagnosed the cancer he had so long dreaded, fear seemed to vanish, but not his sense of humour. Talking about the removal of a nipple he joked, "I won't be needing that anyway."

When he died in 1975 at the age of sixty the Community mourned a man of enormous personal charm, who never wore his piety on his sleeve. A certain sparkle had been extinguished, though not completely, for the many anecdotes surrounding him have passed into Mirfield's history. In his cell were left his few possessions, two dog-eared photograph albums, which nobody ever claimed, one or two newspaper cuttings, some books and his copy of the Guinness family tree. It passed into the hands of Peter Guinness, youngest grandson of Henry Grattan, when he became a curate in West Yorkshire, almost as if he had known that one day one of the family would come for it.

If ever there was such a thing as the archetypal Guinness, in his charm, drive and enormous *joie de vivre*, in his continual inner struggle for truth and integrity, in his intense humanity, with all its failures and achievement, Father Jack probably came the closest. He lies buried in the gardens of Mirfield which he loved so dearly. There is an unmistakable tranquillity about the graveside, sheltered by trees, an atmosphere very different from that which surrounds the family vault at Leixlip. Could it be that this the poorest of all the Guinnesses was in fact the richest?

Whatever the answer no false humility made Jack disguise his pride in the family name. It is an invincible pride which for brewers, bankers and clergymen alike can survive any scandal, so that whether they like the black stuff or not, almost any member would happily echo Rupert Guinness' only speech in the House of Lords.[9] When one indignant peer complained that everywhere he went he was unable to see the beautiful British countryside for billboards alleging that "Guinness is good for you", ninety-year-old Lord Iveagh rose to his feet and in the words of the posters which Jack Guinness acquired en masse from the brewery and plastered on the walls of every church where he held a mission, shouted only five words: "Guinness is good for you."

Postscript

Towards the end of the Second World War, Cecil Edward Guinness, known in the family as Edward, was invalided out of the army with a badly wounded arm and the worry of finding peacetime employment. Edward was a son of Cecil Cope Guinness and grandson of Arthur Cecil Cope, Adelaide Guinness' blacksheep of an elder brother, who inherited from their mother the pretensions of an aristocrat without the means to fulfil them. Cecil went to seek his fortune in Australia and America, but died in America in penury, leaving his second wife with two small children to support. She appealed to Adelaide for help, and at Sir Edward Cecil's suggestion returned to England with John Cecil, aged six and Mildred, aged three. Adelaide took Mildred under her wing, as with Geraldine and Lucy, she liked grooming girls. Mildred, who in later life became Lady Henrietta's beloved "Aunt Gunn", was compliant and often appeared in the background of family photographs taken at Elveden.

John Cecil by contrast was left to fend for himself and received a patchy education. Life was a constant struggle. After serving in the Great War and being wounded three times he found employment in the booming cotton trade in Lancashire, experiencing some prosperity for the first time in his life. It was a temporary interlude. In the early thirties the industry collapsed. Despite the sacrifice involved, John Cecil was determined that his five children, of whom Edward was the eldest, should have the education he had never had. That, he said, was the best investment he could give them. Each would then have to make his or her own way in life.

When Edward found himself posted to a rehabilitation hospital near Aldershot, he remembered that his godfather Ernest Guinness lived nearby. "Uncle" Ernest, who had given him a pair of binoculars for his christening, had since then seemed oblivious of his existence, but he decided to go and see him all the same. At that time he was generally known as Ted, which down a crackling wartime phone sounded very like Ned. Since Ned was a Guinness relative who was decidedly *persona non grata* at the time, Edward was given a polite but firm brush-off. With the inherited persistence of his forebears he made the situation clear and was invited to spend a thirty-six hour leave at Holmbury House with the Hon. Ernest and his wife Chloe.

During the Saturday afternoon and evening Ernest quizzed him very closely about his career at school and in the army, and at teatime on Sunday Rupert and Gwenny suddenly appeared. Their son Viscount Elveden had died only two months before. Without a son between them the two brothers were desperately anxious about the succession at the brewery. A strong family presence was vital, and though Edward's descent was from Samuel the goldbeater, not Arthur the brewer, his grandfather's sister had been their mother, and two of his grandfather's brothers had been respectively Chairman and Managing Director of the brewery. For his part Edward was unaware that he was being assessed for his managerial potential, but a series of interviews at Park Royal followed, and when he was finally offered the post of junior brewer he accepted at once, hardly daring to believe his good fortune.

That one chance telephone call led to forty-three years in the company, the last fifteen as Chairman of Harp Lager, the lager off-shoot of Guinness. On the day he entered Park Royal, October 1st, 1945 he was put on the 2 p.m. till 10 p.m. shift and issued with overalls and wellington boots, so that he could help the process workers clean out the enormous mash tuns, coppers, fermenting tuns, vats and other vessels, all then cleaned by hand. As had always been the case, anyone aspiring to a senior position in the company, including the Board, had to qualify as a brewer first.

From the first day Edward was conscious of being a member of a family firm whose hallmark was integrity. He was as shocked as everyone else when forty-two years later the Department of Trade and Industry walked into Guinness's head office in Portman Square.

There had been many changes in the management of the brewery over the years. The first Earl of Iveagh had exercised tight personal control in every area of the firm. Though he allowed Ernest the opportunity to exercise his inventive engineering talents, Rupert was never encouraged to be involved in the same way. When Rupert became Chairman in 1927 his experience was in agriculture, and he knew little about brewing. Ernest became the Vice-Chairman, but the day to day running of the company had to be entrusted to an outside manager. But the family still remained very much in control. The tradition grew that on the eve of a board meeting the Managing Director would meet "the family" at what was called a "Tea Party", where he would give an account of his stewardship.

For some years all was well. The Managing Director was Sir Hugh Beaver, who had been the consulting engineer during the building of Park Royal. He was the first non-brewer to fulfil the role, but his knowledge of both the Irish and English breweries was comprehensive and he had an abiding respect for the Guinness family. Rupert and Ernest were wholly committed to the company. Until his death in 1949 Ernest would go up to Park Royal three times a week demanding to see Edward, so that he could be shown around some new plant or development. And at weekends at Holmbury Ernest would share with Edward lessons learnt from the past and his hopes for the future. When he died his nephew Bryan Guinness, Lord Moyne, inherited the Vice-Chairmanship. So far so good: the dynastic succession had been preserved.

By 1962 Rupert was eighty-eight and, spurred on no doubt by Gwenny, was more than ready to hand over the chairmanship of the company. His grandson, Arthur Francis Benjamin, known as Benjamin, was only twenty-five. He had scarcely had time to serve an apprenticeship in the brewery, and no opportunity to decide on his own future. Shy and retiring, finding public occasions something of a strain, Benjamin was the epitome of a man who had greatness thrust upon him. When the first Arthur Guinness' eldest son decided to become a clergyman, the second Arthur had taken his place. When the second Arthur's eldest son became a clergyman and the second son a poet, Benjamin Lee stepped into the gap. When Benjamin Lee's eldest son, Lord Ardilaun, resigned from the partnership Edward Cecil was more than able to take over. Edward Cecil had three sons, two of whom made exceptional contributions to the firm. He also drew in his wife's family. So the descent from father to son had been preserved for five generations and two hundred years. Benjamin Iveagh had no say in his destiny. He could not choose to be a clergyman or a poet, a doctor or a postman for that matter. The buck stopped with him.

To compound a difficult situation Hugh Beaver had had a heart attack and was anxious to retire. Recognising how much Benjamin needed support, Alan Lennox-Boyd, the husband of his Aunt Patricia, known as Patsy, resigned his seat in the Cabinet as Colonial Secretary and became the Managing Director. He was a man of outstanding ability, but ill-health necessitated his retirement in 1967, the same year that Rupert died.

The seventies were difficult years for Benjamin. Not only did he carry full responsibility for the brewery, he had also inherited many of his grandfather's other outside commitments. He was dogged by ill-health and in order to establish his status as an Irish citizen, there was a period of five years when he was not allowed to set foot in England. This meant that he was unable to chair the Annual General Meetings, always held at Park Royal, because Guinness was a British-registered company. His absence denied him the opportunity to establish the authority and direction necessary in running a family business. Since it is the Chairman who holds the ultimate responsibility for the decisions of the company, who sanctions managerial policies and stimulates new initiatives, experience and confidence are vital.

For a time a strong family presence remained on the Board. Benjamin's uncles, Alan Boyd and Bryan Moyne, were Vice-Chairmen. His aunts Maureen and Patsy, along with his cousin, Bryan's son Jonathan Guinness, were directors. Peter Guinness of Guinness Mahon, brother of John Henry who later died on Snowdonia, had been appointed to the Board in 1964. And Edward took his place there in 1971, as Chairman of Harp Lager. But by the end of the seventies Alan Boyd, Bryan Moyne and Maureen, Marchioness of Dufferin and Ava, had retired. Patsy followed soon after. The regular "Tea Party" fell into abeyance.

For Benjamin fulfilling the role of Chairman became increasingly difficult during the enormous expansion of Guinness in the mid-eighties. In 1983 Guinness' net assets were £250 million. By 1987 with the acquisition of Bell's and the old Distillers' Company they had multiplied four times, to a total of £1 billion. Inevitably this had affected the family shareholding. In the early eighties it had been 20 per cent, very high for a firm the size of Guinness, but the first Earl of Iveagh had charged his contemporary family and their descendants never to sell their shares under any circumstances. After the acquisition of Bell's it was reduced to 12 per cent, and after Distillers' to a mere 5 per cent. In one year Guinness had become one of the major international companies and the responsibilities of the chairmanship were formidable.

In mid-1986 the inevitable moment arrived when Benjamin, the third Earl of Iveagh, informed his colleagues on the Board that he had decided to stand down and accept the title of President. For the first time in the history of Guinness the chairmanship passed from family hands. The Chief Executive, Ernest Saunders, was created Chairman in the Earl of Iveagh's place. The arrangement lasted only a few months.

Not only has the brewery survived the storm, but it is branching out in new directions. Non-alcoholic lager is the latest venture, one of which the Guinness ancestors would no doubt have approved. Lord Moyne had never approved of the takeover of Bell's Whisky. Generations of brewers had refused to have anything to do with hard spirits: "It has been painful to see this family tradition shattered," he says[1]. But whether Guinness will ever again truly be a family firm, who can say? Edward Cecil, one of only two family members to remain on the board, is the father of three daughters. Older members of the staff still retain a considerable affection for the members of the family they knew. Their portraits, and those of their illustrious ancestors, line the corridors of the Park Royal and Dublin breweries, reminding the current employees of the giants of the past who turned a small brewery into the largest in the world and set new standards in the welfare of their staff.

With the tragic death of John Henry Guinness the Guinness family connection with the Dublin branch of Guinness Mahon comes to an end. What of the future of the brewery? Will the precious silver salver be entrusted to one of Benjamin's two sons? Will some distant cousin of the senior, Grattan or banking line suddenly emerge from obscurity to mastermind the next fifty years? If he does he will have to be an exceptional individual with more than an average share of ability to exercise control over his managers. A tall order, but where the Guinness family is concerned, by no means impossible.

1 Lord Moyne to author, July 18th, 1988.

Notes

1 1759–1803 Arthur the First, Founder of a Dynasty

1 The pedigree of the Guinness family was subject to detailed scrutiny by Henry Seymour Guinness in *Richard Guinness of Celbridge*. Only a few copies exist in private circulation within the family.
2 An anecdote recounted to the author by a Manchester journalist, who heard it from a relative of Oliver St John Gogarty.
3 From Wesley's Journals, May 12th, 1748. Quoted in *John Wesley's England* compiled by Richard Bewes.
4 *Freeman's Journal*, March 12th, 1765.
5 Patrick Lynch and John Vaizey, *Guinness' Brewery in the Irish Economy, 1759–1876*, p. 73.
6 ibid. p. 72.
7 ibid. p. 72.
8 ibid. p. 58.
9 ibid. p. 104.
10 Plunkett Papers, June 4th, 1798.
11 Lynch and Vaizey, op. cit. p. 73.
12 *Dublin Evening Post*, January 25th, 1803.

2 1803–1842 Captain John the Gentleman Soldier

1 From an account by T. P., "Grattan Guinness: an echo of a great duel", *T. P.'s Weekly*, July 8th, 1910.
2 Harry Grattan Guinness, *In Memoriam: Henry Grattan Guinness*, RBMU, 1911, p. 3.
3 From Charles Chevenix Trench, *The Great Dan*. Jonathan Cape, p. 92–3
4 *T. P.'s Weekly*, op. cit.
5 *Dublin Journal*, February 2nd, 1815.
6 From Henry Grattan Guinness' journals, quoted in *In Memoriam*, op. cit. All subsequent quotes of Henry Grattan Guinness are from his journals.
7 W. E. Adams, quoted by S. Blake and R. Beacham in *The Book of Cheltenham*. Buckingham, 1982.

3 1815–1855 The Life and Times of Arthur the Second

1 Farmleigh MS.
2 Plunkett Papers, February 9th, 1816.

3 ibid. March 12th, 1849.
4 Lynch and Vaizey, op. cit. p. 126.
5 Undated letter to Mrs Jane Guinness. Farmleigh MS.
6 To John V. Topp, 1844 in Lynch and Vaizey, op. cit. p. 112.
7 Lynch and Vaizey, op. cit. p. 143.
8 Martelli, *Man of His Time: a life of the First Earl of Iveagh, KP, GCVO*, 1975, p. 21.
9 Lynch and Vaizey, op. cit. p. 106.
10 ibid.
11 *Pilot*, quoted in ibid. p. 107.
12 Letter to P. V. Fitzpatrick, August 16th, 1839 in *Correspondence of Daniel O'Connell*, ed. W. J. Fitzpatrick. p. 199.
13 1851. Lynch and Vaizey, op. cit. p. 17.
14 ibid. p. 114.
15 Farmleigh MS. March 12th, 1849.
16 M. S. Alexander to Arthur Guinness, 1842. Park Royal MS.
17 Farmleigh MS. May 3rd, 1849.
18 ibid. November 22nd, 1851.
19 ibid. May 9th, 1849.
20 *Freeman's Journal*, August 19th, 1831.

4 1855–1860 Henry Grattan and Benjamin Lee, Stars in their Ascendancy

1 Lynch and Vaisey, op. cit. p. 178.
2 Frederick Mullally, *The Silver Salver*, p. 22.
3 From an Elvedon MS.
4 F. S. L. Lyons, *Irish Historical Studies*, p. 374.
5 *Christian*, June 30th, 1910.
6 From "Septima" (pseud. for Grace Grattan Guinness), *Peculiar People*, Heath Cranton, 1934.

5 1860–1872 Trials and Testings

1 *New York Herald Tribune*, undated.
2 Quoted in *Barnardo*. Memoirs by Mrs S. Barnardo and James Marchant, p. 17.
3 Farmleigh MS. June 1st, 1862.
4 ibid. January 1st, 1863.
5 Lynch and Vaizey, op. cit. p. 181.
6 ibid.
7 Letter dated February 16th, 1866, from the Hudson Taylor Archives of the Overseas Missionary Fellowship. Quoted by courtesy of A. J. Broomhall.
8 *The Times*, May 29th, 1868, quoted in Mullally, *The Silver Salver*, op. cit.
9 Temperance pamphlet quoted in *The Silver Salver*, op. cit. and in Martelli, *Man of his Time*.
10 Kate Drew, *The Escape Upward*.

6 1872–1880 To the Great Metropolis

1 *Barnardo*, op. cit. p. 104.
2 The Mildmay Hospital, founded in 1866 for the victims of cholera, still exists today and is in the forefront of the treatment of AIDS sufferers.
3 Farmleigh MS. October 1871.
4 From John Pollock, *Shaftesbury, the Poor Man's Earl*, Hodder and Stoughton, 1985, p. 155.
5 C. W. Mackintosh, *Dr Harry Guinness*, RBMU, 1916.
6 From Joy Guinness, *Mrs Howard Taylor, Her Web of Time*. All subsequent anecdotes and quotes relating to Henry Grattan Guinness' children are drawn from their respective biographies, or are passed down by the family.
7 From Mrs Howard Taylor, *Guinness of Honan*.
8 From The East London Institute Reports, 1874–9, written by Fanny Guinness.
9 ibid.
10 Anecdote recorded in several places including Elizabeth Pritchard, *For Such a Time as This*.
11 From Alan Moorehead, *The White Nile*, Book Club Associates, 1960, pp. 83–4.
12 ibid. p. 100.
13 Institute Reports, op. cit.

7 1880–1882 A New Generation Grows Up

1 Introduction to *The Approaching End of the Age*.
2 From Martelli, *Man of His Time*, op. cit. p. 67.
3 *Whitehall Review*, 1881.
4 Augustus J. C. Hare, *The Story of My Life*, 6 vols.
5 Private information revealed to Piers Brendon.
6 Lucy's diary, 1880.
7 From Joyce Marlow, *Captain Boycott and the Irish*, Deutsch, 1973, p. 134.

8 1882–1885 The Tasmanian Adventure

1 Martelli, *Man of His Time*, op. cit. p. 111.
2 Martelli, *Rupert Guinness: a life of the 2nd Earl of Iveagh, KG, CB, CMG, FRS*, p. 5.
3 Mary Reed's reminiscences of Lucy Guinness in Irene V. Cleverdon. *Pools In The Glowing Sands*.
4 *Dr Harry Guinness*, op. cit. p. 23.
5 Martelli, *Man of His Time*, op. cit. p. 102.
6 Professor S. R. Dennison and Dr Oliver MacDonagh, *History of Guinness, 1868–1939*, Ch IX, p. 19. Only two copies exist, in manuscript.
7 ibid.
8 Martelli, *Man of His Time*, op. cit.

9 The Building of International Empires

1 Anecdote recounted by Harry's youngest son, Desmond.
2 From *In Memoriam*, op. cit. p. 40.
3 From Lucy Guinness, *The Marathon of Today* and *Which House?*
4 A conscience-stricken Frederick Charrington of the Charrington Brewery donated a fortune to combat alcoholism.
5 *The Times*, November 20th, 1889.
6 Martelli, *The Elveden Enterprise*, Faber and Faber, 1932, p. 50.
7 Martelli, *The Story of My Life*, op. cit.
8 A private letter from Lord Moyne to the writer.
9 Martelli, *Man of His Time*, op. cit. p. 258.
10 ibid. p. 13.

10 1890–1900 Adventures Overseas

1 Martelli, *Rupert Guinness*, op. cit. p. 24.

11 1900–1908 The Dawn of the Edwardian Age

1 "Septima", *Peculiar People*. "Septima" was Grace Hurditch Guinness, and the book is her autobiography. In its time it sold well, as an antidote to *Father and Son*, by Edmund Gosse.
2 The belt of Tippu Tib, made of beaten metal and studded, was given by him as a gift to Ruth Hurditch Fisher and now belongs to my sister-in-law, Margaret.
3 Martelli, *Rupert Guinness*, op. cit. p. 28.
4 Gwendolin's diary is quoted at the end of Martelli, *Man of His Time*, p. 311.
5 *The Times*, 1903, quoted in Martelli, *Rupert Guinness* op. cit. p. 50.
6 From *The Congo Crisis*, one of three polemical works Harry Guinness wrote on slavery in the Congo. The other titles are *Rubber is Death* and *Congo Slavery*.

12 1910–1918 War and the End of an Era

1 Private recollection in a letter received by author.
2 Farmleigh MS. June 12th, 1925.
3 Sinn Fein is gaelic for "We, ourselves".
4 Katherine Everett, *Bricks and Flowers*, Reprint Society, 1951, p. 162.
5 ibid. p. 195.
6 ibid. p. 194.
7 Martelli, *The Elveden Enterprise*, op. cit. p. 52.

13 1914– Tragedy and Triumph

1 *Reminiscences of Sport and War*, Eyre and Spottiswoode, London, 1939, pp. 229–30.

2 Martelli, *The Elveden Enterprise*, op. cit. p. 87.
3 Private recollection of his father by the Hon Bryan Guinness, 2nd Lord Moyne.
4 Mary Soames, *Clementine Churchill*. By her daughter (Penguin, 1979), p. 376.
5 Neither Lord Moyne nor his sister Lady Normanby has any recollection of the Churchills spending a holiday on their father's yacht the *Rosaura*, but in her biography of her mother, Mary Soames maintains that they did. Clementine's further trips on the *Rosaura* are well documented both in her letters to Winston and in her journal.
6 Bryan Guinness, *Personal Patchwork 1939–1945*, Cygnet, 1986, p. 219.
7 Gerald Frank, *The Deed*. Simon and Schuster, New York, 1963.
8 November 13th, 1944. *Personal Patchwork*, op. cit. p. 216.
9 Private letter to author's father-in-law, February 13th, 1979.
10 Following an operation on his tongue, the second Lord Iveagh suffered from a speech impediment which made him difficult to understand.

Postscript

1 *See* Preface p. xiii

Bibliography

Original Source Material

Most of the original files on members of the family, containing letters and other documents used by Lynch and Vaizey for their history of the brewery, have disappeared from the store-room at Park Royal. Some are now at Farmleigh, the home of Lord Iveagh, and are referred to as Farmleigh MS. Farmleigh also houses the Plunkett Papers and the diary of Gwendolin Guinness, Lady Iveagh. I am indebted to Piers Brendon for giving me access to his notes on these documents.

Guinness of Dublin, Volume IV, Pedigree and Charts, is compiled by H. S. Guinness and Brian Guinness.

The East London Institute Reports by Fanny Guinness, and Harry Guinness' diary of 1887 belong to Ann Guinness of Bournemouth.

Lucy Guinness' diaries are in the keeping of her grandson Karl Kumm. Her letters to her husband Karl Kumm belong to her son, Dr Henry Kumm of Pennsylvania, USA.

Letters from Geraldine Guinness Taylor to her nephews Henry and Karl are in the possession of Henry Guinness of Redbourne, Herts.

Correspondence between Henry Grattan Guinness and Hudson Taylor are from the archives of the Overseas Missionary Fellowship, courtesy of A. J. Broomhall.

The letter from Jane Lucretia Guinness to her husband Captain John Grattan Guinness; Henry and Fanny's letter to their brother and sister-in-law, Wyndham and Dora; other correspondence by Geraldine Guinness; Grace Hurditch's letters to her sister Ruth; and the love letters of Henry Grattan Guinness and Grace Hurditch Guinness are in the possession of the author.

Biographical Material on the Guinnesses

1 W. D. Armstrong, *Sunrise on the Congo*. (Never printed. In manuscript form at the offices of the RBMU.)
2 Piers Brendon, *Head of Guinness* (A life of Rupert Guinness, 2nd Earl of Iveagh). Privately printed, 1979. 30 copies only.
3 Professor S. R. Dennison and Dr Oliver MacDonagh, *The History of Guinness, 1886–1939*. (Never printed. In manuscript form.)
4 Lucy Guinness, *Enter Thou: pages from the life story of Fanny E. Guinness*, RBMU.

5 Bryan Guinness, *Personal Patchwork 1939–1945*. Cygnet, 1986.

6 H. Grattan Guinness, *Lucy Guinness Kumm, Her Life Story*. RBMU, 1907.

7 H. Rundell Guinness, *A Short History of Guinness Mahon and Co.* (Never printed. In manuscript form.)

8 H. S. Guinness, *Richard Guinness of Celbridge*. Privately printed (only 25 copies), 1934.

9 Howard Guinness, *Journey Among Students*. Australia, AIO, 1977.

10 Joy Guinness, *Mrs Howard Taylor, Her Web of Time*. CIM, 1949.

11 *In Memoriam: H. Grattan Guinness. DD, FRAS* (a compilation of memoirs edited by his son). Regions Beyond Missionary Union, 1911.

12 Ivy Frances Jones, *The Rise of a Merchant Bank*. Privately printed, Dublin, 1974.

13 Patrick Lynch and John Vaizey, *Guinness' Brewery in the Irish Economy 1759–1876*. Cambridge University Press, 1960.

14 C. W. Mackintosh, *Dr Harry Guinness*. RBMU, 1916.

15 George Martelli, *The Elveden Enterprise*. Faber and Faber, 1932.

16 George Martelli, *Man of His Time: a life of the First Earl of Iveagh, KP, GCVO*. Privately printed. Copies only with the Guinness family.

17 George Martelli, *Rupert Guinness: a life of the 2nd Earl of Iveagh, KG, CB, CMG, FRS*. Privately printed. Copies only with the Guinness family.

18 Frederick Mullally, *The Silver Salver*. Granada, 1981.

19 "Septima" (Grace Hurditch Guinness), *Peculiar People*. Heath Cranton, 1934.

20 Mrs Howard Taylor, *Guinness of Honan*. China Inland Mission, 1930.

Some Books by the Grattan Guinnesses

HENRY GRATTAN GUINNESS
The Approaching End of the Age. Hodder and Stoughton, 1878.
Light for the Last Days. Hodder and Stoughton, 1886.
Romanism and the Reformation. Hodder and Stoughton, 1887.
The Divine Programme of World History. Hodder and Stoughton, 1888.
The City on the Seven Hills. Morgan and Scott, 1891.
Creation Centred in Christ. Hodder and Stoughton, 1896.
Key to the Apocalypse. Hodder and Stoughton, 1899.
History Unveiling Prophecy. Fleming Revell, 1905.
On This Rock. Morgan and Scott, Fleming Revell, 1909.

GERALDINE GUINNESS (MRS HOWARD TAYLOR)
Hudson Taylor. A biography in 2 vols. China Inland Mission, 1918; abridged edn. Hodder and Stoughton, 1965 (still in print).
In the Far East. Marshall, Morgan and Scott, 1889.
Pastor Hsi

BIBLIOGRAPHY

LUCY. E. GUINNESS
South America, the Neglected Continent, 1894.
Across India at the Dawn of the 20th Century. Religious Tract Society, 1898.
Motherhood. Longmans, 1929. Poems.
The Marathon of Today.
Which House.

Other Printed Sources

Barnardo, Mrs Syrie and James Marchant, *Barnardo*. Memoirs. Hodder and Stoughton, 1907.

Bewes, Richard, ed., *John Wesley's England*. Hodder and Stoughton, 1981.

Broomhall, A. J., *Hudson Taylor and China's Open Century*. Hodder and Stoughton, 1981–8.

Cleverdon, Irene, V. *Pools in the Glowing Sands*, Robertson and Mullens, 1936.

Everett, Katherine, *Bricks and Flowers*. Reprint Society, 1951.

Hare, Augustus J. C., *The Story of My Life*. George Allen, 1896.

Holmes, Kenneth, *The Cloud Moves*. RBMU, undated (c.1965).

Longford, Elizabeth, *Wellington: the years of the sword*. Weidenfeld and Nicholson, 1972.

Moorehead, Alan, *The White Nile*. Book Club Associates, 1960.

Orr, J. Edwin, *The Second Evangelical Awakening*, Marshall, Morgan and Scott, 1952.

Pollock, John, *Shaftesbury, the Poor Man's Earl*. Hodder and Stoughton, 1985.

Pritchard, Elizabeth, *For Such a Time*. Victory Press, 1973.

Index

INDEX